HARVARD ECONOMIC STUDIES

VOLUME XCI

AWARDED THE DAVID A. WELLS PRIZE FOR THE YEAR 1949–50
AND PUBLISHED FROM THE INCOME OF THE DAVID A. WELLS
FUND. THIS PRIZE IS OFFERED ANNUALLY, IN A COMPETITION
OPEN TO SENIORS OF HARVARD COLLEGE AND GRADUATES OF
ANY DEPARTMENT OF HARVARD UNIVERSITY OF NOT MORE
THAN THREE YEARS' STANDING, FOR THE BEST ESSAY IN CER-
TAIN SPECIFIED FIELDS OF ECONOMICS.

THE STUDIES IN THIS SERIES ARE PUBLISHED BY THE DEPART-
MENT OF ECONOMICS OF HARVARD UNIVERSITY, WHICH, HOW-
EVER, ASSUMES NO RESPONSIBILITY FOR THE VIEWS EXPRESSED

CITY MILK DISTRIBUTION

R. G. Bressler, Jr.

HARVARD UNIVERSITY PRESS · CAMBRIDGE · MASSACHUSETTS

1952 ——

To

The Department of Agricultural Economics
University of Connecticut

ACKNOWLEDGMENTS

The present study of city milk distribution has involved the coöperation and assistance of many people. While it is impossible to give specific credit and thanks to all, the author would like to express his gratitude to a few who were closely connected with the work. To begin with, the project was part of the program of the Storrs Agricultural Experiment Station at the University of Connecticut. Director William L. Slate has been especially helpful, and his constant reminder to "be a judge, not an advocate" will carry far beyond the limits of this study.

Frederick V. Waugh and Harold B. Rowe contributed to the development of many of the basic ideas through their interest in the milk-marketing research program of the New England Research Council. Donald O. Hammerberg was in constant touch with the work, first as Head of the Agricultural Economics Department at the University of Connecticut and later as Connecticut Milk Administrator. The late Alan MacLeod of the New England Research Council helped to plan the work and carried much of the responsibility for the study in rural markets. The late Leonard W. Parker aided in exploring many of the theoretical aspects of efficient marketing and distribution. Some of these theoretical sections were discussed with members of the Littauer Agricultural, Forestry, and Land Use Seminar, and Professor John D. Black's continued interest was largely responsible for the completion of the work in thesis form.

Basic data for the study were obtained almost entirely from Connecticut milk distributors. Special mention should be made of C. R. Brock and A. E. Hall of the Brock-Hall Dairy, A. C. Fisher of the National Dairy units in Connecticut, A. W. Acker of Highland Dairy, T. E. McManus of A. C. Petersen's Dairy, and J. R. Thim of the New Haven Dealers' Association for their interest, active coöperation, and constructive criticism. W. B. Woodburn of the Bureau of Milk Control, California Department of Agriculture, made available a number of studies of route and plant costs. Farm Market Relations, Inc., helped to finance out-of-state travel in connection with the studies of wholesale delivery.

All of the Agricultural Economics group at Connecticut contributed directly or indirectly to the project. Stanley K. Seaver, David A. Clarke, Jr., Clarence J. Miller, William F. Henry, Gordon A. King, and George E. Frick were directly involved, carried out most of the field work, and assisted greatly in the analyses. Philip J. Thomas, Miss Maryrose Dondero, and Miss Ruby Chappelle drew the graphs.

Miss Sophia Bernat deserves a special note of appreciation, for the success of the entire project was in no small part due to her efforts. She supervised all of the office work, and made the statistical computations and the preparation of the manuscript her personal responsibilities.

These and many others have contributed to the formulation of the project, to the collection of basic data, and to the analysis and presentation. The author must, however, and gladly does, accept sole responsibility for the end product and for all its limitations of formulation, scope, methods, and conclusions.

R. G. B., Jr.

CONTENTS

Contents

PART ONE ———

INTRODUCTION

1 —

THE ROLE OF MARKETING IN THE MODERN ECONOMY

The growth of our marketing system

Until the middle of the nineteenth century, the United States economy was dominantly one of subsistence farming. Population was concentrated along the Atlantic seaboard and, although the agricultural frontier had been pushed to the west, less than one-third of the land now in use between the coastal states and the Mississippi River was then under cultivation. Out of a total population of seventeen million in 1840, nine million people lived on farms, six million more in rural communities and small towns, and only two million in the larger towns and cities. While local trade and small industries had developed, as well as shipping along the coast and to Europe, nearly 80 percent of all gainfully employed workers were in agriculture. The stage was set, however, for the development of an industrial economy. The technological and resource bases for industry were available, while the vast and fertile acres of the Midwest could sustain a commercial agriculture capable of feeding large urban populations as well as contributing raw materials for industry.

This interdependent expansion of commercial agriculture and growth of industrial and trading centers was retarded primarily by the lack of an adequate marketing and transportation system. Over-the-road transportation of agricultural commodities from the Midwest to the Coast was both slow and costly, and conditions were not greatly improved until the opening of the Erie Canal in 1825. This was followed by a growth of river and canal

4 Introduction

traffic and by the railroads. Total railroad trackage increased
from 3,000 miles in 1840 to 30,000 in 1860, and the first trans-
continental line was completed in 1869. The period that followed
was one of tremendous change — the opening of the West and
the development of regional specialization in agriculture, the
growth of cities and industries, and the expansion and growing
complexity of the marketing and transportation system that ties
these segments together into a modern industrial economy. By
1940 total population amounted to 131 million, with 30 million

TABLE 1. Estimated allocation of gainfully employed workers to
production, distribution, and service, United States, 1870–1930.*

Year	Estimated number of workers			
	Production	Distribution	Service	Total
	(millions)	(millions)	(millions)	(millions)
1870	9.7	1.5	1.7	12.9
1880	12.9	2.3	2.2	17.4
1890	16.2	3.8	3.3	23.3
1900	19.1	5.6	4.4	29.1
1910	23.7	7.6	6.1	37.4
1920	26.2	9.7	6.5	42.4
1930	26.5	13.0	9.4	48.8

* Taken from P. W. Stewart and J. F. Dewhurst, *Does Distribution Cost Too Much?
The Factual Findings* (The Twentieth Century Fund, New York, 1939), 378, Appendix,
Table C.

on farms, 27 million rural nonfarm, and an urban population of
74 million. During this 100-year period, then, farm population
declined from 53 to 23 percent while urban population increased
from 11 to 56 percent of the total. Gainful employment in agriculture dropped from 80 to less than 20 percent of total employment.

In spite of the decline in the proportion of the population engaged in agriculture, farm production kept pace with the growth
in total population. In addition, there was a great increase in
industrial production and other nonagricultural activities. The

result was a steady increase in the per capita volume of goods and services available in the United States. This increasing standard of living was the net effect of two more or less divergent tendencies: (1) a marked increase in the productivity of workers in agriculture and industry; and (2) an increasingly large proportion of the population engaged in such facilitating activities as transportation and trade. Economic specialization or the division of labor between individuals, industries, and geographic regions meant that the task of exchanging products was becoming more complex. No longer was each family largely self-sufficient or able to obtain its requirements by bartering with neighbors. Furthermore, consumers were beginning to demand more services and to insist on buying in small and more convenient units. The marketing process required a growing host of country buyers, wholesalers, retailers, credit agencies, and all types of transportation workers.

A general picture of this trend may be had from the employment estimates made by Stewart and Dewhurst (Table 1).[1] Such estimates are necessarily somewhat arbitrary, for many of the classifications reported by the Occupation Census include both marketing and production activities. In the present case, the estimates were made by grouping classes that were primarily production, marketing, or service in nature, and allocating among these three the clerical workers. This procedure probably underestimated the importance of marketing because of such items as the sales activities carried on by manufacturing and industrial concerns.

With these limitations in mind, the data indicate that the increase in the total number of gainful workers between 1870 and 1930 was approximately 280 percent. This was the net result of an increase of 170 percent in production, 770 percent in marketing and transportation, and 450 percent in public and private service. Comparing these estimates with changes in the physical volume of goods produced, Stewart and Dewhurst concluded that the output per worker in production had increased about 230

---

[1] P. W. Stewart and J. F. Dewhurst, *Does Distribution Cost Too Much? The Factual Findings* (The Twentieth Century Fund, New York, 1939), 8–14, 377–379.

percent while the volume of goods distributed per worker in marketing and transportation had remained about constant. The combined effect was an increase of approximately 160 percent per worker in production plus distribution.

The distribution of gainfully employed workers by industries

TABLE 2. Distribution of gainfully employed workers by industries, United States, 1940.*

Industry	Gainfully employed	Distribution
	(thousands)	(percent)
Agriculture, forestry, and fishery...............	8,476	18.8
Mining......................................	913	2.0
Construction...............................	2,056	4.6
Manufacturing..............................	10,573	23.4
Subtotal..............................	22,018	48.8
Transportation, communication, and public utility	3,113	6.9
Wholesale and retail trade....................	7,539	16.7
Finance, insurance, and real estate............	1,468	3.2
Subtotal..............................	12,120	26.8
Business and repair services..................	864	1.9
Personal services............................	4,009	8.9
Amusement, recreation, and related services.....	395	.9
Professional and related services..............	3,318	7.3
Government.................................	1,753	3.9
Industry not reported........................	689	1.5
Subtotal..............................	11,028	24.4
Total.................................	45,166	100.0

* Based on data from *16th Census of the United States, 1940. Population, Second Series, United States Summary* (U. S. Department of Commerce, Washington, D. C.), 42.

in 1940 is given in Table 2. Again, these classifications do not permit an exact determination of the employment in marketing, but they do indicate that such activities as transportation and trade constitute very important sectors of the economy.

Census data on the value of raw materials and the value added by manufacturing and marketing activities have been used in a number of studies to estimate the total cost of marketing. As in the employment figures just described, such cost estimates involve a number of arbitrary allocations. Nevertheless, they may be accepted as approximate indications of the quantitative importance of marketing under present-day conditions.

Black and Galbraith estimated that retail marketing cost about $13.8 billion in 1929, wholesaling $7.0 billion, and that manufacturers' marketing costs amounted to $3.6 billion.[2] Adding $3.8 billion for transportation, the total cost of marketing and transportation was approximately $28.2 billion. This total is almost exactly equal to the estimated 1929 value added by manufacture exclusive of manufacturers' marketing costs. Converse estimated that 52 percent of the money spent for goods by the household consumer went to pay the costs of marketing and transportation.[3] Stewart and Dewhurst estimated the cost of commodity distribution at approximately 59 percent of the total cost of producing and distributing commodities.[4] Malenbaum, criticizing the previous estimate because of the failure to take net capital formation into account, estimated that marketing and transportation costs amounted to 51 percent of the total value of commodities.[5]

Food marketing costs show about the same relative importance as marketing costs for all commodities. On the basis of average food purchases or "market basket" for a family of three, marketing charges accounted for 51 percent and the farmers' share to 49 percent of the consumers' food dollar in 1949.[6] Food marketing charges are less flexible than farm prices, however, and consequently assume greater relative importance in periods of depression. During 1932–33, for example, marketing charges averaged 68 percent of the consumers' dollar, while in 1945 they amounted to only 46 percent. Marketing charges also differ in relative importance among the different food commodities, in general reflect-

---

[2] J. K. Galbraith and J. D. Black, "The Quantitative Position of Marketing in the United States," *Quarterly Journal of Economics*, XLIX (1935), 394–413.

[3] P. D. Converse, *The Elements of Marketing* (Prentice-Hall, New York, 1936), 11–12, 983–985.

[4] Stewart and Dewhurst, *Does Distribution Cost Too Much?*, 116–119.

[5] Wilfred Malenbaum, "The Cost of Distribution," *Quarterly Journal of Economics*, LV (1941), 55–70.

[6] *Agricultural Outlook Charts — 1950* (U. S. Department of Agriculture, October 1949), 14–18.

ing such factors as bulkiness, perishability, distance from producing centers to markets, and the amount of processing involved
in converting the farm raw material into the finished food product.
Thus in 1949 marketing and processing charges accounted for 27
percent of the retail price for eggs, 39 percent for all meats, 45
percent for dairy products, 64 percent for fruits and vegetables,
and 84 percent for bread.

Details of the problem of estimating costs and of the exact
magnitude of marketing costs need not concern us here. The
above estimates are similar enough to justify the statement that
distribution is as important as production in the national bill for
commodities.

City milk distribution

While marketing conditions differ for every commodity, the
development of milk marketing may be used to illustrate the general evolution. A century ago the relatively small volume of fluid
milk consumed in city markets came either from very limited
districts around the cities or was actually produced within the
city boundaries, frequently by cows fed on distillery wastes.
About 1840, shipments by rail were inaugurated with the transportation of milk in wooden churns from country areas to Boston
and New York. This product proved to be of higher quality than
the supplies normally available and milk consumption and city
milksheds gradually expanded until today fluid milk is transported hundreds of miles to the major markets. In this period a
complicated system developed to collect the product from farms,
transport it to city milk plants, process and bottle it under rigid
conditions of sanitation and refrigeration, and deliver it to homes,
stores, and restaurants.

Milk is an extremely perishable product and can be an ideal
medium for the multiplication of bacteria. Growing realization
of this fact and of the importance of milk and dairy products in
the human diet led to the development by state and local governments of elaborate regulations to insure the quality of the
product and to protect the public health. In addition, it was
gradually recognized that the marketing system was a far-from-
perfect mechanism for the making of prices. This led to a system

of administered prices in most markets, either through collective bargaining by dealer and producer groups or through state and federal governments.

City milk distribution is commonly defined to include all operations and functions involved from the time the product is received at city plants until it is delivered to the consumer. This definition has been used in the present study, despite the fact that such operations as pasteurizing and bottling may be more correctly considered production than marketing. The particular operations involved fall naturally into plant and delivery classes. Plant operations include receiving milk; weighing, testing, and keeping producer records, unless these operations are transferred to country receiving and shipping stations; pasteurizing and bottling, although some milk is sold in the raw or unpasteurized form; storing and refrigerating the milk until it is loaded on trucks and wagons for delivery; and general supervisory and administrative activities. Delivery may be either on a retail basis to consumers' homes or wholesale to stores, restaurants, schools, industrial plants, and similar outlets. Delivery route operations include loading the delivery trucks; transporting the milk from the city plant and delivering it to the consumer's doorstep; and keeping consumer records. In addition, route drivers usually collect payments from customers and solicit new business.

Some idea of the cost of city milk distribution may be gained from a consideration of milk prices and price margins. The average spread between the prices that consumers pay and that farmers receive for milk in the United States has increased more than 50 percent since the 1932–33 depression years. This does not mean, however, that milk distribution has become *relatively* less efficient and more costly. In general, milk distribution margins have increased about half as rapidly as producer prices, an increase in producer prices from 4.0 to 8.0 cents per quart, for example, being typically associated with an increase in price spread for distribution from 6.0 to 8.0 cents per quart. Moreover, milk distribution margins are no higher today relative to the marketing charges for all foods than they were during the decade of the 1920's. This is illustrated by the trends summarized in Fig. 1 and Table 3, where index numbers of milk marketing and food

marketing charges are traced for the period from 1922 through
1949. Considering only the more recent period, the index of milk
distribution margins (1935–1939 = 100) increased from 93
in 1933 to 121 in 1942, and then fell off to 115 in 1945 as a result
of wartime restrictions and such developments as alternate-day
delivery. With the relaxation of controls, especially on wages,
the postwar period brought a sharp increase to an index of 144
in 1949. Food marketing charges increased less rapidly in the
prewar period, moving from an index of 91 in 1933 to 105 in 1942.
Wartime efficiencies were not as effective in holding back marketing charges for all foods as they were for milk, however, with

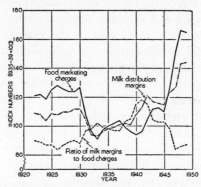

Fig. 1. Index numbers of food marketing charges and milk distribution margins, United States, 1922–1949.

the result that the index rose to 112 in 1945, and then spurted
upward to a peak of 166 in 1948.

These conflicting trends mean that the charges for milk distribution *relative* to the charges for all food marketing were moving
significantly upward until interrupted by the war developments.
During and since the war, however, milk margins relative to all
food marketing charges have moved rapidly downward. This
performance by the dairy industry must be recognized as one of
the most spectacular and important improvements in relative
"efficiency" that our marketing system has experienced in many
years. It has completely offset the upward drift of the 1930's and
has returned the fluid-milk marketing industry to a position comparable to that of the 1920's.

TABLE 3. Index numbers of food marketing charges and
milk distribution margins, United States, 1922–49.*

Year	Food marketing charges†	Milk distribution margins‡	Ratio of milk margins to food charges
1922	121	109	90
1923	122	108	89
1924	119	104	87
1925	125	109	87
1926	128	108	84
1927	126	110	87
1928	124	110	89
1929	124	112	90
1930	127	112	88
1931	108	105	97
1932	96	94	98
1933	91	93	102
1934	97	96	99
1935	100	98	98
1936	102	99	97
1937	104	101	97
1938	99	102	103
1939	96	101	105
1940	94	108	115
1941	96	113	118
1942	105	121	115
1943	112	117	104
1944	113	116	103
1945	112	115	103
1946	126	123	98
1947	151	127	84
1948	166	143	86
1949	165	144	87

* Index: 1935–1939 = 100.
† Agricultural Statistics 1949 (U. S. Department of Agriculture), 619.
‡ Based on data from The Dairy Situation (U. S. Department of Agriculture, Mimeograph DS–210, May 1950), 45, 51.

Details of the current situation are given in Table 4, where
January 1950 producer prices and distribution margins are summarized for 90 United States cities. For these markets, producers
received an everage of 10.8 cents per quart for milk delivered to

TABLE 4. Producer prices and price spreads in milk distribution, 90 United States cities, January 1950.*

Producer prices		Retail margin		Wholesale margin		Store margin		Wholesale plus store		Store differential	
Cents per quart	Number of cities	Cents per quart	Number of cities	Cents per quart	Number of cities	Cents per quart	Number of cities	Cents per quart	Number of cities	Cents per quart	Number of cities
6.5– 7.4	2	6.5– 6.9	1	4.5–4.9	1	0.5–0.9	2	6.5– 6.9	2	†	3
7.5– 8.4	12	7.0– 7.4	—	5.0–5.4	8	1.0–1.4	2	7.0– 7.4	7	0 –0.4	42
8.5– 9.4	12	7.5– 7.9	4	5.5–5.9	12	1.5–1.9	15	7.5– 7.9	16	0.5–0.9	18
9.5–10.4	19	8.0– 8.4	18	6.0–6.4	19	2.0–2.4	51	8.0– 8.4	15	1.0–1.4	23
10.5–11.4	10	8.5– 8.9	16	6.5–6.9	17	2.5–2.9	16	8.5– 8.9	12	1.5–1.9	1
11.5–12.4	15	9.0– 9.4	20	7.0–7.4	15	3.0–3.4	3	9.0– 9.4	15	2.0–2.4	1
12.5–13.4	14	9.5– 9.9	13	7.5–7.9	9	3.5–3.9	1	9.5– 9.9	12	2.5–2.9	2
13.5–14.4	2	10.0–10.4	8	8.0–8.4	3			10.0–10.4	5		
14.5–15.4	3	10.5–10.9	1	8.5–8.9	2			10.5–10.9	1		
15.5–16.4	1	11.0–11.4	5	9.0–9.4	2			11.0–11.4	2		
		11.5–11.9	—	9.5–9.9	2			11.5–11.9	—		
		12.0–12.4	2					12.0–12.4	3		
		12.5–12.9	1								
		13.0–13.4	1								

Average producer prices and price spreads

10.8		9.3		6.8		2.0		8.8		0.5	

* Based on data from "Fluid Milk and Cream Report" (Bureau of Agricultural Economics, U. S. Department of Agriculture, January and February 1950).

† Store prices exceeded home-delivered prices by amounts ranging from 0.5–0.9 cents per quart. This means that the store differential would be a minus quantity or less than zero for the three cities indicated.

city plants, but individual markets ranged from less than 7.0 to more than 15.5 cents per quart. The price spread for home-delivered milk ranged from less than 7.0 to more than 13.0 cents and averaged 9.3 cents; thus an average of 54 percent of the consumers' dollar went to the farmer and 46 percent to distribution agencies. The spread between the producer price and the price charged stores ranged from 4.5 to 9.5 cents and averaged 6.8 cents per quart. The storekeepers' margins varied from 0.5 to 3.5 cents in these cities, and averaged about 2.0 cents per quart. This means that the combination of wholesale delivery plus store charges averaged 8.8 cents, and that the store "differential" (the difference between the price charged consumers at the store and the price for home-delivered milk) averaged 0.5 cents per quart. In nearly half of these markets, however, the store and home-delivered prices were identical, while in three markets the reported out-of-store price was actually higher than the price for milk delivered to the home.

Prices, margins, and marketing efficiency

While the foregoing descriptions provide quantitative indications of the importance of marketing in our whole economy and more specifically in the dairy industry, they cannot indicate whether or not the marketing function is performed efficiently. It is true that the volume of goods handled per worker in transportation and trade has not increased materially while the output per worker in production has expanded rapidly. The volume of goods is a poor indicator of the magnitude of the marketing job, however, for physical products have been associated with an increasing amount of service. It is possible to point out that the growing complexity of marketing was a necessary adjunct to the specialization of production and increased demands for service, but the data cannot reveal whether or not the increased employment in marketing has been greater or smaller than the change in the character of the function would require.

In dairy marketing, low consumer prices may reflect efficient distribution. On the other hand, they may indicate that farm production is being carried on efficiently and under favorable circumstances or that the prices received by farmers for their product have been unduly depressed for any of a number of reasons. Nor will price margins between the consumer and the producer measure marketing efficiency. Such factors as the concentration of consuming areas, the street network, and the per capita consumption of milk vary within and between markets, and give rise to unavoidable differences in the cost of distribution. Differences in living conditions may be reflected in wages and so contribute to differences in distribution costs. Finally, a monopolistic position on the part of any group in the market may result in high (or low) levels of prices, profits, or wages; such monopolistic gains will be

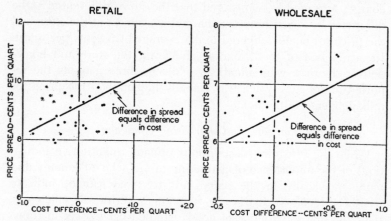

Fig. 2. Price spreads and differences in delivery route labor costs, retail and wholesale milk distribution, 30 United States cities, 1949–50.

reflected in distribution margins but certainly will not represent improvements in efficiency.

For all of these reasons it is impossible to say, for example, that the existence of markets where milk is distributed with a price spread of 7 cents per quart means that many other markets are operating with margins that are excessive by amounts ranging from 25 to 100 percent. Nor is it possible to make simple adjustments to the gross margins that will permit such generalizations. Figure 2 shows the results of such attempts, where information on delivery-route volumes and wages as shown in Table 5 have been used to adjust the reported price spreads for 30 markets scattered throughout the United States. Differences

TABLE 5. Milk distribution margins and delivery route wages and volumes, 30 United States cities, 1949–50.*

Market number	Retail delivery				Wholesale delivery			
	Price spread per quart	Daily route		Route labor cost per quart	Price spread per quart	Daily route		Route labor cost per quart
		Quarts	Wages			Quarts	Wages	
	(cents)		(dollars)	(cents)	(cents)		(dollars)	(cents)
1	8.4	485	13.50	2.78	6.2	960	10.33	1.08
2	8.2	630	11.60	1.84	6.2	1125	11.60	1.03
3	8.6	500	12.00	2.40	6.6	700	12.00	1.71
4	8.6	500	13.00	2.60	6.6	700	12.00	1.71
5	9.3	500	11.00	2.20	7.3	1100	9.00	0.82
6	8.3	470	14.20	3.02	5.8	1200	10.80	0.90
7	8.3	500	15.00	3.00	5.8	1200	10.80	0.90
8	8.5	500	13.00	2.60	6.0	1100	12.00	1.09
9	8.5	525	12.00	2.29	6.0	1200	11.00	0.92
10	8.5	475	13.00	2.74	6.0	1000	12.00	1.20
11	8.3	540	17.00	3.15	5.3	1300	14.75	1.13
12	9.2	500	15.40	3.08	6.4	1300	15.00	1.15
13	7.9	535	12.00	2.24	5.4	1100	11.00	1.00
14	11.0	440	16.60	3.77	7.5	1375	22.00	1.60
15	11.0	440	16.60	3.77	7.5	1375	22.00	1.60
16	10.0	380	16.00	4.21	6.0	1645	19.00	1.16
17	9.1	565	14.15	2.50	6.1	1940	15.65	0.81
18	9.8	635	13.20	2.08	6.8	1915	13.85	0.72
19	8.7	715	14.15	1.98	6.4	1480	13.85	0.94
20	9.8	545	12.35	2.27	6.8	1430	12.15	0.84
21	9.5	505	14.40	2.85	6.5	2475	14.80	0.60
22	9.4	595	11.95	2.01	7.2	1390	12.65	0.91
23	9.2	465	14.40	3.10	6.0	2260	14.60	0.65
24	8.2	550	12.85	2.34	6.7	1200	12.85	1.07
25	9.3	540	14.80	2.74	6.0	1575	14.80	0.81
26	9.8	500	15.00	3.00	6.6	1540	15.00	0.97
27	9.6	580	14.00	2.41	6.8	1560	14.00	0.90
28	9.5	570	14.40	2.53	6.8	1520	14.40	0.95
29	9.5	580	12.50	2.15	6.2	1675	12.50	0.75
30	8.0	450	10.00	2.22	5.5 *	850	10.00	1.18

* Price margins from *The Fluid Milk Report* (U.S.D.A. Mimeographs, 1949–50); Wage and route volume data from personal correspondence with various agricultural economists, milk dealers, and state and federal agencies.

in delivery costs have been computed by dividing daily average route wages by daily average route volumes, and expressing the results as deviations from the average for the group. In spite of the fact that delivery costs are the major component of milk-distribution costs, and that route labor is the dominant element in delivery costs, these diagrams indicate that there is no consistent or obvious relation between existing price margins and these cost and efficiency factors. While the addition of other markets to the sample might modify our conclusions, these results suggest either that other costs are dominant (a doubtful hypothesis, as indicated above) or that the pricing mechanisms (automatic or administered) in these markets are operating in arbitrary and capricious ways. In any event, they stress the fact that insights into matters of milk-distribution efficiency must come from more specific and detailed studies.

2 ——

THE STUDY OF CITY MILK DISTRIBUTION

Marketing efficiency and the general welfare[1]

Most students of economics have agreed that, at least with present knowledge, it is impossible to specify a unique set of conditions or organizations that will maximize social welfare. This failure stems from a variety of sources, but especially from the problems of interpersonal comparisons and the nonmeasurability of utility. It is possible to define useful concepts of economy or efficiency, however, and such definitions and their application in agricultural marketing research are the subject of the present study. For our purposes, we will consider efficiency to be a relative concept by which two situations may be compared or by which any given situation may be rated relative to some defined ideal. More specifically, efficiency will be measured in terms of the relations between input-output ratios. An "efficient" organization, then, will be one that yields a greater output for a given input than does some alternative organization or, conversely, that requires a smaller input to obtain a given output. It follows, of course, that the *most* efficient organization will be represented by that alternative which maximizes the output for a given input or minimizes the input for a given output.

Since several factors of production are ordinarily involved in

[1] This section is taken in large part from the introductory pages of "Efficiency in the Production of Marketing Services," a paper prepared by the present author as a contribution to a seminar sponsored by the University of Chicago and the Social Science Research Council during the summer of 1950.

any productive process and there is frequently more than one output, the application of this efficiency definition will not be as simple as the preceding sentences imply. While partial measurements will sometimes be useful — output per man-hour of labor, for example — our most important problems will require the balancing off of one factor or commodity against another in order to determine efficient combinations. This necessarily involves us in some system of weights by which factors of production may be combined into an index of input and products into an index of output. Any desired system of weights could be specified and efficient organizations determined in terms of these weights. But the results would be valid only in terms of these arbitrary specifications and so might have very limited usefulness.

In this study we will define efficiency in terms of price weights, although we hasten to add that we view these prices as subject to many imperfections and limitations. Nevertheless, they involve a working out and balancing off of different desires and tastes of millions of consumers on one hand and of technology and scarce resources on the other, and so appear to be less arbitrary than the particular weights that any individual might devise. We stress that our efficiency measures will be only as valid as these price weights, however, and our reluctance in accepting them is reflected in the limitations imposed on the application and interpretation of efficiency discussed below.

Although no attempt is made to identify efficiency as defined with the concept of general welfare, the writer has personal convictions that (1) efficiency has an important bearing on general welfare, and (2) improved efficiency will *usually* be consistent with generally accepted welfare goals. It can be demonstrated that an increase in efficiency will mean an increase in the total output of goods and services from given resources. This means that it would be *possible* for everyone to have more economic goods (leisure included), and thus strongly suggests that efficiency will be in line with welfare. However, where achieving efficiency would require marked changes in social and economic institutions or would impose on values outside the market mechanism, society may well choose less efficient organizations. If maximum efficiency requires strict control over many economic activities or the socialization of certain sectors of the economy, for example, we *may* choose to have more freedom and less efficiency. To repeat, efficiency is only one aspect of general welfare and cannot alone be used to define a unique set of goals and policies for society.

It may be worth stressing that the possibilities for discrepancies between efficiency and welfare increase as we consider higher and higher levels of economic organization. Thus there appear to be only limited departures between individual and social objectives in achieving efficiency within a particular plant. The combination of plant and transportation functions involves greater disturbances to institutional arrangements and more interpersonal comparisons, while the efficient organization or reorganization of an industry may bring the conflict between efficiency and social welfare into sharp focus. Changes in the allocation of resources among major sectors of the economy further multiply these difficulties. In view of this, we reëmphasize that the concept of efficiency is submitted as only one — albeit an important — consideration in social welfare. When presented to society, descriptions of alternative organizations in terms of their relative efficiencies and the social and economic changes required to achieve efficiency will not *define* the social choice, but they will permit the choice to be made in an informed and intelligent manner. This also defines our concept of the role of the research economist — to select areas where he believes society to be interested in efficiency and to describe possible alternatives so that society will have a better basis on which to make decisions.

In the pages that follow, our considerations are directed toward efficiency in the production of marketing services — specifically, the efficiency of milk marketing or distribution. Selection of this field is largely a matter of personal interest and preference, but these are buttressed by such developments as the continued and expanded public financial support for marketing research and by a long history of public investigation and control in milk marketing. These actions by local, state, and federal governments afford some evidence that society is concerned with milk distribution, and that here efficiency is one of our socially desired — and sometimes conflicting — goals. In a general way, however, much that we shall do has broader application, and in this sense the study of milk distribution is presented as indicative of the types of problems encountered throughout the field of marketing. Our broadest objective will be to explore appropriate research procedures and to test them through application in a series of carefully integrated studies of the various aspects of milk distribution.

Specific objectives for the study

It has long been apparent that monopolistic and competitive forces are combined and intermingled in city milk distribution. In many ways the industry has been intensely competitive, and many firms have been forced out of business by aggressive sales promotion or price cutting on the part of their competitors. In spite of these competitive aspects of the market, the addition of monopolistic elements in the form of brand names and advertising, the dominant position of small groups of handlers, and a tendency toward relatively inflexible prices through mutual agreement or public administration result in a mixture that has neither the advantages of perfect competition in assuring efficiency nor the obvious disadvantages of monopoly that might assure regulation in the public interest.

From these conditions we expect on theoretical grounds that the industry will be characterized by such inefficiencies as excess and unutilized plant and delivery capacity, duplicating sales and delivery efforts, and an excessive number of firms. Common observation of milk delivery in any city confirms the presence of such inefficiencies. It follows, therefore, that costs will be higher and, to the extent that monopolistic rather than monopolistic-competitive forces are involved, that profits will be higher than under more perfectly competitive conditions.

But more specific descriptions than this are needed. It is not sufficient to know that an operation is organized inefficiently. To be of real use, this knowledge must be expressed in quantitative terms. The important question is: how inefficient is it? Or, better still: how much more efficient would other organizations be? The main purpose of the present study is to give quantitative answers to these questions.

The specific objectives of the study may be stated concisely:

(1) To describe the existing organization of milk distribution in sample markets;

(2) To determine the fundamental relations governing physical inputs and economic costs in milk distribution;

(3) To synthesize these elements into alternative organizations of distribution;

(4) To test such hypothetical reorganizations by comparing inputs and costs for present and reorganized systems;

(5) To further test the projected systems against consumer preferences and demands; and

(6) To generalize from the above as to desirable reorganization programs for the industry.

Procedures

The procedures followed in this study are suggested by the objectives just enumerated. First, detailed descriptions of milk-delivery operations were obtained for a number of sample markets. This information served two purposes: (1) it provided a description of the present distribution system against which to check reorganization proposals; and (2) it gave in detail the geographic patterns of total milk deliveries that were essential to following syntheses of alternative organizations. In most cases, this material was obtained directly from dealers operating in the sample areas, an effort being made to obtain information from all dealers in the market. The information included the number, volume, and daily miles for all milk routes, the total wholesale and retail deliveries made by each dealer, and the location of all customers.

Concurrent with the sample area studies, analyses were made of the physical inputs and economic costs involved in milk distribution. These included studies of milk-truck costs, time studies of wholesale and retail delivery operations, route labor requirements and costs, and studies of plant operations. The truck and route labor studies were made with the coöperation of a limited sample of dealers, while the plant studies were based largely on syntheses of available economic and engineering data. All of these studies were so designed as to indicate the effects of changes in the important elements on the several cost items. Wherever possible, the analyses were made first in physical terms and then converted to economic functions by the application of suitable cost rates. This was done to emphasize the basic nature of the relations and to permit revisions of the economic functions to fit changing price and cost-rate patterns. The value of the results can be increased and prolonged by this method, barring important technological developments, and its application is illustrated by the revision of some of the results of the 1940–1943 studies to fit postwar conditions.

After the first two groups of studies were completed, their results were combined in order to estimate costs under the present system of milk distribution. At the same time, all of the elements needed for synthetic studies of alternative systems were available and these reorganization studies were inaugurated. Logical considerations such as those developed in Chapter 8 recommended a formulation of the synthetic studies around the idea of increasing delivery densities. To that end, major emphasis in these studies was on various methods of zoning markets or allocating delivery territories to particular dealers in order to reduce route duplication, increase delivery densities, and so to reduce distribution costs. As a more or less logical extension of this idea, the potentialities of complete market monopoly under public-utility status or public ownership were investigated.

The results of these studies were then generalized by relating the various physical and economic functions to market densities. These relations were used to make estimates for other markets and to describe the "optimum" form of market organization from the standpoint of production economics.

Finally, as was emphasized in the previous section, it was realized that efficiency in the production or supply side of the problem could not by itself determine desirable adjustments. Consumers were involved, and their demands and preferences were needed in order to round out the picture. Since most of the programs under consideration differed in significant ways from the existing form of milk distribution, there was no possibility of studying consumer reactions directly. The only method available was to ask consumers to express their preferences among the several alternatives. To accomplish this, surveys were made of a sample of consumers in selected markets. In order to approximate quantitative demand schedules, these consumers were asked to estimate the monetary savings that would be necessary to induce them to accept milk distribution under each of the hypothetical circumstances.

The Connecticut studies of milk marketing efficiency

In 1937 the Storrs Agricultural Experiment Station inaugurated three projects in milk marketing. Dealing primarily with country phases of the problem, the results of these projects were published as a series under the general title *Efficiency of Milk Marketing in Connecticut*. The individual bulletins are listed below:

1. *Supply and Price Interrelationships for Fluid Milk Markets*, D. O. Hammerberg, L. W. Parker, and R. G. Bressler, Jr., Bulletin 237 (1942).
2. *The Transportation of Milk*, D. O. Hammerberg and W. G. Sullivan, Bulletin 238 (1942).
3. *Economics of the Assembly of Milk*, R. G. Bressler, Jr., and D. O. Hammerberg, Bulletin 239 (1942).
4. *Retail Distribution of Milk by Producers*, D. O. Hammerberg, I. F. Fellows, and R. H. Farr, Bulletin 243 (1942).

In 1941, a project statement was submitted to the Storrs Station covering city aspects of milk marketing. The general statement was along the lines indicated in the previous sections. Specific subprojects outlined studies of alternate-day delivery, delivery-route costs, plant costs, and milk distribution in selected markets. These were later supplemented by subprojects dealing with war-time changes in milk distribution and consumer reactions to proposed changes in milk distribution.

This project was approved by Director W. L. Slate of the Experiment Station and by the Office of Experiment Stations in Washington. In addition, it was approved by the Governor's Office and was financed in part by special grants for emergency marketing research work from that office. The bulletins resulting from this project are listed below. They are a continuation of the series just mentioned.

5. *Economics and Biology of Alternate-Day Milk Delivery*, R. G. Bressler, Jr., E. O. Anderson, D. A. Clarke, Jr., and E. N. Bilenker, Bulletin 247 (1943).
6. *Truck Costs and Labor Requirements on Milk Delivery Routes*, D. A. Clarke, Jr., and R. G. Bressler, Jr., Bulletin 248 (1943).
7. *Milk Delivery in Rural Connecticut*, Alan MacLeod and C. J. Miller, Bulletin 249 (1943).
8. *Possible Milk Delivery Economics in Secondary Markets*, S. K. Seaver and R. G. Bressler, Jr., Bulletin 252 (1944).
9. *Conservation Possibilities in Retail Delivery in Major Markets*, R. G. Bressler, Jr., D. A. Clarke, Jr., and S. K. Seaver, Bulletin 253 (1944).
10. *Consumer Demands and Preferences in Milk Delivery*, R. G. Bressler, Jr., Bulletin 257 (1948).
11. *Economies of Scale in Specialized Pasteurizing and Bottling Plants*, W. F. Henry, R. G. Bressler, Jr., and G. E. Frick, Bulletin 259 (1948).
12. *Wholesale Milk Distribution*, G. A. King and R. G. Bressler, Jr., Bulletin 273 (1950).

These studies provide the essential basis for the material reported in the following chapters. Except for minor revisions and for editing to achieve better integration, large sections of the published bulletins have been used directly. In these cases, no specific references or quotations have been given. Where materials are reported from other studies, of course, appropriate references and credits have been included.

PART TWO ————

THE PRESENT ORGANIZATION
OF MILK DISTRIBUTION

3 ——

THE MILK MARKETS
OF CONNECTICUT

Rural, secondary, and major markets

Any system of market classifications is necessarily arbitrary. For purposes of this study, milk markets in Connecticut were classified according to population when the problems of supply and farm-to-market transportation were being investigated. This classification seemed appropriate because the volume of milk delivered to the market was an important factor and population data provided readily obtained measures that were highly correlated with total volume. In the studies of city distri-

TABLE 6. Distribution of Connecticut towns according to the density of milk deliveries, 1940.

Delivery density (quarts per mile)*	Market classification	Number of towns
0– 7	Rural	63
8– 14	Rural	36
15– 29	Rural	26
30– 59	Secondary	20
60– 89	Secondary	13
90–119	Secondary	3
120–149	Major	1
150–179	Major	2
180–209	Major	3
210 and over	Major	2
Total		169

* Daily retail and wholesale milk deliveries by licensed dealers, divided by number of miles of improved streets and roads in the town.

bution, however, the density of milk deliveries per mile of street is more important than the total volume, and so market classifications have been based on that measure. Rural markets have been defined as those towns (townships) where less than 30 quarts of milk was delivered daily per mile of road or street in 1940. Secondary markets include those towns with delivery densities ranging from 30 to 119 quarts per mile. Major markets are those with densities of 120 quarts or more per mile.

In applying to the Connecticut Milk Administrator for licenses, every milk handler in the state must submit information concerning his daily average sales of milk and cream and the approximate distribution of sales by towns. Data submitted in the spring of 1940 were summarized to obtain the approximate volume of milk delivered in each town in the state; these volumes were divided by the numbers of miles of surfaced roads and streets to obtain delivery densities. The results of these computations are shown in Table 6. Of the 169 towns in the state, 125 had milk delivery densities in 1940 of less than 30 quarts per mile and so have been designated as rural markets, 36 fell into the secondary-market range with densities between 30 and 119 quarts per mile of street, and the remaining eight with densities of 120 quarts or more per mile of street were by definition the major markets. The geographic distribution of these markets is indicated in Figure 3.

In more familiar terms, the rural markets had populations ranging up to 10,000 and commercial milk distribution ranging up to approximately 3,000 quarts per day. The secondary markets for the most part included those towns with populations ranging from 8,000 to 30,000 and with 1940 milk deliveries ranging from 2,500 to 10,000 quarts daily. The major-market populations ranged up to 160,000 while daily milk deliveries ranged up to 55,000 quarts. The delineations were not clear-cut in terms of population and volumes of milk delivery, of course, for the classification was based on delivery densities as explained above.

Some aspects of milk distribution in these markets

A general description of milk distribution in Connecticut markets in 1940 is given in Table 7. Rural markets, with approxi-

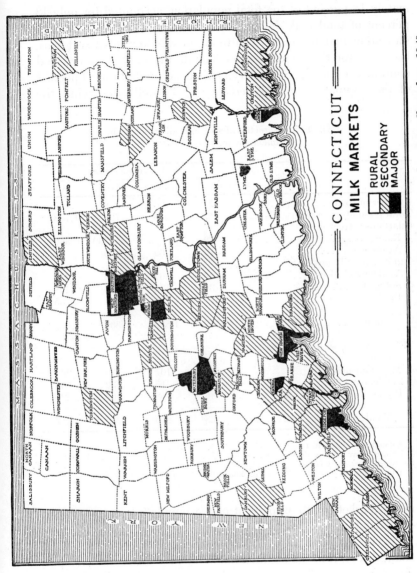

Fig. 3. Classification of towns in Connecticut into rural, secondary, and major milk markets, 1940.

mately 18 percent of the total population, accounted for only 13 percent of total milk deliveries. This should not be taken as an indication that per capita consumption was low in these towns, however, for the figures do not include the milk produced and consumed on farms. Secondary markets accounted for 39 percent of the population and 41 percent of milk deliveries, while the

TABLE 7. Characteristics of milk distribution in
Connecticut markets, 1940.*

Item	Market classification			
	Rural	Secondary	Major	All
Number of towns..............	125	36	8	169
Total population in thousands.....	317	666	725	1,708
Quarts per street mile				
Range.......................	0–29	30–119	120–300	1–300
Average.....................	10	60	206	46
Number of milk dealers†				
Merchant-dealers..............	139	307	183	304
Subdealers...................	36	173	199	258
Producer-dealers‡.............	1,394	1,109	421	2,135
Total.....................	1,569	1,589	803	2,697
Milk delivered per day (thousands of quarts)				
Merchant-dealers..............	17	107	139	263
Subdealers...................	3	15	32	50
Producer-dealers‡.............	48	88	68	204
Total.....................	68	210	239	517

* Based on reports to the Connecticut Milk Administrator.
† Since many dealers deliver milk in more than one town, the number of dealers in the several markets will not total to the number reported for the entire state.
‡ Including producer-dealers-limited, who deliver 10 quarts or less daily.

major markets, with 42 percent of the population, accounted for 46 percent of commercial distribution.

Several types of milk dealers operate in these markets. Merchant-dealers buy all of their milk supplies from farmers; producer-dealers produce some or all of the milk they distribute on their own farms; subdealers neither produce milk nor buy from farmers but obtain their supplies from other dealers, usually after it has been processed and bottled.[1] From the standpoint of numbers, producer-dealers constituted by far the most important group, including approximately 90 percent of all handlers in rural markets, 70 percent in secondary markets, and 50 percent in the major markets. In terms of the volume of milk distributed, however, the importance of producer-dealers dropped from about 70 percent in rural markets to less than 30 percent in major markets. For the state as a whole, merchant-dealers distributed 51

TABLE 8. Distribution of milk dealers and of total volume by the volume per dealer per town, Connecticut secondary milk markets, 1940.

Daily quarts per dealer*	Percent of dealers	Percent of total volume
1– 100	69	20
101– 200	16	17
201– 300	5	9
301– 400	3	6
401– 600	3	12
601–1,000	2	10
1,001–1,400	1	7
1,401–2,200	1	7
2,201 and over	0.5	12
Total	100	100

* These volumes represent the amounts delivered in the market and differ from dealer volume in that a dealer may deliver in several towns.

percent, subdealers 10 percent, and producer-dealers 39 percent of all fluid milk sold.

As seems to be generally the case, Connecticut milk markets are typically dominated by one or two relatively large dealers. While the average dealer in rural markets delivered only 8 percent of the market volume in 1940, the largest dealer in each market handled an average of 31 percent. In the major markets, 66 percent of the dealers delivered 5,000 quarts or less per month and this group accounted for only 14 percent of the total de-

[1] Producers distributing less than 10 quarts daily are designated as "producer-dealers-limited" under the Connecticut law and are exempt from some of the provisions of milk control. About one-third of the producer-dealers in Connecticut fall into this category.

liveries. On the other hand, more than 50 percent of the business was concentrated in the hands of that 5 percent of the dealers who delivered more than 25,000 quarts per month. A similar situation held in the secondary markets (Table 8).

Sample markets for detailed study

To obtain more specific information about milk distribution in these markets, 24 towns and cities in the state were selected

TABLE 9. Summary of milk delivery statistics for sample Connecticut markets.*

Town	1940 population	Number of distributors	Daily deliveries (quarts)	Delivery density (quarts per street mile)
Rural markets				
Ashford.............	704	2	13	0.4
Harwinton.........	1,112	5	81	1.7
Old Saybrook......	1,985	5	120	2.6
Willington.........	1,223	9	144	2.8
Brookfield.........	1,345	6	193	3.4
Bridgewater.......	537	5	98	4.5
Mansfield.........	3,459†	17	338	5.7
Ellington..........	2,479	9	361	6.6
Somers............	2,114	12	395	7.3
Woodbridge.......	2,262	8	451	8.8
Orange............	2,009	12	601	12.0
Chester...........	1,676	15	369	12.3
Ridgefield........	3,900	14	993	12.4
East Windsor......	3,967	16	979	15.8
North Haven......	5,326	12	1,451	18.8
Essex.............	2,859	20	676	23.3
Saybrook..........	2,332	13	901	27.3
Secondary markets				
Hamden...........	23,373	46	8,357	57
Willimantic.......	13,824	54	4,291	59
East Haven.......	9,094	27	4,592	73
Torrington........	26,988	62	9,623	75
West Haven.......	30,021	46	9,917	106
Major markets				
New Haven.......	160,605	91	50,737	232
Hartford..........	166,267	149	55,434	301

* Based on reports made to the Connecticut Milk Administrator, and not on detailed surveys.
† Not including 1,100 inmates of the Mansfield Training School.

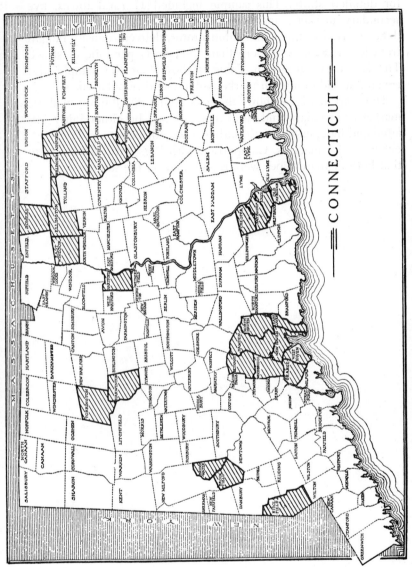

Fig. 4. Sample markets for detailed studies of milk distribution.

for detailed study. This sample included 17 rural towns, five secondary markets, and two major markets. According to the data reported to the Milk Administrator, delivery density ranged from less than one to more than 300 quarts per mile of street. The summary figures in Table 9 show that the sample also covered a wide range in market volume and population.

The map in Fig. 4 shows the geographic distribution of these markets. Secondary and rural markets may be either fairly isolated and independent or suburban areas adjacent to and dependent on major markets. Comparison with Fig. 3 will demonstrate that both of these types were represented in the sample.

4 —

MILK DISTRIBUTION IN RURAL MARKETS

The number, size, and type of milk dealers

Almost all rural areas in Connecticut produce more milk than is consumed locally, the surplus usually being sold at wholesale and "exported" to urban markets. Even on the basis of retail sales, there is a marked tendency for local dealers to spread their deliveries over more than one town. The following descriptions, however, refer only to the operations within the selected rural markets.

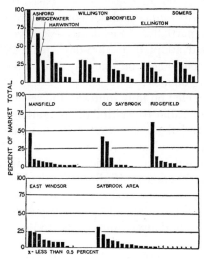

Fig. 5. *Percentage sales by individual distributors in each of 12 rural markets.*

Distributors in these sample markets varied in size from those peddling 5 or 6 quarts daily to those selling hundreds of quarts in several adjoining towns. More than half of the handlers in the sample areas delivered less than 50 quarts daily within the areas, while only 15 percent delivered more than 150 quarts per day. This is the characteristic situation in milk markets, with a large number of small dealers and a small group of relatively large dealers that dominate the markets. The tendency is illustrated graphically in Fig. 5 for the sample rural markets.[1] Most of these distributors were producer-dealers (dairy farmers who retail milk), although commercial or merchant-dealers were occasionally encountered, especially in suburban areas near major markets or in summer vacation districts.

Mileage requirements for daily and alternate-day delivery

In the summer of 1942, alternate-day delivery was not required in most of the rural areas of the state. As a result, the adoption of this program in the sample markets was far from uniform. The larger distributors in the larger rural markets were almost universally on an alternate-day basis, but in the smaller markets some distributors had not converted to this basis or had converted only partially. Some dealers with volumes under 200 quarts daily had adopted a "skip-day" plan, delivering double volumes to all customers on one day and making no deliveries on the following day.

The miles traveled on milk routes in the seventeen sample markets are given in Table 10. With daily operations, dealers in these markets had traveled 1,582 miles per day to make their deliveries. When the sample studies were made in 1942, alternate-day delivery had resulted in a reduction to 986 miles per day, or a saving of about 38 percent. If all dealers had been operating on an alternate-day delivery basis, it is estimated that mileage requirements would have totaled 900 miles per day, or a reduction of 43 percent below daily requirements. Individual dealers' mile-

---

[1] Excluding three rural markets in the New Haven area; these have been treated as part of the New Haven metropolitan market and are discussed in a later section.

age reductions depended on the nature of their routes, the completeness with which they had converted to alternate-day operations, and the type of alternate-day operations that they had selected. Where "skip-day" operations were practical, reductions amounted to 50 percent. With the more usual program of dividing

TABLE 10. Miles traveled on retail milk routes in making daily and alternate-day deliveries under the existing system of milk delivery, rural Connecticut markets, 1942.

Town	Quarts per day*	Route miles per day		
		Daily delivery	Summer 1942†	Alternate-day delivery
Ashford................	9	5	5	3
Bridgewater............	65	26	18	18
Harwinton.............	98	31	25	22
Willington.............	113	26	19	13
Brookfield.............	263	69	43	37
Ellington.............	363	55	42	30
Orange................	483	108	60	60
Somers................	488	74	37	37
Woodbridge............	554	116	68	68
Mansfield.............	583	118	80	63
Old Saybrook..........	782	88	59	57
Ridgefield.............	1,155	172	102	89
East Windsor..........	1,214	154	105	88
North Haven..........	1,699	281	162	162
Saybrook Area‡........	2,271	259	161	153
Total.............	10,140	1,582	986	900

* Differ from data in Table 3.5 in two respects: (1) 1942 rather than 1940 figures, and (2) these are the volumes actually reported and located within each market by dealers covered in sample studies.

† Alternate-day delivery was not required in rural areas at the time of the study, with the result that milk was being delivered on both a daily and an alternate-day basis.

‡ Including Saybrook, Chester, and Essex.

routes and servicing one-half on one day and the balance on the following day, mileage reductions averaged about 40 percent.

The total miles traveled daily by individual dealers increased with daily volume at a decreasing rate, but the relation was not close (Fig. 6). The scatter of individual observations reflected such factors as the density of milk consumption in the area, the extent to which the dealer had limited his operations, and the location of his plant relative to the majority of his customers. In

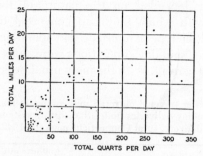

Fig. 6. Relation of miles traveled per dealer to quantity of milk distributed.

spite of this scatter, it is quite apparent that, on the average, larger dealers had higher delivery densities per mile of route: 50-quart dealers averaged about 10 quarts per mile of route while dealers handling 200 quarts or more averaged about 20 quarts per mile in these rural markets.

Duplication of delivery routes

Maps showing the existing systems of milk-delivery routes were made in each market. The map of alternate-day delivery routes for the Chester-Essex-Saybrook area is reproduced in Fig. 7.[2] From this it is quite clear that, while some duplication would be unavoidable under any home-delivery system, the competitive development of routes has resulted in a considerable amount of duplication and cross-hauling. How much of this could be avoided will be discussed in following chapters.

The total number of quarts delivered per mile of improved road in the sample rural markets is compared with the number delivered per mile of route under daily operations in Fig. 8. Route density was found to increase with market density, but at a much slower rate. While the distance traveled by delivery routes will necessarily exceed the number of miles of streets and roads on which deliveries are made because of such factors as return trips and unavoidable duplication with other routes, the very pronounced lag between the two measures can be explained

[2] Because most of the milk dealers in this area serve all three towns, they have been treated as a unit in the rural market studies.

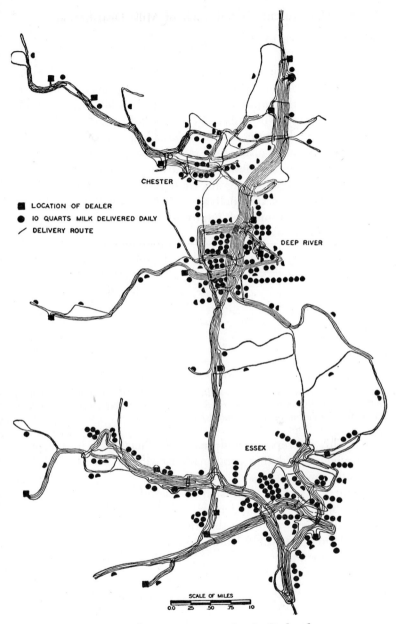

LOCATION OF DEALER
10 QUARTS MILK DELIVERED DAILY
DELIVERY ROUTE

CHESTER

DEEP RIVER

ESSEX

SCALE OF MILES
0.0   .25   .50   .75   10

*Fig. 7. System of truck routes in operation in Saybrook area, summer
1942.*

only by excessive route duplication such as existed in the Say-brook area.

It should be pointed out that measuring market delivery densities in terms of quarts per mile of improved road is an approximation that must be given relative rather than absolute interpretation in towns with small volumes of milk deliveries. This is true because deliveries are made on only a portion of the roads in such towns, thus causing total miles of improved road to depart significantly from the miles of roads on which deliveries are made. In the foregoing diagram, route densities in the low ranges are not higher than true delivery densities, but they are higher than densities per mile of improved road, for the reason just

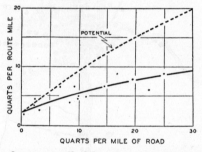

Fig. 8. Relation between milk deliveries per mile of road and per mile of route travel with daily delivery, rural Connecticut markets, 1942. See Chapter 13 for derivation of the potential curve.

given. This discrepancy will cause no difficulty if it is kept in mind when considering rural markets with relatively small volumes and low densities.

Figure 8 includes a regression line based on the reorganization studies discussed in later chapters. For the time being, it will not be described except to say that this line represents the approximate relation that would hold between market density and route density *if avoidable route duplication were eliminated.* The discrepancy between this line and the actual regression, then, reflects route inefficiency in the present organization of milk distribution in rural markets. In low-density ranges where only one or two dealers are now operating and where natural segregation has prevented route duplication, the two lines are about at the same level. As market density increases and more dealers enter the picture, however, duplication and cross-hauling become increasingly important. In the larger rural markets, this has reduced route efficiency to approximately half of its potential level.

Milk distribution as a supplementary enterprise

Almost all milk dealers in rural markets handled volumes too small to provide capacity utilization of manpower and equipment. As a result, milk distribution was usually a supplementary enterprise, with a large share of the operator's time devoted to other activities. While industrial or business employment was not

TABLE 11. Distribution of producer-dealers according to the percent of man-work-units used in the retail enterprise, Connecticut, 1937.*

Percent of man-work-units	Number of cases
0– 9.9	8
10–19.9	15
20–29.9	38
30–39.9	66
40–49.9	46
50–59.9	6
60–69.9	5
Total	184

* D. O. Hammerberg, I. F. Fellows, and R. H. Farr, *Efficiency of Milk Marketing in Connecticut, 4. Retail Distribution of Milk by Producers* (Storrs Agricultural Experiment Station, Bulletin 243, 1942). The man-work-unit is a measure of labor requirements.

uncommon in this connection, the dominant combination was dairy farming and milk distribution. Approximately 90 percent of the dealers in the rural markets of Connecticut were also dairy farmers (Table 7).

A study of the operations of 184 producer-dealers in 1937 revealed the side-line nature of milk distribution. These producer-dealers typically spent about one-third of their time in retailing milk, while in only a few cases was the delivery enterprise as important in terms of labor requirements as the farm operation (Table 11). Frequently the route was operated by a member of the family or a hired man who also worked on the farm and in the milk plant.

This nonspecialization also applied to much of the plant and delivery equipment. Trucks were commonly of the pickup type and were used around the farm when not in use on the delivery route. In most cases very little was required in the way of specialized buildings and equipment for plant operations, for only a few of these dealers handled enough volume to justify elaborate bottling equipment, and pasteurization equipment was even more unusual.

In short, milk distribution by these relatively small dealers was primarily an enterprise that had been added to provide productive employment for labor and equipment that was already available but incompletely utilized. As a consequence, entrepreneurial decisions were on a basis that differed significantly from that for the larger, specialized milk dealers. Opportunity costs and available alternatives were the dominant considerations, with many of the inputs of a noncash and indirect type. As a result, it is difficult to establish significant measures of costs for these dealers. This problem will be explored more completely in Part Three.

5 —

MILK DISTRIBUTION IN SECONDARY MARKETS

The Torrington market, 1942

Torrington, with a population of some 27,000 in 1940, is a city of brass and metal-working industries. It is located in northwestern Connecticut, about 20 miles from any other city. The surrounding rural area is fairly typical of the dairy farming found in the western Connecticut highlands, and the milkshed for the market lies for the most part within eight miles of the city. In September 1942, 51 milk handlers delivered more than 12,000 quarts daily in the area. Because of its isolated location, all but one or two of these handlers restricted their operations to Torrington and the immediately adjacent rural areas.

Individual handler volumes ranged from a few quarts to more than 3,000 quarts of milk daily. There were 39 handlers delivering less than 250 quarts daily, nine delivering from 250 to 500 quarts, and only three that delivered more than 500 quarts daily. These last three handled approximately one-half of the deliveries for the entire market. Classified according to type of dealer, there were: nine producer-dealers-limited [1] delivering a total of 54 quarts daily; 35 producer-dealers with an aggregate volume of 4,979 quarts; two subdealers delivering a total of 1,119 quarts; and five merchant-dealers with a combined volume of 6,073 quarts daily.

[1] Producer-dealers-limited deliver less than 10 quarts of milk daily. Because of their small size and the common practice of delivering only to neighbors, they were not included in the detailed study.

Details of route organizations and of consumer locations were obtained from 36 handlers delivering 8,631 quarts of retail and 3,054 quarts of wholesale milk daily. The total of 11,685 quarts daily represented 95 percent of all milk delivered in the market. Approximate plant locations and volumes for these handlers are indicated in Fig. 9, where subdealer volumes have been combined in the totals for the plants where the milk was processed. Only

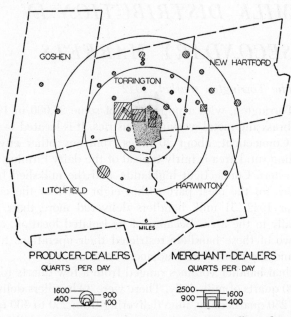

Fig. 9. Location of plants serving the Torrington milk market, 1942.

four plants are located within the first taxation district (for all practical purposes the urban market), and these are in the northern sections. The remaining plants, originating about half of the milk, are located outside of this district at distances ranging up to seven miles. While nearly three-quarters of the milk delivered in the market is pasteurized, only eight plants have pasteurizing equipment. Seven other handlers have all or part of their milk pasteurized at these plants on a custom basis.

The general pattern of consumer locations is shown in Fig. 10, where total milk deliveries per thousand feet of street have been plotted. This map is based on a division of the urban market into 50 subareas. Density of deliveries in these areas ranged from 3 to 260 quarts and averaged 27 quarts per thousand feet of street for the entire urban district. As is to be expected, densities were

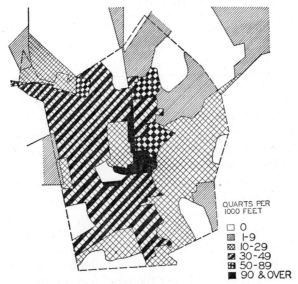

QUARTS PER
1000 FEET

☐ 0
▨ 1-9
▧ 10-29
▨ 30-49
⊞ 50-89
■ 90 & OVER

Fig. 10. Quarts of milk delivered per thousand feet of street on retail and wholesale routes, Torrington, 1942.

greatest in the central or business districts where they typically exceeded 50 quarts per thousand feet.

Duplication of Torrington routes

The duplication of milk-delivery routes under the present system is suggested by the frequency distribution in Table 12. The urban district was divided into 300 individual streets or sections of streets averaging one-quarter mile in length and the numbers of dealers serving each street were determined. Some streets were served by more than 20 of the 36 dealers studied, while the average for the entire market was eight dealers per street. Much of the duplication was related to the density of total deliveries on the

TABLE 12. Number of streets served by specified
numbers of milk dealers, Torrington, 1942.

Number of dealers delivering on street	Number of streets*
1– 4	110
5– 8	73
9–12	60
13–16	32
17–20	21
21–24	4
Total	300

* Long streets have been subdivided into sections of approximately one-half mile. The average length of street in this tabulation was about one-quarter mile.

streets in question, as is indicated in Fig. 11. Since long streets
tend to have more dealers than short streets when density is held
constant, this diagram includes only streets between 1,000 and
2,000 feet long. The number of dealers per street is found to increase with increases in density, but at a slightly decreasing rate.
This means that delivery densities for the average dealer were not
much higher in the areas of concentrated population than in the
less densely populated sections. According to the diagram, five
dealers typically served streets where total density was 10 quarts
per thousand feet, while 16 dealers were typical when the total
density averaged 50 quarts per thousand feet. Delivery densities
for individual dealers then averaged approximately 2 quarts when

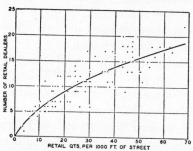

Fig. 11. Relation between delivery density and number of dealers per
street, Torrington, 1942. This figure is based on retail milk and includes
only those streets between 1,000 and 2,000 feet long. Most of the scatter
around the regression line is due to this variation in street length and the
associated total volume per street.

total density was 10 quarts, and 3 quarts when total density was 50 quarts per thousand feet of street. In other words, the competitive development of milk distribution has tended to eliminate the natural advantages associated with heavy concentration of population.

Probably the best indication of delivery duplication is the comparison of the miles actually traveled by delivery routes with the miles of streets in the area. The 36 handlers for which detailed information was obtained traveled a total of 1,384 miles making deliveries on a daily basis and 853 miles daily on an alternate-day delivery basis. Surfaced streets and roads in the town measure 128 miles, while milk was actually delivered on only 82 miles of these streets. Considering only the distances traveled within the urban section of the market and not the distances traveled to and from plants located outside this area, Torrington dealers averaged about 10 quarts of milk per mile of delivery route. The total market density, as mentioned above, was about 27 quarts per thousand feet, or more than 140 quarts per mile of street in the urban section. While it would be impossible to deliver milk without some duplication, it is clear that actual delivery densities are only a fraction of those that would be possible under an efficient delivery system.

Route miles

With daily delivery, only four Torrington dealers used more than one delivery route. In total the 36 dealers operated 45 retail and mixed routes and three wholesale routes, covering 1,384 miles daily. With the low volumes per dealer that characterized the market, most of the routes provided neither capacity utilization of the delivery equipment nor a full day's employment for the driver. When the Connecticut Milk Administrator made alternate-day retail delivery compulsory in this and other urban areas, the route travel was decreased to 853 miles, a saving of 38 percent. The utilization of equipment and labor improved in a few cases, as the number was reduced to 43 retail and three wholesale routes per day.

Distances traveled by individual dealers varied from 12 to 175 miles daily with daily delivery and increased with dealer volume at a decreasing rate. Large dealers were generally more efficient than small handlers with respect to delivery density, as is indicated in Fig. 12. Density tended to increase rapidly as dealer volume increased to 400 quarts, and then at a slower rate as volume continued to increase. At any given volume there was a fairly wide range in actual densities, reflecting differences in the efficiency of route organization within the area and in the extent to which the dealers concentrated their operations in sections of the market. Hauling distances to and from the market have been eliminated in constructing this diagram, but would have resulted in even wider dispersions if they had been included in calculating

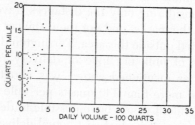

Fig. 12. Relation between dealer volume and quarts per mile of delivery routes, Torrington, 1942.

delivery densities. Even the most efficient dealers, it should be noted, were far below the average total density of 140 quarts per mile.

Milk distribution in Willimantic, 1943

In February 1943 a study of milk marketing in Willimantic was undertaken to supplement the study made in Torrington. The city of Willimantic had a population of about 12,000 in 1940 while the town of Windham, which includes the city of Willimantic, had a population of about 14,000. This milk market is much smaller than the Torrington market, but it is in many respects similar. It is located 25 miles from any major market and 15 miles from the nearest secondary market. With the exception of a few quarts delivered in rural areas outside the town of Windham, dealers in general confined their deliveries to the Willimantic market.

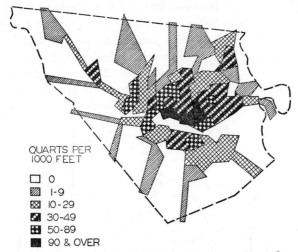

QUARTS PER
1000 FEET

☐ 0
▨ 1-9
⊠ 10-29
▨ 30-49
⊞ 50-89
■ 90 & OVER

Fig. 13. Quarts of retail and wholesale milk delivered per thousand feet of street, Willimantic, 1943.

The market is served mainly by producer-dealers living at some distance from Willimantic. At the time the study was made 40 dealers were delivering slightly more than 6,900 quarts per day. Twelve of these 40 were producer-dealers-limited delivering a total of about 70 quarts of milk. Because of their small size and the fact that in their normal operation little or no mileage is involved in delivery, they were omitted from the study. Of the remaining 28, records were obtained from 25 dealers. Twelve delivered less than 100 quarts per day, five delivered between 100

TABLE 13. Distribution of areas in Willimantic milk
market according to density of milk delivery, 1943.

Quarts per 1,000 feet of street	Number of areas
0– 9	19
10–19	11
20–29	12
30–39	13
40–49	7
50 and over	18
	—
Total	80

and 200 quarts, five between 200 and 500 quarts, and only three
delivered more than 500 quarts of milk per day. The largest dealer
in the market delivered more than 2,500 quarts daily. Only two
of the sample dealers were merchant-dealers and they delivered
a total of 2,941 quarts. The remaining 23 were producer-dealers
with a combined total of 3,803 quarts daily. The amount of milk
delivered daily by all dealers in the sample was 6,744 quarts or

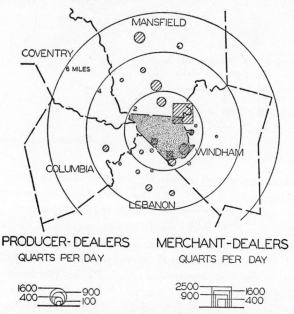

PRODUCER-DEALERS   MERCHANT-DEALERS
QUARTS PER DAY   QUARTS PER DAY

Fig. 14. Location of plants serving the Willimantic milk market, 1943.

97 percent of all the milk delivered in the market. Of this total,
34 percent was wholesale and 66 percent retail.

The location of the areas of heaviest consumption is shown in
Fig. 13. This map is based on a division of the urban market into
80 areas. Density in these areas ranged from less than 1 to 200
quarts per thousand feet of street and averaged 35 quarts per
thousand feet considering only the urban area (Willimantic).
Density is highest in the central and eastern sections of the city.

The location of dealers and their approximate size is shown in
Fig. 14. Only four plants were located within the city limits of

Willimantic, and the largest dealer in the area was located just outside the city. While 70 percent of the milk in the market was pasteurized, only five dealers had pasteurizing equipment.[2] In contrast with Torrington, where a number of dealers carried custom-pasteurized milk, only one dealer did so in Willimantic.

Route mileage and duplication in Willimantic

Information was obtained from each dealer regarding the amount of milk delivered in each of the 80 areas. Some idea of the amount of duplication can be gained from Table 14, where

TABLE 14. Number of areas served by specified numbers of milk dealers, Willimantic, 1943.

Number of dealers delivering in area	Number of areas*
1– 4	19
5– 8	24
9–12	25
13–16	10
17–20	2
Total	80

* The average area contained less than 0.5 mile of paved streets.

the areas are classified by the number of dealers serving them. Two of the areas were served by 17 or more of the 25 coöperating dealers while 45 percent of the areas were served by nine or more dealers.

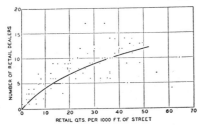

Fig. 15. Relation between delivery density per thousand feet of street and number of retail dealers serving the area, Willimantic, 1943.

[2] Since the study was made one additional dealer has installed pasteurizing equipment.

It can be seen from Fig. 15 that some of the duplication was related to density. As the density of consumption increased, the number of dealers per area increased. However, they did not increase in the same proportion but at a decreasing rate, and as a result dealers' densities of delivery did not increase greatly in areas of high consumption. This means that high density of delivery, a very important factor in saving mileage, has been practically dissipated in the areas where it could be highest.

With all dealers on daily unrestricted delivery, a total of 703 miles was traveled by milk trucks. Individual dealers ranged from 2 to 190 miles per day. When the field work was under way, the dealers in Willimantic were partially on alternate-day delivery. Some dealers were delivering every other day, some were delivering part of a route every day and part every other day, and some dealers were delivering every day. Under this system the distance traveled by all dealers was 508 miles, or a saving of 28 percent. If all dealers had been on alternate-day delivery, the saving would have been considerably larger.

There are 73 miles of paved and surfaced roads in Windham, including Willimantic, and only 55 miles on which delivery of milk was made. With daily delivery, each mile on which delivery of milk was made was traveled an average of 13 times. In the case of the mixed daily and alternate-day delivery, the average street was covered about nine times. Even though some duplication is necessary, this amount appears to be high.

Most of the dealers had only one route and that was usually operated either by themselves or by a member of the family. With daily delivery, the 25 dealers operated 30 retail and three wholesale routes. When the study was made, alternate-day delivery had been partially adopted and the number of routes changed to 28 retail and four wholesale. Under such a delivery system very little saving in manpower and equipment was possible through consolidating routes and increasing loads for individual dealers.

6 —

MILK DISTRIBUTION IN MAJOR MARKETS

Milk distribution in Hartford, 1940

Hartford, with a population of more than 166,000 in 1940, is the largest city in Connecticut. Because of its size and the availability of milk-consumption data, it was the first town in the state to be covered by the studies of milk marketing efficiency. Basic data for the study were obtained from three principal sources: (1) sales reports and license applications made to the Connecticut Milk Administrator; (2) published and unpublished results of milk consumption surveys made by the Hartford Board of Health;[1] and (3) route volume and mileage reports obtained from a sample of dealers in connection with studies of alternate-day milk delivery. The data from the Milk Administrator were used to determine the number and location of dealers serving the city of Hartford and the approximate volumes they distributed in Hartford and nearby towns. The Board of Health surveys gave a detailed description of the pattern of total deliveries by all dealers on the various streets of the city. The sample survey data on retail routes, when coupled with total volume data, made it possible to estimate the equivalent number of routes serving Hartford and the miles traveled with daily and alternate-day delivery.

In March 1940 there were 149 handlers delivering milk to homes, stores, restaurants, and factories in Hartford. These deal-

---

[1] Louis Horwitz, "Survey of Daily Milk Consumption in the City of Hartford," Hartford Board of Health Mimeograph (1940).

TABLE 15. Distribution of milk dealers by type and size, Hartford, March 1940.*

| | Type of dealer | | | | | | | | | |
| Quarts per day† | Merchant | | Producer | | Sub | | Total | | Percent | |
	Number	Volume	Number	Volume	Number	Volume	Number	Volume	Number	Volume
1– 166	24	2 017	46	3 234	20	1,733	90	6,984	60	12
167– 333	11	2 413	14	3,195	7	1,542	32	7,149	21	13
334– 499	3	1,115	4	1,805	2	892	9	3,812	6	7
500– 666	2	1,199	3	1,734	—	—	5	2,933	3	5
667– 833	—	—	4	2,751	—	—	4	2,751	3	5
834–1,666	2	2,001	1	837	—	—	3	2,838	2	5
1,667–3,333	—	—	2	4,746	—	—	2	4,746	1	9
3,334 and over	3	20,076	1	4,145	—	—	4	24,221	3	44
Total	45	28,821	75	22,447	29	4,166	149	55,434	100	100
Percent	30	52	50	40	20	8	100	100		

* Based on data from the Connecticut Milk Administrator.
† Volume of milk delivered within the city limits of Hartford.

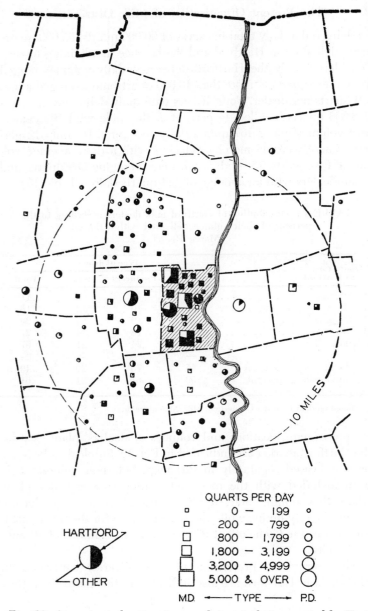

QUARTS PER DAY

□	0 — 199	○
□	200 — 799	○
□	800 — 1,799	○
□	1,800 — 3,199	○
□	3,200 — 4,999	○
□	5,000 & OVER	○

HARTFORD

OTHER

M.D. ◄——— TYPE ———► P.D.

Fig. 16. Approximate location, type, and size of plants operated by Hartford milk dealers, with the proportion of total plant volume delivered in Hartford, March 1940.

[55]

ers delivered a daily total in excess of 90,000 quarts, 55,000 quarts being delivered in Hartford and the balance in adjoining towns.[2] Considering only the Hartford deliveries, daily volumes ranged from a few quarts to more than 10,000 quarts and averaged about 370 quarts per dealer. Four dealers with daily deliveries in excess of 3,333 quarts handled 44 percent of the milk, while 90 dealers with volumes under 167 quarts daily accounted for only 12 percent. There were 45 merchant-dealers with a daily average volume of 640 quarts, 75 producer-dealers averaging 299 quarts, and 29 subdealers with an average of 144 quarts daily (Table 15).

TABLE 16. Distribution of Hartford milk dealers according to the percent of their volume delivered within the city, March 1940.*

Percent of deliveries in Hartford	Type of dealer			
	Merchant	Producer	Sub	Total
1– 20	6	4	1	11
21– 40	4	10	2	16
41– 60	8	19	1	28
61– 80	5	18	4	27
81–100	22	24	21	67
Total	45	75	29	149
Weighted average percent	59	61	81	61

* Based on data from the Connecticut Milk Administrator.

Approximate locations and volumes of dealers' plants serving the Hartford market are indicated in Fig. 16. Subdealers have not been indicated separately in this map, but their volumes have been included with the merchant- and producer-dealer plants where they obtain their supplies. Only 20 plants were located within the city limits, while the balance were for the most part to the west of the Connecticut River and within a radius of 10 miles of the city.

The approximate proportions of total deliveries that were actually made in Hartford are also indicated in this map. Even those

[2] License applications gave the approximate percentage distribution by towns. As these were used to determine the total volume for Hartford, this figure is admittedly only an approximation.

dealers located in the city usually delivered substantial proportions of their sales in other towns. As is to be expected, there was
some tendency for the proportion of Hartford deliveries to decrease as distance from the city increased. When considered according to type of handler, it was found that both merchant- and
producer-dealers averaged about 60 percent of their sales in Hartford and 40 percent in nearby towns. Subdealers limited their
operations to a greater extent, delivering an average of less than
20 percent outside of the city limits (Table 16).

As already mentioned, the Hartford Board of Health survey of
milk consumption gave the volumes of milk delivered on the
various streets in the city. To put these data into a more con-

TABLE 17. Frequency distribution of Hartford subdivisions
according to the density of total milk deliveries per
thousand feet of street.°

Quarts per 1,000 feet of street	Number of subdivisions
10– 29	19
30– 49	25
50– 69	31
70– 89	45
90–109	16
110 and over	14
Total	150

° Based on data from the Hartford Board of Health.

venient form, the city was divided into 150 small tracts containing
on the average 1.25 miles of streets and in which about 350 quarts
of milk were delivered. Density of consumption (total deliveries)
in these tracts ranged up to 800 quarts per mile of street (more
than 150 quarts per thousand feet). A frequency distribution of
the tracts according to density is given in Table 17, while the
geographic variations are indicated in Fig. 17.

The total volume of milk deliveries included in the Board of
Health survey was 52,497 quarts per day. This compares with an
estimate of 55,434 based on records submitted to the Milk Administrator. In view of the necessary limitations of both estimates,
this agreement must be considered remarkably close. In most of

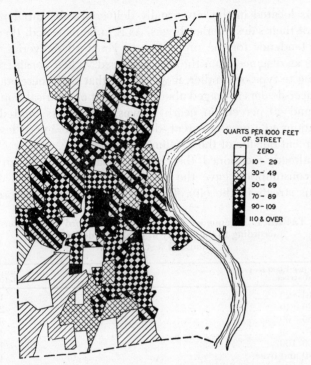

QUARTS PER 1000 FEET
OF STREET

ZERO
10 - 29
30 - 49
50 - 69
70 - 89
90 - 109
110 & OVER

Fig. 17. Geographic variations in the density of total milk deliveries, Hartford, 1940.

the computations that follow, the Board of Health data have been used. This selection has been necessary because a detailed geographic pattern of deliveries was essential to the work; it does not indicate that one estimate is more reliable than the other.

Route volumes and mileages in Hartford

Estimates of route volumes and mileages were obtained from a sample of 16 dealers in the Hartford area who delivered more than 48,000 quarts daily. Of this total, about 28,000 quarts were delivered in Hartford proper, so the sample accounted for more than half of all Hartford deliveries. Distances traveled on the sample routes totaled 5,675 miles per day with daily delivery, for an average delivery density of 8.6 quarts per mile of route travel. With alternate-day delivery and the elimination of special deliveries, density was increased to an average of 15.4 quarts per mile. Wholesale routes in this area averaged about 40 quarts per mile of delivery route.

By dividing the total volume of milk deliveries in Hartford by the above average delivery densities, it is possible to estimate the miles of milk routes in Hartford. Total deliveries, according to the Board of Health survey, were 52,497 quarts per day. About 81 percent of this total represented home deliveries, while the balance, 19 percent, represented wholesale deliveries. Applying the density rates, estimates are obtained of about 5,130 miles per day with daily delivery and 2,970 miles per day with alternate-day delivery. As these estimates are only for the city proper, while the density rates are for the metropolitan area (routes extended into suburban towns), it may seem reasonable to assume that the results overstate the mileage requirements. There is a pronounced tendency for route duplication to increase with total delivery density, however, so that average densities per mile of route are not much higher for central sections than for the entire district. Other studies have indicated that the upward bias as a result of this procedure is less than 3 percent.[3] This would be counterbalanced by the fact that the sample dealers were larger than average, for dealers with large volumes tend to have higher than average delivery densities. Modifications for these factors would probably be small, however, and present purposes may be served by stating that daily milk deliveries in Hartford required about 5,000 miles of delivery-truck travel in 1940, while alternate-day deliveries required approximately 3,000 miles per day.

These distances were traveled in an area containing only 184 miles of city streets. While some streets would be traveled by more than one route even under ideal conditions, route mileages 27 times as large as street mileages with daily delivery and 16 times as high with alternate-day delivery indicate pronounced route duplication. Few of the dealers serving the market confined their operations to any one section of the city. Even dealers with small volumes had routes that extended into many sections. This is

[3] In the New Haven area, as reported in following sections, daily delivery densities averaged 8.3 quarts per route mile for the city and 8.1 quarts per route mile for the seven-town metropolitan district.

illustrated by the data in Table 18, where the numbers of tracts served by each of seven dealers are summarized. Dealer A, with only 0.2 percent of the total Hartford deliveries, served customers in nearly one-third of the 150 tracts into which the city was

TABLE 18. Daily volume of milk deliveries and number of tracts in which deliveries were made, seven Hartford milk dealers, 1940.

Dealer	Daily volume* (quarts)	Tracts served† (number)
A	125	47
B	735	117
C	1,649	141
D	2,699	149
E	3,782	149
F	3,818	149
G	11,195	150

* Excluding milk delivered outside of the Hartford city limits.
† As explained in the text, the city was divided into 150 small areas or tracts, containing an average of 1.25 miles of streets.

divided. Similarly, dealer B delivered only 1.4 percent of the milk but entered about three-quarters of the tracts. The other dealers, handling from three to 22 percent of total sales, delivered milk in all or practically all of the subdivisions.

Milk distribution in the New Haven metropolitan market, 1942

The city of New Haven, located on Long Island Sound, had a population of 161,000 in 1940. From the standpoint of milk marketing, this major market was the center of a metropolitan district consisting of seven towns and cities with an aggregate population in excess of 230,000. In addition to New Haven, the metropolitan district included the secondary markets of Hamden, West Haven, and East Haven and the rural markets of North Haven, Orange, and Woodbridge. Because many dealers operate in all seven of the towns and most dealers in the area deliver milk in at least several of them, these towns constitute in most respects a single milk market. While some discrepancies are found in the local health ordinances concerning milk, especially in that New Haven requires the pasteurization of Grade B milk, the metropolitan

TABLE 19. Proportions of dealers and of milk deliveries included in the study of the New Haven metropolitan milk market, 1942.*

Town and item	Merchant-dealer Number	Merchant-dealer Daily quarts	Producer-dealer Number	Producer-dealer Daily quarts	Subdealer Number	Subdealer Daily quarts	Producer-dealer-limited Number	Producer-dealer-limited Daily quarts	All dealers Number	All dealers Daily quarts
New Haven										
Sample	16	39,878	13	5,030	22	3,846	—	—	51	48,754
Total	18	40,394	20	5,871	36	5,861	—	—	74	52,126
Percent in sample	89	99	65	86	61	66	—	—	69	94
Hamden										
Sample	13	8,403	12	728	12	197			37	9,328
Total	15	8,699	18	900	16	309	2	6	51	9,914
Percent in sample	87	97	67	81	75	64			73	94
West Haven										
Sample	14	8,143	8	736	8	124			30	9,003
Total	16	8,427	12	875	14	322	2	7	44	9,631
Percent in sample	88	97	67	84	57	39			68	93
East Haven										
Sample	12	2,481	5	498	5	136			22	3,115
Total	12	2,481	5	498	7	244	2	14	26	3,237
Percent in sample	100	100	100	100	71	56			85	96
North Haven										
Sample	9	1,543	7	108	2	48			18	1,699
Total	9	1,543	11	228	2	48	3	20	25	1,839
Percent in sample	100	100	64	47	100	100			72	92
Woodbridge										
Sample	3	216	3	325	1	13			7	554
Total	3	216	4	336	2	21	2	16	11	589
Percent in sample	100	100	75	97	50	62			64	94
Orange										
Sample	5	376	4	107					9	483
Total	5	376	5	117	1	26	5	24	16	543
Percent in sample	100	100	80	91	—	—			56	89
Seven Town Total										
Sample	16	61,040	16	7,532	23	4,364			55	72,936
Total	18	62,136	31	8,825	38	6,831	14	87	101	77,879
Percent in sample	89	98	52	85	61	64			54	94

* Data for dealers not included in the study were obtained from records of the Connecticut Milk Administrator.

area is subject to similar economic factors, obtains its milk from one milkshed, and is generally served by the same group of dealers. The studies of milk distribution in this area, therefore, have considered the seven towns as a single metropolitan market.

Basic data for the studies were obtained directly from coöperating dealers. They included records on the number, volume, and mileage of delivery routes. In addition, route books were examined to obtain detailed descriptions of the location of deliveries. Such information was secured for a sample estimated to include 94 percent of all deliveries made in the market.

During the 1942 period, the city of New Haven was served by 74 dealers (Table 19). In addition, 27 other handlers (including 14 producer-dealers-limited, each of whom distributed less than 10 quarts daily) operated in the suburban towns but not in New Haven. These 101 dealers distributed nearly 78,000 quarts of milk daily in the metropolitan district. Detailed information was obtained from 55 dealers handling a total of nearly 73,000 quarts, 51,000 of which were retail deliveries. This sample has been used as the basis for the following descriptions and analyses of the New Haven milk market.[4]

The locations of dealer and producer-dealer plants are given in Fig. 18, with approximate indications of size. The volumes handled by subdealers have been included with the volumes of the plants supplying the milk in this diagram. Deliveries ranged from a few quarts to nearly 20,000 quarts of retail and wholesale milk daily. The location of consumers, on the other hand, is shown in Fig. 19, where daily quarts of milk per thousand feet of street have been indicated. These delivery densities have been based on an arbitrary division of the market into nearly 1,000 subdivisions. The subdivisions formed a regular grid of squares about 2,100 feet on a side, so that each small square contained roughly 0.16 square mile of area. Milk deliveries were made in only 510 of these squares. Delivery density averaged about 20 quarts per thousand feet of street. Highest densities were about

[4] In fairness to the excellent coöperation extended by practically all dealers in the area, it should be pointed out that the omissions in the sample were due almost entirely to time and personnel limitations of the research staff. A number of small dealers actually submitted their detailed records by mail after the field work had been completed.

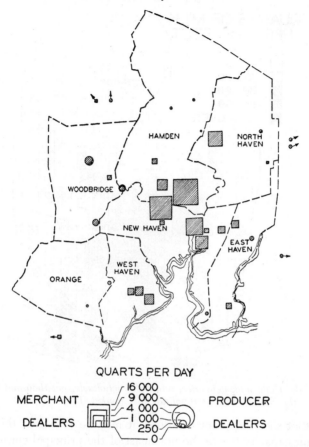

QUARTS PER DAY

MERCHANT DEALERS

16 000
9 000
4 000
1 000
250
0

PRODUCER DEALERS

Fig. 18. *Approximate location, type, and size of dealers' plants serving the New Haven metropolitan milk market, 1942. Deliveries made by subdealers have been included with the volumes handled by the merchant-dealers who processed and bottled the milk.*

85 quarts per thousand feet of street for retail sales and 95 quarts per thousand feet for wholesale sales. Heaviest total deliveries occurred in the downtown sections of New Haven, where retail plus wholesale sales reached a maximum of 120 quarts per thousand feet of street. There were also fairly dense delivery areas corresponding with population concentrations in East Haven, West Haven, and Hamden. Comparing the delivery density map

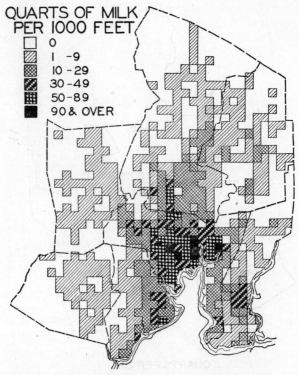

Fig. 19. Daily milk deliveries, retail plus wholesale, per thousand feet of street in the New Haven metropolitan milk market, 1942.

with that showing plant locations, it may be seen that the bulk of plant capacity lies to the northeast of the principal consuming areas. Plants are scattered throughout the entire area, however, with a number of relatively small plants on the periphery of the market.

The present delivery system

Under the present system, routes operated by the dealers included in the study covered about 9,045 miles with daily delivery. Alternate-day delivery and the elimination of special deliveries reduced this to 5,284 miles per day, or a saving of 42 percent. These served an area with only 700 miles of streets. Average delivery densities were about 8 quarts per route-mile with daily delivery and 14 quarts per route-mile with alternate-day delivery (Table 20). In spite of pronounced variation from town to town in deliveries per mile of street, as shown in Fig. 19, deliveries per mile of route were much more stable. They ranged from 4.5 quarts per route-mile with daily delivery in the rural town of Orange, for example, to 9.3 quarts per route-mile in Hamden.

Individual dealers differed widely from the market average density. This is shown by the data in Table 21, where dealers have been classified according to their volume and route density. As volume increased, there was a natural tendency for delivery den-

TABLE 20. Milk route miles and delivery densities in the
New Haven area, 1942.

Town	Daily volume (quarts)	Route miles*		Route density†	
		Daily	Alternate-day	Daily (qts./mile)	Alternate-day (qts./mile)
New Haven........	48,754	5,890	3,454	8.3	14.1
Hamden..........	9,328	1,000	580	9.3	16.1
West Haven.......	9,003	1,200	700	7.5	12.9
East Haven.......	3,115	450	260	6.9	12.0
North Haven......	1,699	281	162	6.0	10.5
Woodbridge.......	554	116	68	4.8	8.1
Orange...........	483	108	60	4.5	8.0
Total.........	72,936	9,045	5,284	8.1	13.8

* The breakdown of total miles among the seven towns is only approximate. Where routes operated in several towns, the delivery portions of the routes were divided according to the actual route organization, while hauling miles were allocated between towns in proportion to volume.

† Total deliveries divided by route miles.

sity to increase. Dealers with less than 500 quarts daily averaged about 3.5 quarts per route-mile. Those with more than 6,000 quarts, on the other hand, had an average density of about 12 quarts per route-mile. It is significant, however, that some relatively small dealers confined their operations sufficiently to attain delivery densities comparable with the larger handlers.

A measure of the concentration of present delivery areas is given in Fig. 20, where dealer volumes have been plotted against the number of market subdivisions in which deliveries were made. This diagram shows that the areas served by individual dealers

TABLE 21. Cross-classification table showing the distribution of
New Haven milk dealers by volume and density classes, 1942.

Quarts per route mile	Dealer volume—quarts per day						
	0-499	500-999	1,000-1,999	2,000-2,999	3,000-5,999	6,000 and over	All
	(No.)	(No.)	(No.)	(No.)	(No.)	(No.)	(No.)
0.1– 2.0	9	—	—	—	—	—	9
2.1– 6.0	16	1	—	—	—	—	17
4.1– 6.0	5	3	1	1	—	—	10
6.1– 8.0	2	4	—	1	2	—	9
8.1–10.0	—	—	2	—	—	—	2
10.1–14.0	2	2	1	—	—	3	8
All	34	10	4	2	2	3	55

increased with volume, but at a decreasing rate. It also shows the
tendency for some dealers to concentrate their deliveries in a
small district while others served customers in many subdivisions.
Several dealers with volumes between 500 and 1,000 quarts, for
example, confined their operation to about 30 subdivisions while
others in the same volume range served as many as 120 subdi-

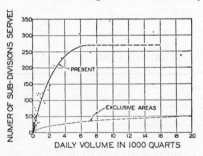

Fig. 20. *Effect of dealer volume on the number of market subdivisions in
which milk deliveries were made, New Haven market, 1942. The broken line
near the bottom of the diagram is based on the number of subdivisions that
would have been required if all dealers had been assigned exclusive delivery
areas, as discussed in following chapters.*

visions. All dealers who delivered more than 2,500 quarts daily
operated in more than 200 subdivisions, with two of these dealers
delivering to customers in more than 300 of the small areas. It
will be recalled that the metropolitan market contained 510 subdivisions in which milk deliveries were made in 1942.

Duplication in the New Haven area

With 9,000 miles of route travel on 700 miles of streets, it is clear that route duplication was very important in this market. Another measure of duplication is given in Table 22, where the subdivisions of the market are classified according to the number of dealers serving the areas. While the metropolitan area averaged about eight dealers per subdivision, nearly one-quarter of the

TABLE 22. Numbers of dealers delivering milk in subdivisions of the New Haven metropolitan milk market, 1942.*

| Number of dealers per subdivision | Number of subdivisions in | | | | | | | |
	New Haven	Hamden	West Haven	East Haven	North Haven	Wood-bridge	Orange	Total
1– 4	4	63	15	28	59	53	44	266
5– 8	12	21	15	15	5	2	1	71
9–12	17	14	17	7	3	—	—	58
13–16	16	8	16	5	—	—	—	45
17–20	17	5	3	—	—	—	—	25
21–24	11	1	—	—	—	—	—	12
25–28	13	—	—	—	—	—	—	13
29–32	13	—	—	—	—	—	—	13
33–36	6	—	—	—	—	—	—	6
37–40	1	—	—	—	—	—	—	1
Total	110	112	66	55	67	55	45	510
Weighted average†	19	6	9	6	3	3	3	8

* The seven-town area was divided into 993 squares approximately 2,100 feet on a side. Milk deliveries were made in 510 of these subdivisions. The remaining 483 represented parks, rural areas, and other uninhabited sections of the market.
† Weighted average number of dealers per subdivision, rounded to whole numbers.

small squares were served by 13 or more handlers and 4 percent were served by more than 28 dealers. Average duplication differed significantly from town to town, ranging from three dealers per subdivision in the rural towns to 19 dealers per square in the city of New Haven.

Some of the foregoing comparisons suggest that the degree of duplication was associated with delivery density per mile of street, and this was indeed the case. As shown in Fig. 21, there was a marked tendency for the number of dealers to increase with increases in total density.[5] This competition for sales offset to a considerable extent the natural delivery advantages associated with heavy concentration of population. In the city of New Haven, to illustrate this, six dealers typically served areas with retail delivery densities of 5 quarts per thousand feet of street, while the average number was 17 where density averaged 30 quarts per thousand feet. Density for the average dealer, then, only doubled while total density for all dealers increased sixfold.

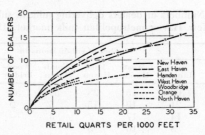

Fig. 21. Net effect of total retail deliveries per mile of street on the number of dealers serving subdivisions of the New Haven metropolitan milk market, by towns, 1942.

It is evident that milk-delivery routes in the New Haven area duplicate extensively under the present system, and that route mileages are excessive. Unrestrained competition for customers has resulted in more than 9,000 miles of milk routes on 700 miles of streets, in 15, 20, or even 30 dealers serving customers in many small subdivisions of the market, and in average delivery densities of about 8 quarts per route-mile in a market where total delivery density averaged more than 100 quarts per mile of street.

[5] To hold constant the influence of variations in miles of street per subdivision, only those areas containing from 0.8 to 1.2 miles of street were used in constructing these regression lines. Curvilinear correlation coefficients (corrected for parameters) were: New Haven, 0.79; Hamden, 0.93; West Haven, 0.94; East Haven, 0.65; North Haven, 0.77; Woodbridge, 0.82; and Orange, 0.46.

7 —

SUMMARY DESCRIPTION OF THE PRESENT DISTRIBUTION SYSTEM

Effect of market density on route mileages

The sample studies reported in previous chapters covered 17 rural towns where total delivery densities were less than 30 quarts per mile of improved roads, five secondary markets with densities ranging from 30 to 119 quarts per street mile, and two major markets with densities between 200 and 300 quarts per mile. The findings of these studies with respect to daily and alternate-day delivery mileages are summarized in Fig. 22. Route-miles per quart of milk delivered, the reciprocal of route delivery density, decreased approximately from 0.4 to 0.1 with daily delivery and from 0.2 to 0.07 with alternate-day delivery as market densities increased from 1 to 400 quarts per mile of street.

These regressions made it clear that route operations were most concentrated and efficient in heavily populated areas where total deliveries per mile of street were high. The competitive development of routes, however, had nullified to a large extent the natural advantage associated with high density. In areas where total milk deliveries averaged less than 10 quarts per street mile, natural segregation had prevented excessive route duplication so that the quarts delivered per mile of route compared favorably with total delivery densities. In city areas with total deliveries averaging more than 100 quarts per street mile, on the other hand, daily delivery routes averaged only 10 quarts per mile of travel,

Instead of bringing high levels of efficiency, the limited type of competition in milk distribution has resulted in low efficiency regardless of the natural conditions.

Alternate-day delivery affected milk routes in several ways. In the first place, it had the effect of doubling the effective delivery density, with a consequent reduction in delivery-route mileages. Second, under some situations such as the adoption of "skip-day" deliveries, it reduced the miles traveled between plants and the delivery areas. Finally, it reduced delivery-time requirements both through reducing route miles and by doubling the volume

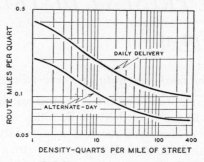

Fig. 22. *Effects of total delivery density on daily and alternate-day delivery mileages under the present system of milk distribution, Connecticut markets. These regression lines have been based on detailed studies made in 24 Connecticut towns and cities. Markets with densities below 30 quarts per mile of street have been defined in these studies as rural markets, those with densities from 30 to 119 quarts as secondary markets, and those with densities of 120 quarts or more as major markets.*

delivered at each stop. Savings in time meant improved labor efficiency, and permitted important increases in route loads; this further reduced total delivery mileage and also decreased the number of trucks and men required to deliver a given total volume of milk.

The regressions in Fig. 22 indicate that alternate-day delivery reduced route miles about 50 percent in rural areas, where many dealers were able to use the "skip-day" type of organization. In general, the reduction resulting from the program decreased as total market density increased, approaching 35 percent as density approached 400 quarts per street mile. In all areas, however, the alternate-day delivery program was very effective and undoubtedly has been the most significant development in milk distribution since the introduction of deliveries in bottles rather than in bulk.

Estimates of milk delivery miles for the entire state

Estimates for any individual market based on these regressions will be subject to a considerable range of error.[1] The standard error of estimate for the daily-delivery regression was 25 percent, while for the alternate-day-delivery curve it was 29 percent. Since there was a marked tendency for relatively high daily-delivery miles per quart to be associated with high alternate-day-delivery miles per quart, the use of these regressions to estimate the *percent reduction* in delivery miles that resulted from alternate-day operations was more precise, with a standard error of estimate of only

TABLE 23. Estimates of milk-delivery mileages under the present system for rural, secondary, and major markets in Connecticut.

Type of market	Number of towns	Daily quarts*	Estimated delivery miles per day†	
			Daily	Alternate-day
Rural............	125	67,633	9,641	5,338
Secondary.......	36	209,663	25,738	15,406
Major..........	8	238,363	25,710	16,210
Total.......	169	515,659	61,089	36,954

* Based on 1940 records of the Connecticut Milk Administrator.
† Estimated from the relations given in Fig. 22.

10 percent. These standard errors mean that, while any individual estimate may deviate from the true delivery mileage because of such factors as the number and size of dealers serving the market, the estimates may be expected to fall within 25, 29, or 10 percent of the true values in approximately two-thirds of the cases considered.

When estimates for a number of markets are combined, the totals for the group are much more reliable than the individual estimates. This is because positive and negative errors in the

[1] These relations may be subject to some criticism since total market volume is involved in both the dependent and the independent variable. For this reason, correlation may be partially spurious, and so coefficients have not been calculated. The form of the relation is particularly well adapted to the analysis of milk-delivery requirements, however, and has been used in this and following chapters.

TABLE 24. Summary of daily and alternate-day retail delivery operations for 100 Connecticut milk dealers, 1942.

Sub-classification	No. of dealers	Daily delivery			Alternate-day delivery			Percent reduction in miles	Percent change in volume
		No. of routes	Daily quarts	Daily miles	No. of routes	Daily quarts	Daily miles		
All routes.........	100	440	133,528	16,310	378.5	134,144	9,147	44	0
*Classified by type of adjustment**									
Split-routes.........	62	139	40,266	6,133	139	40,459	3,710	40	0
Consolidation.........	17	271	87,159	9,280	224.5	87,625	4,995	46	+1
Skip-routes.........	21	30	6,103	897	15	6,060	442	51	−1
Classified by type of dealer†									
Merchant-dealer.....	26	279	88,723	9,884	234	88,490	5,442	45	0
Producer-dealer.....	58	135	37,482	5,185	121	38,409	2,986	42	+3
Subdealer...........	16	26	7,323	1,241	23.5	7,245	719	42	−1
Classified by size of dealer in quarts per day									
0– 249........	31	31	4,022	961	25	3,967	535	44	−1
250– 499........	25	29	8,678	1,320	25	8,589	758	43	−1
500– 999........	19	47	13,889	2,059	42.5	14,016	1,179	43	+1
1,000–1,999........	11	47	14,855	2,045	41	14,563	1,226	40	−2
2,000–4,999........	7	68	21,308	2,804	64	22,177	1,610	43	+4
5,000–9,999........	4	80	25,299	3,621	64	25,095	1,874	48	−1
10,000 and over....	3	138	45,477	3,500	117	45,737	1,965	44	+1

* Split routes are routes that have been split into two parts with one delivered on one day and the other on the following day. Consolidation represents a further modification with volume per route increased and the number of routes decreased. Skip routes are those where the normal two-day volume is delivered in one day, with no deliveries on the alternate day.

† Merchant-dealers buy all of their milk from producers; producer-dealers produce some or all of the milk they distribute; and subdealers buy only from other dealers and usually after the milk has been processed and bottled. These definitions are in line with those used by the Connecticut Milk Administration.

individual estimates tend to compensate. With a group consisting of 169 towns, the standard error of the combined estimate for the group will be only two or three percent. Such totals are given in Table 23. They show that dealers in rural Connecticut markets experienced an average reduction of 45 percent in delivery mileages as a result of alternate-day delivery while dealers in secondary and major markets saved 40 and 37 percent respectively. The

TABLE 25. Loads on retail and wholesale routes in adjacent markets during earlier periods, compared with those in Connecticut in May 1946.[*]

		Points per route daily	
Area	Month	Retail	Wholesale
Boston (8 large distributors)[†]......	October 1944	473	1553
Portland, Maine[†] (4 large distributors)........................	October 1944	457	1249
Merrimack Valley, N. H.[‡] (10 large distributors).................	July 1945	438	1174
Upstate New York[**] (25 large distributors in Buffalo, Rochester, Syracuse, Utica, Binghamton, and Albany-Troy-Schenectady)......	October 1944	418	1257
Connecticut (23 large distributors in Hartford, New Haven, Bridgeport, and Waterbury)...........	May 1946	511	1357

[*] Stewart Johnson, *Load Size and Delivery Labor Cost in Milk Distribution* (Storrs Agricultural Experiment Station, Bulletin 264, 1950), p. 14.
[†] G. F. Dow, *Size of Load and Delivery Costs for Labor in Milk Distribution in Boston and Portland* (Maine Agricultural Experiment Station, Bulletin 437, 1945).
[‡] *Size of Loads and Delivery Costs for Labor in Milk Distribution in the Merrimack Valley of New Hampshire for 10 Large and 9 Small Distributors* (New Hampshire Agricultural Experiment Station, 1945).
[**] Stewart Johnson, *Milk Distribution in Six Large Cities of Upstate New York* (Cornell University Bulletin, A.E. 517, 1945).

weighted average reduction for the whole state is estimated to have been about 40 percent, with daily delivery miles totaling about 61,000 and alternate-day delivery totaling about 37,000 miles per day.

A rough check of these estimates may be had from a state-wide survey of 100 dealers made in 1942. The results of this survey, given in Table 24, show an average reduction in delivery mileage of 44 percent through the alternate-day delivery program. Average route densities were 8.2 and 14.7 quarts per mile, as compared to state-wide estimates of 8.5 and 14.0 quarts per mile. This correspondence is fairly close, especially in view of the fact that the 100-dealer survey did not adequately sample the smaller dealers in rural markets. With a large number of routes under a single management, alternate-day operations frequently made possible important route consolidations, with added savings in mileage, manpower, and equipment.

This tendency for routes to be consolidated and route volumes to increase under alternate-day operations is emphasized by the changes following 1943. Johnson reported that in May 1946, 23 Connecticut dealers operating a total of 471 retail routes had route volumes averaging 463 quarts of milk and 511 points of all products.[2] That this increase was widespread and not limited to Connecticut was indicated by Johnson's summary of studies in other markets (Table 25).

Milk prices and margins

According to the findings of the Federal Trade Commission, milk prices in Connecticut prior to 1933 "were arrived at through conference between the executive committee of the Connecticut Milk Producers' Association and a conference committee of the Connecticut Milk Dealers' Association. The conferences were informal, usually being called to order by the President of the Connecticut Milk Producers' Association and presided over by a representative of the dealers. No minutes of the conference were kept, and references to the proceedings are very meager in the minutes of the two associations." [3]

In 1933 this monopolistic pricing mechanism was formally recognized and given legal status and public responsibility through the establishment of the Connecticut Board of Milk Control, made up of representatives of producers, dealers, and (presumably) the public. This Board established minimum producer and consumer prices for milk until it was replaced by the Connecticut Milk Administrator in 1935. From 1935 until 1941, the Administrator

[2] Stewart Johnson, *Load Size and Delivery Labor Cost in Milk Distribution* (Storrs Agricultural Experiment Station, Bulletin 264, 1950), p. 12.

[3] *Report of the Federal Trade Commission on the Sale and Distribution of Milk Products, Connecticut and Philadelphia Milksheds* (House Document No. 152, 74th Congress, 1st Session, Washington, 1935), 23–27.

established minimum producer prices for the several classes of milk, and also set the minimum retail price to be charged consumers in a number of Connecticut markets. It will be noted that these consumer prices were minima and not maxima, for the effort was primarily to "stabilize" the market and prevent "unfair" competition rather than to reduce prices to the consumer. Important revisions were made in the milk legislation in 1941, and since then the Administrator has fixed only the producer prices. Power to regulate consumer or retail prices is still contained in the law, but this power has not been exercised.

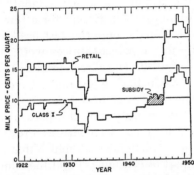

Fig. 23. Retail and Class I prices for family-grade milk in Connecticut markets, 1922–1950. Prior to 1933, producer prices were established by bargaining between the Connecticut Milk Producers' Association and the Connecticut Milk Dealers' Association; since 1933, they have been fixed by the State. Minimum resale prices were fixed during the 1933–1941 period, but have not been subject to direct control since that time.

It is quite clear that prices in these markets have been determined under conditions far removed from true competition. The administered character of the established prices is revealed by the data in Fig. 23, where producer and consumer prices for family-grade (Grade B) milk are summarized. Except for a few months, the Class I price was stabilized at 9.5 cents per quart from 1924 through 1930, with a delivered price to consumers of 16 cents per quart.[4] The depression of the early 1930's drove Class

[4] Cassels pointed out that Connecticut milk prices were artificially maintained above competitive levels during the 1920's by market exclusion practices by the Connecticut Milk Producers' Association and the Connecticut Dairy and Food Commission. See J. M. Cassels, *A Study of Fluid Milk Prices* (Harvard University Press, Cambridge, 1937), 170–174.

I prices down to 4.5 cents by March 1933, with accompanying reductions in retail prices to 10 cents per quart. This break was undoubtedly responsible for the establishment of the Milk Control Board in May of that year, and with this public assistance prices recovered to 7.75 cents per quart for Class I and 14.0 cents at retail before the end of the year. With minor changes, these levels were maintained until war influences came into play in 1941. At the beginning of that year, the producer price stood at 7.0 cents and the retail price at 14.0 cents per quart.

Prices were advanced twice during 1941, but the upward trend was curbed by the addition of a new regulating agency — the Office of Price Administration. Except for a few minor changes, including a lowering of the butterfat test used as a standard of payment from 4.0 to 3.7 percent, prices were practically stable until the middle of 1946. The direct producer price moved up slowly from about 8.6 in 1942 to just under 8.9 cents per quart in 1944 and 1945. The retail price to consumers apparently was constant at 16.0 cents per quart during this period, but actual prices realized by dealers advanced somewhat as a result of an increase in the sales of premium grades of milk (that was not always voluntary on the part of consumers) and the elimination of some price discounts that had been current.

Of course, the stability of prices during the war period was achieved in part by the payment of government subsidies to producers. These ranged from 1.4 to 1.7 cents per quart in the spring of 1946. With the ending of subsidies and the decontrol of fluid-milk prices, rapid adjustments were made during the summer of 1946. By the end of the year, the producer price for Class I milk had increased to about 13.5 cents per quart while the consumer price had gone up to 21 cents per quart. While the original increases represented the transfer from subsidies to direct payment by consumers, milk prices in Connecticut and generally through the United States continued to move upward with the upsurge in the general price level. Sharp breaks in the prices for manufactured dairy products during the second half of 1948 eventually reacted on fluid-milk markets and prices turned down during 1949 and early 1950. In Connecticut, producer prices reached a peak of 15.3 cents per quart at the end of 1948, with retail prices

of 23.5 cents. By the middle of 1950 these had been reduced to
13.2 and 21.5 cents respectively, but developments in Korea and
the high levels of employment and purchasing power have been
forcing prices up again in recent months.

While producer and consumer prices for milk have been fairly
responsive to general economic conditions, dealers' price margins
have been remarkably stable. Except for short periods when the
margin fluctuated between 6.0 and 7.0 cents per quart, the established spread between producer and consumer prices for milk in
Connecticut markets remained at 6.5 cents per quart from 1922
to 1932. For one month in 1933 this margin fell to 5.5 cents, but it
quickly recovered to 6.25 cents and remained there for several
years. With some decline in producer prices, the margin rose to
6.9 cents per quart in 1938 and finally to 7.4 cents in 1942. Without allowance for changes in quality or the elimination of many
price discounts, the margin then dropped to approximately 7.1
cents per quart in 1944 and held there until the removal of price
controls. With decontrol, margins increased to 7.5 cents by the
end of 1946 and 8.2 cents by the end of 1948. Producer price reductions were not accompanied by lower margins, and the established price spread available to Connecticut dealers averaged
8.3 cents in 1950.

The general conclusion to be drawn from these price and margin movements is certainly that milk distribution costs in Connecticut have moved slowly upward throughout the past quarter
of a century. On the other hand, the increases during the past ten
years are not an indication of decreased efficiency. The general
level of wages increased rapidly in these years, and wages of dairy
workers were no exceptions. Actual physical efficiency in milk
distribution was increased very significantly by the previously
discussed program of alternate-day delivery and by a marked
increase in consumption and in the volumes handled by most
dealers. These factors made it possible for the industry to absorb
the higher costs of labor and supplies with relatively small increases in the price paid for the marketing service.

Relative to the changes in all food marketing charges discussed
in Chapter 1, the "deflated" price margins for Connecticut distributors increased from an average of about 5.3 cents during the

1920's to 6.3 cents in the early 1930's and 7.0 cents for the period from 1938 through 1942. The actual decline in margins plus an increase in food marketing charges reduced the deflated margin to 6.3 cents during the 1944–45 control period. While the increases since the war seem large, they lagged far behind all food marketing charges, with the result that relative margins in the 1947–1949 period averaged only 5.0 cents — lower than at any time since World War I. In comparison with other prices and marketing charges, then, the increase in the margins available to Connecticut milk distributors since 1941 must be recognized as a remarkable improvement in relative efficiency.

Most of the above material applies specifically to conditions in the major markets. In many respects the smaller markets were more competitive, especially through the activities of producer-dealers. As already pointed out, milk distribution is a supplementary enterprise for producer-dealers as well as for many small merchant-dealers. It was not uncommon for these dealers to acquire and keep consumers by cutting prices below the established or going levels. Data covering more than 10,000 customers buying Grade B and Grade A milk from producer-dealers in 1937 indicated that some 32 percent were paying 13 cents, 16 percent were paying 12 cents, and 6 percent were paying from 9 to 11 cents per quart.[5] At this time, the established price for family-grade milk was 14 cents per quart. Of course, most producer-dealers sell raw milk, so that somewhat lower prices may be justified on the basis of processing costs and perhaps on the basis of value to the consumer.

It is difficult if not impossible to obtain meaningful estimates of price margins for these dealers. One of the important reasons that producers retail milk is to obtain a Class I outlet for their product. While the Class I price in Connecticut in 1937 was about 7.1 cents per quart, the composite or weighted-average price received by wholesale producers was only about 6.0 cents per quart and many received less than 5.5 cents. Whatever the explanation of lower prices, it is true that some element of price competition

    [5] D. O. Hammerberg, I. F. Fellows, and R. H. Farr, *Efficiency of Milk Marketing in Connecticut, 4. Retail Distribution of Milk by Producers* (Storrs Agricultural Experiment Station, Bulletin 243, 1942), 16–19.

has been retained in Connecticut milk marketing through the activities of producer-dealers and other small-volume handlers.

Milk distribution costs

The Federal Trade Commission investigations of 1934–35 included some studies of milk distribution costs and profits in Connecticut.[6] Based on samples varying from seven to 13 dealers,

TABLE 26. Rate of return on total capital invested in milk and milk-products business for specified numbers of Connecticut distributors, 1929–1934.*

Year	Number of distributors	Percent return on capital
1929	3 larger companies..........................	21.05
	4 smaller companies.........................	14.74
	Total, 7 companies.......................	20.21
1930	4 larger companies..........................	19.63
	5 smaller companies.........................	13.85
	Total, 9 companies.......................	18.83
1931	5 larger companies..........................	20.07
	6 smaller companies.........................	13.43
	Total, 11 companies......................	19.13
1932	5 larger companies..........................	12.93
	6 smaller companies.........................	8.65
	Total, 11 companies......................	12.31
1933	5 larger companies..........................	6.75
	8 smaller companies.........................	1.27
	Total, 13 companies......................	5.80
1934	4 larger companies..........................	3.98
	6 smaller companies.........................	5.04
	Total, 10 companies......................	4.14

* *Report of the Federal Trade Commission on the Sale and Distribution of Milk Products, Connecticut and Philadelphia Milksheds* (House Document No. 152, 74th Congress, 1st Session, Washington, 1935), 67–68.

[6] Federal Trade Commission Report, 66–74.

these studies indicated that the rate of return on total capital employed in the milk and milk-products business dropped from 20 percent in 1929 to 4 percent in 1934 (Table 26). A more detailed account of sales, operating expenses, and profits on sales is given in Table 27 for eight companies operating in June and July 1934. Out of each dollar sales of milk, cream, and other dairy products, these companies paid 59.3 cents for milk and other raw materials. Operating expenses included: processing, 10.1 cents; delivery, 16.9 cents; selling, 4.3 cents; and administrative and general expenses, 4.2 cents. Raw material costs and operating expenses thus accounted for 94.8 cents out of every dollar of sales, leaving 5.2 cents per dollar for profits.

TABLE 27. Sales, operating expenses, and net profits for three larger and five smaller Connecticut milk distributors, June and July 1934.*

Item	$1,000 per month	Percent of total net sales
Net sales		
Fluid milk and cream....................	$404	81.0
Ice cream and mix......................	53	10.7
Other products.........................	41	8.3
Total net sales	$499	100.0
Cost of raw materials		
Fluid milk............................	$216	43.3
Fluid cream...........................	40	8.0
Other materials........................	40	8.0
Total raw materials..................	$296	59.3
Gross margin...........................	$203	40.7
Operating expenses		
Processing............................	$ 51	10.1
Delivering............................	84	16.9
Selling...............................	21	4.3
Administrative, etc....................	21	4.2
Total operating expenses.............	$177	35.5
Total costs and expenses..................	$473	94.8
Net profit.............................	$ 26	5.2

* Report of the Federal Trade Commission on the Sale and Distribution of Milk Products, Connecticut and Philadelphia Milksheds (House Document No. 152, 74th Congress, 1st Session, Washington, 1935), 72. Totals may not check owing to rounding.

The 1937 study of producer-dealers indicated that costs were a function of dealer volume, decreasing from about 7.7 cents per quart with daily volume of only 25 quarts to 3.5 cents with 375 quarts.[7] With 125 quarts of milk delivered daily, roughly the average for Connecticut producer-dealers, delivery costs amounted to 2.4 cents, plant costs 1.5 cents, and selling costs 0.2 cents per quart. The estimate of total costs of 4.1 cents per quart may be compared with a normal margin of about 6.75 cents per quart for that year. As already pointed out, however, many

TABLE 28. Reported costs for processing and delivering a quart of standard milk, Hartford units of the National Dairy Products Company, year ending October 31, 1947.[*]

Item	Cents per quart
Wages	4.75
Depreciation and repairs	.64
Bottles and caps	.35
Power, fuel, water, ice	.25
Gas, oil, tires, licenses	.24
Supplies	.21
Advertising	.20
Insurance	.20
Taxes (except income tax)	.18
Administrative supervision	.17
Executive salaries	.04
All other expense	.18
Total	7.41
Price spread	7.00

[*] *Hartford Times,* January 17, 1948.

producer-dealers were making retail milk deliveries at prices ranging from 1 to 5 cents below the established level, so this comparison should not be regarded as of great significance.

Published reports of the costs of processing and delivering a quart of regular milk by the Hartford units of the National Dairy Products Company indicate averages of 6.31 and 7.41 cents per quart in 1940 and 1947.[8] The margins between raw-product cost

[7] Hammerberg, Fellows, and Farr, *Efficiency of Milk Marketing in Connecticut,* 4, 42–51.
[8] As published in the *Hartford Times,* January 17, 1948, 5.

and consumer price for these years were reported as 6.29 and 7.00 cents respectively, the company noting that the indicated losses were compensated by small profits on other items and that total profits averaged less than 1½ cents out of every dollar of sales. Details of the reported costs for the 12-month period ending October 31, 1947 are given in Table 28.

Reported costs for home delivery of Grade B milk by a large and relatively efficient Connecticut milk distributor are sum-

TABLE 29. Report of costs and profits on retail sales of Grade B milk, one large Connecticut distributor, 1940–1944 and 1949.

Item	Cents per Quart 1940–1944	1949
Plant costs...............................	1.10	1.48
Sales and administration....................	.99	1.54
Delivery expense		
Vehicle................................	.88	.68
Rent...................................	.03	.02
Containers.............................	.17	.12
Supplies...............................	.09	.02
Payroll taxes, etc........................	.36	.28
Delivery wages..........................	2.06	} 3.00
Relief man, etc...........................	.43	
Totals..............................	6.11	7.14
Gross margin.............................	7.04	7.82
Discount on sales.........................	.27	.01
Adjusted margin..........................	6.77	7.81
Profit before taxes........................	0.66	0.67

marized in Table 29 for the 1940–1944 period and for 1949. For the five-year period, expenses averaged 6.11 cents per quart as compared to a margin (adjusted for sales discounts) of 6.77 cents, or a gross profit margin of 0.66 cents per quart before taxes. The 1949 figures show the influence of increasing costs and prices, and of the previously discussed widening of the established margin between producer and consumer prices. Reported costs totaled 7.14 cents per quart, margins averaged 7.81 cents, and profits before taxes amounted to 0.67 cent per quart.

These cost data serve to illustrate the general situation in Connecticut markets. Further cost computations pertaining to the existing system of milk distribution will be given after the basic relations governing costs are investigated in Part Three.

Conclusions

In spite of the fact that an average of approximately 50 quarts of milk are delivered for every mile of street and improved road in Connecticut, milk-delivery routes averaged only about 8 quarts per mile with daily delivery and 14 quarts with alternate-day delivery. This suggests that delivery routes overlap and duplicate to a considerable extent. Detailed studies in a number of rural and urban markets indicated that this was indeed the case, and that such inefficiencies became more pronounced as market density increased. The prewar organization of milk distribution in Connecticut was characterized by excessive numbers of dealers, milk plants, and milk routes, and by excessive route travel. But these inefficiencies are not peculiar to Connecticut; reports from all sections of the United States make it clear that the Connecticut situation is typical of milk distribution the country over.

Milk prices and margins in Connecticut have long been determined either by arbitration between producer and dealer groups or through the Connecticut Milk Administrator. As a result, they have been slow to change and at times have been maintained above competitive levels. The dealers' margin, or spread between the price paid to producers and the price paid by consumers, has been remarkably stable. Except for a few months, this margin remained between 6.0 and 7.0 cents per quart for the entire period between World War I and World War II. During the recent war period, producer prices increased to about 8.9 cents per quart while consumers paid 16 cents per quart for family-grade milk. The dealers' margin was about 7.1 cents. These levels were about average for milk markets in the United States.

Price increases during the war period were retarded by the Office of Price Administration. Some of the resulting stability, however, was achieved by the payment of governmental subsidies directly to producers. In the spring of 1946, these ranged from 1.4 to 1.7 cents per quart in Connecticut. With the removal of price control and the termination of the subsidy program, producer and consumer prices increased rapidly. By the end of 1946, the Class I price had advanced to about 13.5 cents per quart while the consumer price had advanced to 21 cents per quart. Prices continued to advance through 1947 and 1948, and at the beginning of 1949 were at peaks of 15.3 cents per quart to producers and 23.5 cents for milk delivered to consumers. The trend was reversed by the general easing off of prices for most agricultural products and especially by the sharp break in the markets for manufactured dairy products. During the first half of 1950, the Class I price in Connecticut amounted to 13.2 and the home-delivered price to 21.5 cents per quart. Corresponding to these prices, price margins to cover the costs of milk distribution amounted to 7.5 cents per quart at the end of 1946, 8.2 cents by the end of 1948, and stood at 8.3 cents per quart early in 1950.

While these wartime and postwar increases in the margin were important, they were not as pronounced as the increases in most prices and in the marketing charges for all foods. Relative to these charges for all foods, deflated Connecticut milk-price spreads averaged 7.0 cents per quart for the 1938–1942 period. These were reduced to 6.3 cents for the 1944–1945 period and 5.0 cents for the 1947–1949 period — lower than at any other time since the first World War. This remarkable increase in relative efficiency was largely due to two factors: (1) the marked increase in total milk sales and so in volume for most dealers; and (2) the alternate-day delivery program. Fragmentary reports on distribution costs, while noncomparable in many respects, at least permit the statement that costs have in general moved in fairly close relation to price margins.

Most of these statements refer specifically to the larger distributors in city areas. Producer-dealers and other small distributors have been in a somewhat different situation. In spite of the fact that these small operators are typically among the least efficient when judged on any physical standard such as route density or quarts per man, they have often been an important element making for price competition. This may be the result of many factors, including relatively low costs associated with raw-milk sales, low returns to owned resources and family labor, and a willingness to retail as long as the returns exceed the composite price.

So much for the present state of milk distribution. How can the existing inefficiencies be reduced? What forms of milk distribution would be most efficient? How would reorganization programs affect the physical inputs and the economic costs of distribution? How would consumers react to such programs? These are the main questions to be considered in the chapters that follow.

PART THREE

THE BASIS FOR MARKET REORGANIZATION

8 ——

THE THEORY OF
ECONOMICAL DISTRIBUTION

Efficient delivery as a function of density

The problem of excessive delivery costs and its solution may best be considered in terms of the density of deliveries. It is a truism that delivery distances for individual dealers are high because they deliver relatively few quarts of milk per route mile and per route hour, yet this may be taken as one of the basic tenets of delivery reorganization. Any program that increases delivery density will reduce the miles traveled by milk trucks and the route labor requirements in the delivery area.

One method of increasing density is to make deliveries at less frequent time intervals; this program is familiar in the alternate-day delivery of milk, which has doubled effective delivery densities and reduced total mileages an average of more than 40 percent and route labor requirements about one-third. Another method may be represented by a consolidation of the operations of two dealers. In most cases, the increase in size of the remaining company brings about increased delivery density, although there are marked exceptions to this rule where small dealers have carefully restricted their deliveries or where large dealers have been willing to expand their territory greatly in order to gain relatively small additional volume.

A third method that has been discussed frequently is the pooling of loads wherein each dealer restricts his delivery operations to a small area but delivers milk for all of the dealers who had previously served the area. This proposal has usually been discarded because of the difficulties involved in handling a large number of brands and grades of milk on a single load.

A fourth method of increasing density involves the exchange of customers between dealers in order to shorten existing routes and limit delivery areas. Many milk dealers have tried this at least on a limited scale. Pushed to the logical conclusion, the exchange of customers becomes the allocation of exclusive delivery territories. Under such a plan each dealer would be assigned a section of the market and all other handlers would be excluded. Exclusive territories, sometimes called "zoned deliveries," may be modified to permit the operations of two or more milk dealers. Such modifications are called semiexclusive territories in this report.

Delivery routes may be divided into delivery and hauling sections, where the latter represents the miles traveled between the plant and the delivery area proper. Exclusive delivery territories will result in maximum density and so will minimize the miles traveled in the delivery portions of the routes. To minimize hauling mileages, however, it is necessary to allocate areas in a very particular way. In general, this means a system of areas that tend to group around the particular plants involved. The exact nature of such allocations is the subject of the following section.

Market allocations to minimize delivery miles and costs[10]

The principles involved in the economical allocation of market areas hold for any situation involving geographic distribution of producers or consumers. They may be developed from location theory and the spatial aspects of prices, and will correspond to the principles that would be followed by individual producers or consumers under purely competitive conditions.

Consider the case of a consumer faced with several sources from which he may obtain a given product. After weighing these alternatives, and assuming the product from all sources to be identical, he will select source which will result in the lowest price *at his location*. This price is a function of the price at the source and the transportation (and handling) costs involved in

[10] Much of this section is paraphrased from a production analysis developed by the author in collaboration with D. O. Hammerberg and L. W. Parker and published in *Efficiency of Milk Marketing in Connecticut, 1. Supply and Price Interrelationships for Fluid Milk Markets* (Storrs Agricultural Experiment Station, Bulletin 237, 1942), 13–18.

moving the product from the source to the consumer's home. Thus, if he could buy from several dealers with identical prices at their plants, he would select the one that would involve the lowest transportation cost, for by so doing he would pay the lowest delivered price at his home. If all consumers weighed the alternatives and made their selections in this fashion, the result would be a system of competitively determined market areas that would allocate consumers among the several dealers as efficiently as possible. In fact, this system would not only allocate market areas efficiently but would determine the quantities that would be sold by each dealer and the whole structure of prices through an interdependent, general-equilibrium system of pricing.[11]

The cost of transportation is a function of the distance over which the product must be transported. When factors such as the size of truck and the volume transported are held constant, these costs will increase in a more or less regular fashion with increases in distance. Consequently, consumer prices will tend to increase as the distance from the dealer's plant increases, since they equal the price at the plant plus transportation costs. The structure of prices around a plant may be thought of as a funnellike surface with the lowest price at the plant and with consumer prices increasing on all sides in a manner dependent on the particular relation between transportation costs and distance.

If a plant were isolated or far removed from other plants, this price structure would extend over adjacent consuming areas without interruption. The market area would take the form of a circle centered on the plant. The outer boundary or margin of this competitive area would fall at a distance from the plant where the plant price plus the transportation costs resulted in consumer prices so high that the marginal consumers would be just induced to buy the product while potential consumers more distant would refuse to buy. Or, considering supply and demand conditions simultaneously, this competitive area would involve the adjustment of plant prices (according to marginal costs) so that in equilibrium the operator would be unwilling to expand his production and new and more distant consumers would be unwilling to enter the market.

[11] A demonstration that these "free choice" areas will minimize transportation costs is given in the Appendix.

This equilibrium is illustrated graphically in Fig. 24. In part *A* of this figure, the funnellike structure of consumer prices with the plant as the origin is shown in cross section. The slope of this inverted cone of prices represents the function between transportation costs and distance; this function need not be linear. The

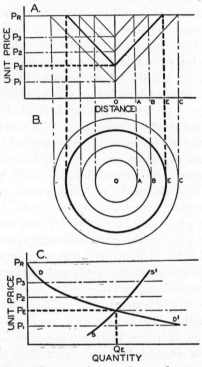

Fig. 24. Competitive determination of the market area for an isolated plant, and of plant and consumer prices: A, sectional view of the structure of prices, with prices increasing because of the addition of transportation costs as distance from plant increases; B, the corresponding outlines of the competitive market areas; C, the final equilibrium of supply and demand.

price P_r represents the consumer's reservation price, that is, the price above which they will refuse to buy the product. As the plant price is successively raised from P_1 to P_3, more and more consumers will be eliminated and the radius of the market area will be contracted from *OC* to *OA* (part *B*). With consumers scattered evenly over the area, this means that the total number served will tend to decrease geometrically as the plant price increases. In a like manner, the quantity of the product sold will decrease as the price increases. The demand curve DD' shown in part C reflects this; the exact form of this curve will depend on the nature of the transportation-cost function, on the geographic distribution of consumers, and on the elasticities of the consumers' individual demand curves.

The quantities that the plant operator would be willing to sell at various prices are represented by his marginal-cost curve SS' in Fig. 24(C). Final equilibrium will involve the equating of supply and demand as indicated. Through this process will be determined the equilibrium price at the plant P_e, the associated

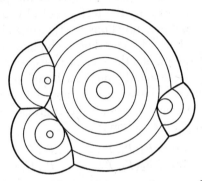

Fig. 25. Price relation and consuming areas for a number of interrelated and interdependent markets. Contour lines are "isotims" showing constant prices, while heavy lines show competitive boundaries between markets.

consumer-price structure around the plant, and the total quantity produced and sold Q_e.

The situation involving several alternative sources of supply is illustrated in Fig. 25, and needs very little additional explanation.[12] The margins between the areas for the several plants are drawn so as to represent equal consumer prices from each of the alternative plants. With given geographic consumption patterns, individual demand elasticities, transport-cost functions, and marginal-cost functions for the plants, the whole structure of plant and consumer prices, plant volumes, and market areas may be determined.

[12] For a similar analysis, see J. M. Cassels, *A Study of Fluid Milk Prices*, 18–40.

In simplified form, the general nature of these interrelations may be indicated by a conventional set of general-equilibrium equations. Suppose we are given an area containing a large number of consumers, and with n plants or sources of supply. At each of these plants, the quantities produced and offered for sale will depend on the price and on the technical organization of production. This may be represented by:

$$S_1 = f_1(P_1),$$
$$S_2 = f_2(P_2),$$
$$\cdots\cdots\cdots\cdots$$
$$S_n = f_n(P_n). \tag{8.1}$$

The subscripts in these equations refer to the particular plants. The functions are given by the technological conditions, and are in fact the marginal-cost functions for the several plants.

The aggregate demand focused on each plant will be a function of the prices at the plants, the cost of transportation, and the individual consumer demand functions based on such factors as tastes, preferences, relative prices, and income. In simplified form, however, we may represent the aggregate demand for the product of each plant as follows:

$$D_1 = F_1(P_1, P_2, \ldots, P_n, C_t),$$
$$D_2 = F_2(P_1, P_2, \ldots, P_n, C_t),$$
$$\cdots\cdots\cdots\cdots\cdots\cdots\cdots\cdots$$
$$D_n = F_n(P_1, P_2, \ldots, P_n, C_t), \tag{8.2}$$

In this set of equations, C_t represents the transportation function. The particular F functions will be quite complex, since they involve geographic relations determined by the interaction of the several prices and transport costs as well as the changing quantities that consumers will take as the price to each consumer changes.

Equilibrium would necessarily involve the equating of supply and demand for each plant, or:

$$S_1 = D_1,$$
$$S_2 = D_2,$$
$$\cdots\cdots\cdots$$
$$S_n = D_n. \tag{8.3}$$

We thus have n equations each of type (8.1), type (8.2), and type (8.3). Involved in these $3n$ equations are $3n$ unknowns; n prices P, n quantities supplied S, and n quantities demanded D. With an equal number of equations and unknowns, it will normally be possible (but involved) to solve for the particular values consistent with equilibrium; that is, the system is determinate. Note that this set of equations represents a system of the "general-equilibrium" type, but that it applies only to a single product in a number of geographically segregated markets. True general equilibrium, of course, would include all products in all markets.

This system of equations illustrates the fundamental idea of general interdependence, with prices and market areas determined simultaneously under conditions of pure competition. As a practical research tool, however, these equations are admittedly unmanageable, for variations in such factors as the geographic distribution and density of consumption would make any mathematical statement extremely complex. The principles involved will be used, nevertheless, through successive graphic approximations similar to those discussed.

The above presentation is based on competitive prices. If prices are not competitively determined, as will be the case when a uniform price holds throughout a geographic area, the general conclusions still hold. Given the volumes sold by each of a number of dealers, the most efficient allocation of consuming areas among the several dealers will still be represented by the theoretical competitive areas, with each area containing a volume of sales equal to the present sales of the particular dealer. Under these conditions, however, the areas will no longer represent "free-choice" areas determined by consumer action. The arbitrary price structure will result in a chaotic situation with respect to the best alternatives available to individual consumers; with uniform consumer prices throughout a city there is no price basis for selecting a dealer and consequently dealer areas overlap and duplicate in a manner that is inefficient from the standpoint of route operations.

If a single agency were to take over milk distribution in any city but were forced to maintain all plants in operation with their present volumes, it would be able to deliver milk most efficiently by allocating the market among the plants in the manner just described. This allocation would permit the lowest average delivery costs for the entire market, and thus the largest saving possible under any system that maintained all existing plants in operation. This is essentially the problem of economical milk distribution unless some dealers are to be eliminated and plant operations consolidated.

Labor efficiency and route volumes

Delivery densities and the allocation of efficient hauling areas are not the only criteria to be followed in planning efficient delivery organizations. Size of the load is important, for with larger loads the total hauling mileage and the input of delivery resources will be reduced. Under past conditions, load size has been determined primarily by labor capacity and by the growing complexity of the job assigned to the route driver. In addition to delivering milk the routeman usually collects payments from customers and promotes the sale of products. Part of his time is spent in soliciting new customers, for competition between dealers for volume is usually keen. Moreover, there has been a tendency for routes to handle a growing variety of grades of milk, of bottle sizes, and of other products. This has increased the time required in delivering the products and in rearranging the load, and has increased the complexity of route bookkeeping.

With given conditions of route volumes and operations to be performed by the routeman, route time will be a function of delivery density. Conversely, the daily volume that can be handled on a delivery route is a function of delivery densities, in general increasing as density increases. The methods of increasing delivery densities discussed in the foregoing sections, therefore, will also be effective in increasing route volumes and so in reducing truck and labor costs of milk distribution.

The allocation of exclusive delivery territories would have an added effect on route volumes. As mentioned above, increasing density will permit increases in route size when the operations to be performed by the routeman are held constant. But exclusive delivery territories would also permit some important changes in the functions of the routeman. Under present conditions a significant portion of the routeman's time is devoted to competitive sales activities. These sales efforts may have some effect on total consumption, but their primary purpose is to shift consumers among dealers. If every dealer were assigned an exclusive delivery area, it is quite apparent that these purely competitive sales efforts would become meaningless and so would be eliminated.

At present, most routemen collect payments from customers. Under a system of exclusive territories or of municipal operation, the collection functions could be greatly simplified or transferred to the central offices where they could be handled more economically. One reason that collections are handled personally under the present system is that consumers who fail to pay can easily shift to new dealers. With the reorganized systems, this shifting would not be possible. Collections could then be made through the mails in the manner customarily used by public-utility companies, and collection failures would be held to a minimum by the power to discontinue the service. From this standpoint, the elimination of collections would permit larger route volumes and probably would reduce bad-debt losses.

Plant operations[13]

Reorganization of milk distribution may involve plant as well as delivery operations. In any city milk plant there will be a particular set of technical conditions that control and determine the relation between inputs of productive factors and outputs of product. These technical relations are basic to the determination of economic costs and returns, since these are generally determined by the application of suitable prices and cost rates to the physical inputs and outputs.

"For any plant the cost elements involved in daily operation may be divided into two general categories: those that are fixed

[13] This and the following section are based largely on R. G. Bressler, Jr., *Economies of Scale in the Operation of Country Milk Plants* (New England Research Council on Marketing and Food Supply in coöperation with the New England Agricultural Experiment Stations and the U. S. Department of Agriculture, 1942); "Research Determination of Economies of Scale," *Journal of Farm Economics*, XXVII (No. 3, August 1945); and "Economics for the Natural Scientist," Storrs Agricultural Experiment Station, unpublished manuscript (1945).

or constant regardless of the volume handled, and those that vary with changes in plant volume. Fixed costs are primarily those associated with land, buildings, and equipment, although there may be a considerable degree of fixity or of discontinuity in such elements as labor and supplies. Fixed costs per unit of output decrease in a hyperbolic curve as plant volume increases, of course, since the total fixed cost is allocated among an increasing number of units. Average variable costs are usually thought of as increasing at an increasing rate with volume increases and the resulting intensification on the fixed factors, although they may be fairly constant per unit for considerable ranges in volume." [14] Such constant unit costs are to be expected when volume is increased by increasing the time dimension rather than by increasing the *rate* of output.

"When fixed and variable costs are combined, average total costs for any plant will ordinarily be found to decrease with volume increases in the low volume range as a result of the reductions in unit fixed costs and finally to increase as the increases in variable costs more than offset the decreases in fixed costs." [15]

The nature of these interrelations may be illustrated by considering a situation where all of the factors of production except one are given and fixed, and where changes in the plant output are a function of the remaining variable factor. Using Q and q to represent the rates of output and input respectively, this general relation may be given as:

$$Q = f(q). \qquad (8.4)$$

The equation showing the average output per unit of input would be:

$$Q/q = f(q)/q. \qquad (8.5)$$

The marginal curve — in finite terms, the additional output per unit of additional input — would be the first derivative of equation (8.4):

$$dQ/dq = f'(q). \qquad (8.6)$$

[14] R. G. Bressler, Jr., *Economies of Scale in the Operation of Country Milk Plants*, 19.
[15] *Ibid.*

These basic physical relations, as mentioned above, may be converted into cost relations by the application of suitable prices or cost rates. In doing this the economist usually expresses the cost functions with output Q as the independent variable, which would involve an inversion of equation (8.4) to the following form:

$$q = F(Q). \tag{8.7}$$

Total variable costs VC are then obtained by multiplying the variable inputs by the appropriate price p_v:

$$VC = qp_v = F(Q)p_v. \tag{8.8}$$

To obtain total combined costs, the fixed costs K must be added:

$$C = K + F(Q)p_v. \tag{8.9}$$

The average or unit cost equation will then be:

$$C/Q = K/Q + F(Q)p_v/Q, \tag{8.10}$$

and the marginal costs will be the first dirivative of the total cost equation (8.9):

$$dC/dQ = d/dQ[F(Q)p_v]. \tag{8.11}$$

Since the several steps in these equations are indicated rather than performed, the general equations necessarily take on many added terms. As a matter of fact, these last three equations would be very similar to the foregoing physical relations. Remembering that the cost equations are based on the physical input-output equations as indicated, they may be simplified into new functions closely related to the original physical functions:

$$C = f(Q), \tag{8.12}$$
$$C/Q = f(Q)/Q, \tag{8.13}$$
$$dC/dQ = f'(Q). \tag{8.14}$$

It should be clear from these functions that a single physical relation may be basic to an unlimited number of cost relations, each differing in the particular rates and prices used to calculate fixed and variable costs. This situation is illustrated in Fig. 26. The solid curve in this diagram represents the "typical" form of a total cost relation, with costs increasing first at a decreasing and finally at an increasing rate. The broken curves illustrate a few of the modifications to the basic relation that would accompany variations in cost rates. If changes are limited to the cost rates applicable to fixed costs, the effects will be to raise or lower the level of the total-cost curve. On the other hand, if the changes are in the price of the variable factor, the effects will be to change the general slope of the curve, with steeper curves resulting from higher prices. Finally, there are all of the possibilities involving both fixed and variable elements, or both the level and the general slope of the curve.

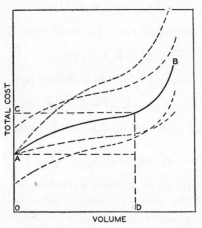

Fig. 26. A family of total-cost curves based on a single production function, illustrating the effects of changes in fixed and variable cost rates.

Mention of the multiplicity of cost curves raises a very important point with respect to both input-output and cost curves. These curves or functions refer to the *greatest* possible output from the given input and to the *lowest* cost for the given output. It goes without saying that there would be a host of less efficient organizations with corresponding functions, but these would be "nonsense" combinations. A given plant output could be produced by using the same fixed factors combined with more labor if the added men merely sat around the plant. It must be remembered that these functions are not based on foolish or ignorant organizations or on mediocre practices, but on the *best* organization under the stated conditions.

Economies of scale in plant operations

The foregoing discussion has referred to the operation of a given plant, where many of the factors of production were fixed. In many situations, however, it would be necessary to consider all factors as variables, and to determine that particular combination of the factors that would be most economical. In other words, it will frequently be necessary to determine the type and size of the plant that will be most economical. What is required is a more general solution that shows output as a complex function of a great many variables. The previous discussion is essentially short-run in nature; the following paragraphs deal with long-run aspects when all factors may be varied.

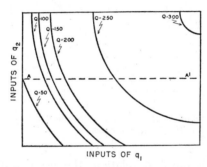

Fig. 27. *Hypothetical production function between factors* q_1 *and* q_2 *and output* Q.

Long-run analysis is concerned with substitution between the several factors of production and, eventually, with the selection of optimum or most economical combinations. This may be illustrated graphically by considering two variable factors, although it should be understood that more than two variables will usually be involved. Figure 27 represents a hypothetical production function between two variable factors q_1 and q_2 and output Q. Each curved line in this diagram shows the various combinations of q_1 and q_2 that will result in a given output. The shape of these "isoquants" is determined by the ease with which one factor may be substituted for the other in the technical processes involved. If two factors were perfect substitutes, the isoquants would appear as straight lines sloping downward and to the right. As the difficulty of substitution increases, the curvature of the isoquants will become more pronounced.

Any cross section of this function such as AA' would hold q_2 constant at OA while allowing q_1 to vary. The trace of this cross section would typically resemble the total input-output relation discussed in the previous section. The present form of the function, then, is simply a summation of all of the possible one-variable functions covering all possible values for the fixed factors.

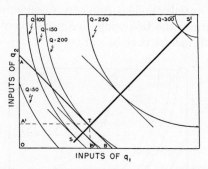

Fig. 28. *Determination of "scale" line ss' showing optimum combination of factors* q_1 *and* q_2 *with given factor prices.*

Given such a physical relation, the economist is concerned with: (1) the determination of the optimum combination of factors for various levels of output, and (2) the conversion of inputs into costs. The optimum combination of factors from an economic standpoint, however, will depend on the relative prices of the factors involved. The graphic approach to this problem may be stated as follows: with given prices for the factors and with a given amount of money to spend, what is the largest output that can be obtained? If the entire amount were spent on factor q_1, OB units could be purchased (Fig. 28). In a similar fashion, it would be possible to obtain OA units of q_2. Furthermore, as long as the prices remain as given it would be possible to purchase any combination of q_1 and q_2 that falls on the straight line connecting A and B; in a price sense there is perfect substitution so that it is always possible to exchange a fixed quantity of q_1 for another fixed and constant quantity of q_2. Now, if the line AB shows all the combinations that can be purchased for a given total expenditure, it is clear that the combination that will be most economical will be OB' of q_1 and OA' of q_2, because this combination will result in the highest total output as represented by the point of tangency T. Of course, if the price of either factor changes, the optimum combination would be affected.

The slope of the straight line AB is OA/OB. But the quantities OA and OB were determined by dividing some given total expenditure by p_1 and p_2, the factor prices. Substituting and simplifying, the slope of the line is found to be the (inverse) ratio of factor prices, or p_1/p_2. This simply confirms what has already been stated — that the most economical combination of factors is a function of relative factor prices. Abandoning the idea of a given total expenditure, the line AB and others parallel to it thus represent the relative factor prices. These "price" lines will define a whole series of tangency points with the isoquants. The locus of these points SS' is ordinarily called the scale line, and it shows the most economical combination of factors to use in producing any output.

It is now a simple matter to select an output (isoquant), to read off the optimum inputs of q_1 and q_2, to multiply these by their respective prices, and so to determine a point on the long-run total-cost curve. The process is similar to that discussed in the previous section, except that there will now be two or more variable elements. Since the analysis has indicated the proportions in which to combine the factors, however, there will be no difficulty in completing the cost computation. It should be clear that the optimum proportions will usually change throughout the range of output.

As in the previous section, it is possible and convenient to indicate a more general solution in terms of mathematical equations. The given data in the problem include (1) the prices $p_1, p_2, \ldots, p_n$ of the n factors of production used in the process, and (2) a physical input-output relation showing the rate of output as a function of a number of variable input rates:

$$Q = f(q_1, q_2, \ldots, q_n). \tag{8.15}$$

This function represents the whole "surface" of the physical relation, and the problem is to define, with the given factor prices, the particular combinations of the factors that are most economical.

The most economical combination is achieved when marginal rates of substitution are equal to the ratios of factor prices. Expressed in equation form, this equilibrium condition will be:

$$dq_1/dq_2 = p_2/p_1 = \frac{\partial Q/\partial q_2}{\partial Q/\partial q_1},$$

$$p_3/p_1 = \frac{\partial Q/\partial q_3}{\partial Q/\partial q_1}, \qquad (8.16)$$

$$\cdots \cdots \cdots \cdots$$

$$p_n/p_1 = \frac{\partial Q/\partial q_n}{\partial Q/\partial q_1}.$$

Note that, in the first of these equations, the first term represents the marginal rate of substitution between the first two factors; the second term is, of course, the inverse ratio of prices; while the last is a ratio of partial derivatives where the numerator represents the marginal productivity of the second factor and the denominator the marginal productivity of the first factor; this ratio also equals the marginal rate of substitution.

The unknowns in this problem are the q's — the inputs of factors — and since there are n factors there will be n unknowns for which to solve. To determine the specific values of these q's that will be consistent with the most economical organization, there are n equations: equation (8.15) plus $n - 1$ equations of type (8.16). With n equations and n unknowns, the problem will ordinarily be determinate. As a matter of fact, the mathematical solution may completely parallel the graphic solution by taking partial derivatives of equation (8.15) with respect to each of the q's, substituting these in equations (8.16) and, finally, establishing values for one of the q's and solving for the others. This will give a schedule of the most economical combinations of the input factors and, when these calculated values are substituted in equation (8.15), a corresponding schedule of outputs. From this point it is a simple matter to multiply the inputs by their respective prices and to sum them in order to obtain a total-cost figure for each output.

A more convenient solution may be given in terms of a single optimum rather than a schedule of combinations of the factors. This involves the production function given in equation (8.15), the factor prices, and, in addition, the unit price P for the product. Total profit G will be the total income less the several input expenses, or:

$$G = PQ - p_1q_1 - p_2q_2 - \cdots - p_nq_n. \qquad (8.17)$$

Taking partial derivatives of equation (8.17) with respect to each of the input elements and setting them equal to zero gives the following set of equations that must hold if profits are to be maximized:[16]

$$\begin{aligned}
\partial(PQ)/\partial q_1 &= p_1, \\
\partial(PQ)/\partial q_2 &= p_2, \\
&\cdots\cdots\cdots \\
\partial(PQ)/\partial q_n &= p_n.
\end{aligned} \qquad (8.18)$$

There are $n + 1$ unknowns in this problem: Q, q_1, q_2, $\ldots$, q_n. There are also $n + 1$ equations: one of (8.15) plus n of (8.18). Under these conditions, there will ordinarily be at least one set of values that will satisfy the equations. Suppose equation (8.15) is multiplied by P and then differentiated partially with respect to each of the q's. These results may be substituted in the equations of type (8.18) to solve for the particular values of the q's that will correspond with the maximum profit situation. In turn, these results may be substituted back in equation (8.15) to determine the optimum output Q and also in equation (8.17) to determine the value of the total profit G.

The heavy curves in Fig. 29 represent long-run cost functions. For comparison, the diagrams include a number of short-run curves. Note that some of these coincide with the long-run curve at one output; this is the output where the particular combination of fixed factors is in optimum adjustment with the variable factor. As output changes, the combination of factors in the

[16] To insure that the solution represents maximum and not minimum profits, the second derivatives must be negative.

short-run situation can only vary by increasing or decreasing the variable factor, and this will result in short-run costs above the long-run level. In addition, there will be other short-run curves that lie entirely above the long-run curve.

It may be desirable to indicate more specifically the application of the long-run analysis to the problem of city milk plants.

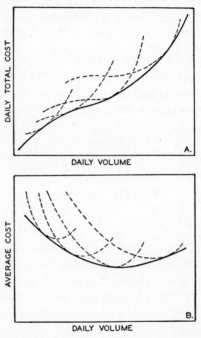

Fig. 29. *Relation between short- and long-run plant cost curves: A, in terms of total costs; B, in terms of average costs. The broken lines represent short-run costs, while the solid lines represent long-run costs — the curves showing economies of scale.*

In any market there will be a number of milk processing and bottling plants. Each of these will be characterized by a particular short-run cost curve. Moreover, the particular cost per quart of milk for each plant will depend not only on the short-run cost curve but on the particular level of output at which the plant is operated. In many plants, average costs could be reduced by increasing daily volume, although there may be some plants that are already operating at or beyond the least-cost volume.

In considering market reorganization, one problem would be to plan an organization of plants that will minimize costs. If all plants are to continue in operation, this means that plant capacities should be adjusted to the existing volumes. The long-run cost curve and the production functions basic to it will indicate the desirable form of this reorganization and the effects that it would have on plant costs. On the other hand, in some reorganizations the existing plants will not be maintained, and the problem will be to adjust volumes and plant capacities so as to result in the optimum number of plants and the lowest possible cost for plant operations. Again, the economy-of-scale curve (long-run cost curve) will indicate the correct adjustment. The least-average-cost point on the long-run curve will represent the optimum size of plant, and the total volume in a market would be handled most economically by a system of plants where each had capacity and volume approximating this adjustment.

"It may be noted that the economy curve has been drawn tangent to the individual-plant cost curves in the diagram. This will be the case if it is possible to have fairly continuous variations in scale. If plant capacities form a discrete series, the economy curve will consist of segments of the plant curves and will have a scalloped appearance. If plant volumes are subject to unavoidable fluctuations, such as those arising from the seasonal variation in milk production, the economy curve will be drawn secant to or intersecting the plant-cost curves. In all cases, however, the economy curve will represent the costs under the most efficient organizations for all volumes. Because it shows the costs that may be achieved with optimum organization and not the costs that may characterize an actual but inefficient system, the curve has sometimes been called a 'planning' curve." [17]

Balancing off plant and delivery costs to determine least-cost organization[18]

The foregoing sections have considered delivery and plant operations separately. In most cases these two aspects of city milk

[17] *Ibid.*, 22.
[18] R. G. Bressler, Jr., "Transportation and Country Assembly of Milk," *Journal of Farm Economics*, XXII, No. 1 (1940).

distribution should be considered simultaneously. As the volume handled through a particular plant is increased, the area served by delivery routes originating at the plant will also increase. Expanding delivery areas will mean longer milk routes. Longer milk routes, in turn, will mean increasing delivery cost. If there are significant economies of scale in plant operation, these can be attained only through diseconomies in delivery operations.

From the standpoint of delivery operations, the most economical organization would probably involve a great number of plants so that routes could be as short as possible. On the other

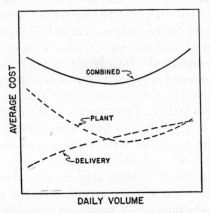

Fig. 30. Combining plant and delivery costs to determine the least-cost organization for the complete distribution system.

hand, plant considerations alone may suggest an organization with a very few plants of very large size. Clearly the optimum organization of the entire distribution system will involve some compromise between these two extremes. The nature of this compromise is illustrated in Fig. 30. Average plant costs in this diagram are taken from the long-run average cost curve given in Fig. 29. Average delivery costs are shown as increasing with plant volume at a decreasing rate, since the radius of the area served will tend to increase with the square root of the volume. Combining plant and delivery costs will indicate the volume where total unit costs are a minimum, and so the optimum type of organization for the complete system.

It would be possible to include delivery operations with plant operations in a mathematical formulation similar to that given in the previous section. Once the appropriate modifications are made in the production function, however, the following steps will be exactly as before. For this reason, the equations will not be duplicated here.

9 —

DELIVERY-TRUCK COSTS

Cost studies for retail trucks

To determine the physical and economic inputs included in the operation of retail milk trucks, several hundred truck records covering operations in 1940 and 1941 were obtained from a group of Connecticut dealers. Many of these records gave details by months as well as annual totals, and all included the operating costs for gasoline, oil, tires, and repairs, and the overhead costs for depreciation, general garage, insurance, taxes and licenses, storage, and interest. Each record also gave the number of days the truck was operated, miles traveled, and the make and age of the truck. Whenever possible, supplemental information on the physical inputs was obtained. The data were analyzed and the resulting descriptions of truck operating costs for the prewar period are summarized in the following pages. In addition, costs for the 1947 period have been estimated by applying postwar prices to the prewar relations.

It is recognized that the relations presented here will not be strictly applicable to any particular truck, because trucks identical in size, make, and age give widely varying performances. Factors not subject to quantitative presentation, such as conditions of roads traveled and the skill of the driver, influence the operating costs. These deviations have a compensating effect, however, so that the residual error, when applied to groups of trucks, will be small. The relations are presented, therefore, as describing hypothetical but typical truck operations. In all cases, the actual dispersions coincident with the relations have been reflected in correlation coefficients.

Gasoline inputs and costs

The amount of gasoline used by retail milk trucks is, of course, a function of the miles traveled. Because of such factors as motor idling and stop-and-go driving, however, some of the gasoline used is not associated with mileage. For the principal types and sizes of milk trucks, it was found that gasoline consumption could be explained quite exactly in terms of a rate per mile plus a fixed amount per day. The results of the analyses are summarized in Table 30.

Variable gasoline consumption per mile for retail trucks aver-

TABLE 30. Effect of mileage and days of operation on gasoline consumption, retail milk-delivery trucks.*

| Make and type† | Number of records | Gasoline consumption (gallons) | | $\bar{R}$ |
		Variable per mile	Fixed per day	
A.................	37	0.086	1.50	0.953
B.................	91	.075	2.26	.961
C.................	81	.085	2.70	.973
Other..............	131	.103	1.17	.956
All................	340	.093	1.76	.950

* Constants determined from mathematical correlation using type equation: Gasoline = *a* (days) + *b* (miles). Correlation coefficients have been corrected for numbers of parameters in estimating equation.
† Retail milk trucks equipped with special bodies. Actual capacities approximate 42 cases. Make A had a rated capacity of ¾ ton, B of 1 ton, and C of 1½ tons. Most of the miscellaneous makes had manufacturer's ratings of 1½ tons, although they ranged from ½ to 1½ tons.

aged 0.093 gallon (approximately 11 miles per gallon) for the entire group. In addition to the gasoline associated with distances traveled, these trucks used a "fixed" quantity averaging 1.76 gallons per day. While there was a wide variation in truck operations and performances, the two factors of miles per day and number of days operated explained 90 percent of the variance in total annual gasoline consumption, as indicated by the multiple correlation coefficient of 0.950. Different makes of retail milk trucks ranged from less than 10 to more than 13 miles per gallon of gasoline, but the three most common makes gave fairly consistent performances of 12 or 13 miles per gallon. Fixed gasoline consumption per day ranged from 1.5 gallons for make A to 2.7 gallons for make C, and apparently was influenced by the rated capacity of the truck and motor. The miscellaneous group of trucks averaged only about 1.2 gallons per day, possibly because of somewhat smaller loads and fewer stops per day. For each make the days operated and the miles traveled explained more than 90 percent of the variance in annual gasoline consumption (Table 30).

Gasoline costs depend on the physical relations mentioned and on the unit price of gasoline. For commercial operators a price of $0.15 per gallon appeared appropriate under Connecticut conditions during the period covered by the records, while the price averaged about $0.18 per gallon in 1947. Using the prewar rate, average gasoline costs for retail milk trucks on daily delivery routes may be represented by a constant of $0.264 per day plus $0.0140 per mile traveled. For the postwar period, costs may be represented by $0.327 per day plus $0.0202 per mile.

Oil consumption

Annual oil consumption is primarily a function of the mechanical condition of motors and of annual mileage. Mechanical con-

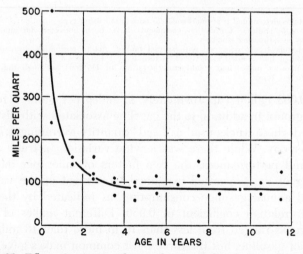

Fig. 31. *Effect of age of truck on miles traveled per quart of oil for retail milk trucks. Plotted observations represent age-group averages for several makes of trucks.*

dition is not subject to direct measurement, however, so some associated measure must be used. Age is such an index and, while subject to important limitations, has been used in the present analysis. Increases in age are generally associated with poorer mechanical condition and consequently with increased oil consumption per mile. Annual oil consumption, then, is a joint function of annual mileage and age.

The relation between age and miles per quart of oil for retail trucks is given by the curve in Fig. 31. This function has been derived from 229 annual operating records for retail milk trucks. Trucks less than one year old averaged 450 miles per quart of

TABLE 31. Effect of make of truck on miles per quart of oil
for retail milk trucks.

Make and type*	Number of records	Deviation in miles per quart of oil†	Average miles per quart of oil‡
A	38	−38	145
B	87	+5	160
C	34	−7	127
Other	70	+44	227
All	229	—	173

* All retail trucks with specialized milk truck bodies, usually with capacities of about 42 cases. Manufacturers' ratings ranged from ½ to 1½ tons. Make A was rated as ¾ ton, make B as 1 ton, and make C as 1½ tons.
† Average deviations from the regression given in Fig. 31.
‡ Based on relation given in Fig. 31, average miles per quart, and the expected length of life as given in Table 33.

oil, while the rate dropped to 175 and 115 miles per quart for trucks in their second and third years. In the fourth year the rate averaged 92 and it remained relatively stable at 85 miles per quart in succeeding years, although individual trucks gave wide variations from this level as a result of differences in motor repairs and replacements. In terms of total mileage, the rate leveled off at about 50,000 miles.

Some variation from the average performance was associated with the make of truck. Average deviations in rates per quart for the three most common makes of retail trucks are indicated in Table 31, together with the average for all other makes included in the sample. In terms of annual oil consumption, this factor, age, and mileage explained more than 50 percent of the variance.[1]

Oil costs may be obtained by applying prices or cost rates to the physical relations described. Because commercial operators frequently used a grade of oil that cost about $0.15 per quart in quantity lots, that rate has been used for the prewar period, while $0.18 has been used for the 1947 period. The cost is relatively unimportant, of course, averaging about $0.001 per mile in both periods.

Tires

Tire and tube cost records for any year are subject to misleading variations because such expenditures are not continuous. Tires are replaced only at rather long intervals, and annual records may therefore fail to represent true costs. To avoid this difficulty, life records of tire costs for a group of 25 retail delivery trucks have been used for analysis. The sample included all the common types and sizes of retail trucks and covered an aggregate of nearly 70 years of service. With adjustments for the value of original equipment and the partially used values of tires in service when the records ended, these resulted in the following cost equation:

$$T = \$12.72 + \$0.003R, \qquad (9.1)$$

where T represents the annual cost and R the annual mileage.[2]

These costs are based on prewar operations, and must be modified to fit postwar conditions. Tire prices averaged about $15 for retail trucks in the period studied. By 1947, this had increased to about $18. On the basis of such price changes, it would appear that the tire and tube costs should be increased about 20 percent. This will modify the annual cost equation to

$$T = \$15.26 + \$0.0036R. \qquad (9.2)$$

In physical terms, the life of a tire in years will be approximately represented by:

$$Y = \frac{20,000}{R + 4,240}, \qquad (9.3)$$

---

[1] The coefficient of correlation between annual oil consumption of retail trucks and the variable factors age, make, and mileage was 0.723.
[2] $\bar{r} = 0.912$.

where Y represents the years of life and R the miles per year.[3] If the annual rate of travel R is known, the years of life Y may be calculated, and so the estimated life of tire in miles RY. The estimates of physical life may not apply exactly for very small values of R, since there were no extremely short routes included in the sample. However, such factors as deterioration, sidewall damage, and stop-and-go wear would be fairly constant regardless of mileage, so the equation logically can be expected to hold approximately even for short routes. If it errs, tire life would be somewhat underestimated with annual travel as low as 2,000 miles.

Repairs

Repairs, like oil consumption, are a function of miles traveled and age. For an individual truck, motor repair costs per mile tend to increase with age at an increasing rate until it is necessary or economical to rebuild or replace the motor. After this large expenditure, cost per mile is lowered but increases again with added use. Repair costs per mile thus follow a wavelike pattern with cycles corresponding to the number of times that the motor is rebuilt. Combining the records for a number of trucks could be expected to show costs increasing at an increasing rate with age in the early years of operation and then leveling off as the rebuilding cycles averaged out into a more or less constant average cost.

Repair costs per mile were obtained from 282 retail-milk-truck records. When related to age they indicated a discontinuous function such as that described above. During the first four years costs per mile increased at an increasing rate from an average of $0.010 during the first year to $0.033 per mile in the fourth year,

[3] This equation may be derived from the cost equation as follows. A set of four new tires for trucks of this type cost approximately $60. The years of service from these tires will then be represented by the total cost divided by the annual cost, or

$$Y = \frac{\$60}{\$12.72 + \$0.003R}. \tag{9.3a}$$

This simplifies into the equation given above. The expected life in miles per tire RY will be $20{,}000 - 4{,}240Y$, or total miles will be relatively small for tires traveling relatively low anual mileages. This is, of course, the result of deterioration and wear associated with time.

and then remained approximately at that level. This is indicated
in Fig. 32, where the plotted observations represent age-group
averages for the several makes of retail trucks. The breaking
point in the fourth year corresponds to an average total travel of
about 50,000 miles. Make of truck was significantly related to
repair costs, with average deviations as indicated in Table 32.
Make and age together explained about two-thirds of the variance
in repair costs per mile.[4] Because of the discontinuity of costs,

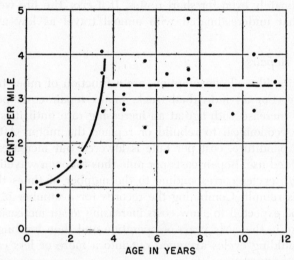

Fig. 32. *Effect of age of truck on repair costs per mile for retail milk
trucks. Plotted observations represent age-group averages for several makes
of trucks.*

rates for individual trucks were subject to important distortion.
In some cases, rebuilding a motor or other major repair jobs resulted in apparent repair costs of more than $6 per mile in the
given year. To obtain more continuous and representative data,
averages by make and age groups were used in the analysis.
Based on the individual truck records, the coefficient of multiple
correlation would be only 0.596 in terms of costs per mile. Similarly, annual repair costs for individual trucks were related to the
three factors age, make, and annual mileage, and resulted in a
coefficient of 0.592.

[4] $\bar{R} = 0.815.$

Representative repair costs per mile for the several makes and types of milk trucks are given in the last column of Table 32. These have been calculated from the relations discussed and the expected life of the various trucks as presented in a following section on depreciation. For retail trucks, repair costs average about $0.026 per mile during the useful life of the truck. Rates

TABLE 32. Effect of make of retail-milk-delivery truck on repair costs per mile.

Make and type	Records (number)	Cost deviation per mile* (cents)	Average repair cost per mile† (cents)
A.....................	38	+2.57	4.59
B.....................	92	−.11	2.28
C.....................	82	+.25	2.91
Other.................	70	−.44	1.58
All..................	282	—	2.60

* Average deviations from the regressions given in Fig. 32.
† Based on Fig. 32 and average deviations by makes, with expected life as given in Table 33.

for the lightest retail trucks (make A) were nearly twice as high as the average, while rates for the miscellaneous group were nearly 40 percent below the average. Study of repair costs for a number of trucks during the postwar period failed to reveal any consistent difference from the prewar averages, so these figures have been used for both periods.

General garage and storage

In addition to repairs, there are a number of general garage expenses in the operation of milk trucks. They include such items as washing, servicing, and painting, and are primarily functions of time. For the group of trucks studied, these miscellaneous costs averaged $108 per year. In addition, storage costs ranged from $5 to $10 per month, although appropriate rates for rural areas would probably be somewhat lower. For the state as a whole, storage costs may be represented approximately by $75 per year. General garage and storage costs, then, totaled $183 per year for retail trucks. The estimated cost in 1947 was $270, reflecting primarily the increase in labor costs.

Depreciation

Depreciation represents the cost of repaying the investment in equipment or of providing capital for replacement when present equipment is worn out. Common accounting procedures depreciate milk delivery trucks over a five-year period, and make no further charge for depreciation if the truck is used beyond that point. While this may be satisfactory as a bookkeeping method, a more useful method of determining actual costs in any year is to allocate the amount to be depreciated over the entire useful life of the truck.[5] This procedure has been followed and is reported in Table 33.

TABLE 33. Investment, life, and depreciation cost for retail milk trucks in the prewar period.

Make and type	Original investment* (dollars)	Salvage value (dollars)	Average useful life (years)	Annual Depreciation costs† (dollars)
A	900	100	5	160
B	1,300	100	7	171
C	2,000	100	10	190
Other.	1,000	100	5	180
All‡	—	—	—	175

° Less tires and tubes.
† Based on original investment less salvage value and on the useful life.
‡ Weighted average.

In general, the more expensive trucks have slightly higher depreciation costs, although most of the differences in original values are offset by years of useful life. Depreciation costs for retail trucks ranged from about $160 for make A to $190 for make C, while the average for all trucks was $175 per year (Table 33). Costs for individual trucks can be expected to vary around these averages, depending on such factors as the amount of money spent on repairs and the care taken in their operation.

Again, these estimates refer to the prewar situation, and prices and costs have changed materially since then. The average original investment for these trucks (less tires and tubes) amounted

[5] Over the life of the truck these two methods give similar results, since both allocate a given total investment.

to approximately $1300 in the prewar period covered by the original records. By 1947 this had increased to some $2000. With an allowance of $200 for salvage value to represent the increase in the used-truck market, depreciation costs for retail milk trucks for the postwar period would average about $270 per year.

Insurance[6]

Milk delivery trucks, in common with other users of the streets and highways, are sometimes involved in accidents. The costs of these risks may be borne directly by the operator or indirectly by insurance companies in return for certain stipulated payments.

TABLE 34. Basic rates for personal-liability and property-damage insurance for retail milk trucks in Connecticut markets.[*]

Markets	Basic insurance rates[†]
Hartford	$96
New Haven	96
Bridgeport	79
Stamford	66
Danbury	48
New London	47
Middletown	43
Mansfield	32

[*] Data from Aetna Casualty and Surety Company and the Travelers Insurance Company.
[†] Rates based on $20,000/$40,000 personal liability and $5,000 property damage.

In either event, the established insurance rates are the best available indications of the magnitude of this cost. Rates vary in accordance with such factors as the locality, the number of trucks operated by the concern, and the accident record of the concern. The risks to be covered by this analysis will be confined to the liability responsibilities of the truck owners; costs that would be covered by collision insurance and other types of protection to the owner's own property have been included under the heading of repairs.

[6] Information on rates obtained through courtesy of the Aetna Casualty and Surety Company and the Travelers Insurance Company, Hartford, Connecticut.

Basic rates for a few typical Connecticut markets are indicated in Table 34. These are for a maximum liability of $20,000/$40,000 for bodily injury and $5,000 for property damage — legal requirements in Connecticut. In rural areas, the basic rates for retail trucks are $32 per year. In small markets, these rates are approximately $45 per year. The highest rates in Connecticut are for New Haven and Hartford and amount to $96 per year for retail milk trucks.

Basic rates are subject to a number of reductions. Fleet reductions range from 1.7 percent for six vehicles to 16 percent for 100 vehicles, while all over 100 are allowed a 25 percent discount. Exposure and experience discounts, based on the number of trucks and the losses in some past period, range in extreme cases up to 40 percent. Other reductions, including rebates from mutual or coöperative insurance companies, are possible.

From the above it is apparent that no single rate will apply in all markets or to all milk dealers. A study of Connecticut dairy farmers who retailed milk reported a range similar to that noted above and an average annual cost of $55.[7] Merchant-dealers would undoubtedly have somewhat higher costs since many of the producer-dealers come under the rural rates. In general, an annual cost of $68 is fairly representative of Connecticut conditions, and this rate has been used in the present study for all makes of retail trucks and in both time periods. Individual operators, of course, may have costs above or below these levels.

Taxes and license fees

Property taxes depend on local tax rates and assessment practices. In Connecticut, tax rates range from less than 10 to more than 30 mills and average about 26 mills.[8] Assessment practices vary, but in general truck assessments follow the values established by the National Automobile Dealers' Association for used cars and trucks. Approximate prewar average assessment values over the life of delivery trucks are indicated in Table 35. Property

[7] Hammerberg, Fellows, and Farr, *Efficiency of Milk Marketing in Connecticut, 4.*

[8] *Information Relative to the Assessment and Collection of Taxes* (Public Document No. 48, Taxation Document No. 312, State of Connecticut, 1946), p. 104.

taxes, then, ranged from $12.50 for retail trucks of make *A* to
$26.25 for trucks of make *C*, and averaged about $18.35 for all
retail milk trucks studied.

Connecticut registrations for motor trucks of this size cost $0.30
per hundred pounds of gross weight, and average about $15 for
retail trucks (Table 35). The Federal Use Tax added $5 to an-
nual costs, but this wartime tax was discontinued in 1946.

TABLE 35. Taxes and license fees per year for retail
milk trucks, 1940–41.

Make and type	Average assessment*	Property tax†	State registration‡	Total
Retail trucks				
A.................	$ 500	$13.00	$12.00	$25.00
B.................	700	18.20	14.40	32.60
C.................	1,050	27.30	18.00	45.30
Other..............	550	14.30	13.50	27.80
All**..............	—	18.30	15.00	33.30

° For the 1940–41 period. Postwar values would be about 40 percent higher.
† An average rate of 26 mills, as reported by the Office of the Connecticut Tax Com-
mission.
‡ At $0.30 per hundred pounds gross.
°° Weighted averages.

Total prewar costs for taxes and license fees ranged from $25.00
for trucks of make *A* to $45.30 for make *B*, and averaged about
$33.30 for all retail trucks. Allowing for the postwar increase in
truck prices of about 55 percent, property taxes would average
about $28, and total tax and registration costs $43 per year.

Interest

Interest payments must be made on the unamortized portion
of the investment in trucks. Annual costs depend on the original
investment, the years of useful life, and the interest rate. In formula form, interest costs are:

$$I = (P - S) \frac{(r)}{2} \frac{(n + 1)}{n} + S(r), \qquad (9.4)$$

where *I* represents the annual cost, *P* the original investment (less
tires and tubes), *r* the rate of interest, *n* the number years of ex-

pected use, and S the salvage value at the end of the useful life. Using the formula above, and a rate of 5 percent, interest costs have been calculated and are summarized in Table 36. Annual

TABLE 36. Prewar interest costs for retail milk trucks.

Make and type	$(P - S)^*$ (dollars)	n (years)	Annual interest costs† (dollars)
A	800	5	29.00
B	1,200	7	39.29
C	1,900	10	57.25
Other	900	5	32.00
All‡	—	—	41.10

* Original investments less $100 salvage value.
† At rate of 5 percent.
‡ Weighted average.

prewar interest costs for retail trucks ranged from $29 to $57.25 and averaged $41.10, while for the postwar period the average would be about $62 per year.

Total costs for retail milk-delivery trucks

The elements of costs discussed in the preceding pages are brought together in Tables 37 and 38. They fall into three broad categories: (1) overhead costs that tend to be constant per year regardless of the number of days of use or miles traveled; (2) operating costs that are constant per day of use; and (3) operating costs per mile. Operating costs per mile have been represented by an average value per mile traveled, as indicated by the foregoing regression analyses. This does not mean that the operation of milk trucks is not subject to diminishing returns and increasing costs, but rather that such increases would stem from intensification in the *rate* of operation, that is, increases in the speed at which the truck is driven. The regressions given apply to average or typical rates of operation, with increases in mileage resulting from increases in the driving-time period rather than from increases in speed.

In these tables, overhead costs have been reduced to a daily

TABLE 37. Summary of costs of operating retail milk trucks, 1940–41.*

| | Costs (dollars) | | |
| | | Operating | |
Items	Overhead per day†	Fixed per day	Variable per mile
Gasoline‡................	—	0.264	0.0140
Oil**....................	—	—	.0009
Tires....................	—	.042†	.0030
Repairs..................	—	—	.0260
General garage and storage..	0.610	—	—
Depreciation††............	.583	—	—
Insurance................	.227	—	—
Taxes and license††........	.111	—	—
Interest††................	.137	—	—
Total................	1.668	0.306	0.0439

* All types and makes of retail trucks included in the sample.
† Assuming 300 days of use per year.
‡ Based on a price of $0.15 per gallon.
** Based on a price of $0.15 per quart.
†† Based on average truck price of $1,300, exclusive of tires and tubes.

TABLE 38. Summary of costs of operating retail milk trucks, 1947.*

| | Costs (dollars) | | |
| | | Operating | |
Items	Overhead per day†	Fixed per day	Variable per mile
Gasoline‡................	—	0.327	0.0202
Oil**....................	—	—	.0010
Tires††..................	—	.051†	.0036
Repairs..................	—	—	.0260
General garage and storage..	0.867	—	—
Depreciation‡‡............	.900	—	—
Insurance................	.227	—	—
Taxes and license‡‡........	.143	—	—
Interest‡‡................	.207	—	—
Total................	2.344	0.378	0.0508

* All types and makes of retail trucks included in the sample.
† Assuming 300 days of use per year.
‡ Based on a price of $0.18 per gallon.
** Based on a price of $0.18 per quart.
†† Based on 20 percent increase above prewar.
‡‡ Based on average truck price of $2,000, exclusive of tires and tubes.

cost basis by assuming an average operation for 300 days per year. If trucks were operated for more or fewer days per year, corresponding modifications in the daily costs would be required. With this limitation in mind, overhead and fixed operating costs per day have been combined into a single constant to give the following summary cost equations:

$$1940\text{--}41 \quad C = \$1.974 + \$0.0439D, \qquad (9.5)$$
$$1947 \qquad C = \$2.722 + \$0.0508D, \qquad (9.6)$$

where D represents the daily mileage and C the daily truck costs. Note that the constant term increased about 38 percent and the variable term about 16 percent during the period from 1940–41 to 1947. Further consideration of the effects of changes in prices and cost rates is postponed to a later section.

Wholesale-delivery-truck costs

To determine costs appropriate for the operation of wholesale-milk-delivery trucks, records were obtained on 31 trucks operating in Connecticut in 1940–41 and on 34 trucks operating in a number of northeastern markets for the period from 1945 to 1947. These 65 records provided annual data on variable operating costs as well as on the magnitude of overhead costs. The information obtained included make of truck, manufacturer's rated tonnage, and annual mileage. The analyses proceeded along lines similar to those reported for retail trucks, and so require no further elaboration at this point. For the same reason, the discussion of the various cost elements will be brief.

The records referred to three types of trucks: (1) type D (1945–1947), rated by the manufacturer as a 1.5-ton truck with a maximum load weight of 3 tons; (2) type E (1945–1947), rated as a 1.5-ton truck but with a maximum load weight of 4 tons; and (3) type F (1940–41), rated as 2 tons with a maximum load of 4 tons. Although types D and E have similar manufacturers' ratings, type E more nearly resembles type F as far as load characteristics are concerned. For the purposes of this study, then, types E and F have been combined to represent 4-ton-capacity trucks.

Gasoline costs for wholesale routes

Gasoline consumption on wholesale milk routes, as on retail routes, is a function of the days of operation, the mileage, and the size of the truck. Regression analyses for the three types of wholesale trucks are summarized in Table 39. If it is assumed for purposes of illustration that these trucks will travel approximately 10,000 miles per year, or 32 miles per day of operation, the equations indicate that 3-ton trucks will average about 8

TABLE 39. The effects of days of operation and distance traveled on gasoline consumption for wholesale delivery trucks.

Type of wholesale truck	Number of records	Manufacturer's tonnage rating (tons)	Maximum gross load (tons)	Gasoline consumption (gallons)*		
				Fixed per day	Variable per mile	$\bar{r}$
D	11	1.5	3	1.33	0.086	0.877
E	23	1.5	4	1.90	.102	.875
F	31	2.0	4	1.76	.112	.954
E and F†	54	—	4	1.83	.107	—

* Constants determined from mathematical correlation using equation $G = aP + bD$, where G represents annual gasoline consumption in gallons; P represents number of days truck operated per year; and D represents annual mileage.
† Simple average of types E and F to represent typical 4-ton trucks.

miles to the gallon and 4-ton trucks will average about 6 miles to the gallon.

Gasoline costs may be determined by applying current prices paid by distributors to the physical relations determined above. In 1947, a price per gallon of $0.18 was indicated as representative for Connecticut conditions. Using this price, the above physical relations correspond to the following cost equations for 3- and 4-ton trucks, where the average of types E and F is used to represent 4-ton trucks:

$$3\text{-ton trucks: } T = \$0.2394N + \$0.01548R, \qquad (9.7)$$
$$4\text{-ton trucks: } T = \$0.3294N + \$0.01926R, \qquad (9.8)$$

where T represents annual gasoline costs, N the number of days the truck was operated in the year, and R the annual mileage.

Oil costs for wholesale trucks

Although age of truck in years is far from a perfect indication of mechanical condition, as pointed out in an earlier section, it is the only index available and so has been used as a factor in explaining variation in oil consumption. The results of this analysis for wholesale trucks are given in Fig. 33, indicating that truck

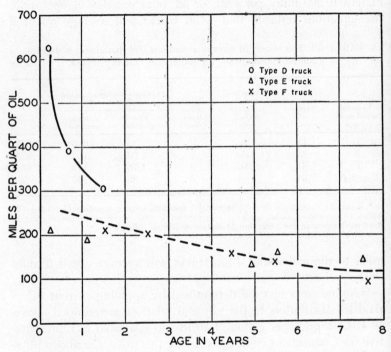

Fig. 33. *Effect of age of truck on miles traveled per quart of oil for wholesale milk trucks.*

miles per quart of oil drop rapidly with increases in age for the first year or two and then at a more gradual rate. The plotted observations in this diagram represent age-group averages rather than observations for individual trucks. Truck types *E* and *F*, with load capacities of 4 tons, followed a reasonably consistent pattern. Truck type *D*, with 3-ton capacity, gave significantly higher mileage per quart of oil, but the records covered only

1- and 2-year trucks and so permit no definite conclusions as to the rate of oil consumption that would be expected as motors further deteriorate. It seems probable, however, that the rapid decline indicated for the first two years will bring this type more into line with the results obtained for the larger trucks.

With an average age of about 5 years, the heavier trucks would travel about 150 miles per quart of oil. With allowance for more economical rates of operation in early years, it has been estimated that the lighter trucks would give an average performance of 200 miles per quart. These may be converted to costs per mile for the 1947 period by applying an average price of $0.18 per quart for truck oil in fairly large quantities. With this price, oil costs would average about $0.0009 per mile for the light trucks and about $0.0012 for the heavier trucks.

Tire costs

The annual costs for tires and tubes for wholesale milk trucks depend primarily on the distances traveled, although such factors as the speed at which the truck is operated, weather and road conditions, and the size of the truck are obviously important. Since many of these factors are difficult to measure and not subject to control, they have been averaged in the present study and costs related only to mileage and truck size.

Figure 34 presents two sets of annual tire expense and mileage data for 4-ton trucks: (1) 19 annual records for type E trucks, and (2) 38 annual records for type F trucks. It should be emphasized that these data show annual *expenses* rather than *costs*, and that individual observations will depart significantly from costs. This is particularly pronounced on low-mileage routes, where a number of records will show very low expenses, and a few records — where new tires were purchased during the given year — will show abnormally high expenses. If inventory values for tires and tubes had been available at the beginning and end of each year, it would have been possible to develop accurate data on annual costs for individual routes. Such data were not available, however, and so it was necessary to combine all of the records and to obtain an average cost per mile. This procedure disregards the influence of time on tire deterioration, but it is the only approach possible with the available data. The regression lines in Fig. 34 represent such averages, and for the combined data indicate a cost of $0.0052 per mile.

Data on tire and tube expenses were not available for 3-ton trucks. At 1947 prices, however, a complete set of tires and tubes for trucks of this size would have cost about 54 percent of the

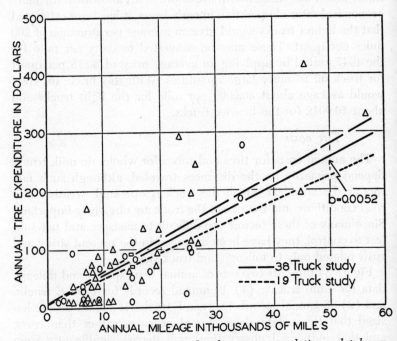

Fig. 34. *Average effect of annual mileage on annual tire and tube expenses for 4-ton wholesale-milk-delivery trucks.*

tire and tube cost for the 4-ton trucks. Data on milk *collection* trucks indicate that annual tire costs for 3-ton trucks would be about 60 percent of the costs for 4-ton trucks.[9] In view of these facts, tire and tube costs for the 3-ton trucks have been estimated at $0.0030 per mile, although this appears low relative to the retail-truck costs.

[9] R. G. Bressler, Jr. and D. O. Hammerberg, *Efficiency of Milk Marketing in Connecticut, 3,* 33–37.

Repair costs for wholesale trucks

The effect of age on repair costs per mile for wholesale milk trucks is shown in Fig. 35, where age-group averages have again been plotted rather than actual observations. The curved regression line refers specifically to the data for type *F* trucks. The re-

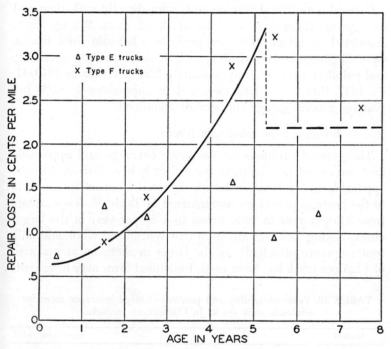

Fig. 35. *Effect of age of truck on repair costs per mile for wholesale-milk-delivery trucks.*

sults from the study of 36 type *E* trucks are also summarized in this diagram. It will be noted that the age-group averages for both studies are fairly consistent for ages of less than 4 years. As was suggested in an earlier section, repair costs in the higher age groups are extremely variable, and they have been represented by an average figure of $0.024 per mile. For an average age of 5 years and an even distribution from 1 to 10 years, the relation given in Fig. 35 would correspond to an average repair cost of $0.0193 per mile for 4-ton trucks. Studies of milk *collection* trucks indicate that repair costs for 3-ton trucks are about 10 percent below the 4-ton level, and so these have been estimated at $0.0174 per mile.[10]

General garage and storage costs

General garage and storage costs vary directly with time and so may be classed as fixed or overhead costs. Storage costs amounted to about $120 per year for wholesale milk trucks. General garage costs, including such items as washing, servicing, and painting, averaged approximately $205 per year in 1940–41. By 1947, these costs had increased to approximately $390 per year for general garage and storage combined.

Insurance for wholesale trucks

The general problems of insurance coverage and applicable fleet and experience discounts have already been discussed. Rates applicable to wholesale trucks in selected Connecticut markets in the postwar period are summarized in Table 40. These range from $45 per year in rural towns to $136 per year in the larger cities. Taking into consideration that specialized wholesale milk routes operate principally in the larger markets, an annual cost of $125 per truck has been used. Individual firms may have costs

TABLE 40. Personal-liability and property-damage insurance rates for wholesale milk trucks in Connecticut markets.*

Market	Insurance rate†
Hartford	$136
New Haven	136
Bridgeport	112
Stamford	95
Danbury	68
Torrington	68
Middletown	49
Mansfield	45

* Travelers Insurance Company.
† Rates based on $20,000/$40,000 personal liability and $5,000 property damage.

[10] *Ibid.*

above or below this rate, of course, depending on their specific location, the number of trucks operated, and previous insurance and accident records.

Depreciation

The annual depreciation charge on an investment in equipment is the decrease in value associated with increased use and age. Specifically, annual depreciation costs may be computed by dividing the original investment in the equipment minus salvage

TABLE 41. Investment, life, and depreciation cost for wholesale milk trucks.

Type	Original investment*	Salvage value	Average useful life in years	Depreciation costs per year†
D	$2,040	$250	10	$179
E	2,000‡	250	10	175
F	2,300	250	10	205
E and F	2,150	250	10	190

* Less tires and tubes.
† Based on original investment less salvage value and on the useful life.
‡ Average price for three common makes, includes price of body.

value by the estimated useful life of the equipment in years. Table 41 summarizes data on original investments, salvage values, and estimated depreciation costs for three types of wholesale milk trucks. Useful life has been estimated at 10 years; this is not high in view of wartime experiences, although it is higher than normal prewar performance. The table indicates that depreciation costs would average about $179 per year for type D trucks with 3-ton capacities and about $190 for type E and F trucks with 4-ton capacities.

Taxes, registration fees, and interest costs

Average assessments for the several types of wholesale trucks are indicated in Table 42, together with property taxes calculated at a rate of 26 mills. These costs average $29.90 per year for 3-ton trucks and $31.30 for 4-ton trucks. Registration fees, calculated at the rate of $0.30 per hundred pounds of gross weight, would amount to $36 per year for the 3-ton trucks and $48 per year for the 4-ton trucks. Interest costs, calculated at the rate

TABLE 42. Annual taxes, registration fees, and interest costs for wholesale milk trucks in Connecticut, 1947–48.

Truck group	Average assessment	Property tax*	State registration†	Interest costs‡
D	$1,150	$29.90	$36.00	$61.72
E	1,125	29.25	48.00	60.62
F	1,275	33.15	48.00	68.88
E and F	1,200	31.20	48.00	64.75

* An average rate of 26 mills: *Information Relative to the Assessment and Collection of Taxes* (Public Document No. 48, Taxation Document No. 312, State of Connecticut, 1946), p. 104.

† At $0.30 per hundred pounds gross.

‡ With original investments, salvage values, and useful life as shown in Table 41, and an interest rate of 5 percent.

of 5 percent on the undepreciated balance, would average nearly $62 per year for the lighter trucks and $65 per year for the heavier trucks over the estimated 10-year life span.

Summary of wholesale-milk-delivery-truck costs

The immediately preceding pages have developed in some detail the variable and fixed costs of operating 3- and 4-ton wholesale-milk-delivery trucks in 1947. These costs are summarized in Tables 43 and 44, where overhead costs per year have been reduced to a daily basis by assuming 300 days of use per year. With this simplification, which would require modification if actual use deviated significantly from 300 days, daily costs may be described by the following equations:

$$C_3 = \$2.979 + \$0.0368D, \tag{9.9}$$
$$C_4 = \$3.159 + \$0.0450D, \tag{9.10}$$

where C represents daily truck costs, D the daily mileages, and the subscripts identify the size of the truck.

While the detailed studies have been limited to these more common truck sizes, certain types of wholesale operations permit very large daily route volumes and so require larger trucks. In order to give some indication of the costs involved in the operation of these larger trucks, studies of 6- and 10-ton milk *collection*

TABLE 43. Summary of costs of operating 3-ton wholesale milk delivery trucks, 1947.

	Costs (dollars)		
	Overhead per day*	Operating	
Items		Fixed per day	Variable per mile
Gasoline†..................	—	0.2394	0.0155
Oil‡......................	—	—	.0009
Tires.....................	—	—	.0030
Repairs...................	—	—	.0174
General garage and storage..	1.300	—	—
Insurance.................	.417	—	—
Depreciation..............	.597	—	—
Taxes and registration......	.220	—	—
Interest..................	.206	—	—
Total.................	2.740	0.2394	0.0368

* Assuming 300 days of use per year.
† At a price of $0.18 per gallon.
‡ At a price of $0.18 per quart.

TABLE 44. Summary of costs of operating 4-ton wholesale milk delivery trucks, 1947.

	Costs (dollars)		
	Overhead per day*	Operating	
Items		Fixed per day	Variable per mile
Gasoline†..................	—	0.3294	0.0193
Oil‡......................	—	—	.0012
Tires.....................	—	—	.0052
Repairs...................	—	—	.0193
General garage and storage..	1.300	—	—
Insurance.................	.417	—	—
Depreciation..............	.633	—	—
Taxes and registration......	.264	—	—
Interest..................	.216	—	—
Total.................	2.830	0.3294	0.0450

* Assuming 300 days of use per year.
† At a price of $0.18 per gallon.
‡ At a price of $0.18 per quart,

TABLE 45. Estimated costs of operating 6-ton wholesale milk
delivery trucks, 1947.

| | Costs (dollars) | | |
| | Overhead per day* | Operating | |
Items		Fixed per day	Variable per mile
Gasoline†	—	0.4860	0.0259
Oil‡	—	—	.0011
Tires**	—	—	.0083
Repairs††	—	—	.0235
General garage and storage‡‡	1.430	—	—
Insurance***	.833	—	—
Depreciation†††	.863	—	—
Taxes and registration‡‡‡	.381	—	—
Interest****	.294	—	—
Total	3.801	0.4860	0.0588

* Assuming 300 days of use per year.

† Based on physical relation derived from data in R. G. Bressler, Jr., and D. O. Hammerberg, *Efficiency of Milk Marketing in Connecticut, 3. Economics of the Assembly of Milk* (Storrs Agricultural Experiment Station, Bulletin 239, 1942), 36–37, and gasoline consumption data on 3- and 4-ton wholesale delivery trucks; $G = 2.70P + 0.144D$, where G represents annual gasoline consumption in gallons, P, represents fixed consumption per day of operation, and D represents annual mileage. Costs computed at $0.18 per gallon.

‡ Based on data for 3- and 4-ton trucks, adjusted for data on 6-ton trucks in R. G. Bressler, Jr. and D. O. Hammerberg, *op. cit.* Cost computed at $0.18 per quart.

** Based on 160 percent of tire costs for 4-ton wholesale delivery trucks, as suggested by relation in R. G. Bressler, Jr. and D. O. Hammerberg, *op. cit.*

†† Based on 122 percent of repair costs for 4-ton wholesale delivery trucks, as suggested by relations in R. G. Bressler, Jr. and D. O. Hammerberg, *op. cit.*

‡‡ Based on 110 percent of storage costs for 4-ton trucks.

*** Based on Hartford, Connecticut rates, which approximately double for loads of 9,500 pounds and over.

††† Based on an original investment, less tires and tubes, of $2,930, salvage value of $340, and 10-year useful life.

‡‡‡ Property taxes based on average assessment of $1,630 and a rate of 26 mills. Registration at $0.30 per hundred pounds of gross weight.

**** Based on interest rate of 5 percent.

trucks have been modified to give an approximation of costs under wholesale delivery conditions. The adjusted data and the bases for adjustments are summarized in Tables 45 and 46. These calculations reduce to the following cost equations:

$$C_6 = \$4.287 + \$0.0588D, \qquad (9.11)$$
$$C_{10} = \$5.775 + \$0.0707D, \qquad (9.12)$$

where the letters represent the same variables as above.

TABLE 46. Estimated costs of operating 10-ton wholesale
milk delivery trucks.

Items	Costs (dollars)		
	Overhead per day*	Operating	
		Fixed per day	Variable per mile
Gasoline†	—	0.6300	0.0319
Oil‡	—	—	.0014
Tires**	—	—	.0140
Repairs††	—	—	.0235
General garage and storage‡‡	1.586	—	—
Insurance***	.833	—	—
Depreciation†††	1.542	—	—
Taxes and registration‡‡‡	.655	—	—
Interest****	.529	—	—
Total	5.145	0.6300	0.0708

* Assuming 300 days of use per year.
† Based on physical relationship derived from data in R. G. Bressler and D. O. Hammerberg, *Efficiency of Milk Marketing in Connecticut*, 3, 37, and gasoline consumption data on 3- and 4-ton wholesale delivery trucks; $G = 3.50P + 0.177D$, where G represents annual gasoline consumption in gallons, P represents fixed consumption per day of operation, and D represents annual mileage. Cost computed at $0.18 per gallon.
‡ Based on consumption data for 3- and 4-ton trucks, adjusted for data on 10-ton trucks in R. G. Bressler, Jr. and D. O. Hammerberg, *op. cit.* Cost computed at $0.18 per quart.
** Based on 270 percent of tire costs for 4-ton wholesale delivery trucks, as suggested by relations in R. G. Bressler, Jr. and D. O. Hammerberg, *op. cit.*
†† Based on 122 percent of repair costs for 4-ton wholesale delivery trucks, as suggested by relations in R. G. Bressler, Jr. and D. O. Hammerberg, *op. cit.*
‡‡ Based on 130 percent of storage costs for 4-ton wholesale delivery trucks.
*** Based on Hartford, Connecticut rates which approximately double for loads of 9,500 pounds and over.
††† Based on an original investment, less tires and tubes, of $5,250, salvage value of $625, and 10-year useful life.
‡‡‡ Property taxes based on average assessment of $2,940 and a rate of 26 mills. Registration at $0.30 per hundred pounds of gross weight.
**** Based on interest rate of 5 percent.

Truck costs in rural areas

Most dealers in rural areas are farmers who operate small retail routes. Trucks are usually of the pick-up type and are used for general purposes on the farm when not in use on the retail route. Such items as insurance rates, taxes, depreciation, and garage costs are usually lower than in city areas. Studies were made of 141 trucks operated by producer-dealers in 1937, and the results are summarized in Table 47.

In linear terms, the average relation between route miles and route volume for producer-dealers was approximately $V = 7D - 70$, while the average daily sale per customer was about 1.8 quarts. Using these to convert the effect of number of custom-

TABLE 47. Costs of operating trucks on milk delivery routes, Connecticut producer-dealers, 1937.*

Size of truck (tons)	Fixed costs per day	Variable costs per	
		Mile	Customer
0.50	$0.343	$0.0246	$0.0019
.75	.348	.0257	.0019
1.00	.411	.0263	.0019
1.50	.512	.0285	.0019
2.00	.617	.0323	.0019
Average	$0.446	$0.0275	$0.0019

* Adapted from Table 11, D. O. Hammerberg, I. F. Fellows, and R. H. Farr, *Efficiency of Milk Marketing in Connecticut, 4.* Using daily mileage, number of customers, age of truck when purchased, and size of truck to explain variations in truck costs resulted in a coefficient of multiple correlation of 0.862.

ers to a mileage basis, the average cost of operating such milk trucks was approximately $0.372 per day plus $0.035 per route mile. Applying the percentage increases found for urban retail routes, approximate postwar costs may be estimated at $0.52 per day plus $0.041 per mile.

Modifications affecting truck operating costs

The foregoing cost descriptions are based on delivery conditions and cost rates that were in effect in Connecticut at the time the records were made. Differences in delivery conditions as well as variations in prices and cost elements from those typical of the periods and markets studied will, of course, modify these descriptions. In the following paragraphs such variations are considered and some of their effects are indicated. Consideration will be limited to differences in conditions and cost rates that will, within their normal range of variation, have an appreciable influence on the cost schedules.

Differences in delivery conditions are, in general, of two types — those that affect the total route distance traveled, and those that affect the number of delivery stops per day. Operating cost per mile, in so far as differences in delivery distances are concerned, will be unaffected. Lowered mileage will probably result in increased life of the truck, especially if the changes are radical departures from normal operations. As a practical matter, it seems unwise to increase the estimates of useful life beyond 10 years because of technological obsolescence. To the extent that the useful life of a truck is increased, the overhead costs per day for depreciation and interest will be reduced. Over the life of the equipment, of course, total depreciation costs will be the same while total interest payments will be increased.

The major effect of differences in the number of delivery stops made per day is upon gasoline consumption. Records of trucks operating on an alternate-day system of delivery indicate that about one-half of the fixed gasoline consumption is due to the number of delivery stops. The percent change in daily fixed gasoline consumption will, therefore, be one-half of the percent change in the number of stops. In terms of the retail trucks studied, fixed gasoline consumption averaged 1.76 gallons per day, or about 0.88 gallons per day due to delivery stops. With an average of 180 daily delivery stops, this means that each stop required roughly 0.005 gallons of gasoline. Changes in the number of stops will thus change daily fixed gasoline consumption by about 0.005 gallons per stop.

Most prices and cost rates are subject to variation, both geographically and through time. Therefore, estimates based on any particular rates will be limited in value to the particular areas and time periods when such prices prevailed. To minimize these limitations, the basic physical production functions have been described in so far as possible. Appropriate cost rates may be applied to these physical inputs to obtain revised cost functions. The procedure has been illustrated by the conversion of 1940–41 cost relations for retail delivery trucks to functions appropriate for 1947. Such calculations may be made for any set of prices and, so long as the basic technology does not alter significantly, the cost relations thus adapted to any specific conditions.

Daily average costs of operating a truck, as distinct from the basic cost relations, will depend not only on the physical relations and the appropriate prices, but on such factors as the size and type of truck and the length of route. As a result, it is impossible to present any single set of data that will correctly represent changes in daily costs. Nevertheless, it is a matter of some interest to see the general trends in such costs since 1940. Index numbers of such changes have been computed and are presented in Table 48.[11] These have been obtained by assuming a length of route of 30 miles per day, and computing costs accord-

TABLE 48. Estimated changes in milk delivery truck costs, United States, 1940–1950; index numbers: 1940–41 = 100.

Year	Prices of motor supplies*	Prices of motor trucks†	Wages per hour‡	Milk truck costs**
1940............	99	98	96	98
1941............	101	102	104	102
1942............	108	106	119	108
1943............	111	107	132	111
1944............	113	110	140	114
1945............	113	121	142	117
1946............	115	129	155	122
1947............	127	145	177	135
1948............	142	163	193	148
1949............	144	164	202	151
1950††..........	148	161	207	152

* Based on data published in *Agricultural Prices* (Bureau of Agricultural Economics, U. S. Department of Agriculture).

† Based on data reported in *Wholesale Prices* (Bureau of Labor Statistics, U. S. Department of Labor).

‡ Based on average hourly earnings of all manufacturing labor, as reported by the Bureau of Labor Statistics, U. S. Department of Labor.

** Based on the following relative weights: motor supplies, 44 percent; motor trucks, 25 percent; hourly wages, 15 percent; other items (assumed to remain constant), 16 percent.

†† Preliminary estimates.

ing to the foregoing relations. Using 1940–41 as a base period, and using an average of retail and 4-ton wholesale trucks, costs have been divided into the following four categories: (1) operating costs for gasoline, oil, tires, and repairs, with a relative weight of 44 percent; (2) depreciation, taxes, and interest as costs that

[11] For similar index-number calculations for milk-collection routes, see Stewart Johnson and William F. Henry, "Formulas for Adjusting Milk Transportation Rates," Storrs Agricultural Experiment Station Mimeograph, November 1950.

change with changes in truck prices, with a weight of 25 percent; (3) general garage expenses with a weight of 15 percent; and (4) insurance and storage charges, with a weight of 16 percent. To represent the approximate changes in these costs, the following available series have been used for the corresponding categories: (1) index numbers of the prices paid by farmers for motor supplies, as reported by the U. S. Department of Agriculture; (2) index numbers of the wholesale prices of motor trucks, as reported by the U. S. Department of Labor; (3) since general garage expenses are primarily for labor, this component has been represented by index numbers of hourly earnings of all manufacturing labor, as reported by the U. S. Department of Labor; and (4) since insurance and storage costs were relatively stable during the period, they have been entered as a constant term in the calculations.

It will be clear from the above that these calculations can only represent changes in milk-delivery-truck costs in a very general way, and that they are not presented as precise indicators of changes for any market. With these limitations in mind, the index of truck costs increased about 4 percent per year from 1940 through 1946. With the rapid postwar increases in prices and wages, the cost index rose 13 percentage points per year during 1947 and 1948, and since then has continued to move upward but at a reduced rate. During the decade, truck costs increased in total by more than 50 percent.

10 —

ROUTE LABOR
REQUIREMENTS AND COSTS

Time studies for retail milk routes

The time involved in retail milk delivery is an important element in delivery costs. In this chapter, data from other studies are summarized to give a general picture of time requirements. In addition, special time studies have been made to determine the effects of such adjustments as alternate-day delivery and exclusive delivery territories on delivery and driving time. Detailed observations were taken on five retail routes operating on an alternate-day basis. Information was collected on the elapsed time for driving and for delivery and collection stops, the distances covered by the route, the number of quarts delivered at each stop, the flights of stairs climbed by the deliveryman, and the distances traveled from the truck to consumers' doors and return. Results of the analyses of these data are presented in the following pages.

Total retail route time

Anderson and Spencer, in a study of ten mixed routes in Ithaca, New York, found total route time averaging about 8 hours daily.[1] Mortenson, reporting on 274 routes in Wisconsin cities, found almost the same average.[2] Bergfeld, studying six New Haven,

[1] R. Anderson and L. Spencer, "Ways of Conserving Tires and Reducing Other Expenses in the Distribution of Milk," New York State College of Agriculture Mimeograph A. E. 386 (January 1942).

[2] W. P. Mortenson, *Milk Distribution as a Public Utility* (University of Chicago Press, Chicago, 1940), 48–57.

Connecticut, retail routes for periods of a week, reported an average route time exclusive of personal stops of slightly more than 7.5 hours.[3]

These totals are broken down according to route operations in Table 49. With allowance for minor differences in the nature of route operations and in accounting procedures, the three reports are fairly consistent. Driving time for the Wisconsin routes was

TABLE 49. The time required for daily milk deliveries by retail routes, selected markets.

Route operation	Daily route time (minutes)				
	Ithaca*	Wisconsin†	New Haven‡	Average	
					(percent)
Loading..........	29	9	19	19	4
Driving..........	135	89	138	121	25
Delivering........	190	139	141	156	33
Collecting........	39	144	80	88	19
Unloading**......	37	43	42	41	9
Miscellaneous††....	51	56	37	48	10
Total.........	481	480	457	473	100

* R. Anderson and L. Spencer, "Ways of Conserving Tires and Reducing Other Expenses in the Distribution of Milk," New York State College of Agriculture Mimeograph A. E. 386 (January 1942).

† W. P. Mortenson, Milk Distribution as a Public Utility (University of Chicago Press, Chicago, 1940). The total hours given in Table 3, page 49, were allocated among the several operations by using the data given in Table 6, page 56.

‡ A. J. Bergfeld, A Study of Milk Distribution in New Haven with Recommendations (Stevenson, Jordan, and Harrison Report, June 1939). Bookkeeping and checking were reported together in this study, but have been divided arbitrarily and equally between unloading and miscellaneous operations in the above table to be approximately comparable with the other studies.

** Includes checking at the plant.

†† Includes shifting load and route bookkeeping.

relatively low while the time spent in collecting bills and soliciting was high, but in neither case are the discrepancies unusual in view of reports from other cities.[4] In general, it appears that

[3] A. J. Bergfeld, A Study of Milk Distribution in New Haven with Recommendations (Stevenson, Jordan, and Harrison Report, June 1939).

[4] A study of 745 milk routes in New York City, for example, indicated that collections required an average of 143 minutes per day. C. Blanford, An Economic Study of the Costs of Selling and Delivering Milk in the New York Market (Cornell University Agricultural Experiment Station Bulletin 686, 1938), 24.

delivery stops accounted for about 33 percent of the route time, driving to and from the route and between customer stops for about 25 percent, collecting and soliciting about 19 percent, and other operations for the remaining 23 percent of route time.

These averages will describe any given route only by chance, with respect to either total time or time for a particular operation. The time required to operate a retail milk route will depend on such factors as the length of the route, the number of collection and delivery stops, the total volume delivered, the type and location of the houses and buildings served, traffic conditions, and the personal characteristics of the deliveryman. Some of the factors are discussed and analyzed below.

Time per delivery stop

The time required to make a delivery stop is primarily a function of the distance traveled by the deliveryman. Factors such as the number of quarts delivered and the flights of stairs to be climbed are also important, while the characteristics of the man himself obviously have some influence. To determine the quantitative effects of these factors, time and motion data were analyzed for 339 stops where the only operation performed was milk delivery. A delivery stop was defined as the time from the removal of the full bottles from the case until the return of the empties. These times were related to the round-trip distance from the truck to the entrance of the house or building, the flights of stairs climbed, and the number of quarts delivered. The results are summarized in Table 50.

In four of the five retail routes studied, these independent factors were closely associated with elapsed time per delivery stop. Because of the human element, however, the effect of each factor varied somewhat from route to route. Time per foot of delivery travel varied from 0.16 to 0.32 seconds, time per quart from 2.7 to 6.1 seconds, and time per flight of stairs from 13.9 to 32.8 seconds. When all routes and observations were thrown together, however, total time could be expressed fairly accurately as:

$$T = 0.18D + 6.1V + 25.2F, \qquad (10.1)$$

where T represents the time for the stop, D the round-trip distance from truck to building in feet, V the quarts delivered, and F the number of flights of stairs climbed. This regression resulted in a corrected coefficient of multiple correlation of 0.838.

The regression equation indicates that deliverymen travel at an average pace of about 4 miles per hour. Climbing stairs is a slower process, of course. If a flight of stairs is thought of as approximately equal vertical and horizontal distances, 1 vertical foot requires approximately as much time as 8 horizontal feet. The remaining factor, the volume delivered, has been expressed as a continuous and linear function. Logically the effect appears somewhat irregular, with time increasing slowly for the first two or three quarts and then by a series of erratic increases as it

TABLE 50. Effects of distances traveled, quarts delivered, and flights of stairs climbed on time (seconds) per stop for retail deliveries.

Routes	Time per foot	Time per quart	Time per flight	$\bar{R}$	Estimated time per average stop
1................	0.27	3.8	13.9	0.907	69
2................	.32	5.4	23.5	.930	90
3................	.27	5.9	17.7	.854	76
4................	.17	6.1	16.8	.182	58
5................	.16	2.7	32.8	.854	64
Combined.........	0.18	6.1	25.2	0.838	67

becomes necessary to fill one or more carriers and as the load becomes heavy enough to have a significant effect on the man's speed. Analyses failed to reveal any consistent pattern of discrete changes, however, and so the linear function was used.

While individual drivers differed in their rates of performing the various jobs, there was some tendency for high performance in one element to be offset by low performance in another. Thus the driver on route No. 1 was relatively slow with respect to distance traveled but fast with reference to volume and stairs, while the driver on route No. 5 was fast with respect to distance and volume but slow on stairs. As a result the time per stop did not vary so greatly between drivers as the rates for the several elements might suggest. The last column of Table 50 gives the computed time for the average stop, where the distance was 185 feet, the volume 3.6 quarts (alternate-day delivery), and with an average of 0.9 flights of stairs. For the five routes studied this time ranged from 58 to 90 seconds; that is, the slowest performance required 55 percent more time than the most efficient. With respect to the several elements, however, slowest performances exceeded the time required for the most rapid performance by 100 to 136 percent.

Delivery time per stop has sometimes been expressed on a per

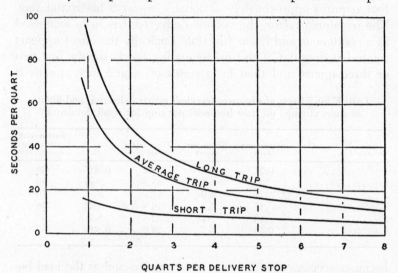

Fig. 36. *Effect of size of delivery on time per quart for delivery stops, retail milk routes. The average delivery stop involved 185 feet of walking distance plus 0.9 flights of stairs. For comparison, long- and short-trip performances have been included, with long trips involving 470 feet of travel and short trips 50 feet of travel.*

quart basis. Anderson and Spencer, for example, reported that "the greatest reduction in serving time per quart comes from the increase from one to two quarts, and within the limits of the data from this study, little reduction in serving time seems to be possible by increasing the size of delivery beyond four quarts to a customer." [5] The preceding analysis leads to somewhat similar conclusions, with savings per quart stemming from the allocation of the walking time over a larger number of quarts. The exact

[5] Anderson and Spencer, "Ways of Conserving Tires and Reducing Other Expenses in the Distribution of Milk."

magnitude of the economies will depend on the distance to be traveled and the stairs to be climbed, with relatively pronounced savings for long trips or trips involving several flights of stairs. Reductions in direct delivery time per quart with increases in volume are illustrated in Fig. 36 for several assumed situations. While the curve for a long delivery trip is based on a distance of 470 feet it also describes the savings that would result if the delivery required 50 feet of walking from truck to building plus three flights of stairs and return, as these two situations require about the same amount of time.

Time per collection stop

Many retail routemen spend part of their day making collections from customers. The total amount of time devoted to collection calls depends on the number of calls and the average time spent per call. Although the time per call is influenced by such factors as the distance to be covered and the flights of stairs to be climbed, as in the case of delivery calls, it is subject to seemingly random fluctuations that stem from the human element. In the previously mentioned time studies made by Bergfeld, a number of observations of collection calls were made. Original records of these studies have been made available by Stevenson, Jordan, and Harrison, management engineers, and are summarized in Table 51. For specialized collection calls, the average time for a successful call was 3.7 minutes. When calls did not result in payment, the average time was only 1.9 minutes, for in many of these cases the customer was not at home and little time was required other than to walk to the door and return. The scatter around these averages was very large, as indicated in the table, ranging up to one-half hour in some cases.

The above data refer to specialized collection trips, which were common before the war. Orders issued by the Office of Defense Transportation, however, outlawed call-backs for delivery or collection during the war, and these reforms have carried over into the postwar period. Many routes are now operating entirely on a daylight schedule so that collections can be made as part of the delivery calls. A number of such combined stops were observed as part of the present study of five alternate-day delivery routes. Elapsed time for these calls ranged up to 7 minutes and averaged 2.7 minutes. When reduced by the delivery time as indicated in the foregoing section, the added time for collection averaged 1.5 minutes, and in 80 percent of the cases the extra time was less than 2 minutes. These included both successful and unsuccessful collection stops.

About 73 percent of the collection stops noted by Bergfeld resulted in a payment. This success ratio indicates that average collection requires about 1.6 calls or, when weighted by the

TABLE 51. Time per stop for successful and unsuccessful collection trips, retail milk routes.*

Time per stop (minutes)	Collection stops	
	Successful (percent)	Unsuccessful (percent)
0.0–0.9	1	19
1.0–1.9	28	42
2.0–2.9	47	23
3.0–3.9	23	4
4.0–4.9	10	4
5.0–5.9	8	—
6.0–6.9	3	2
7.0–7.9	5	4
8.0–8.9	2	—
9.0–9.9	1	—
10.0 and over	7	2
Total	100	100

* Based on data from A. J. Bergfeld of Stevenson, Jordon, and Harrison, management engineers.

average time, that successful collection of a bill by specialized calls requires about 4.8 minutes. With combined delivery and collection calls, however, the added time for collection normally amounts to 2.4 minutes, a saving of 50 percent in collection time. When applied to the data given in Table 49, the time reduction on a normal route is 44 minutes per day. Such adjustments as biweekly and monthly collections and collections through the mails would result in further reductions in route collection time.

Driving time

According to the data presented in Table 49, the average daily retail milk route included more than 2 hours of driving time daily.

For any particular route the amount of driving time is basically a function of the total distance covered, with modifications for such factors as traffic conditions and distances between stops. The driver influences time requirements by his manner of starting and stopping the truck and his usual cruising speed. In general, the time required to drive from customer to customer or to and from the plant increases with distance at a decreasing rate. This curvilinearity is a reflection of the increasing and decreasing speeds that accompany starting and stopping. When the distance

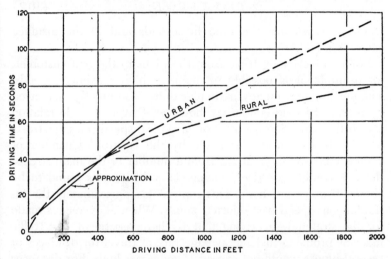

Fig. 37. *Relations between driving distance and time, retail milk routes. Broken lines indicate the curvilinear nature of the regressions in the lower distance ranges and the differences between urban and rural driving in the higher ranges. The solid straight line is the approximation used for distances between customer stops and covers a distance range that includes about 90 percent of these trips for the sample routes.*

covered is long enough for the truck to reach a more or less constant cruising speed, however, added distance increases time at a constant rate and the total-time curve rises with a constant slope.

Distance and time observations were taken on several hundred trips between customer stops. These were on city routes and in areas of fairly dense population. The average distance between stops was 280 feet, with 50 percent of the stops less than 200 feet apart and approximately 90 percent less than 600 feet. When

these distances were plotted against elapsed time, the relation
was found to follow the general pattern set forth above. The
curved broken line in the lower distance ranges in Fig. 37 is based
on these data. As a simplification that does little violence to the
facts, the relation may be taken as a linear function for the range
that would include most truck movements between customer
stops. About two-thirds of the time variance between such trips
could be explained by the solid line given in Fig. 37, or by the
following equation:

$$T = 5.3 + 0.08D, \tag{10.2}$$

where T represents the time in seconds and D the distance
covered in feet.[6]

For relatively long trips, from the plant to the first customer,
for example, it is possible to maintain higher average speeds.
The performance on any particular route is so greatly influenced
by traffic and road conditions, however, that any single relation
is of little value. Some indication of typical speeds on city streets
may be had from studies made by the Hartford Chamber of
Commerce.[7] By observations from a number of the main streets,
the net average speed of commercial vehicles was found to be
about 30 miles per hour. This represents approximately the instantaneous speed past selected points. When allowance is made
for the stop-and-go driving that is characteristic of city traffic
it seems probable that the average rate of travel for distances of
several blocks would not exceed 15 miles per hour. For distances
in excess of 1,000 feet, the five retail routes studied gave results
consistent with this average. When routes follow open highways,
as is true for many producer-dealers driving to and from market,
average speeds maintained for these distances might well be
twice this rate. In Fig. 37, the broken lines in the higher distance
ranges indicate the effect of this traffic factor. The top line is
based on a speed of 15 miles per hour and may be taken as
roughly representative of city conditions, while the lower line,
based on a speed of 30 miles per hour, is more typical of rural and
suburban areas.

[6] $\bar{r} = 0.860$.
[7] The author is indebted to the Hartford Chamber of Commerce for having
made available the results of its surveys.

Summarizing the foregoing discussions and converting the relations into terms of total driving time per route, city routes may be represented approximately by the following equation:

$$T = 240D_1 + 420D_2 + 5.3N, \qquad (10.3)$$

where T represents the driving time in seconds, D_1 the miles traveled from the plant to the first customer and from the last customer to the plant, D_2 the miles traveled between the first and last customer stops, and N the number of customer stops. If the plant is located in a rural area, the first term would be changed to $120D_1$ to correspond to an average speed of 30 miles per hour, or to some other rate representative of local driving conditions.[8]

Time for other retail operations

Detailed investigations have not been made of the time relations involved in such route operations as loading and unloading, adjusting the load, and bookkeeping. The data summarized from other studies in Table 49 indicate that 108 minutes were devoted to these operations daily, or an average of about 22 seconds per quart. While alternate-day delivery and other adjustments can be expected to reduce some items such as route bookkeeping time, the over-all effect will not be great and 22 seconds per quart has been used in all cases.

Summary for all retail route operations

By using average values for some factors such as the distance walked by the routeman in making a delivery, it is possible to summarize the previously discussed time relations into relatively simple expressions for daily route requirements. As shown in Table 52, total time may be expressed as four component parts related to volume, number of stops, distance from plant to the delivery section of the route and return, and distance from the first to the last customer. In equation form and expressed in minutes, this can be represented approximately by:

$$T = 0.46V + 1.71N + 4.0D_1 + 7.0D_2, \qquad (10.4)$$

[8] This definition of D_1 and D_2 is arbitrary. For routes with very scattered customer stops, it would be better to measure D_1 relative to the distance from the plant to the principal delivery area.

where T is the estimated time in minutes, V the route volume in quarts, N the number of stops, D_1 the distance to and from the plant in miles, and D_2 the distance between the first and last stops in miles. This equation refers to city operations with special trips for collection. With collections made in conjunction with delivery stops, the added time per stop would be reduced from 1.71 to 1.36 minutes. With complete elimination of soliciting and collection on the part of the routeman, as might be feasible under some reorganization plans, the time per stop would be further reduced to 1.02 minutes.

This relation may be simplified by combining the distance

TABLE 52. Summary of route time requirements for city retail milk routes with special collection stops.

Operations	Seconds per quart (V)	Seconds per stop (N)	Seconds per mile (D_1)	Seconds per mile (D_2)
Delivering*..........	6.1	56.0	—	—
Collecting†..........	—	41.2	—	—
Driving.............	—	5.3	240	420
Other..............	22.0	—	—	—
Total..........	28.1	102.5	240	420

* Based on average walking distance per stop of 185 feet and an average of 0.9 flight of stairs.
† Based on average of 1.6 trips to make collection, and allocated evenly over a seven-day week.

components into a single term and by allocating the time per stop to the volume factor. As previously explained, the distance factors refer to speeds under urban conditions, and rates as low as 2.0 minutes per mile would be appropriate for rural, inter-urban, or urban "freeway" traffic. It is quite clear that the appropriate rates will depend on local conditions, but present purposes may be served by using the single rate of 4.0 minutes per mile for all route travel as more or less typical. The allocation of time per stop to the volume factor involves appropriate values for volume per stop. In the foregoing studies, this appeared to be 1.8 quarts with daily delivery and 3.6 quarts per customer with alternate-day delivery. Using 1.8 quarts per customer, the following simplified equations may be derived for daily delivery:

$$T_1 = 1.41V + 4.0D, \qquad (10.5)$$
$$T_2 = 1.22V + 4.0D, \qquad (10.6)$$
$$T_3 = 1.03V + 4.0D, \qquad (10.7)$$

where the subscripts refer to: (1) prewar conditions with special collection trips; (2) present conditions with combined collection and delivery trips; and (3) reorganized conditions with no soliciting or collecting by the routeman.

The determination of appropriate simplifications for alternate-day delivery involves several further modifications. It will be recalled that the time per stop involved several elements directly related to the number of stops, *plus* collection time that represented an average per stop allocated over a period of time. This was because collections are not usually made at every delivery, but on some less frequent basis such as once a week or month. As a consequence, the allocated time per quart for collection should not be reduced by alternate-day delivery, and only 61.3 seconds or 1.02 minutes per stop will be divided by the average volume of 3.6 quarts per stop, while collection time is continued at the same level as for daily delivery. Moreover, "other route time" when allocated on a per-quart basis will amount to approximately 0.24 minutes rather than 0.37 minutes. With these modifications, the simplified equations for alternate-day delivery will be:

$$T'_1 = 0.99 + 4.0D, \qquad (10.8)$$
$$T'_2 = 0.80 + 4.0D, \qquad (10.9)$$
$$T'_3 = 0.61 + 4.0D. \qquad (10.10)$$

Time studies of wholesale routes

Information on wholesale milk delivery route-time requirements and the breakdown of total time requirements according to operations has been obtained from four sources: (1) a study of five specialized wholesale routes in New Haven during 1939;[9] (2) a summary of studies of 63 California routes made in the period from 1940 to 1943;[10] (3) a study of five Hartford routes made as part of the present project in 1942; and (4) detailed time

[9] A. J. Bergfeld, *A Study of Milk Distribution in New Haven.*
[10] Bureau of Market Enforcement, California State Department of Agriculture, mimeographed reports (1940–43).

TABLE 53. Average daily time requirements for delivery by wholesale milk routes.

Operation	New Haven* (minutes)	New Haven* (percent)	West Coast† (minutes)	West Coast† (percent)	Present study 1942 (minutes)	1942 (percent)	1947 (minutes)	1947 (percent)
Load	15	3	28	6	23	5	‡	—
Drive	167	31	144	30	122	27	144	28
Receive order	‡	—	48	10	‡	—	21	4
Arrange load	‡	—	**	—	‡	—	53	11
Load dolly	‡	—	**	—	‡	—	7	2
Deliver	49	9	113	24	45	10	32	6
Return	‡	—	††	—	‡	—	12	2
Service refrigerator	‡	—	6	1	‡	—	22	4
Empties	24	4	63	13	48	10	33	7
Bill	139	26	46	10	43	9	63	12
Miscellaneous	122	23	**	—	150	33	113	22
Walk from cab	‡	—	**	—	‡	—	12	2
Unload	23	4	29	6	27	6	‡	—
Total	539	100	477	100	458	100	512	100

* Average for five routes, adapted from A. J. Bergfeld, A Study of Milk Distribution in New Haven with Recommendations.
† Averages for 63 routes summarized from mimeographed reports of the Bureau of Market Enforcement, California State Department of Agriculture (1940–1943).
‡ Included in miscellaneous time.
** Included in delivery time.
†† Included in time for empties.

studies for ten routes in Connecticut, California, Pennsylvania, and New Jersey made in 1947 as part of the present project. Although all of these studies were not made in exactly the same manner, the results are fairly consistent. The total time per route averaged about 8.25 hours per day (Table 53). The breakdown of total time according to operations indicates that loading and unloading accounts for about 8 per cent, driving 30 per cent, arranging the load and making deliveries 20 per cent, handling empty cases and bottles 10 per cent, billing and collecting 10 per cent, and miscellaneous operations 22 per cent of total route time.

The following pages analyze time requirements for each of the major operations, and indicate the effects of various factors on these time requirements.

Driving time

The time spent in driving on any wholesale route is related most closely to the total distance traveled, but it is also affected by such factors as the number of customer stops, traffic conditions, and the particular characteristics of the driver. For present purposes, driving time has been considered a function of distance and of the number of customer stops, as these two factors appear to be most important and may be measured easily in quantitative terms. Traffic conditions were taken into account only in so far as they would be reflected in differences in the time requirements for routes operating in urban and in rural or intermarket areas. The primary analysis was based on data for the 63 California routes mentioned above. This analysis was supplemented, and to some extent modified, by a study of the driving time and distance between individual stops for three of the routes included in the field work of the present study.

For each of the 63 California routes, data were available on the total driving time, the total miles traveled, and the number of customers served. These were divided into three groups according to the number of customers: (1) those routes serving fewer than 30 customers; (2) routes serving from 30 to 39 customers; and (3) routes serving 40 customers or more. For each of these groups driving time was related to distance, with the results shown in

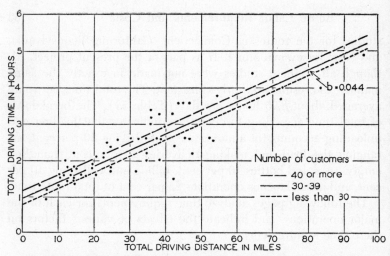

Fig. 38. *Net effect of driving distance on driving time for 63 California wholesale milk routes.*

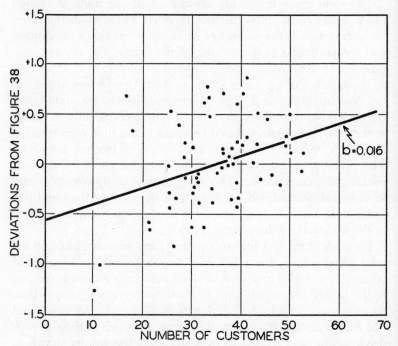

Fig. 39. *Net effect of the number of customers on driving time for 63 California wholesale milk routes.*

Fig. 38, indicating that each additional mile adds 0.044 hours to driving time.

Using the 30–39 customer regression as a base, deviations were then related to the number of customers, as shown in Fig. 39. The wide scatter of points in this diagram is undoubtedly due in large part to the fact that average speeds were not equal on all of the routes so that the distance-time regression is only approximately correct when applied to any particular route. In spite of this scatter, there is some observable tendency for driving time to increase with increases in the number of customers, each additional customer increasing the time by an average of 0.016 hours. It should be noted that the number of customers is not a very satisfactory measure, for driving time will be influenced by the number of customer *stops* rather than the actual number of customers. Since several customers may be served at a single stop in some cases while in others a route may stop at a single customer more than once, it is clear that the use of the number of customers as a factor in the analysis is subject to some limitations.

To summarize, the above analysis indicates that total route driving time may be expressed in terms of the following linear equation:

$$T = 0.390 + 0.044D + 0.016C, \qquad (10.11)$$

where T represents driving time in hours, D represents the total route miles, and C the number of customers served by the route.[11]

In view of the wide scatter in Fig. 39, an attempt was made to check on the above equation by analyzing the data obtained for three routes on driving times and distances between individual customer stops. Relating distance between stops to driving time for these three routes resulted in the following linear equations:

$$t = 0.016 + 0.061d, \qquad (10.12)$$
$$t = 0.013 + 0.029d, \qquad (10.13)$$
$$t = 0.049 + 0.032d, \qquad (10.14)$$

where t represents the driving time between individual stops in hours and d the distance between stops in miles.[12] These relations are shown in Figs. 40 and 41.

[11] $\bar{R} = 0.876$.
[12] $\bar{r}_2 = 0.881$; $\bar{r}_3 = 0.980$; $\bar{r}_4 = 0.956$.

In order to put these in a form comparable to the results of the 63-route analysis, they must be converted into equations giving total driving time. This may be done by multiplying each equation by the number of customer stops *plus one* — the extra stop being used to represent the return trip from the last customer to

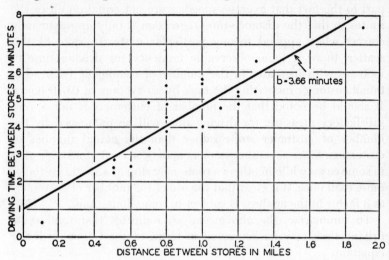

Fig. 40. *Effect of distance between stops on driving time between stops for a single route operating under urban conditions.*

the plant. Remembering that $T = t(C + 1)$ and $D = d(C + 1)$, the above equations may be converted into the following:

$$T = 0.016 + 0.061D + 0.016C, \quad (10.15)$$
$$T = 0.013 + 0.029D + 0.013C, \quad (10.16)$$
$$T = 0.049 + 0.032D + 0.049C. \quad (10.17)$$

In comparing equation (10.11) with equations (10.15), (10.16), and (10.17), it must be remembered that equation (10.11) represents average conditions on a relatively large sample of 63 routes while each of the other equations is derived from a number of observations on single routes. As a result, the latter may be greatly affected by the characteristics of the particular routes and routemen. With this in mind, it may be noted that the indicated effects of the number of customers on driving time are quite similar for equations (10.11), (10.15), and (10.16) and only in equation

(10.17) is there a marked difference. In view of this evidence, the original value of 0.016 hour per customer has been accepted as a reasonable approximation for typical cases, but with the realization that individual differences may result in marked departures on particular routes.

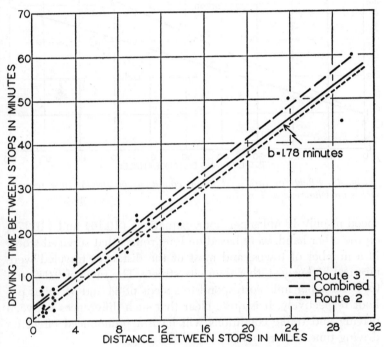

Fig. 41. Effect of distance between stops on driving time between stops for two routes operating under rural and intermarket conditions.

Comparisons of the indicated effects of distance on driving time in the four equations fails to reveal any marked similarity. This is to be expected, for the various routes operated under significantly different traffic conditions. The 63 routes on which equation (10.11) was based are a sample of urban driving conditions, and the rate of 0.044 hour per mile corresponds to an average over-all speed of about 23 miles per hour. Equation (10.15) is based on a route that operated in a congested district, and the rate of 0.061 hour per mile corresponds to an average

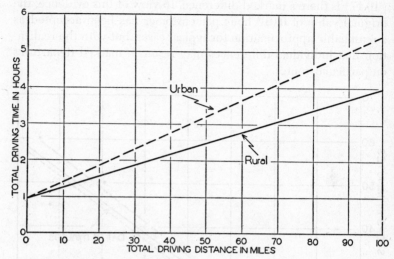

Fig. 42. Effects of rural and urban conditions on driving-time requirements for wholesale milk routes.

speed of only 16 miles per hour. Equations (10.16) and (10.17), on the other hand, were based on long routes that serviced stores in a number of towns, and most of the distances traveled were on rural highways rather than city streets. The rates of 0.029 and 0.032 hour per mile correspond to speeds of 34 and 31 miles per hour respectively. It is quite clear that such differences between driving and traffic conditions will have a pronounced effect on driving-time requirements.

To conclude this section, and in view of the above-mentioned

TABLE 54. Total driving time (hours) varying with driving conditions, rural or urban, number of customer stops, and route mileage.

Number of customer stops	Urban*			Rural†		
	25 mi.	45 mi.	65 mi.	25 mi.	45 mi.	65 mi.
25	1.89	2.77	3.65	1.54	2.14	2.74
35	2.05	2.93	3.81	1.70	2.30	2.90
45	2.21	3.09	3.97	1.86	2.46	3.06

° Values computed from equation (10.11).
† Values computed from equation (10.18).

differences between rural and urban conditions, we have selected two general equations to approximate typical driving-time requirements on wholesale-milk-delivery routes:

$$T_u = 0.390 + 0.044D + 0.016C, \qquad (10.11)$$
$$T_r = 0.390 + 0.030D + 0.016C. \qquad (10.18)$$

The first of these is the original equation derived from the analysis of 63 route records, and may be taken as representative of urban conditions. The second differs from the first only in the effect of distance on time, and here an average speed of 33 miles per hour has been used as representative of driving conditions on rural and intermarket routes. These two relations are shown graphically in Fig. 42, where the number of customers is assumed to be constant at 35 stops per route. The combined influences of numbers of customers and of route mileage are indicated by the driving-time estimates given in Table 54.

Arranging products for delivery

The time required to arrange milk and other products for delivery was observed on 152 customer stops, together with the associated volumes of the products delivered. While other factors such as the size and type of container and the rate at which the driver worked undoubtedly influence arranging time, they have not been considered specifically in this study.

Analysis of these data indicated that the arranging time for deliveries of milk only could be represented by the equation

$$t = 0.21 + 0.08V, \qquad (10.19)$$

and that the addition of a single case of miscellaneous products increased the time by approximately 0.73 minute while the addition of two cases of miscellaneous products resulted in an increase of 1.67 minutes.[13] It was found that the miscellaneous cases averaged 14 labor units of products in the single-case deliveries and 15 units in the double-case deliveries.[14] Correcting for these differences, it appears that each additional case of mis-

---

[13] $\bar{R} = 0.667$.
[14] See Appendix for a definition of labor units.

cellaneous products added approximately 0.78 minute to arranging time. In equation form, then, the final relation between volume and arranging time will be

$$t = 0.21 + 0.08V + 0.78M, \qquad (10.20)$$

where M represents the number of cases of miscellaneous products.

Time per delivery trip

Delivery time is defined in this study as the time required to carry the milk and other products from the truck to the storage area in the store or restaurant. The time required to service the refrigerator is not included in delivery time and will be discussed in a following section. Time, distance, and volume data were available from studies of 12 wholesale routes (including two routes studied in 1942) covering a total of 500 individual delivery trips. These data were used to determine appropriate relations describing delivery time.

The distance from the truck to the storage area is the major factor influencing delivery time. Analysis of the data mentioned above indicated that this factor accounted for 66 percent of the variance in time per delivery trip and that the regression between time and distance was

$$t = 0.08 + 0.0047D, \qquad (10.21)$$

where t represents delivery time in minutes and D the delivery distance in feet.[15]

While volume per trip appeared to have a significant effect on delivery time for several routes, this factor proved to be of very minor importance in an analysis based on all 500 observations. Table 55 summarizes the results of simple and multiple correlation studies for the 12 sample routes and for all routes combined. It will be noted that the inclusion of both distance and volume as independent factors had little effect on the accuracy of the description except in the case of route 11, and that for the combined analysis the multiple correlation accounted for about 69 percent of the total variance in time as compared to 66 percent for

[15] $\bar{r} = 0.811$. See Appendix for details.

the simple correlation.[16] It should be emphasized, however, that these results refer to delivery *trips* and that a stop where a large volume is delivered will involve a number of such trips.

The foregoing multiple regression expresses delivery time per trip as an additive linear function of delivery volume and distance. It may appear more reasonable to consider time as a joint or multiplicative function of the two independent variables, on the ground that increases in volume will result in slower rates of travel rather than in constant additions to time. Such a function

TABLE 55. Correlation coefficients between X_1, delivery trip time, X_2, delivery trip distance, and X_3, delivery volume.

Route number	$\bar{r}_{12}$	$\bar{R}_{1.23}$	$\bar{r}_{13.2}$*
1....................	0.821	0.840	0.311
2....................	.817	.811	.000
3....................	.637	.711	.410
4....................	.870	.870	.000
5....................	.738	.747	.171
6....................	.893	.892	.092
7....................	.906	.906	.000
8....................	.965	.974	.504
9....................	.510	.563	.277
10....................	.839	.892	.557
11....................	.473	.834	.780
12....................	.945	.945	.000
Combined.............	0.811	0.828	0.285

* See M. Ezekiel, *Methods of Correlation Analysis* (Wiley, New York, 1941).

$$\bar{r}^2_{13.2} = \frac{(1 - \bar{r}^2_{1.2}) - (1 - \bar{R}^2_{1.23})}{1 - \bar{r}^2_{1.2}}$$

might take the form $t = a + bDV$, where bV represents the time per foot and will increase with increases in volume. Functions of this type were fitted to the observations for several of the sample routes, but the results were not as accurate descriptions as those obtained in the previous analyses.[17]

As a final check on the influence of volume on delivery time, an analysis was made of the time to return from the store to the truck without loads. Data on the time for return trips were avail-

[16] $\bar{R} = 0.828$.
[17] Coefficients of joint correlation were 0.650 for route 2 and 0.634 for route 3. Compare these with the results shown in Table 55.

able for only five of the sample routes. For these routes the equations for delivery time (10.22) and return time (10.23) are given below:[18]

$$t_d = 0.081 + 0.0038D, \qquad (10.22)$$
$$t_r = 0.077 + 0.0041D. \qquad (10.23)$$

It will be noted that these two equations are very similar and that, as a matter of fact, the indicated time per foot is slightly higher for the empty return trip than for the loaded delivery trip.

To summarize, it appears that delivery-trip time is primarily a function of delivery distance, and that volume has little or no influence. Time requirements for return trips do not differ significantly from those for delivery trips, and both may be represented by equation (10.21).

Loading dolly

One of the reasons that volume per trip did not appear to be an important factor in explaining time requirements in the foregoing analysis of delivery time was that hand trucks or dollies were frequently used for the larger-volume stops. This tendency

TABLE 56. The effect of volume per stop on the frequency with which deliveries were made using a dolly or hand truck.

Delivery conditions	Percent of stops where dolly was used
Unload at platform	0
1 case	0
2 cases	4
3 cases	16
4 cases	37
5 cases and over	66
All stops	20

is illustrated by the data in Table 56. Where deliveries were made simply by unloading from the truck to a platform or where the total volume was only one case of milk and dairy products, dollies were not used. With volumes of two cases, however, the dolly was occasionally used and the use increased with volume increases until two-thirds of the stops with volumes of five cases or more

[18] $\bar{t}_d = 0.788$ and $\bar{t}_r = 0.850$.

were serviced with these hand trucks. Combining all volumes, the dolly was used to service an average of 20 percent of all customer stops.

Where the dolly was used, the time to load the cases on the dolly was found to be a linear function of the number of cases:

$$t = 0.10 + 0.104V, \qquad (10.24)$$

where t represents the time to load dolly in minutes and V the number of cases delivered per stop. This equation accounted for 42 percent of the time variance, indicating that unmeasured factors were of considerable importance.[19]

Handling empty containers

The time to handle empty containers has been defined in this study as the time required to sort empty bottles in the store and to load them on the truck. The time required to carry empty containers from the store to the truck is not included in this

TABLE 57. The effect of type of container on the time per trip required to sort and load empty containers.

Type of container	Number of routes	Average time to sort, carry, and load empties (minutes)	Distance to truck (feet)	Estimated average time to carry (minutes)	Estimated average time to sort and load empties (minutes)
Paper..........	6	0.873	68	0.400	0.473
Mixed..........	2	1.238	48	.306	.932
Glass..........	2	1.852	75	.432	1.420
Combined.......	10	1.146	65	.386	.760
Hartford routes*	5	0.800	58	0.353	0.447†

* Five wholesale routes in Hartford, Connecticut studied in 1942.
† Not comparable with the results above because time to load empties is not included. Other data indicate that time to load averages about 0.34 minute, so a comparable average for these routes would be about 0.79 minute per trip.

category, for it has already been accounted for as the return trip. The average times per customer trip spent in handling empty containers are summarized in Table 57 for the sample routes. The second column in this table shows the average time for handling empties and for carrying them back to the truck. The third col-

[19] $\bar{r} = 0.651.$

umn gives the average distance from the store to the truck, while the fourth estimates carrying time per trip according to equation (10.21). The last column is the difference between the second and fourth columns, and so represents an estimate of the time per trip spent in handling empty containers.

As indicated in this table, the time to handle empties is significantly affected by the type of containers used. On routes where paper containers are used, little time is required except occasionally to pick up damaged containers; the average time per trip for six routes handling only paper was 0.473 minute. Where glass bottles are used, on the other hand, the containers must be counted and the stores credited for returned bottles and cases; the average time required for these operations on two routes handling only glass containers was 1.420 minutes per trip. Where both paper and glass containers are used, the time requirements will fall somewhere between the above two extremes, depending on the proportion of each type of container; the average time for two mixed routes was 0.932 minute per trip. Combining all ten sample routes, the time required to sort empty containers and to load them on the truck averaged 0.760 minute per trip.

Time records were also available for the five Hartford wholesale routes studied in 1942, but for the most part these records only indicated the time required to sort empty containers in the store and did not include the time to load them. As the last line in Table 57 indicates, the average time to sort empties on these routes was 0.447 minute. Data on the time to load empties were obtained separately on one route, however, indicating that this operation required approximately 0.34 minute per trip. Thus these data result in a combined estimate of the time to sort and load empty containers that is almost exactly the same as the average for the ten sample routes.

Other route operations

In addition to the route operations already discussed, there are a number of operations that either are of relatively minor importance or tend to be constant rather than varying with such factors as volume, number of customers, and length of route. They include billing and collecting, getting the customer's order, servicing the refrigerator, time spent in walking from the cab to the back of the truck, loading and unloading the truck and checking the load, and miscellaneous interruptions. The time requirements for these operations are discussed briefly in the following paragraphs.

Billing and collecting includes the time required to make out the sales slip, to obtain the customer's signature, and to receive payment where sales are on a cash basis. Before the war, much of the billing and collecting involved special stops, but this practice was eliminated during the war as a conservation measure. On the ten sample routes studied in 1947, 95 percent of the billing and collecting was performed in connection with regular customer stops, while special collection stops were required for only

TABLE 58. Average time to bill and collect on wholesale milk delivery routes.

Source of data	Number of routes	Average time per customer stop (minutes)
California routes, 1940–1943................	63	1.33
Connecticut routes, 1942...................	5	1.14
Sample routes, 1947.......................	10	1.75
Combined................................	78	1.37

5 percent of the customers. As is indicated in Table 58, the average time for billing and collecting was 1.37 minutes per customer.

On the ten sample routes, special trips from the truck to the store to get the order for the day's delivery were made for 23 percent of the customers. These trips required an average of 2.29 minutes, of which 1.30 minutes were actually devoted to taking the order while the balance was spent in walking to the store and returning to the truck.

While the time required to arrange milk in the store refrigerator is affected by such factors as the type of refrigerator and the number of products handled, the volume per stop is the dominant factor. Routemen serviced refrigerators at approximately 20 percent of the customer stops on the sample routes, and time requirements per stop may be approximated by use of the equation

$$t = 0.38 + 0.77V, \qquad (10.25)$$

where t represents the time *per customer* in minutes and V the volume per customer in case equivalents. This equation explained about 76 percent of the variance in time requirements.[20]

A certain amount of time is required at each stop for the routeman to walk from the cab to the rear of the truck and to open the doors, as well as to close the truck and to return to the cab when the delivery is completed. The time studies made on the sample routes indicated that these requirements averaged 0.57 minute per stop.

Loading, unloading, and checking are usually performed by plant rather than route personnel, but minor elements of these duties are performed by the routemen. Data on these operations were not obtained for the 10 sample routes, but the results of the studies of 63 California routes were available and were used. For these routes the average time required for these loading and unloading operations was 57 minutes per day. While it seems reasonable to expect that such factors as route volume and the types of products handled would influence these time requirements, attempts to explain the variance on the basis of such factors failed to reveal significant relations — perhaps because of the above-noted fact that the routemen perform only part of these operations. As a consequence, the time has been entered in the route summaries as a constant of 57 minutes per day.

Finally, there are a number of miscellaneous interruptions that contribute to the time requirements for any wholesale route. For the sample routes these miscellaneous items have been defined to include all time requirements not specifically covered in the foregoing categories. They averaged 58.92 minutes per route, including the time to eat lunch on nine of the ten sample routes. Excluding lunch time, miscellaneous time would amount to a constant of 31.92 minutes per day for wholesale delivery routes.

Summary of wholesale-route time requirements

The previous pages have indicated that wholesale milk delivery-time requirements are a complex function of constant and

[20] $\bar{r} = 0.871.$

variable elements involving route volume, route distance, number of customers, number of delivery trips, volume per customer, type of containers, and walking distance from the truck to the delivery point. While all of these factors have independent effects, the time function may be simplified to express requirements for typical situations. In Table 59, such factors as walking distance

TABLE 59. Summary of the time requirements for wholesale Milk routes operating under urban conditions.

| Operation | Time requirements (minutes) | | | | |
	Per day	Per mile (D)	Per customer (C)	Per case (V)	Per trip (B)
Driving*................	23.40	2.640	1.027	—	—
Arranging load†.........	—	—	0.225	0.171	—
Delivering‡.............	—	—	—	—	0.771
Loading dolly**.........	—	—	.021	.021	—
Handling empties††.....	—	—	—	—	.760
Other operations‡‡......	88.92	—	2.685	.154	—
Total..............	111.32	2.640	3.958	0.346	1.531

* Based on equation (10.11), with allowance for the fact that there were 7 percent more customer stops than customers on the sample routes.
† Based on equation (10.20), with 87 percent of the volume in terms of cases of milk and 13 percent in terms of cases of miscellaneous products, and with 7 percent more stops than customers.
‡ Based on equation (10.21), and an average distance from truck to store of 65 feet, and including the time to deliver and to return.
** Based on equation (10.24), with allowance for the facts that the dolly was used on only 20 percent of the stops, that there were 7 percent more stops than customers.
†† Taken from Table 57.
‡‡ Billing and collecting, 1.37 minutes times 107 percent; getting order, 2.29 minutes for 23 percent of the customers; servicing refrigerator, based on equation (10.25), for 20 percent of the customer stops and with 7 percent more stops than customers; walking from cab, 0.57 minute times 107 percent; loading and unloading, 57 minutes per day; miscellaneous time, 31.92 minutes per day.

and type of container have been averaged for this purpose. In equation form, this summary table may be expressed as:

$$T = 111.32 + 2.640D + 3.958C + 0.346V + 1.531B, \quad (10.26)$$

where T represents the daily route time in minutes, D the daily mileage, C the number of customers served, V the route volume in case equivalents, and B the total number of delivery trips from the truck to delivery points in customers' establishments.

With any given conditions with respect to average deliveries per customer, daily mileage, or average volume per delivery trip, it would be possible to simplify this equation. Such factors may be subject to important changes under different systems of milk delivery, however, and so further simplifications will be delayed until later and more appropriate sections.

Wages and labor costs for milk delivery routes

It is possible to estimate many of the costs of milk delivery by determining the physical input requirements and then combining these with appropriate factor prices or cost rates. This may be more difficult, however, for labor and labor costs. Wages for route drivers are the result of negotiations between drivers and distributors, either on an individual basis or through labor organizations. While these negotiations may result in a wage per day or week that may be applied to the time requirements to determine costs, they frequently take the form of various combinations of base pay plus commissions on sales or collections. Such differences will have obvious effects on the influence of route volume on labor costs. Moreover, contracts frequently call for minimum payments per day or week, and specify overtime rates for hours over stated daily or weekly bases.

The retail wage arrangements used by a number of Connecticut milk distributors in 1942 are indicated in Fig. 43. A number of dealers reported straight salaries ranging from $25 to $43 and averaging $35 per week. With allowances for relief drivers and for vacations with pay, these salaries corresponded to costs varying from $0.014 to $0.028 and averaging about $0.020 per quart. Arrangements of this type were reported only by dealers with relatively small volumes and for the most part were limited to the minor markets. Large dealers in the major markets reported wage contracts for retail routemen based on commissions on collections or a combination of commission and salary. Straight commissions were typically 12.5 percent which, with home delivered prices of $0.16 per quart and allowances for relief drivers and vacations, corresponded to labor costs of $0.025 per quart. While there were a variety of combinations of salary and commission arrangements, they resulted in fairly uniform weekly earnings and labor costs per quart under daily delivery. The average arrangement involved $11 per week plus 10 percent commission on collections. This brought about an average labor cost of approximately $0.026 per quart. The higher costs under these arrangements are not basically due to the type of wage contract, of course, but are reflections of the higher living costs, better alternatives for employment, and better bargaining position of labor in the larger markets.

The average retail driver in the major markets earned about $44 per six-day week under daily delivery conditions. Costs

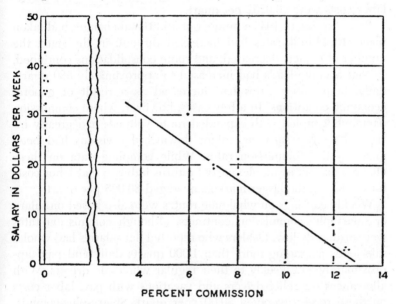

Fig. 43. *Retail wage contracts for a number of Connecticut milk dealers, 1942. The observations at the left of the diagram represent dealers paying on a straight wage basis; those to the right represent arrangements involving combinations of wages and commissions on collections. For the most part the straight salary arrangements are typical of the smaller markets while the commission arrangements are found in the larger cities.*

averaged $0.0257 per quart on this basis, with two-thirds of the cases falling between $0.0246 and $0.0268 per quart. In short, both weekly earnings and route-labor costs per quart were fairly uniform under daily delivery. After alternate-day delivery had been in effect for several months, the situation changed somewhat. Labor costs per quart were still fairly uniform, but there were pronounced variations in the size of loads and in weekly earnings. Dealers paying primarily on a commission basis had consolidated routes and increased average loads by 77 quarts daily. As a consequence, weekly earnings for regular deliverymen were approximately $56, while labor costs averaged $0.0254 per quart. On the other hand, dealers who paid a combination of salary and commission increased loads only 26 quarts. On the average, this increase resulted in weekly earnings of $46 and costs per quart of $0.0250. For both groups combined, average labor costs were $0.0252 per quart.

By the spring of 1943 a number of additional changes had taken place. Fluid-milk sales had increased throughout the state, the number of dealers decreased, and route consolidations continued, so that average loads had increased to approximately 380 quarts daily. Some wage rates had increased as a result of general economic conditions. In a few cases, however, where commission payments coupled with expanded route volumes had greatly increased weekly earnings, minor downward revisions had been made in the commission rates. While complete data on these changes are not available, partial returns indicate that labor costs for dealers in the larger markets averaged $0.025 per quart.

Weekly earnings on wholesale routes were also based on salary or salary-plus-commission contracts, although commission rates were ordinarily low. Dealers who reported flat salaries had wholesale loads averaging more than 1,000 quarts daily and paid approximately $42 weekly to their regular wholesale drivers. With allowances for relief drivers and vacations with pay, labor costs on these routes averaged $0.007 per quart. Salary-plus-commission arrangements were more common and averaged about $34 per week plus 1.5 percent on sales. With wholesale prices of $0.13 per quart and average loads of 1,425 quarts, these routes had a labor cost slightly less than $0.006 per quart. Within the group two fairly distinct types of routes could be distinguished — routes serving stores and restaurants and those delivering primarily to factories or other large institutional stops. With a larger number of smaller stops, the store and restaurant routes averaged only 1,100 quarts per day and had labor costs ranging from $0.007 to $0.008 per quart. The institutional routes averaged more than 1,500 quarts daily and had labor costs ranging from $0.005 to $0.007 per quart.

Many routes that are primarily retail included some whole-sale deliveries. When the amount of wholesale milk was very small it was frequently covered under the same contract as the retail deliveries. In a number of cases, however, special contracts were established for the wholesale milk on mixed routes. On the average these called for commissions of 5 percent on wholesale deliveries and, with a price to stores of $0.13, resulted in labor costs of $0.008 per quart.

In a recently issued report of the Storrs Agricultural Experiment Station, Stewart Johnson has described postwar wage and labor costs for milk delivery in Connecticut markets.[21] His findings with respect to retail and wholesale routes are quoted in part below:

The labor requirements on retail routes in Connecticut include the regular drivers who usually make six trips per week, and foremen or relief drivers who replace the regular drivers on their one day off each week. Extra help also is needed to operate routes for men who are sick or on vacation.

Under these conditions the labor requirement per retail route is slightly in excess of one man. In May 1946 a total of 587 retail route-men were employed by the 23 distributors who coöperated in this study. These men operated a total of 471 retail routes, an average of 1.25 men per route.

Average earnings of these 587 routemen in May 1946 were $77.12 per week. The average cost per route for drivers' wages was $96.40 per week, or $13.77 per day. With an average load of 511 points per route, the delivery labor cost was 2.69 cents per point.

Earnings of routemen varied considerably among the 23 distributors, averaging as low as $46.45 per week for the two distributors whose routemen earned the least to as high as $88.50 per week for the three distributors whose routemen earned the most . . . [Table 60]

With no Sunday deliveries, each wholesale route usually was taken care of by one man. A few distributors employed foremen or helpers to assist the regular routemen, but this was the exception rather than the rule. Only five of the 20 distributors used helpers for their regular men on wholesale routes. In May 1946, a total of 116 men were employed on wholesale routes by the 20 distributors whose records were analysed. These men operated a total of 97 wholesale routes, an average of 1.20 men per route.

Average earnings of the 97 regular routemen in May 1946 were

[24] Stewart Johnson, "Load Size and Delivery Labor Cost in Milk Distribution," 6–7, 10–11.

$60.37 per week, and of the 19 helpers were $39.53 per week. The average cost per route for delivery labor was $68.11 per week or $11.35 per day. With an average load of 1375 points per route, the delivery cost was 0.83 cent per point . . . Although the point systems were somewhat different as between retail and wholesale routes, the value of one point per quart bottle of home delivered milk was the

TABLE 60. Variation among groups of distributors in weekly earnings of routemen and in delivery labor cost per point.*

Distributor† Group	Weekly earnings of men employed on routes	Number of employees per route	Points per route	Delivery labor cost per point (cents)
1	$46.45	1.14	429	1.77
2	53.90	1.29	349	2.86
3	59.48	1.26	402	2.66
4	68.35	1.22	429	2.78
5	71.97	1.23	492	2.57
6	74.88	1.31	480	2.92
7	78.52	1.28	508	2.82
8	88.50	1.20	586	2.68
All groups	$77.12	1.25	503	2.73

* Stewart Johnson, *Load Size and Delivery Labor Cost in Milk Distribution* (Starrs Agricultural Experiment Station, Bulletin 264, March 1950), Table 3.
† Distributors were grouped according to average earnings of men on retail routes, with the two distributors whose routemen's earnings were the least in Group 1 and with three distributors in each succeeding group.

same as for the quart bottle of milk delivered to stores from wholesale routes.

Earnings of regular wholesale routemen varied from as low as $38.00 per week for one of the 20 distributors to as high as $80.32 per week for another. For 14 of the 20 distributors, average earnings of the regular wholesale routemen fell in the range between $50.00 and $70.00 per week.

Finally, we may return to Table 5 for a summary of 1949–50 route earnings as reported for 30 markets in the United States. These reported wages are plotted against their corresponding average route volumes in Fig. 44, together with the 1946 averages reported for Connecticut. It is apparent that wages vary widely from market to market, and that they show no important relation to such factors as route volumes. Taking all markets together, the simple average earnings of regular routemen was $13.67 per day for retail routes and $13.55 per day for wholesale routes. As indicated above, the daily earnings of regular routemen in Connecticut in 1946 averaged $12.85 for retail routemen and $10.06 for wholesale routemen.

In view of the above findings, and allowing for some increase following May 1946, labor costs in the pages that follow will be computed on the basis of earnings of regular routemen for an 8-hour day of $13.00 for retail routes and $12.50 for wholesale routes. As in the case of any other factor of production, the use of these "prices" does not imply that they are the "equitable" or "just" levels but only that they are typical of the given conditions.

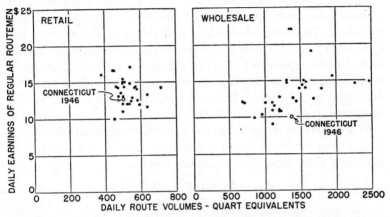

Fig. 44. Average route volumes and average earnings of regular routemen, retail and wholesale milk delivery, 30 United States cities, 1949–50. (See Table 5.)

Moreover, other rates will certainly be appropriate in other markets and for other time periods. Again, suitable rates can be selected for any given situation, and cost functions modified by the application of these rates to the physical time requirement equations.

Before proceeding to the cost equations, several additional elements must be considered. To begin with, the above wages apply only to regular routemen and should be modified to allow for the higher wages of relief drivers. The typical retail route week will require six days of work by the regular routeman plus one day by the relief man. Additional relief drivers are required to take care of vacations, holidays, and sick leave, and this will increase requirements about 6 percent. The total labor per route week will thus be about 7.42 man-days, or 24 percent in addition to the regular routeman — compare this with Johnson's 1.25 men per route. Allowing for relief men's wages about 10 percent higher than regular drivers, the daily average labor cost will be 8 percent higher than the wages for the regular routeman. These direct labor costs must be increased about 5 percent to allow for Social Security, unemployment compensation, and workmen's compensation payments.

Finally, several minor elements of route costs, while not part of route labor, may be added here rather than requiring separate treatment. The labor of checkers and shippers will increase the total labor cost by about 8 percent, while route supplies may be added as the equivalent of about 4 percent. In total, then, retail route labor costs per day may be represented by increasing regular wages by 25 percent. This will result in a daily cost of $16.25, or approximately $0.034 per minute.

When this rate is applied to the simplified equations (10.6) and (10.9) representing present retail route-time requirements, the following daily labor cost equations result:

$$C_{1d} = \$0.0415V + \$0.136D, \qquad (10.27)$$
$$C_{1a} = \$0.0272V + \$0.136D, \qquad (10.28)$$

where V again represents the daily route volume, D the daily mileage, C_1 the daily labor cost or expense, and the subscripts d and a refer to daily and alternate-day delivery. In a like manner, equations (10.7) and (10.10) may be converted to the following labor-cost equations under reorganized conditions:

$$C'_{1d} = \$0.0350V + \$0.136D, \qquad (10.29)$$
$$C'_{1a} = \$0.0207V + \$0.136D. \qquad (10.30)$$

Similar computations are necessary for wholesale routes, and will differ mainly in that such routes typically operate on a six-day basis and so require no regular relief driver. Vacations, holidays, and sick leave will again increase labor requirements by about 6 percent — note that this is lower than the previously reported 1.20 men per wholesale route because helpers are not included. With allowances for the higher wages of relief men and the inclusion of the costs for shippers and checkers and for route supplies, the total will again approximate 25 percent above regular route wages. This corresponds to a cost of $15.62 per day or about $0.0325 per minute.

When applied to the wholesale time requirements as given by equation (10.26), the following cost equation will result:

$$C_1 = \$3.62 + \$0.086D + \$0.129V + \$0.050B, \quad (10.31)$$

where D represents the daily route mileage, V the route volume in case equivalents, B the number of delivery trips, and C_1 the daily wholesale route labor costs or expense.

Labor requirements and costs on rural routes

Time studies of routes operated by producer-dealers have indicated that route hours increase by about 0.12 for each added route mile and 0.01 per customer.[22] Converting these to minutes and with an average of 1.8 quarts per customer, daily delivery time for these routes was approximately 0.33 minute per quart plus 7.2 minutes per mile, exclusive of collection time. If collection time is added, the time per quart would be increased to approximately 0.75 minute. With alternate-day delivery, time per quart would be about 0.5 minute for routes of this type.

While city routemen in Connecticut are usually paid at least partially on a commission basis, rural drivers are usually paid on a flat weekly basis. In addition, they are frequently employed as general workers on producer-dealer farms, and are expected to help with the work on the farm or in the dairy plant as well as on the milk route. Of course, in very many cases the route driver is not hired but is the producer-dealer himself or a member of his family.

Weekly wages for hired routemen in small markets and rural areas averaged about $35 in 1942. In most cases these men were expected to work seven days a week and, as already mentioned, to perform duties in addition to their route operations. With this in mind, a figure of $5.00 per day or $0.70 per hour may be used as fairly typical for milk-route drivers in rural districts prior to the

[22] Hammerberg, Fellows, and Farr, *Efficiency of Milk Marketing in Connecticut, 4.*

176   **The Basis for Market Reorganization**

war, while a rate of $1.25 per hour would be more appropriate for
1947. With this rate, labor costs may be approximated by the following equations:

$$C_{1d} = \$0.0158V + \$0.151D, \qquad (10.32)$$
$$C_{1a} = \$0.0105V + \$0.151D, \qquad (10.33)$$

where C_1 represents daily route-labor costs under rural conditions,
V the volume per day, D the route miles per day, and the subscripts d and a refer to daily and alternate-day delivery.

11 —

PROCESSING AND BOTTLING PLANTS

The number and size of city milk plants in Connecticut

While there were some 2,000 milk distributors operating in Connecticut in 1940, only 338 or about 17 percent operated pasteurizing plants.[1] These pasteurizing dealers, however, handled more than 400,000 quarts daily or nearly 80 percent of all the fluid milk distributed in the state. By 1946, the total number of dealers had dropped to 1,220 and the number of pasteurizing dealers to 268, while total Class I sales had increased by more than 50 percent. Moreover, the consumption of pasteurized milk increased by 75 percent so that the pasteurizing dealers handled about 700,000 quarts of milk daily or 86 percent of total Class I sales.

These changes are indicated by the data in Table 61, where pasteurizing dealers are classified according to daily volumes in 1940 and 1946. Even in the postwar period most of these dealers handled relatively small volumes while a few accounted for the bulk of the deliveries: 50 percent of the dealers who pasteurized milk handled 800 quarts or less daily and accounted for only 8 percent of total milk deliveries by pasteurizing dealers, while the 9 percent of the dealers who handled more than 6,000 quarts daily accounted for 62 percent of the total volume. As a result of these shifts, the daily average volume per pasteurizing dealer increased from 1,200 quarts in 1940 to 3,400 quarts in 1946.

[1] These numbers do not include producer-dealers-limited, who distribute less than 10 quarts daily.

Excess plant capacity apparently is the rule in milk distribution. Tucker, studying country pasteurizing plants in New York, found an average of 20 percent of unused floor space.[2] In Milwaukee it was found that plants with investments in equipment under $10,000 used only 31 percent of their pasteurizing capacity, 18 percent of their bottling capacity, and 16 percent of their bottle-washing capacity "based on the assumption that operations over a period of 5.5 hours daily constitute full utilization."[3]

TABLE 61. The percentage distribution of Connecticut pasteurizing dealers by size, 1940 and 1946.

Daily volume (quarts)	1940		1946	
	Percent of dealers	Percent of milk	Percent of dealers	Percent of milk
240 or less........	26	4	5	*
241– 400..........	23	6	19	2
401– 800..........	24	11	26	6
801–1,200..........	9	8	13	5
1,201–1,600..........	4	4	10	5
1,601–2,000..........	*	*	5	4
2,001–2,400..........	3	5	3	3
2,401–4,000..........	} 11	62	{ 7	8
4,001–6,000..........			3	5
6,000 and over.......			9	62
Total..........	100	100	100	100

* Less than 0.5 percent.

Marshall found that the utilization of plants in California averaged from 24 to 75 percent of capacity.[4]

Mortenson studied a number of plants in Wisconsin cities. "Information obtained in this study indicates that only a very small percentage of the milk-distributing companies are operating at more than 80 percent of plant capacity. Many are operating at

[2] C. K. Tucker, *The Cost of Handling Fluid Milk and Cream in Country Plants* (Cornell Agricultural Experiment Station, Bulletin 473, 1929).

[3] *A Survey of Milk Marketing in Milwaukee* (Dairy Section, Agricultural Adjustment Administration, U. S. Department of Agriculture, Marketing Information Series DM-1, 1937).

[4] J. Marshall, Jr., "Changes in Methods of Operation of Milk Distributors in California Which Will Conserve Rubber, Automotive and other Equipment and Reduce Costs of Operation," California State Department of Agriculture Mimeograph (1942).

from 60 to 80 percent, with the majority of these nearer the 60 than the 80 percent mark. Operations at 50 percent capacity or below are not uncommon, and many plants are running as low as 30–40 percent of their optimum output. If the aggregate of all distributors in the market were considered, the operation now common in the markets of the size studied is probably in the neighborhood of 50–70 percent of the optimum." [5]

The data on the number and size of Connecticut pasteurizing dealers do not give a direct indication of the importance of excess plant capacity, but they stress the fact that most of the dealers handled quite small volumes even in 1946 and that many were too small to utilize effectively even the smaller pasteurizing equipment. In addition, it seems quite clear that excess capacity must have been very prevalent in 1940, for otherwise it would have been impossible to increase the aggregate volume 75 percent while reducing the number of operators 18 percent. While the wartime shifts undoubtedly absorbed much of the existing excess capacity, it is probable that this type of inefficiency still persists in many plants and will continue to be a problem in the future.

The objectives of the present chapter are to describe the relations between volume and costs for individual plants and so to indicate the influence of such factors as excess capacity on costs, and then to use these results to determine the relation between plant capacity and plant costs when the plants are operating at optimum volumes. This last-mentioned relation between capacity and costs will indicate the economies or diseconomies of scale.

Research procedures [6]

The nature of short- and long-run plant cost curves has already been discussed. As indicated in Fig. 29, average short-run cost curves first decrease with the spreading of fixed or overhead costs but finally increase if subject to diminishing returns as more of the variable factors are combined with the fixed factors. A series of such short-run curves representing a gradation in capacity will

[5] W. P. Mortenson, *Milk Distribution as a Public Utility* (University of Chicago Press, Chicago, 1940).

[6] This section is based largely on R. G. Bressler, Jr., "Research Determination of Economies of Scale," *Journal of Farm Economics,* XXVII (1945), 526–539.

define the long-run curve. If continuous variation in scale is possible, the long-run curve showing the economies and diseconomies of scale will be tangent to the short-run curves. If changes in scale are discontinuous, then the economy-of-scale curve will consist of segments of the several short-run curves and will have a scalloped appearance.

This is the curve that is needed for intelligent planning, for it shows the advantages or disadvantages of prospective plants of various sizes. Several methods have been used by research workers in attempting to approximate the economies-of-scale curves. Perhaps the most common approach has been to determine average costs and volumes for each of a group of sample plants. These cost-volume data are then summarized in a table or diagram to show the average regression between plant volume and costs. Unfortunately, such average regressions combine and confuse cost changes that result from the more complete utilization of a plant of given scale with the cost changes that accompany changes in scale. As a consequence, it is a correct representation of neither.

This difficulty may be avoided by selecting a sample of plants that are well designed and operating approximately at capacity. In view of the prevalence of excess capacity, however, such a direct approach may not be as practical as might at first appear. Maladjustments within the sample plants, both with respect to the integration of the several processes and items of equipment and to the adjustment of volume to capacity, will usually make some modifications necessary. These will take the form of budgetary or synthetic adjustments to actual plants in order to approach hypothetical organizations meeting the required conditions.

In the present study, the research has been based almost entirely on such syntheses. Plant designs and equipment lists have been obtained from dairy-plant experts. These have been used to estimate investments and fixed costs. Job analyses have been used to indicate the amount of labor needed. Other variable costs have been projected on the basis of known cost data and on the principles of physics and engineering. These elements finally have been combined to indicate the relations between costs and volume for each of a group of plants with capacities ranging up to 4,800 quarts daily, and the plant or short-run curves then have been used to determine the long-run relation showing the economies of scale.

The previous section indicated that the range in plant volume up to 4,800 quarts per day will include the great majority of Connecticut operations. Although varying considerably from market to market and greatly influenced by the total market volume, this same situation holds in most fluid-milk markets. Nevertheless, the relatively few distributors with larger volumes usually dominate the market in terms of their share of the total volume and it is important, therefore, to describe cost relations for the larger-volume range. The long-run curve developed by the detailed syntheses has been extended to larger volumes on the basis of costs obtained for a small sample of large and relatively efficient plants. In the light of the objections raised to average cost-volume data, this procedure may seem questionable. The most important economies of scale will fall in the small-volume range, however, and "it is likely to be only the very small plants which show materially higher costs causally traceable to their small size, while most plants are in a range of size which shows little or no downward trend with increased size." [7] Because of the tendency for both the short- and long-run average-cost curves to flatten out in relatively large-volume ranges, the scatter of costs based on actual plants will narrow and approach the long-run curve. This scatter will be further reduced by the deliberate selection of relatively efficient plants. For these reasons, it has seemed unnecessary to make detailed syntheses for large-volume plants. It must be admitted, however, that this section of the curve might well have been modified somewhat by more detailed study.

It will become apparent in the following pages that the major job of estimating cost relations is the determination of the basic physical relations. Most of the work is technical rather than economic, but, as explained in the preceding section, these technical relations must be known before the appropriate cost relations can be developed. Theoretically, the economist takes these technical functions as a part of his given data; practically, it is frequently

[7] J. M. Clark, "Toward a Concept of Workable Competition," *The American Economic Review*, XXX (1940), 241–256.

true that appropriate functions are not available and must be developed as a part of the job of economic analysis. This is the case in milk distribution, although many phases of the following syntheses have been possible only because of a satisfactory background of technical knowledge.

One further point should be made before proceeding to the results of the plant studies. The theoretical sections in Chapter 8 have emphasized the increases in costs that would accompany increases in input-output rates. In highly mechanized plants that involve close integration of a number of elements and machines in a "line" of production, changes in rates may be of little importance and output variations must be obtained primarily through expanding or contracting the time period during which the plant is operating.[8] This is the case in milk plants, where a flow of milk passes through a number of mechanized stages with little change in rate within a given plant. This rate is not only fixed within relatively narrow ranges by the technological integration of the plant, but it is also fixed by legal restrictions on pasteurizing methods. Laws and regulations specify that the milk must be heated to specified temperatures and held there for specified lengths of time, thus fixing the rate (continuous for the "flash" process and discontinuous for the "vat" process) at which the plant operates. For this reason, average variable and marginal cost curves will tend to be linear rather than curvilinear functions when expressed in terms of daily volumes rather than instantaneous rates.

Designs and construction costs
for small pasteurizing plants

Designing a series of pasteurizing plants is not a very exact procedure. Certain features of construction and arrangement are required by law, while others are essential to efficient operation. Within this framework, a variety of designs are possible. Plants should have hard-surfaced floors, properly graded and drained. All doors and windows should be screened, and walls and ceilings

[8] R. G. Bressler, Jr., "Efficiency in the Production of Marketing Services," Economic Efficiency Series Paper No. 7, Social Science Research Council Project in Agricultural Economics, University of Chicago Mimeograph, 1950.

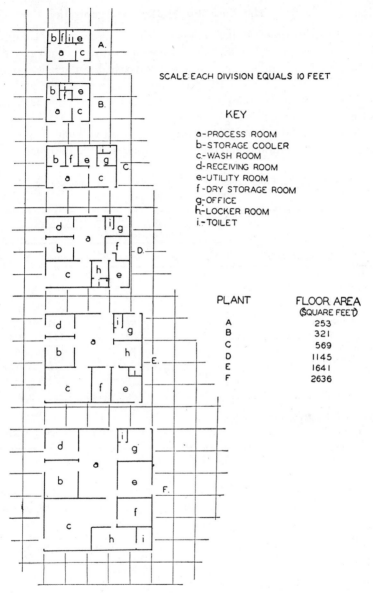

SCALE EACH DIVISION EQUALS 10 FEET

KEY

a-PROCESS ROOM
b-STORAGE COOLER
c-WASH ROOM
d-RECEIVING ROOM
e-UTILITY ROOM
f-DRY STORAGE ROOM
g-OFFICE
h-LOCKER ROOM
i-TOILET

PLANT	FLOOR AREA (SQUARE FEET)
A	253
B	321
C	569
D	1145
E	1641
F	2636

Fig. 45. Floor plans for six hypothetical pasteurizing and bottling plants with daily capacities ranging from 240 to 4,800 quarts per day.

should be dustproof. Boiler rooms should be separate from milk-handling rooms, and toilets should not open directly into rooms where milk is handled or equipment is washed. Sufficient space should be allowed for setting up, operating, and cleaning the equipment, and the room arrangements should facilitate the flow of milk and bottles through the plant.

The actual layout and construction of a plant will vary depending on local conditions and on the preferences of the designer and

TABLE 62. Floor areas for six hypothetical milk pasteurizing and bottling plants.

	Square feet of floor in plant*					
	Plant capacity (quarts per day)					
Section of plant	A 240	B 400	C 800	D 1,600	E 2,400	F 4,800
Process room.............	108	123	190	273	352	549
Storage cooler.............	20	31	56	112	165	260
Bottle washing.............	48	77	118	252	336	684
Receiving room...........	—	—	—	102	140	192
Utility room..............	41	54	81	127	190	248
Storage room.............	19	19	54	101	144	202
Office...................	—	—	52	83	127	192
Locker room..............	—	—	—	49	134	210
Toilet...................	17	17	18	46	53	99
Total.................	253	321	569	1,145	1,641	2,636
Square feet per quart of daily capacity...............	1.05	0.80	0.71	0.72	0.68	0.55

* Exclusive of walls and partitions.

owner. Much of this variation, however, will not have a very significant effect on plant operating costs. For the purposes of the present study, a series of plant designs that meet the general requirements and the typical recommendations of dairy experts will provide an adequate basis for further computations. By following a uniform type of construction and layout for each plant in the series, the effects of size may be emphasized rather than minor variations in design or material.

Following the general recommendations of equipment manufacturers and the plans for a number of existing plants, rough designs were set up for six hypothetical pasteurizing plants. These plants have capacities of 240, 400, 800, 1,600, 2,400, and 4,800 quarts daily. The floor plans for the several plants are shown in Fig. 45, while the approximate floor area for each plant is given in Table 62. Plant A, with a daily capacity of 240 quarts, would require about 253 square feet of floor space or 1.05 square feet per quart of daily capacity. At the other extreme, plant F, with a capacity of 4,800 quarts per day, would have an area of 2,636 square feet or 0.55 square feet per quart.

The method used to estimate construction costs is similar to the procedure followed by architects and contractors, where costs are synthesized from details of material and labor requirements. This may be illustrated by the details of the estimate of the costs of constructing concrete floors for plant D:

Gravel fill under floor.

Floor area exclusive of partitions, 817 square feet. Gravel fill, 8 inches thick or approximately 20 cubic yards.

20 cubic yards at $2.00 = ... $40.00

Unskilled labor can spread gravel at a rate of about 1.3 cubic yards per hour. With wages of $1.35 per hour, labor costs will be $1.04 per cubic yard.

20 cubic yards at $1.04 = ...   20.80

Concrete work.

Concrete 4 inches thick over 817 square feet, or about 10 cubic yards. Materials, using 1:2:3 mix, cost about $8.70 per cubic yard.

10 cubic yards at $8.70 = ...   87.00

Two men, one skilled and one unskilled or semiskilled, can mix and pour 1 cubic yard of concrete in about 1 hour. With wages of $2.10 and $1.35 per hour, the labor cost per cubic yard will be about $3.45.

10 cubic yards at $3.45 = ...   34.50

Estimated total cost $182.30

Similar procedures were followed in estimating the costs for the various items in building construction for the six hypothetical plants, with the results summarized in Table 63. Under postwar conditions, construction costs ranged from $3,150 for plant A to $12,000 for plant F, and appeared to increase with capacity at a decreasing rate. In terms of building investments per quart of daily capacity, the range is from $13.12 for plant A to $2.69 for plant F. Under prewar conditions, plant investments would have ranged from $8.12 per quart of capacity in plant A to $1.64 for

TABLE 63. Estimated building investments for six hypothetical milk pasteurizing and bottling plants.*

	Postwar building investment in plant					
	Plant capacity (quarts per day)					
Item	A 240	B 400	C 800	D 1,600	E 2,400	F 4,800
Concrete work............ $	330	$ 370	$ 550	$ 950	$1,190	$ 1,595
Walls and partitions........	650	715	1,010	1,450	1,780	2,235
Roof......................	210	260	470	940	1,350	2,0 60
Doors and windows.........	470	470	600	1,010	1,085	1,200
Plumbing.................	620	650	880	1,075	1,310	1,810
Electrical work............	50	50	60	90	100	110
Storage cooler.............	300	390	550	840	1,170	1,730
Total................	$2,630	$2,905	$4,120	$6,355	$7,985	$10,740
Estimated investment†.....	$3,150	$3,500	$4,950	$7,650	$9,600	$12,900
Investment per quart of daily capacity						
Postwar..............	$13.12	$ 8.75	$ 6.19	$ 4.78	$ 4.00	$ 2.69
Prewar‡..............	$ 8.12	$ 5.38	$ 3.81	$ 2.94	$ 2.44	$ 1.64

* Construction prices of 1947.
† Including approximately 20 percent to cover contractor's overhead costs and profits.
‡ See Appendix for details.

plant F. These data indicate that construction costs increased more than 60 percent during the war period.

The decline in building investment per quart of capacity as capacity increases is the result of two principal factors: (1) plant area does not increase as rapidly as capacity; and (2) construction costs per square foot of floor area decrease with increase in size. The first of these reflects the tendencies for certain minimum amounts of working space to be required in any plant, and for the physical size and space requirements for equipment to increase less rapidly than the capacity of the equipment. The second reflects the decreasing relative importance of walls and partitions as floor area increases — that "circumference" increases less rapidly than area. Both of these give rise to important economies of scale for city milk plants.

Investments in equipment

Lists of the necessary equipment were made for these six plants and detailed cost and price estimates were obtained from a number of dairy-equipment manufacturers. Characteristics of the major items of equipment are summarized in Table 64. Vat-type

TABLE 64. Principal items of equipment for six milk pasteurizing and bottling plants.*

Item	Plant capacity (quarts per day)					
	A 240	B 400	C 800	D 1,600	E 2,400	F 4,800
Pasteurizing vats						
Number................	1	1	1	2	2	2
Gallons................	30	50	100	100	150	300
Milk cooler						
Pounds per hour.........	525	900	1,800	1,800	2,600	5,200
Bottle washer						
Bottles per minute.......	10	12	18	20	28	40
Compressor						
Capacity in tons.........	0.5	0.75	1.0	1.5	2.5	4.5
Boiler						
Horsepower............	3.5	5	9	9	13	25

* See Appendix for a detailed equipment list for plant D.

pasteurizers were specified for all plants, with capacities ranging from one 30-gallon vat in plant A to two 300-gallon units in plant F. Milk coolers ranged in capacity from 525 to 5,200 pounds of milk per hour. Hand-operated bottle fillers were specified for the three smallest plants, while automatic fillers were recommended for plants D, E, and F. Refrigeration compressors ranged in capacity from 0.5 to 4.5 tons, while boilers ranged from 3.5 to 25 horsepower.

Estimates of the necessary investments in equipment are summarized in Table 65, and range from $4,200 for plant A to $24,950 for plant *F* under postwar conditions. In terms of the equipment investment per quart of daily plant capacity, these correspond to $17.50 for plant *A* and $5.20 for plant *F*. Under prewar conditions, equipment investments were estimated at $10.62 and $3.25

TABLE 65. Estimated investment in equipment for hypothetical milk pasteurizing and bottling plants.*

	Postwar equipment investment in plant					
	Plant capacity (quarts per day)					
Item	*A* 240	*B* 400	*C* 800	*D* 1,600	*E* 2,400	*F* 4,800
Receiving...............	$ 80	$ 80	$ 500	$ 840	$ 840	$ 1,540
Pasteurizing.............	1,010	1,080	1,235	2,425	2,760	3,650
Cooling†.................	1,060	1,245	1,675	1,925	2,610	3,630
Bottle filling.......... ′..	190	225	330	1,170	1,600	2,500
Bottle washing...........	250	325	825	2,485	3,000	3,900
Boiler...................	620	685	845	880	970	1,340
Bottles, cases............	160	270	530	1,005	1,590	3,180
Miscellaneous...........	130	170	250	410	565	1,045
Total..............	$3,500	$4,080	$6,190	$11,140	$13,935	$20,785
Estimated investment‡...	$4,200	$4,900	$7,450	$13,350	$16,700	$24,950
Investment per quart of daily capacity						
Postwar...........	$17.50	$12.25	$ 9.31	$ 8.34	$ 6.96	$ 5.20
Prewar**...........	$10.62	$ 7.62	$ 5.81	$ 5.06	$ 4.35	$ 3.25

* See Appendix for details of equipment costs for plant *D*.
† Including the costs of brine tanks and refrigerating coils.
‡ Including approximately 20 percent to cover shipping and installation charges.
** See Appendix for details of prewar investments.

per quart for these two plants, so these items also increased more than 60 percent during the war period. The marked decreases in the investment per quart that accompany increases in capacity represent an important advantage for the larger city milk plants.

Fixed costs of plant operation

Estimates of the total investments for the six milk plants are given in Table 66. In addition to the previously discussed investments in buildings and equipment, Table 66 also includes estimates of the investments in land. These last are arbitrary, since the actual land values will vary widely from one market to another and from one section to another within any market. The reported values vary from $410 to $1,020, with the differences based entirely on the variations in land area requirements for the several plants. Total investments range from $7,760 for plant *A* to $38,870 for plant *F* under postwar conditions, and these figures are about 60 percent higher than prewar levels.

Dairy plants and equipment are durable goods that are not completely used up or destroyed in a single production period. As a result, it is necessary to allocate investments over a number

TABLE 66. Total investments for six hypothetical milk pasteurizing and bottling plants.

	Postwar total investment for plant					
	Plant capacity (quarts per day)					
Item	*A* 240	*B* 400	*C* 800	*D* 1,600	*E* 2,400	*F* 4,800
Building	$3,150	$3,500	$ 4,950	$ 7,650	$ 9,600	$12,900
Equipment	4,200	4,900	7,450	13,350	16,700	24,950
Land	410	440	510	600	680	1,020
Total	$7,760	$8,840	$12,910	$21,600	$26,980	$38,870
Total investment per quart of daily capacity						
Postwar	$32.33	$22.10	$ 16.13	$ 13.50	$ 11.24	$ 8.10
Prewar*	$20.46	$14.10	$ 10.26	$ 8.38	$ 7.08	$ 5.10

* See Appendix for details.

of years of useful life, and to calculate fixed costs on the basis of depreciation rates based on the expected life. In addition to depreciation, fixed plant costs include interest, repairs and maintenance, insurance, and taxes. In all cases, the annual costs are functions of total investment, and may be estimated by applying suitable rates to the investment figures.

While the method of computing fixed costs is relatively simple, the determination of appropriate rates is quite complex and necessarily arbitrary in many respects. The useful life of a building or piece of equipment cannot be forecast with accuracy, for it will depend on such factors as the care given to the item in question and on new technological developments. While past experience will provide some guide, depreciation rates can be only approximations at best. Tax rates are established by the appropriate local and state governments, but they vary from locality to locality and from time to time. Moreover, tax rates have meaning only in connection with established assessment practices, and

TABLE 67. Fixed cost rates for dairy plants.

Item	Annual rate as a percent of the original investment
Depreciation*	
Buildings...	4.3
Equipment	
Receiving.......................................	13
Pasteurizing....................................	10
Cooling...	7
Filling..	8
Washing..	8
Boiler..	7
Miscellaneous...................................	8
Interest†...	3
Repairs..	5
Insurance‡..	0.5
Taxes**..	1.0

* Generalized from a number of studies and reports, including: Depreciation rates recommended by the American Association of Creamery Butter Manufacturers (1932); Depreciation rates recommended by the International Association of Ice Cream Manufacturers (1929); Depreciation studies made by the Bureau of Internal Revenue; C. K. Tucker, The Costs of Handling Fluid Milk and Cream in Country Plants (Cornell Agricultural Experiment Station, Bulletin 473, 1929), 22; and G. F. Dow, An Economic Study of Milk Distribution in Maine (Maine Agricultural Experiment Station, Bulletin 395, 1939), 626–627.
† Approximately equivalent to a rate of 5 percent on the undepreciated balance.
‡ Based on information from the New England Fire Insurance Rating Association, Hartford, Connecticut.
** The tax rate in Connecticut as of August 1, 1945, ranged from about 9 to 33 mills, and averaged about 20 mills for all towns in the state. With an assumed assessment ratio of 50 percent of the original investment, the tax rate would amount to 10 mills.

these may vary by 50 percent or more. Insurance rates also are variable, and the selection of a single rate necessarily averages out differences that will be important in any particular locality.

The rates used to calculate fixed costs in this study are summarized in Table 67. These are expressed relative to the original investment, and so may be applied directly to the estimated investments given in the previous table. The results of such calculations

are presented in Table 68. In annual terms, fixed costs for the
postwar plants under consideration ranged from $1,126 in plant A
to $5,699 in plant F. Reduced to a daily basis and expressed as
average fixed cost per quart of capacity, these are equivalent to
about $0.0128 for plant A, $0.0088 for plant B, $0.0065 for plant

TABLE 68. Estimated fixed costs for six hypothetical milk
pasteurizing and bottling plants.

	Postwar annual fixed costs in plant					
	Plant capacity (quarts per day)					
Item	A 240	B 400	C 800	D 1,600	E 2,400	F 4,800
Depreciation*......... $	410	$ 461	$ 690	$ 1,202	$ 1,462	$ 2,063
Interest†.............	233	265	387	648	809	1,166
Repairs*.............	368	420	620	1,050	1,315	1,892
Insurance*..........	37	42	62	105	132	189
Taxes†..............	78	88	129	216	270	389
Total........... $	1,126	$ 1,276	$ 1,888	$ 3,221	$ 3,988	$ 5,699
Fixed costs per quart of daily capacity						
Postwar.........	$0.0128	$0.0088	$0.0065	$0.0055	$0.0046	$0.0032
Prewar‡.........	$0.0080	$0.0056	$0.0041	$0.0034	$0.0029	$0.0021

* Based only on investments in buildings and equipment.
† Based on total investment in land, buildings, and equipment.
‡ See Appendix for details.

C, $0.0055 for plant D, $0.0046 for plant E, and $0.0032 for plant
F. Increasing the scale of operation from 240 to 4,800 quarts per
day, then, would result in a saving in fixed costs of nearly $0.01
per quart of plant capacity. Corresponding to the wartime
changes in the total investment, these fixed costs are about 60
percent higher than the prewar levels.

Plant labor

The number of men to be employed in each plant and their
working hours have been determined by job analyses of the various operations and processes. The actual time involved in any
operation is determined by the nature of the operation and by
the type and size of machinery involved. Where more or less

automatic machine operations are involved, time requirements are fixed within narrow limits and so are relatively easy to estimate. In operations such as setting up the milk pumps and sanitary piping, tending the boiler, and cleaning the plant and equipment, time requirements have been based on data gathered from observation of these operations in actual plants, on estimates made by dairy technicians, and on the results of published studies.[9]

The following list shows the details of operations for plant *D*, more or less in chronological order. A graphic summary of the daily labor distribution according to the job and the worker is given in Fig. 46.

Setting up equipment and raising steam.

Manager opens the plant and spends approximately 30 minutes in setting up equipment and 30 minutes in checking out retail milk loads. Assistant helps in setting up the equipment.

Receiving milk and washing cans.

Manager dumps and weighs the milk while an assistant washes cans. This process requires about 12 minutes for each of four vats to be pasteurized.

Pasteurizing.

Milk is piped from the receiving room to the pasteurizing vats, where it is heated to a temperature of 143°F. and held at that temperature for 30 minutes. This entire process requires about 1 hour, but it involves only occasional attention by the plant labor staff.

Drawing, cooling, and bottling milk.

These three operations are performed simultaneously as a continuous process. Assistant tends the bottle filler while the manager stores the filled bottles in the cooler. Total time required averages about 30 minutes per vat.

[9] E. H. Rinear, *Milk Distribution Costs of Producer-Distributors and Sub-Dealers in New Jersey* (New Jersey Agricultural Experiment Station, Bulletin 663, 1939), 46; C. E. Clement, *Operation and Management of Milk Plants* (U. S. Department of Agriculture, Circular 260, 1933), 16–17; J. B. Rodgers, D. R. Theophilus, H. Beresford and J. L. Barnhart, *Distribution of Steam, Electrical Power, and Labor in Representative Idaho Creameries* (Idaho Agricultural Experiment Station, Research Bulletin 12, 1936).

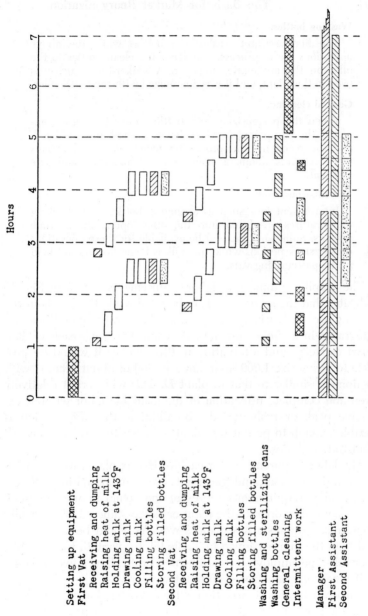

Fig. 46. Plant operations and use of labor in plant D.

Washing bottles.

The first assistant washes the bottles while the above operations are in process, and sends the clean bottles to the filler on the automatic conveyor. A soaker-type washer is used in this plant, and it is synchronized with the bottle filler.

General cleaning.

When the pasteurizing and bottling operations are completed the equipment is taken down, washed and sterilized, and the receiving and processing rooms are cleaned. This work requires about 2 hours for the manager and one assistant.

Miscellaneous work.

Intermittent jobs such as arranging bottles and checking temperatures are fitted into the other operations as time permits. Sufficient time will be available for these operations during slack periods while the milk is being heated and held in the pasteurizing vats.

The graphic summary of labor requirements shown in Fig. 46 indicates that the second vat is to be filled while the first is in the holding or pasteurizing stage, and that other operations are integrated in a similar manner. By using two vats, each of 400-quart capacity, and alternating in this manner it would be possible to pasteurize 1,600 quarts in a period of about 4 hours with equipment similar to that in plant *D*. This will permit relatively even and complete utilization of the available labor without excessive peak or rush periods. In addition, the organization is flexible enough to permit the plant manager to carry out his administrative duties.

The labor requirements for each of the six plants were synthesized in this manner, and the results are summarized in Table 69. These labor requirements represent the actual number of man-hours needed to operate the plant each day. Since dairies usually operate seven days a week, more workers would be on the payroll than the number given in Table 69. In plant *E*, for example, four full-time employees would be needed to allow a five and one-half day work week for each plant worker.

Since vat-type pasteurization is legally defined as holding milk at a temperature of 143°F. for a period of 30 minutes, these phases of the work will necessarily be fairly uniform in the several plants. The use of larger vats in the larger plants, and economies in preparatory and cleaning work, however, will result in greater labor efficiency in the larger plants. The output per man-hour would be about 44 quarts in plant A, and would increase with increases in plant capacity until it averaged 120 quarts per man-hour in plant F. These estimates appear reasonable when compared to the results of other studies of dairy-plant labor requirements.

To convert these physical labor requirements into estimates of labor costs, it is necessary to apply suitable labor rates. The de-

TABLE 69. The number of workers and hours worked daily in hypothetical milk pasteurizing and bottling plants.

Plant	Daily capacity (quarts)	Worker	Daily hours	Total man-hours per day	Quarts per man-hour
A.	240	I	5.5	5.5	44
B.	400	I	7.0	7.0	57
C.	800	I	7.5		
		II	2.5	10.0	80
D.	1,600	I	8.0		
		II	7.0		
		III	3.0	18.0	89
E.	2,400	I	9.0		
		II	8.0		
		III	8.0	25.0	96
F.	4,800	I	8.0		
		II	8.0		
		III	8.0		
		IV	8.0		
		V	8.0	40.0	120

termination of wage rates, however, is subject to some difficulty. Wages of dairy-plant workers change from time to time in response to changes in general economic conditions. In a growing number of city milk plants, the specific rates are determined through collective bargaining. Rates vary from plant to plant, however, and from market to market. In general, the wages paid at plants located in smaller towns and rural areas are lower than those paid at plants located in the larger cities, even though the milk processed by the former may be sold in the larger markets. Finally, much of the labor in small plants is supplied by the operator himself or by members of his family without formal wage payments.

For these reasons it is not possible to select a single rate that would be representative in the sense that an average price would represent conditions in a more perfect market. Labor costs have been computed on the basis of two assumed rates: (1) $1.00 per hour, selected as fairly typical of postwar labor costs for major Connecticut markets; and (2) $0.70 per hour, selected as more or less typical of postwar conditions in the smaller markets or of prewar conditions in major markets.[10] These rates cover wages plus an allowance of approximately 8 percent for Social Security taxes,

TABLE 70. Estimates of labor costs for six hypothetical milk pasteurizing and bottling plants.

| | Hours of labor | | Estimated costs for plant labor at* | | | |
| | | | $0.70 per hour | | $1.00 per hour | |
Plant	Per day	Per quart	Per day	Per quart	Per day	Per quart
A	5.5	0.0229	$ 3.85	$0.0160	$ 5.50	$0.0229
B	7.0	.0175	4.90	.0122	7.00	.0175
C	10.0	.0125	7.00	.0088	10.00	.0125
D	18.0	.0112	12.60	.0079	18.00	.0112
E	25.0	.0104	17.50	.0073	25.00	.0104
F	40.0	.0083	28.00	.0058	40.00	.0083

* Hourly rates cover wages, Social Security taxes, workman's unemployment insurance, and the allocated costs of vacations with pay.

workman's unemployment insurance, and the allocated costs of vacations with pay. Labor costs based on these rates are summarized in Table 70. Under postwar conditions for major markets, the labor costs for plant A would amount to approximately $0.0229 per quart. Economies of scale in the use of labor are quite pronounced, as indicated by the foregoing discussion of output per man-hour, and labor costs would amount to only $0.0083 in plant F. These costs are about 42 percent above those based on the prewar rates.

[10] "Union Demands, with Retail Drivers Now Averaging Over $84 per Week Would, if Met, Boost Retail Prices at Least 2¢ per Quart," *Hartford Times* (January 17, 1948), p. 5. See Appendix for calculations based on other rates per hour.

Electricity requirements and costs[11]

Dairy plants use electric power for lighting and to operate the motors for pumps, bottle washers, conveyors, and automatic bottle fillers. Mechanical refrigeration is the biggest job, however, accounting for roughly three-quarters of all electric power used in plants of the type under consideration. After the pasteurizing operations are completed, the temperature of the milk must be reduced to approximately 40°F., and the bottled milk must be kept in a refrigerated room or storage cooler until it is loaded on the trucks for delivery. These cooling operations involve the transfer of heat from the milk (and equipment) to a refrigerant. By determining the total heat transfer, it is possible to estimate the hours of operation for the compressor and so to estimate electricity requirements.

Such computations are illustrated below in the case of plant *D*. After pasteurization, the milk is passed over a tubular cooler. Well or tap water will be circulated through the upper sections of this cooler in an amount that is sufficient to reduce the temperature of the milk from 143°F. to 65°F.[12] The lower sections of the cooler will contain refrigerated brine, and this will reduce the milk temperature to the required 40°F. Since the specific heat (the quantity of heat required to raise the temperature of 1 lb of a substance by 1 degree) of milk in the temperature ranges here involved is approximately 0.94 Btu/lb deg F., each pound of milk cooled will involve a transfer of about 23.5 British thermal units to the brine. Cooling 1,600 quarts each day will thus require a total heat transfer of 80,800 Btu.

Similar computations have been made for all of the cooling operations for plant *D*, with the results summarized in Table 71.

The output of a refrigeration compressor may be varied over a

[11] This section is based largely on the following publications: J. T. Bowen, *Refrigeration in the Handling, Processing, and Storing of Milk and Milk Products* (U. S. Department of Agriculture, Miscellaneous Publication 138, 1932), and A. W. Farrall, *Dairy Engineering* (Wiley, New York, 1942).

[12] These temperatures and the calculations based on them represent average conditions throughout the year; power requirements will be higher in certain seasons of the year and lower in others.

considerable range by changing the speed of operation or the
back pressure in the suction lines. With a compressor rated at 1.5
tons, the refrigeration load of 193,500 Btu per day could be
carried by operating the compressor approximately 18 hours each
day.[13] Compressors of this size are usually equipped with a
2-horsepower motor, so that this operation would theoretically involve 26,856 watt-hours of electricity. Owing to motor inefficiencies, however, each horsepower will require about 1,000 watts
rather than the theoretical 746 watts, and the daily use of electricity for this purpose will average about 36 kilowatt-hours.

Estimates of the various electrical loads have been made in this
manner for the six hypothetical plants, and are summarized in

TABLE 71. Refrigeration load (Btu per day) for plant *D*.

Item	Load
1. Cooling milk after pasteurization	80,800
2. Cooling milk in storage cooler	16,300
3. Cooling cans, bottles, cases, etc.	30,800
4. Refrigeration losses through walls	37,400
5. Blower motor heat	10,600
6. Line losses	17,600
Total	193,500

Table 72. Total kilowatt-hours per day would range from 14 for
plant *A* to 111 for plant *F*. In terms of daily plant capacities, the
use of electricity would decrease at a decreasing rate from approximately 0.06 kwh in plant *A* to 0.02 kwh per quart in plant *F*.

The cost of electrical power is subject to wide variations, depending on geographic location and the amounts used each
month. Average rates for commercial power service in Connecticut are represented in Fig. 47, with some indication of the range
that existed in 1946.[14] Using average rates that are consistent with
the monthly consumption of electricity in the several plants, costs

[13] If larger compressors were used, the hours of operation and the power
requirements per quart would be reduced, but these savings would tend to
be offset by somewhat higher equipment costs.
[14] Based on data given in the *35th Annual Report of the Public Utilities
Commission, State of Connecticut, 1946* (State of Connecticut, 1947).

have been estimated at $0.0028 per quart for plant A, $0.0022 for plant B, $0.0019 for plant C, $0.0013 for plant D, $0.0011 for plant E, and $0.0008 per quart for plant F (Table 72). While some items in the cost of electricity would tend to be fixed, regardless of plant volume, it is estimated that nearly 90 percent of the

TABLE 72. The estimated use and cost of electricity for six hypothetical milk pasteurizing and bottling plants.

| | Kilowatt-hours per day in plant | | | | | |
| | Plant capacity (quarts per day) | | | | | |
Item	A 240	B 400	C 800	D 1,600	E 2,400	F 4,800
Agitator............	0.25	0.50	0.50	2.00	2.00	2.00
Milk pump..........	.50	.50	.50	0.50	0.50	0.50
Bottle filler..........	—	—	.25	.50	.50	1.00
Conveyor...........	—	—	—	.50	.50	0.50
Bottle washer........	.12	.12	2.25	1.33	1.66	3.00
Dump unit..........	—	—	0.03	0.06	0.20	0.38
Compressor..........	9.00	13.50	27.00	36.00	54.00	90.00
Cooler fan...........	0.90	0.90	0.90	2.25	2.25	4.50
Brine pump.........	.25	.25	.25	0.50	0.50	0.50
Water pump.........	1.00	1.00	1.00	1.25	1.50	2.50
Lights..............	2.16	2.16	2.82	4.23	4.83	5.73
Total............	14.18	18.93	35.50	49.12	68.44	110.61
Kwh per quart........	0.059	0.047	0.044	0.031	0.028	0.023
Cost per kwh........	$ 0.047	$ 0.046	$ 0.043	$ 0.041	$ 0.039	$ 0.036
Cost per quart						
Postwar..........	$0.0028	$0.0022	$0.0019	$0.0013	$0.0011	$0.0008
Prewar*..........	$0.0030	$0.0023	$0.0020	$0.0014	$0.0012	$0.0009

* Based on prewar rates as indicated in Fig. 47.

total use of electricity is a direct function of the plant volume. In the light of this, electricity has been treated as a variable cost in this study.

Estimates of electrical power costs under prewar conditions are also given in Table 72, and run slightly higher than the postwar levels. This is owing entirely to the fact that power rates in Connecticut dropped about $0.003 per kilowatt-hour between 1939 and 1946 (Fig. 47).

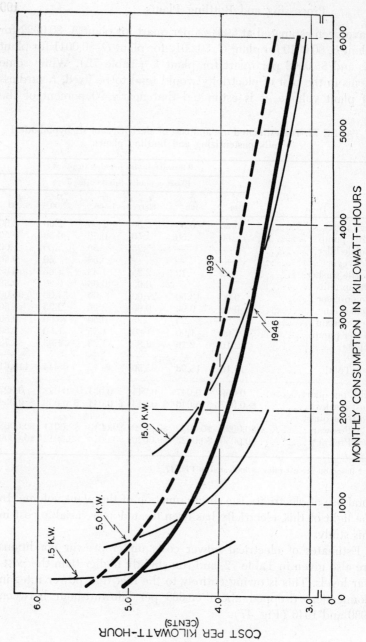

Fig. 47. Effect of monthly consumption of electricity on commercial power rates per kilowatt-hour, Connecticut, 1946.

Steam requirements and fuel costs[15]

Steam is used in city milk plants for several purposes, chief of which is to raise the temperature of the milk in the pasteurizing process. Other uses include heating the water and supplying live steam for washing and sterilizing bottles and cans, for cleaning the plant and equipment, and for plant heating. Steam requirements for these operations may be synthesized by methods similar to those used to estimate the use of electricity in the previous section.

Estimates of the heat and steam requirements for pasteuriza-

TABLE 73. Estimated heat and steam requirements for pasteurization, six hypothetical milk pasteurizing and bottling plants.

| Plant | Heat required (thousands of Btu per day) | | | | Estimated pounds of steam per day[†] |
	Heating milk	Heating medium	Heat loss[*]	Total	
A	46	40	17	103	103
B	76	54	26	156	156
C	152	79	46	277	277
D	304	159	93	556	556
E	456	204	132	792	792
F	912	312	245	1,469	1,469

[*] Losses from pipes and walls of vats estimated at 20 percent.
[†] Each pound of steam would supply about 1,000 Btu.

tion are summarized in Table 73 for the six hypothetical plants. Heat requirements were calculated from the quantities of milk and water (the heating medium) to be heated, the original and final temperatures, and the specific heats of the several materials. With allowance for heat losses in the process, these requirements may be translated into steam requirements by dividing by the number of British thermal units that will be available from each

[15] Based on a number of studies of steam requirements in dairy plants, including, O. M. Camburn, *Steam Usage in Vermont Coöperative Creameries* (Vermont Agricultural Experiment Station, Bulletin 339, 1932); Rodgers, Theophilus, Beresford, and Barnhart, *Distribution of Steam . . . in Idaho Creameries*, R. E. Summers and W. A. Martin, "Proration of Power Uses, Dairy Coöperative Associations," Oregon Agricultural Experiment Station unpublished manuscript (1937).

pound of steam. With steam at 80 pounds pressure and with a maximum temperature of 143°F. for the milk, each pound of steam would supply about 1,000 Btu. With total requirements of 556,000 Btu in plant D, for example, steam requirements for pasteurization would average about 556 pounds per day.

Steam requirements for other operations have been based on the results of other studies, and are reported in Table 74.[16] Fuel

TABLE 74. Average steam and fuel requirements, and estimated fuel costs per quart of milk, for six hypothetical milk pasteurizing and bottling plants.

| | Pounds of steam per day* | | | | | |
| | Plant capacity (quarts per day) | | | | | |
Item	A 240	B 400	C 800	D 1,600	E 2,400	F 4,800
Pasteurization........	103	156	277	556	792	1,469
Can washing†.........	40	65	125	250	375	725
Bottle washing‡.......	60	100	67	134	200	400
General Cleaning**....	84	107	189	382	547	879
Heating††...........	68	73	107	166	222	314
Total...........	355	501	765	1,488	2,136	3,787
Daily gallons of oil‡‡..	4.2	5.9	9.0	16.2	23.2	41.2
Gallons of oil per quart of milk..........	0.0175	0.0148	0.0112	0.0101	0.0097	0.0086
Estimated fuel costs per quart						
Postwar***.......	$0.0018	$0.0015	$0.0011	$0.0010	$0.0010	$0.0009
Prewar†††........	$0.0011	$0.0009	$0.0007	$0.0006	$0.0006	$0.0005

* These estimates refer to situations where the plants are operating at capacity. Reductions in the volumes handled would be accompanied by more or less proportionate reductions in steam requirements.

† Estimated on the basis of one can for every 70 pounds of milk received, and with steam requirements of 5 pounds per can.

‡ On the basis of 3 pounds of steam per case of bottles for the steam-type bottle washers used in plants A and B, and 1 pound per case for the soaker types used in the other plants.

** This category includes miscellaneous uses, and has been estimated on the basis of 1 pound of steam for every 3 square feet of floor area.

†† Based on average temperatures in Connecticut during the heating season, with steam requirements prorated over the entire year.

‡‡ Based on 1 gallon of fuel oil for every 85 pounds of steam in the first three plants, and 1 gallon for every 92 pounds in the three larger plants.

*** With a delivered price of $0.10 per gallon for Number 2 fuel oil.

††† With a delivered price of $0.06 per gallon.

[16] *Ibid.*

requirements were then derived from these by using an average heat content of fuel oil of 160,000 Btu per gallon and assuming 60 percent boiler efficiency for the three smaller plants and 65 percent efficiency for the three larger plants. On this basis, 1 gallon of oil would be required for every 85 pounds of steam in the smaller plants and for every 92 pounds in the larger plants. The fuel requirements were converted into costs by applying a price of $0.10 per gallon for Number 2 fuel oil in the postwar period and a price of $0.06 per gallon in the prewar period. Postwar fuel costs ranged from $0.0018 per quart of milk in plant A to $0.0009 per quart in plant F, and these levels were 67 percent above prewar costs. As in the case of electricity, these costs are for the most part a direct function of plant volume and so have been treated as variable costs in this study.

Other variable costs

In addition to the costs already considered, plant supplies and plant loss or shrinkage are important costs of operating pasteurizing and bottling plants. Supplies include such items as washing powder, soap, chemicals for sterilization, brushes, caps, bottle replacements, and postage and office supplies.

The most important of the supply costs are those for caps and bottle replacements.[17] The cost for caps is directly associated with plant volume, of course, but the magnitude of the cost will depend on the type of cap used. Plug-type caps cost about $0.70 per thousand, clean-seal caps $2.50, and hood or crown types cost about $4.00 per thousand. These would correspond to costs of about $0.0007, $0.0025, and $0.0040 per quart of milk handled.

Breakage and loss of bottles occur in all milk plants and seem to be related to general plant efficiency and bottle care rather than to the size of the operation.[18] Clement reported that milk bottles had an average life of 35 trips, with extreme cases ranging from 6 to 91 trips.[19] According to the University of Connecti-

---

[17] A basic number of bottles have been considered as part of the equipment for each plant, and included in original investments.

[18] C. E. Clement, *Milk Bottle Losses and Ways to Reduce Them* (U. S. Department of Agriculture, Circular 469, 1939).

[19] C. E. Clement, *Effect of Plant Arrangement, Equipment, and Methods of Operation in Relation to Breakage of Bottles in Milk Plants* (U. S. Department of Agriculture, Technical Bulletin 280, 1932).

cut Department of Dairy Industry, however, this figure is too low for small dealers under Connecticut conditions. Computations in this study are based on an average rate of 45 trips per bottle. With bottles costing about $50.00 per thousand in the postwar period, costs would thus average about $0.0011 per quart of milk handled.

The costs of other supplies are relatively minor with respect to any particular item, and have been estimated on the basis of available prewar data to total about $0.0010 per quart.[20] Postwar changes in the general price level would increase these costs to an estimated $0.0019 per quart. Total supply costs for all items in the postwar period would average about $0.0037 per quart if plug caps were used, $0.0055 for clean seal, and $0.0070 per quart if crown-type caps were used, representing increases of from 50 to 70 percent above prewar levels.

In the normal operation of every milk plant, the amount of milk reported as received at the plant is not exactly equal to the amount of milk bottled. This difference is usually a loss but, as a result of accounting, weighing, and testing procedures it may sometimes appear as an "overage." Actual physical loss results from spillage and breakage, leakage from cans and equipment, evaporation, and adhesion to cans and equipment. In addition, there may be either a reported loss or an overage due to errors in weighing and testing when the milk is received at the plant.

According to available reports, plant loss is subject to more or less chance variation but averages from 1 to 2 percent of the volume in most plants. Dow estimated plant loss at 2.0 percent in Maine plants, while Rittenhouse reported an average of 1.25 percent for Boston.[21] Clement reported averages ranging from 1.4

[20] E. H. Rinear, *Milk Distribution Costs . . . in New Jersey;* E. M. Hughes, *The Business of Retailing by Producer-Distributors in New York State* (Cornell Agricultural Experiment Station, Bulletin 741, 1941); G. F. Dow, *An Economic Study of Milk Distribution in Maine Markets;* S. L. Maxtant and C. C. Taylor, *Marketing Fluid Milk in Four Virginia Cities* (Virginia Polytechnic Institute, Bulletin 275, 1930); *A Survey of Milk Marketing in Milwaukee;* Hammerberg, Fellows, and Farr, *Efficiency of Milk Marketing in Connecticut,* 4.

[21] Dow, *op. cit.;* C. F. Rittenhouse, "Summary Report on the Cost of Distributing Milk in the Boston Market," prepared for the Massachusetts Milk Control Board (1936).

to 4.1 percent, but found that these losses could be reduced significantly and that "while the amount of shrinkage will differ at different plants, plants which are well arranged and equipped and efficiently operated will usually keep it down to about 1 percent of the quantity of milk handled, or less." [22] In view of this and of the low margins reported during the war when milk supplies were short, a figure of 1 percent has been used in calculating plant loss or shrinkage in the present study.

Normal amounts of plant loss may be reported and paid for as Class II milk in most markets. Prices for this "surplus" milk vary, depending on the uses to which it may be put. In Connecticut markets, the established Class II milk prices are based on a for-

TABLE 75. Class II milk prices in Connecticut, 1937–1947.*

Year	Average price per hundredweight	Year	Average price per hundredweight
1937	$1.77	1944	$2.87
1938	1.61	1945	2.91
1939	1.44	1946	3.74
1940	1.61	1947	3.83
1941	2.11	1948	4.18
1942	2.40	1949	3.01
1943	2.85	1950	2.99†

* Summarized from reports of the Connecticut Milk Administrator. The prices during the war period represent the amounts paid by dealers, and do not include subsidy payments to producers.
† Preliminary.

mula involving the market price of cream in Boston. Recent changes in the Class II price are indicated in Table 75. In the prewar period, Class II prices averaged about $1.71 per hundredweight. During the war they increased to $2.91 exclusive of subsidy payments to producers, while with the removal of price controls the yearly average rose to $3.74 per hundredweight in 1946 and to $3.83 per hundredweight in 1947. Using the prewar average, the cost of plant loss would amount to less than $0.0004 per quart. Under 1947 prices, however, this loss would represent a cost of more than $0.0008 per quart, an increase of nearly 125 percent.

[22] Clement, *Operation and Management of Milk Plants,* 30.

The effects of plant volume and scale on operating costs

The several items of plant operating costs are summarized in Table 76. Under postwar conditions, fixed costs per day would increase from $3.08 for plant *A* to $15.61 for plant *F*. Labor costs at full capacity would increase from $5.50 to $40.00 per day for

TABLE 76. Summary of costs for six hypothetical milk pasteurizing and bottling plants.

	Postwar operating costs in plant					
	Plant capacity (quarts per day)					
Item	*A* 240	*B* 400	*C* 800	*D* 1,600	*E* 2,400	*F* 4,800
Fixed costs per year						
Depreciation........ $	410	$ 461	$ 690	$ 1,202	$ 1,462	$ 2,063
Interest............	233	265	387	648	809	1,166
Repairs............	368	420	620	1,050	1,315	1,892
Insurance..........	37	42	62	105	132	189
Taxes..............	78	88	129	216	270	389
Subtotal........ $	1,126	$ 1,276	$ 1,888	$ 3,221	$ 3,988	$ 5,699
Fixed costs per day.... $	3.08	$ 3.50	$ 5.17	$ 8.82	$ 10.93	$ 15.61
Fixed costs per quart..	$0.0128	$0.0088	$0.0065	$0.0055	$0.0046	$0.0032
Labor costs per day*... $	5.50	$ 7.00	$ 10.00	$ 18.00	$ 25.00	$ 40.00
Labor costs per quart..	$0.0229	$0.0175	$0.0125	$0.0112	$0.0104	$0.0083
Variable costs per quart						
Electricity..........	$0.0028	$0.0022	$0.0019	$0.0013	$0.0011	$0.0008
Fuel...............	.0018	.0015	.0011	.0010	.0010	.0009
Supplies†...........	.0037	.0037	.0037	.0037	.0037	.0037
Plant loss‡.........	.0008	.0008	.0008	.0008	.0008	.0008
Subtotal........	$0.0091	$0.0082	$0.0075	$0.0068	$0.0066	$0.0062
Combined cost at full capacity						
Postwar..........	$0.0448	$0.0345	$0.0265	$0.0235	$0.0216	$0.0177
Prewar**.........	$0.0309	$0.0238	$0.0184	$0.0161	$0.0148	$0.0121

* Assuming operation at full capacity and labor rates averaging $1.00 per hour; if plant volumes were reduced enough to reduce the number of batches of milk to be pasteurized, hours of labor and labor costs would be reduced accordingly.

† With plug-type caps; if crown-type caps are used, supply costs will average about $0.0070 per quart.

‡ On the basis of the 1947 value for Class II milk.

** See Appendix for details.

these plants. Variable costs per quart would decrease with the increases in the size of plant, falling from $0.0091 per quart in plant *A* to $0.0062 in plant *F*. When all items are expressed on a unit basis and plants are assumed to be operating at full capacity, combined average costs would amount to approximately

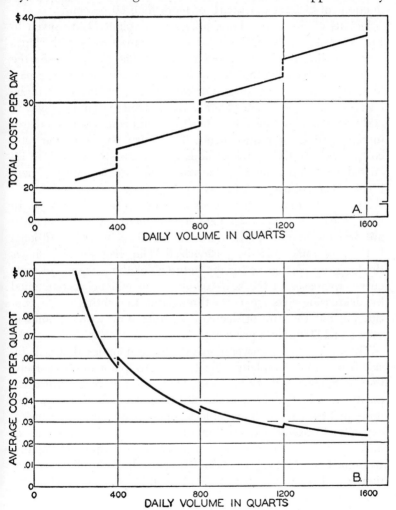

Fig. 48. Relation between volume and costs for plant D: A, *in terms of total costs per day;* B, *in terms of average costs per quart.*

$0.0448 per quart in plant A, $0.0345 in plant B, $0.0265 in plant C, $0.0235 in plant D, $0.0216 in plant E, and $0.0177 in plant F. These costs are about 45 percent higher than the prewar estimates. Increasing the plant capacity and volume from 240 to 4,800 quarts per day, then, will result in unit or average cost reductions of $0.0271 per quart, or more than 60 percent.

Details of the cost-volume relations for plant D are given in Fig. 48. Total costs will increase along straight lines with slopes corresponding to the variable costs of $0.0068 per quart. As the volume increases up to 400 quarts, the capacity of a single pasteurizing vat, pasteurizing and bottle-filling operations will be based on a single batch of milk. Beyond this volume, however, additional batches must be pasteurized, with consequent increases in time and labor requirements. The sharp breaks in the total cost curve (Fig. 48A) reflect added labor costs that must be incurred when additional pasteurizing runs are necessary. These breaks also will occur in the average-cost curve (Fig. 48B).[23]

Average-cost curves for the six plants are shown in Fig. 49. In each case costs decrease as plant volume increases, but the curves are broken by abrupt increases at volumes where additional batches of milk must be pasteurized. The diagram also shows the long-run cost curve for the industry, or the economy-of-scale curve. Increases in the scale of operation will be accompanied by decreasing average costs throughout the entire range considered, but the rate of decrease is quite slow with volumes in excess of 1,200 quarts per day.

The average-cost curves illustrate the economies that will result from more complete utilization of any plant or, conversely, the diseconomies that will result from any failure to utilize capacity completely. Even under the best of conditions, however, it frequently will be impossible to operate without some excess capacity. Consumers do not purchase exactly even amounts of milk throughout the year, and production also varies seasonally. In Connecticut during the 1938–1942 period, fluid milk consumption varied from an index of about 98 in December and January

---

[23] Since labor requirements will vary slightly with volume, even within a batch, this admittedly is a simplification. It will not result in serious distortions, however, especially in the volume ranges approaching capacity.

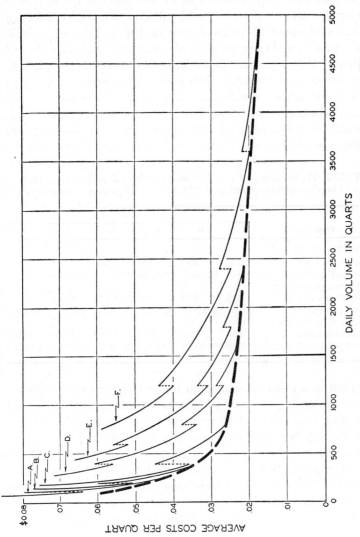

Fig. 49. Average-cost curves for six hypothetical milk pasteurizing and bottling plants. The broken line represents the long-run cost curve.

to 103 in August; milk production, on the other hand, ranged from an index of approximately 94 in November to 107 in June.[24] During the 1943–1946 period, fluid-milk consumption varied from an index of about 93 in December to 104 in July, while milk production ranged from an index of about 90 in November to 112 in June.[25] Under postwar conditions, then, the average plant in Connecticut would operate with unavoidable excess capacity in the fall and winter months even though operations were at full capacity during the spring peak period. While the amount of this unavoidable excess capacity will vary greatly from plant to plant, an average of 95 percent utilization for the entire year may be

TABLE 77. Summary of costs for six hypothetical milk pasteurizing and bottling plants operating at 100, 95, and 75 percent of capacity.

Item	Plant					
	A	B	C	D	E	F
100 percent of capacity						
Quarts per day......	240	400	800	1,600	2,400	4,800
cost per quart......	$0.0448	$0.0345	$0.0265	$0.0235	$0.0216	$0.0177
95 percent of capacity						
Quarts per day......	228	380	760	1,520	2,280	4,560
Cost per quart......	$0.0467	$0.0358	$0.0275	$0.0244	$0.0224	$0.0184
75 percent of capacity						
Quarts per day......	180	300	600	1,200	1,800	3,600
Cost per quart......	$0.0568	$0.0432	$0.0328	$0.0274	$0.0251	$0.0204

accepted as a practical maximum under Connecticut conditions.

Average costs per quart for plants operating with an annual utilization of 95 percent of capacity are given in Table 77 and Fig. 50, together with estimates based on 75- and 100-percent utilization. For the reasons just discussed, the curve based on 95-percent utilization is presented as the basic long-run cost curve. It is interesting to note that increasing amounts of excess capacity decrease average volumes as well as increase average costs, with the result that departures from the basic curve are not pro-

[24] Alan McLeod and D. A. Clarke, Jr., *Some Recent Developments in the Connecticut Milk Markets, I. Milk Production and Consumption Trends* (Storrs Agricultural Experiment Station, Bulletin 254, 1945).

[25] Based on reports of the Connecticut Milk Administrator.

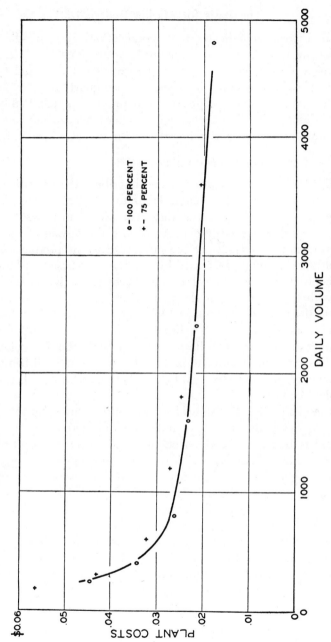

Fig. 50. The long-run average-cost curve for pasteurizing and bottling plants operated at an average of 95 percent of capacity, with points plotted.

nounced. Figure 50 indicates that modifications corresponding to 75-percent utilization would amount to approximately $0.0025 per quart with volumes less than 2,000 quarts per day, and to $0.0010 or less with volumes in excess of 3,000 quarts per day. In short, the basic economy-of-scale curve provides a reasonably accurate description of costs even with some excess capacity, and the accuracy of the description increases with increases in volume.

Laboratory and bookkeeping costs[26]

In addition to the activities already described, the operations of city milk plants usually include laboratory testing and bookkeeping. In small plants such as those considered in this study, laboratory work is primarily concerned with the testing of milk received from producers, since the price paid to the producer is frequently increased or decreased by a differential based on butterfat content. While some of the bookkeeping activities have to do with the accounts for the plant itself, most of this work relates to the producer payroll and to the sales accounts of retail and wholesale delivery routes. For these reasons, the costs for these operations have not been included with the foregoing plant costs. They are legitimate parts of the cost of milk distribution, however, and so have been treated here as additions to the basic plant costs.

Most municipalities and states have established laws and regulations governing the quality of milk and the methods of handling and testing milk. In Connecticut, the State Department of Farms and Markets is responsible for the enforcement of these laws and regulations, and carries on a continuous program of testing as a check on the quality of milk delivered by farmers, the quality of milk in retail channels, and the accuracy of the tests made by dealers. In addition, the Connecticut Milk Administrator has insisted that payments to producers be based on these butterfat tests if the dealer does not test for himself.

Testing and sampling require trained personnel and rather elaborate laboratory equipment and so may be quite expensive

---

[26] The author wishes to express his thanks to the Office of the Connecticut Milk Administrator, and especially to James Devine, for assistance in preparing this section.

for small plants. As a consequence, it is common for small dealers in many markets to dispense with this procedure and to contract with producers to buy milk on a "flat-price" basis without regard to the butterfat test. Under Connecticut regulations, as previously mentioned, dealers who do not test are required to pay for their milk on the basis of the butterfat tests made periodically by the Department of Farms and Markets. These tests are made at least twice and usually three times each month, the dealer paying for each test at the rate of $1.25 per producer. The regulations pro-

TABLE 78. The proportion of Connecticut pasteurizing milk dealers who bought milk on the basis of the state butterfat tests, March 1946.*

Daily volume (quarts)	Total number of pasteurizing dealers	Number of pasteurizing dealers using state test	Percent in each class using state test
240 and less.............	13	13	100
241– 400...............	51	50	98
401– 800...............	69	69	100
801–1,200...............	36	35	97
1,201–1,600...............	27	27	100
1,601–2,000...............	14	13	93
2,001–2,400...............	9	9	100
2,401–4,000...............	18	11	61
4,001–6,000...............	7	5	71
6,000 and over............	24	1	4
Total.................	268	233	87

* Based on data obtained from the Connecticut Milk Administrator.

vide that dealers may share this expense equally with producers, but with the short supply situation of the postwar period most dealers have carried this expense without deductions from the producers' checks.

The data in Table 78 indicate that 87 percent of all dealers who pasteurize milk in Connecticut use the state testing service and that only 13 percent carry on their own testing programs. Only three of the 219 pasteurizing dealers handling volumes of 2,400 quarts per day or less did their own testing, and only in the group with volumes over 6,000 quarts was private testing typical. In view of these facts and of the focus of the present study on plants with volumes of less than 4,800 quarts daily, laboratory and testing expenses have been estimated from the charges made for the State service. With three tests per month and with daily production averaging about 340 pounds per wholesale dairy farm, this cost would average about $0.0008 per quart of milk.[27]

Bookkeeping and accounting procedures are far from standardized in milk distribution, ranging from the small plant operator who keeps his books "in his head," to the elaborate bookkeeping and clerical offices of some of the larger firms. This lack of uni-

TABLE 79. The number of office workers and the hours of office work per hundred quarts of milk, 200 pasteurizing plants.[*]

Daily volume (quarts)	Number of plants	Plant averages		
		Daily volume (quarts)	Number of office workers	Office hours per 100 quarts[†]
400 and less.........	4	340	0	0
401– 1,000..........	18	670	0.5	0.47
1,001– 2,000..........	31	1,560	.8	.32
2,001– 4,000..........	35	3,150	2.7	.54
4,001– 8,000..........	31	6,020	3.6	.38
8,001–12,000..........	21	10,336	5.1	.31
12,001–20,000..........	29	15,744	6.9	.28
20,001–40,000..........	25	29,392	11.8	.25
Over 40,000...........	6	80,000	32.6	.26
Total.............	200	11,235	5.2	0.29

[*] Based on data from C. E. Clement, *Operation and Management of Milk Plants* (U. S. Department of Agriculture, Circular No. 260, 1933), Table 7, p. 47.
[†] Assuming a 44-hour work week.

formity, especially in the low-volume ranges, is illustrated by the data in Table 79, adapted from a report published by the U. S. Department of Agriculture.[28] Based on a survey of 200 dairy plants, this study indicated that plants with daily volumes of 400 quarts or less did not hire bookkeepers and office workers. Within the range from 400 to 8,000 quarts, bookkeeping labor varied erratically from 0.32 hour per 100 quarts for 31 plants with volumes averaging 1,560 quarts per day, to 0.54 hour per 100 quarts

[27] The average production per herd for members of the Connecticut Milk Producers' Association in 1946 was 341 pounds per day.
[28] Clement, *Operation and Management of Milk Plants*, Table 7, p. 47.

for 35 plants with daily average volumes of 3,150 quarts. Only in the range above 8,000 quarts did the averages become stable, with office labor per 100 quarts dropping from 0.31 hour at a daily average volume of 10,336 quarts, to 0.26 hour with volumes of 80,000 quarts per day.

The Office of the Connecticut Milk Administrator regularly audits the books of all milk dealers in the state, and so is familiar both with current practices of the trade and with desirable book-keeping requirements. This Office was asked to indicate the bookkeeping and clerical staff that would be required to do an

TABLE 80. Estimates of the number of office workers and of postwar office labor costs for six hypothetical milk pasteurizing and bottling plants.

Plant	Daily volume (quarts)	Hours of office labor per week*			Hours per 100 quarts	Office labor costs†	
		Book-keeper	Clerks	Total		Per week	Per quart
A	240			8‡	0.48	$ 8.00	$0.0048
B	400			13‡	.46	13.00	.0046
C	800	24		24	.43	24.00	.0043
D	1,600	44		44	.39	44.00	.0039
E	2,400	44	20	64	.38	57.00	.0034
F	4,800	44	68	112	.33	88.20	.0026

* Based on information from the Connecticut Milk Administrator.
† With postwar wage rates averaging $1.00 per hour for plant workers and bookkeepers and $0.65 per hour for clerks. These rates are assumed to cover Social Security taxes, workman's unemployment insurance, and the allocated costs of vacations with pay.
‡ Records kept by the plant manager or owner, and assuming that the records will be comparable to those kept by the larger plants.

adequate job in each of the six sample plants discussed in previous sections of this chapter, with the results summarized in Table 80. According to these estimates, plants handling 240 to 400 quarts daily normally would not hire a bookkeeper or clerk, and all records would be kept by the manager or owner. To keep records comparable with those typical of larger plants would require 0.48 and 0.46 hour per day per 100 quarts respectively, although many plants of this size are operated with adequate records and with much lower bookkeeping labor requirements. The office staffs for the larger plants range from a part-time book-keeper in plant C handling 800 quarts per day, which would correspond to office-labor requirements of 0.43 hour per 100 quarts, to a full-time bookkeeper, a full-time clerk, and a part-time clerk for plant F with a daily volume of 4,800 quarts, or 0.33 hour of office work per 100 quarts of milk. Comparison with the data in Table 79 will indicate that these estimates fall well within the range reported by actual plants of these sizes, and that they appear consistent with the office labor reported by the larger plants.

Wage rates for office workers vary considerably from plant to plant and from market to market, but under postwar conditions rates of $1.00 per hour for bookkeepers and $0.65 per hour for

TABLE 81. Effects of bookkeeping and laboratory costs on plant costs at 95 percent of capacity.

	Postwar operating costs per quart in plant Daily plant volume (quarts)					
Item	A 228	B 380	C 760	D 1,520	E 2,280	F 4,560
Laboratory............	$0.0008	$0.0008	$0.0008	$0.0008	$0.0008	$0.0008
Bookkeeping..........	.0048	.0046	.0043	.0039	.0034	.0026
Subtotal.........	$0.0056	$0.0054	$0.0051	$0.0047	$0.0042	$0.0034
Plant costs*..........	$0.0467	$0.0358	$0.0275	$0.0244	$0.0224	$0.0184
Total.............	$0.0523	$0.0412	$0.0326	$0.0291	$0.0266	$0.0218
Total prewar costs†....	$0.0361	$0.0285	$0.0226	$0.0201	$0.0183	$0.0150

* Obtained from Table 77 with plant volume equal to 95 percent of capacity.
† See Appendix for details.

clerks may be taken as typical of conditions in the major Connecticut milk markets.[29] These rates have been used to convert office-labor requirements into costs, with the results summarized in the last two columns of Table 80. Assuming that even the smaller plants would keep adequate books, the costs for office labor would decrease at a decreasing rate from $0.0048 per quart for plant A with a daily capacity of 240 quarts, to $0.0026 per quart for plant F with a daily capacity of 4,800 quarts.

The estimated costs for butterfat testing and bookkeeping are summarized for each plant and combined with the basic plant

[29] See Appendix for labor costs for bookkeepers and clerks at prewar and postwar wage levels.

costs in Table 81. While laboratory costs remain constant per
quart of capacity, bookkeeping costs decline with increases in
plant capacity and volume. These costs would amount to $0.0056
per quart for plant A and decrease to $0.0034 per quart for plant

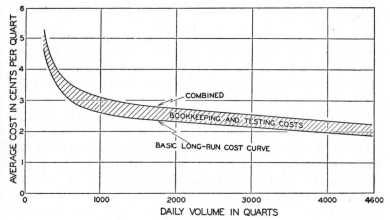

*Fig. 51. Effects of bookkeeping and laboratory costs on the long-run aver-
age-cost curve at 95 percent of capacity.*

F. When combined with the basic plant costs per quart, figured
at 95 percent of capacity, these amount to $0.0523 for plant A,
$0.0412 for plant B, $0.0326 for plant C, $0.0291 for plant D,
$0.0266 for plant E, and $0.0218 for plant F. The basic economy-
of-scale curve and the curve including bookkeeping and laboratory costs are shown in Fig. 51.

Large pasteurizing and bottling plants

While most of the pasteurizing plants in Connecticut fall within
the volume ranges covered by the six hypothetical plants just
discussed, the bulk of the milk is handled by a relatively small
number of larger plants. To determine appropriate cost relations
for these plants and to provide the basis for estimating the plant
costs that would characterize reorganization programs involving
the concentration of all milk in a few large plants, the economy-
of-scale curve must be extended to much higher volume ranges.
It is quite clear from a consideration of the summary tables
and diagrams in the previous section that unit costs will continue

to decrease as plant scale and volume is increased beyond 4,800 quarts daily. Virtually every item that contributes to total cost is increasing at a decreasing rate, indicating that average costs are decreasing. To project the rate of decrease more exactly, however, will require detailed information on the costs of operating larger plants.

A number of studies of the costs of operating city milk plants are available, and will throw some light on this question. Clement and his associates in the U. S. Department of Agriculture, in studying the influence of plant arrangement and methods of operation on labor requirements, describe a number of actual plants with volumes averaging approximately 100,000 quarts per day where the volume handled per plant employee averaged over 1,000 quarts per day.[30] This compares with a maximum of 800 quarts per employee per day for the largest plant previously discussed, and indicates that labor efficiency will continue to increase with expansion in size. Other studies attest to the gains in efficiency with respect to buildings and equipments. In addition to these increases in physical efficiency, external economies will frequently permit larger firms to purchase equipment and supplies at lower prices. These economies will be balanced, in part at least, by the growing complexities of the organization and the consequent need for more elaborate and expensive office and managerial operations. Finally, there may be a tendency for wage rates to be higher in larger plants and for labor to be more organized; this tendency will be disregarded here since it involves problems of income distribution and value judgments that are beyond the realm of this study.

As part of a 1934 study of the feasibility of municipal milk distribution in Milwaukee, plans were drawn and costs estimated for a pasteurizing and bottling plant that would handle 276,000 quarts of milk and cream daily.[31] The results of this study are summarized in Table 82.

An elaborate study of city milk-plant costs was made in Boston

---

[30] C. E. Clement, P. E. LeFevre, J. B. Bain, and F. M. Grant, *Effect of Milk Plant Arrangement and Methods of Operation on Labor Requirements* (U. S. Department of Agriculture, Technical Bulletin 153, 1929), 36.

[31] *A Survey of Milk Marketing in Milwaukee*, 85–113.

in 1934–35.[32] Costs were reported for the entire market and also for those dealers who handled 2,500 quarts or more daily. Only 7.2 percent of the dealers fell in this category, but their plants handled 83.6 percent of all Class I milk in the market. From data given, it is possible to determine that the average volume for these dealers was about 23,500 quarts daily. Average costs are

TABLE 82. Estimated daily overhead and operating charges for a proposed central pasteurizing and bottling plant, Milwaukee, 1934.[*]

Expense	Estimated costs per day
Depreciation and interest†	
Buildings...	$102.18
Equipment...	127.47
Power and refrigeration.............................	493.42
Management overhead...............................	137.12
Direct overhead.....................................	33.33
Direct labor...	366.50
Insurance‡..	42.96
Advertising**.......................................	118.00
Property tax††......................................	36.83
All other expenses..................................	800.00
Total...	$2,257.81
Cost per quart of milk and cream‡‡.................	$0.00818

[*] A Survey of Milk Marketing in Milwaukee (Dairy Section, Agricultural Adjustment Administration, U. S. Department of Agriculture, Marketing Information Series DM-1, 1937), 101.
† Depreciation calculated at a rate of 2.5 percent per year on buildings and 8 percent on plant equipment; interest charged at the rate of 5 percent. These figures do not include depreciation and interest on power and refrigeration equipment, for these are included in next item.
‡ Includes compensation, public liability, fire, wind, and theft.
** Assumed to represent 0.5 percent of daily gross income.
†† Based on a rate of $17.50 per $1,000, with an appraised value of 80 percent of original investment.
‡‡ Based on 276,000 quarts of milk and cream daily.

summarized in Table 83, and indicate that these dealers operated their plants for approximately $0.0088 per quart of milk.

Reports covering the operation of 20 dealers in New York City who had volumes averaging approximately 40,000 quarts per day in 1937 show an average cost of $0.0061 per quart of Grade B

[32] C. F. Rittenhouse, Summary Report, 5–9, 58–66, and supplementary mimeographed pages.

milk.[33] These costs do not include administration, general and overhead expenses, or container costs, and it is not possible to separate these from other cost summaries.

Spencer found costs for representative New Jersey plants ranging from about $0.011 to $0.016 and averaging about $0.013 per quart. "The variation in costs was due to several factors, such as the location of the plant (whether in the city or in the country), the quantity of milk handled, the variety of products and pack-

TABLE 83. Expenses included in weighted average city milk-plant costs for 7.2 percent of the dealers in the Boston market, 1934–35.°

Expenses	Cost per quart of milk
Labor	$0.0026
Heat, light, and power	.0008
Water and ice	.0001
Depreciation and rent	.0008
Taxes and insurance	.0002
Repairs and maintenance	.0004
Supplies and laundry	.0005
Miscellaneous expenses	.0002
Shrinkage	.0008
Administration	.0009
Containers†	.0015
Total	$0.0088

° C. F. Rittenhouse, *Summary Report on the Cost of Distributing Milk in the Boston Market* (prepared for the Massachusetts Milk Control Board, 1936), 64 and supplementary mimeographed table similar to Table XV-B, but for the 7.2-percent group of dealers.
† Average of wholesale and retail costs, with 63 percent retail and the balance wholesale.

ages turned out, as well as the arrangement, organization and management of the plant from the standpoint of operating efficiency."[34] Costs for several plants, presumably large, were reported at less than $0.010 per quart. Other studies make it clear that many relatively large and efficient plants were operating

[33] J. J. Bennett, Jr., *A Report on the Milk Industry of the State of New York with Particular Reference to the New York Metropolitan Area* (New York Attorney General, 1938), 75–76.
[34] Leland Spencer, "Costs of Distributing Milk in New Jersey," New Jersey Department of Agriculture Mimeograph (1943), 16–19.

with costs of $0.010 per quart or less in the prewar and war period.[35]

Unfortunately, it is difficult or impossible to adjust these results to a basis comparable with the postwar costs discussed in the previous sections. Detailed studies for postwar operations are available, however, from a report by Bartlett and Gothard [36] covering two Illinois plants in 1946 and from the California Bureau of Milk Control for a number of plants during the 1947–48 period.[37] These studies have been standardized to an average wage rate of $1.00 per hour and a plant loss of 1.25 percent, with the results shown in Table 84. It should be emphasized that these have been selected to represent efficient operations and that they are by no means a random sampling of all plant operations. The somewhat erratic changes from plant to plant in particular items of expense indicate that efficiency and perhaps accounting methods are not entirely uniform among the several plants. Nevertheless, these may be accepted as representative of reasonably efficient operations and so used to project the economy-of-scale curve.

Examination of the data in terms of total daily costs indicates that the general relation between costs and volume can be approximated by the following equation:

$$C_g = \$21.00 + \$17.43P - \$0.0388P^2, \qquad (11.1)$$

where C_g represents the daily total cost for plants bottling in glass containers, and P the plant volume in thousand quarts per day. Table 84 also indicates that fiber-container costs exceed glass-container and case costs by an average of $0.0148 per quart for the six plants reporting both packages. Part of this difference is offset by labor and equipment economies, however, and average

---

[35] See, for example, the figures drawn from a number of studies and summarized in the Appendix of R. W. Bartlett, *The Milk Industry* (Ronald, New York, 1946).

[36] R. W. Bartlett and F. T. Gothard, "Measuring the Efficiency of Milk Plant Operations," Illinois Agricultural Experiment Station Mimeograph (1950).

[37] Mimeographed reports and hearing records, Bureau of Milk Control, California Department of Agriculture.

TABLE 84. Reported plant costs for large pasteurizing and bottling plants.

	F	R	S	T	U	V	W	X	Y	Z
					Plant*					
Daily volume (1,000 quarts)†										
	4.6	13	19	21	51	71	83	107	126	140
Plant cost (cents per quart) in glass										
Fixed........	0.32			0.48	0.18	0.48	0.41	0.17	0.25	
Labor‡.......	.83			1.15	.69	.42	.48	.42	.54	
Container.....	.51			0.28	.36	.33	.30	.40	.30	
Plant loss**...	.08			.08	.08	.08	.08	.08	.08	
Other........	.44			.19	.34	.14	.16	.14	.17	
Total......	2.18			2.18	1.65	1.45	1.43	1.21	1.34	
Estimate††	2.18	1.85	1.78	1.76	1.59	1.50	1.45	1.35	1.27	1.21
Plant cost (cents per quart) in fiber										
Fixed........		0.26	0.40	0.42	0.11	0.17	0.40	0.41	0.14	0.23
Labor‡.......		.51	.39	.37	.32	.50	.29	.31	.28	.45
Container‡‡ ..		1.75	1.75	1.84	1.75	1.86	1.83	1.80	1.71	1.80
Plant loss**...		0.08	0.08	0.08	0.08	0.08	0.08	0.08	0.08	0.08
Other........		.18	.14	.19	.11	.34	.14	.16	.14	.17
Total......		2.78	2.76	2.90	2.37	2.95	2.74	2.76	2.35	2.73
Estimate***	3.38	3.05	2.98	2.96	2.79	2.70	2.65	2.55	2.47	2.41

* Plant F from Tables 76 and 81. Plants R and U based on 1946 conditions as reported in R. W. Bartlett and F. T. Gothard, "Measuring the Efficiency of Milk Plant Operations," Illinois Agricultural Experiment Station, Mimeograph (1950). All other plants based on 1947–48 data obtained from the California Bureau of Milk Control.

† Excluding bulk sales.

‡ Standardized to an average wage rate of $1.00 per hour.

** Standardized to a plant loss of 1.25 percent, valued at a Class II price of $3.00 per hundredweight.

†† Based on equation (11.1).

‡‡ Standardized to "Canco" containers.

*** Based on equation (11.2).

total plant costs differ only by $0.0120 per quart. If this difference is included in the cost equation, the cost for plants bottling in fiber may be approximated by:

$$C_f = \$21.00 + \$29.43P - \$0.0388P^2. \qquad (11.2)$$

Estimates based on these equations are included in Table 84, and indicate that the projections follow reported costs rather closely. In a few cases, notably where plant operations have been streamlined by reducing the number of products processed, the reported costs are lower than the estimates. In others, lower levels of efficiency result in costs above those projected. In general, however, the projections seem to smooth out differences among plants and to represent reasonable (but not maximum) levels of plant efficiency. These projections are coupled with the previously presented economy-of-scale curve in Fig. 52, indicating that costs

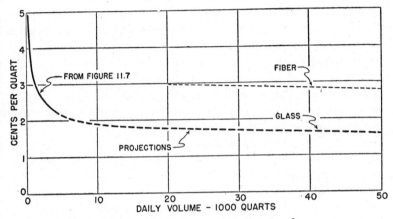

Fig. 52. Projection of curve showing economies of scale.

continue to decrease with increases in plant scale but at a greatly reduced rate. Finally, it should be noted that, while this gives reasonable approximations for the range up to 150,000 quarts per day, the equations should not be used for higher ranges. Because of the parabolic form of the equations, indicated *total* costs decline after 225,000 quarts with equation (11.1) and after 379,000 quarts with equation (11.2).

The effects of changes in prices and cost rates

The previous pages have referred specifically to the costs of operating milk plants under postwar conditions, but frequent references to prewar conditions have stressed the importance of changes in prices and cost rates on operating costs. To summarize briefly, investments in buildings and equipment and the fixed costs associated with these increased about 60 percent during the war period; wages and labor costs increased about 40 percent;

variable costs increased an average of 40 percent, including increases of 67 percent in fuel costs, 60 percent in supplies, 125 percent in plant loss (due to the increase in Class II prices), and a decrease of 2 or 3 percent in electricity rates; and laboratory and bookkeeping expenses increased by an average of 40 percent. The combined effect of all these was to increase total plant operating costs about 45 percent.

Inasmuch as prices and cost rates for the most part are quite variable, both geographically and from time to time, no attempt will be made to indicate the specific effects of particular changes on operating costs. It should be pointed out, however, that the results presented here will need to be modified if they are to be applied under other conditions. For this reason the basic analyses were expressed in physical terms wherever possible and these physical inputs were then converted to costs by applying suitable prices. Adjustments in the results may be made by revising these computations and applying suitable prices to the physical inputs. Approximate revisions may be made quite simply by changing the cost estimates summarized in Table 76 in accordance with the percentage changes in prices or rates. For example, if plant wage rates should increase 20 percent above the levels used in this study, the labor costs for plant C would be increased from $0.0125 to $0.0150 per quart.

Raw-milk plants[38]

Since most small dealers handle only raw milk and many rural areas are served exclusively by such dealers, this chapter would be incomplete without a brief presentation of the cost and volume relations for plants of this type. Raw-milk plant operations are relatively simple, and require little in the way of elaborate buildings or equipment. Many of the smaller dealers have no specialized equipment for washing and filling bottles, and only the larger ones use electrical refrigeration with dry boxes or cold-storage rooms.

A study of the operations of 172 Connecticut producer-dealers in 1937 indicated that 92 had annual costs for buildings and equip-

[38] This section is based entirely on Hammerberg, Fellows, and Farr, *Efficiency of Milk Marketing in Connecticut, 4,* 31–39.

ment of less than $100, 65 had annual costs ranging between $100 and $399, and only 15 had costs of $400 or more per year. About 50 percent of the variance in these costs could be explained by variations in volume, with the relation following the form

$$C = \$0.0329 + \$0.0024P, \tag{11.3}$$

where C represents the equipment and building costs per day and P the daily volume in quarts.[39] Economies of scale are not large in this item of plant costs, for small-volume plants tend to operate with limited amounts of makeshift equipment.

TABLE 85. Estimated labor requirements and costs for small raw-milk plants.*

Daily volume (quarts)	Investment in equipment	Plant labor (hours per day)	Quarts per man-hour	Labor costs per quart
25	$ 250	1.24	20	$0.0346
75	620	1.79	42	.0168
125	990	2.25	56	.0131
175	1,370	2.90	60	.0117
225	1,750	3.44	65	.0108
275	2,110	4.01	69	.0102
325	2,490	4.56	71	.0098
375	2,860	5.11	73	.0094

* Adapted from D. O. Hammerberg, I. F. Fellows, and R. H. Farr, *Efficiency of Milk Marketing in Connecticut*, 4. Costs have been calculated with an assumed wage rate of $0.70 per hour.

Plant labor represents the largest element in the costs of operating raw-milk plants. In physical terms, the data based on the operations of these producer-dealers indicated that daily hours of plant labor could be approximated by the equation

$$H = 1.0 + 0.016P - 0.000066I, \tag{11.4}$$

where H represents the daily hours of plant labor, P the daily volume in quarts, and I the investment in equipment in dollars.[40] The last term in this equation represents the substitution between labor and equipment, or the labor-saving effects of equipment. Average investments and estimated hours of labor are indi-

[39] This regression resulted in a corrected coefficient of correlation of 0.701.
[40] Corrected coefficient of multiple correlation, 0.797.

cated in Table 85 for raw-milk plants with volumes ranging from 25 to 375 quarts per day. Important increases in physical efficiency are apparent, with quarts per man-hour increasing from 20 to 73 as volume increases from 25 to 375 quarts per day. These physical data have been converted into costs by applying a rate of $0.70 per hour, more or less typical of prewar conditions in rural Connecticut areas. Labor costs per quart drop rapidly from approximately $0.035 with 25 quarts per day to $0.013 with

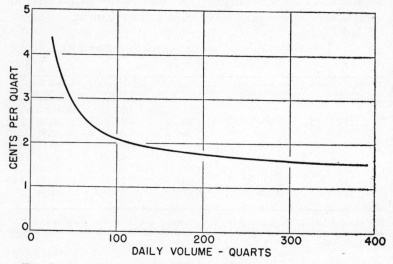

Fig. 53. *Economies of scale in the operation of raw-milk plants in Connecticut, adjusted to postwar conditions.*

125 quarts, and then more slowly to $0.0094 as volume increases to 375 quarts per day.

Total costs for supplies in these plants ranged from $200 to $2,468 and averaged $322 per year. Examination of these costs indicated that they were fairly constant on a per-quart basis regardless of the volume handled, and that the previously established prewar rates of 0.24 and 0.41 cents per quart (depending on the type of bottle cap used) were fairly representative. Assuming that a plug-type cap was used, postwar supply costs would average about $0.0037 per quart.

The effect of volume on average combined costs for raw-milk

plants is indicated in Fig. 53. As the foregoing discussion has indicated, economies of scale are important only in plant labor costs, but the savings in this item are enough to result in a pronounced decline in the combined average-cost curve. With daily average volumes as low as 25 quarts, plant costs will average about $0.042 per quart. Unit costs decrease at a decreasing rate as volume increases, and will average about $0.020 with 125 quarts and approach $0.015 per quart as volume approaches 400 quarts per day. It should be added, however, that many of these costs and especially labor costs may be written down by small dealers and producers on an "opportunity" cost basis. If such resources as family labor are available and unutilized, operations may be carried on even though the returns are considerably less than the $0.70 per hour used in making the above estimates.

12 —

CRITERIA FOR
REORGANIZATION

Retail route volumes under several systems of distribution

The studies summarized in Chapter 10 indicated that the time requirements for retail milk routes are a complex function of route volume, route mileage, the number of delivery stops and volume per stop, the collecting and soliciting included as part of route operations, and the general characteristics of the area served with respect to such factors as the distance that houses are set back from the street and the proportion of deliveries made to upper floors of buildings. In greatly simplified form, however, this function may be expressed as follows:

$$T_d = 1.22V_d + 4.0D_d, \tag{10.6}$$
$$T_a = 0.80V_a + 4.0D_a, \tag{10.9}$$

where T represents daily route time in minutes, V the daily route volume in quarts, D the daily route mileage, and the subscripts d and a refer to daily and alternate-day delivery.

If an eight-hour day is taken as the standard, these equations can be converted to define volume in terms of route mileages:

$$V_d = 393 - 3.28V_d, \tag{12.1}$$
$$V_a = 600 - 5.0D_a. \tag{12.2}$$

Both V and D are functions of delivery density, with V increasing and D decreasing as delivery density increases. Using K to represent delivery density in quarts per route mile, and remembering that D must equal V/K, route volume can be expressed as the following functions of density:

$$V_d = \frac{393}{1 + 3.28/K_d} \qquad (12.3)$$

$$V_a = \frac{600}{1 + 5.0/K_a} \qquad (12.4)$$

These functions are represented by curves I and II in Fig. 54.

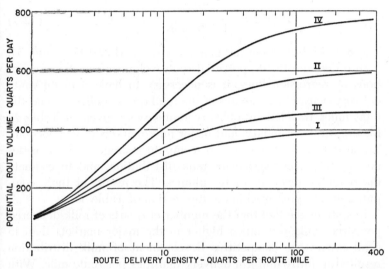

Fig. 54. *Effect of retail route density on potential route volume: I, daily delivery under existing conditions; II, alternate-day delivery under existing conditions; III, daily delivery with collections simplified and soliciting eliminated; IV, alternate-day delivery with collections simplified and soliciting eliminated.*

The foregoing equations refer to delivery under the present more or less competitive system. Typical route operations now include making collections from customers and soliciting new customers. If milk were delivered under reorganized systems based on exclusive delivery territories for each dealer or complete municipal monopoly, competitive sales efforts would be meaningless and collection problems could be greatly simplified and probably would be handled through the mails in a manner similar to that commonly used by public utilities.[1] Allowing for this reduction in route time, the basic equations will then be:

$$T'_d = 1.03V_d + 4.0D_d, \qquad (10.7)$$
$$T'_a = 0.61V_a + 4.0D_a, \qquad (10.10)$$

while the daily-volume functions reduce to

$$V'_d = \frac{466}{1 + 3.88/K_d} \qquad (12.5)$$

$$V'_a = \frac{787}{1 + 6.56/K_a} \qquad (12.6)$$

These revised functions are given as curves III and IV in Fig. 54.

In order to estimate potential route volumes from these equations or regression lines, it is necessary to have data on route delivery densities. Estimates of the total quarts delivered and the total miles traveled by delivery routes were given in Table 23 for the rural, secondary, and major milk markets of Connecticut. These data have been used to compute average route densities under the present system of milk distribution, and to estimate the potential levels of route volumes. The results of these computations are presented in the top section of Table 86.

In spite of the fact that the number of quarts of milk delivered per street mile was much higher in the major markets than in rural towns, the competitive development of milk distribution resulted in fairly uniform delivery densities per route mile. With daily delivery, route densities averaged 7.0 quarts per route mile in rural towns, 8.1 quarts in secondary markets, and 9.3 quarts in major markets. These correspond to potential route volumes of 268, 280, and 290 quarts per day respectively. With alternate-day operations, route densities for these three groups of markets ranged from 12.7 to 14.7 quarts per route mile, while potential route volumes ranged from 430 to 448 quarts per day.

These estimates may be checked against the results obtained from the survey of 100 Connecticut dealers in the 1941–1943

[1] Mortenson estimated that these changes would reduce total route time by 25 percent. W. P. Mortenson, *Milk Distribution as a Public Utility* (University of Chicago Pres, Chicago, 1940), 46–50.

TABLE 86. Estimated route densities and potential route volumes for rural, secondary, and major markets under several systems of milk distribution.

Delivery system and type of market	Route density (quarts per mile)*	Potential route volume (quarts per day)†
Present systems		
Rural towns		
Daily delivery.............	7.0	268
Alternate-day..............	12.7	430
Secondary markets		
Daily delivery.............	8.1	280
Alternate-day..............	13.6	439
Major markets		
Daily delivery.............	9.3	290
Alternate-day..............	14.7	448
Exclusive territories		
Rural towns		
Daily delivery.............	11.6	349
Alternate-day..............	19.6	590
Secondary markets		
Daily delivery.............	31.2	414
Alternate-day..............	45.8	688
Major markets		
Daily delivery.............	69.7	441
Alternate-day..............	101.0	739
Municipal distribution		
Rural towns		
Daily delivery.............	12.5	356
Alternate-day..............	21.8	605
Secondary markets		
Daily delivery.............	39.0	424
Alternate-day..............	64.9	715
Major markets		
Daily delivery.............	91.3	447
Alternate-day..............	143.0	752

* Route densities in quarts per route mile based on data given in Table 23 for the present system, and on material presented in the Appendix for systems involving exclusive territories and municipal distribution. The density figures for reorganized systems are preliminary estimates.

† Estimated from regressions given in Fig. 54; volumes for reorganized systems are based on regressions III and IV.

period.[2] In the winter of 1941 these dealers were delivering on a daily basis, and had route densities averaging 8.2 quarts per route mile and route volumes averaging 303 quarts per day. Ac-

[2] Table 23.

cording to curve I in Fig. 54, the potential volume was about 281 quarts per day. Apparently the regressions underestimate actual performance slightly. The error is undoubtedly due to the over-simplification of the route-time functions, and probably in the time per mile. If all of the error is in this term, the discrepancies between the indicated and the true regressions will decrease with increases in density, and will be less than 5 quarts with route densities in excess of 50 quarts per mile.

Alternate-day delivery was introduced in Connecticut in the spring of 1942, and shortly thereafter route volumes had increased to 354 quarts with densities of 14.7 quarts per mile. One year later, loads averaged about 380 quarts and densities averaged 16.5 quarts per route mile. Potential volumes under alternate-day delivery, according to curve II, were about 450 quarts per day. The failure of actual load sizes to reach the potential levels reflected a lag in the adjustment to the new conditions. While a number of the larger dealers had fully exploited the possibilities of the program and had route volumes averaging around the potential levels, others made the shift more slowly and less completely. By 1946, Connecticut retail routes operated by the larger distributors were averaging 463 quarts and 511 total points,[3] and again the regressions appear to be somewhat conservative.

While estimates of potential route volumes may be made without difficulty when route densities are known, it is another matter to estimate the route volumes appropriate for any new system of milk distribution. The difficulty arises from the fact that route density and route volume are interdependent. As volume increases, the total number of trucks required for milk delivery will decrease and this will reduce the mileages traveled between plants and delivery areas. In other words, route density cannot be determined independently but tends to increase with increases in load size. As a result, estimates of route volumes under reorganized conditions must be obtained through a series of successive approximations.

To solve this problem, the logical development of the analysis must be interrupted. Before reorganization studies can be made, appropriate route volumes must be established; but before route

[3] See page 74.

volumes can be established, preliminary reorganization studies must be made to determine approximate levels of route densities that would characterize the reorganized systems. The procedure followed has been to make preliminary investigations on the basis of assumed maximum loads of 350 quarts with daily delivery and 450 quarts with alternate-day delivery, and to use the delivery densities so determined to establish more suitable route volumes.[4]

The results of this procedure are summarized in the lower sections of Table 86. Using the preliminary route densities, potential route volumes for daily delivery under a system of exclusive or allocated delivery territories would average about 350 quarts for rural markets, 415 quarts for secondary markets, and 440 quarts for major markets. Alternate-day routes could average about 590 quarts per day in rural markets, 690 quarts in secondary markets, and 740 quarts in major markets. If all deliveries were under the control of a single agency, as in the case of municipal distribution, potential daily delivery volumes would range from 355 to 445 quarts per day for the three groups of markets while alternate-day route volumes would range from 605 to 750 quarts per day. As already explained, these are only approximations to the true values, and the increased densities that would accompany loads of these sizes would permit still larger loads. In most cases the additional volume would be relatively small, however, for the regressions are quite flat in the higher density ranges.

In view of these results, the following maximum route volumes have been established for use in the reorganization studies:

	Daily delivery	Alternate-day delivery
Rural towns	325	550
Secondary markets	400	650
Major markets	450	700

[4] Daily delivery loads for rural areas were limited to 325 quarts. Because the nature of the reorganization studies will be discussed fully in following chapters, the details of the preliminary studies are given only in the Appendix.

While municipal distribution would permit slightly higher maximum loads than would exclusive territories, the same limits will be used for both systems. This does not mean that average route volumes will be identical under the two systems, however, for the large number of relatively small dealers in any market will prevent average volumes from reaching the potential levels under a system of exclusive territories. Finally, under certain types of reorganization, such as semiexclusive delivery territories, competitive sales activities will undoubtedly persist. Potential route volumes under such conditions will be represented by curves I and II in Fig. 54. For practical purposes, volumes of 350 quarts with daily delivery and 500 quarts with alternate-day delivery appear appropriate for secondary and major markets.

It should be noted that the route volumes adopted are conservative in the light of the potential levels. Two reasons may be given for this: (1) it seems better to err on the conservative side from the standpoint of the acceptance of the results by the industry; and (2) with loads in excess of 500 quarts, it will normally be necessary to return to the plant to drop off empty bottles and cases and to pick up a supplementary supply of milk. While the development of new trucks with larger capacities would make it possible to handle as much as 700 quarts on a single load, such equipment is not now available. Most routes under reorganized conditions will travel very short distances, but returning to the plant will require some time and so will reduce the potential route volumes somewhat.

Retail-delivery cost functions

Under the conditions that existed before the war, daily retail milk delivery cost about $0.041 per quart in urban Connecticut markets; in 1943, after the alternate-day delivery program had been in effect for some months, delivery costs had been reduced to approximately $0.036 per quart. The saving of nearly $0.005 per quart is not a true measure of the effectiveness of the alternate-day delivery program, however, for it combines the effects of increasing efficiency with those of increasing weekly earnings per man. This was a period when wages were generally rising and it was necessary to increase the earnings of routemen if home deliveries of milk were to be continued. In short, the wartime conservation program not only resulted in the above saving in unit delivery costs, but also permitted weekly earnings per man to increase by from 25 to 50 percent without an increase in dealers' margins.

In order to indicate the net effect of various reorganization schemes, it is necessary to hold weekly earnings constant. The level at which wages are assumed to remain, however, will influence the magnitude of the computed costs and savings. The ultimate saving that would have resulted from alternate-day delivery *if weekly earnings had remained at the prewar level* would have been about $0.014 per quart. On the other hand, if daily delivery had been reinstated after the war and *earnings remained at 1947 levels,* the increase in delivery costs would have averaged more than $0.023 cent per quart.

As has been indicated in Chapter 10, daily earnings of retail routemen in urban Connecticut markets averaged about $13.00 per day in 1947. This rate was increased 25 percent to allow for other payroll costs, and coupled with the basic time-requirement functions to give the following retail route labor cost equations:

$$C_{1d} = \$0.0415V + \$0.136D, \qquad (10.27)$$
$$C_{1a} = \$0.0272V + \$0.136D, \qquad (10.28)$$

where C_1 represents the daily labor cost for retail routes under the present system, V the daily route volume, D the daily miles traveled, and the subscripts d and a refer to daily and alternate-day delivery. Under reorganized systems, streamlined collection and soliciting operations would reduce these equations to

$$C'_{1d} = \$0.0350V + \$0.136D, \qquad (10.29)$$
$$C'_{1a} = \$0.0207V + \$0.136D. \qquad (10.30)$$

Note that all of these equations assume that earnings will vary with daily hours of work. If wage contracts require a fixed payment regardless of hours, then the cost equations would reduce to constants per day reflecting direct wages plus other payroll costs and allowances.

The cost studies reported in Chapter 9 indicated that, under 1947 conditions, truck costs for specialized retail milk-delivery trucks commonly used in urban markets could be represented by the equation

$$C_t = \$2.722 + \$0.0508D, \tag{9.6}$$

where C_t represents the truck costs per day and D the route miles per day. This equation refers specifically to daily-delivery conditions. Alternate-day operations would reduce some elements of truck costs, but expanding route volumes that accompany alternate-day delivery would tend to compensate for these reductions. As a consequence, equation (9.6) will be used to represent both daily and alternate-day delivery.

Combining these truck and labor cost equations, the daily costs of operating urban retail routes under 1947 Connecticut conditions can be approximated from the equations

$$C_d = \$2.722 + \$0.0415V + \$0.1868D, \tag{12.7}$$
$$C_a = \$2.722 + \$0.0272V + \$0.1868D. \tag{12.8}$$

With reorganized systems, and with 1947 wages and cost rates, these equations would be:

$$C'_d = \$2.722 + \$0.0350V + \$0.1868D, \tag{12.9}$$
$$C'_a = \$2.722 + \$0.0207V + \$0.1868D. \tag{12.10}$$

These combined cost equations, in turn, may be reduced to show average costs per quart delivered, as follows:

$$c_d = \$2.722/V + \$0.0415 + \$0.1868D/V, \tag{12.11}$$
$$c_a = \$2.722/V + \$0.0272 + \$0.1868D/V; \tag{12.12}$$
$$c'_d = \$2.722/V + \$0.0350 + \$0.1868D/V, \tag{12.13}$$
$$c'_a = \$2.722/V + \$0.0207 + \$0.1868D/V. \tag{12.14}$$

Since D/V is the reciprocal of delivery density in quarts per route mile, these equations indicate that retail-delivery costs per quart are inverse functions of route volume and route delivery density. Since the previous section has demonstrated that volume is also a function of delivery density, the unit cost equations are in reality inverse functions of route delivery density when volumes achieve the potential levels.

In these urban markets, cost savings stem from reduced route mileages and increased route volumes. In rural areas, on the other hand, the principal savings from reorganization programs stem from reduced route mileages and the freeing of unspecialized labor and equipment for uses not connected with milk delivery. Because rural milk delivery is frequently a sideline enterprise using unspecialized resources, it is difficult to establish significant measures of costs for these operations. Any solution must involve arbitrary allocations of labor and equipment costs between milk distribution and other farm or nonfarm enterprises, and should be interpreted with this in mind. For present purposes, these allocations have been made on the basis of the time devoted to milk distribution, with seven hours per day arbitrarily defined as the full-time equivalent.

According to the material presented in Chapters 9 and 10, truck costs and route time requirements for daily delivery in rural areas may be approximated from the following equations:[5]

$$C_{td} = \$0.52 \ + \$0.041D,$$
$$T_{rd} = \ 0.75V + \ 7.20D,$$

where T_r represents route time in minutes per day and the other letters represent the factors mentioned in the preceding paragraphs. To allocate fixed truck costs in proportion to a seven-hour day, the following modifications are necessary:

$$C_{td} = \frac{(\$0.52) \ (0.75V + 7.20D)}{420} + \$0.041D$$
$$= \ \$0.00093V + \$0.050D. \tag{12.15}$$

With route labor figured at a rate of $1.25 per hour, the route-time equation given above may be converted into the following daily labor cost equation:

$$C_{1d} = \$0.0158V + \$0.151D. \tag{10.32}$$

Combining the truck and labor cost equations:

$$C_d = \$0.01673V + \$0.201D, \tag{12.16}$$

or, in terms of average costs per quart of milk,

$$c_d = \$0.01673 + \$0.201D/V. \tag{12.17}$$

[5] Chapter 9, pp. 135–136 and Chapter 10, pp. 175–176.

In a similar fashion, and using the time function $T_{ra} = 0.5V + 7.2D$, costs under alternate-day delivery may be approximated by the use of the following equation:

$$c_a = \$0.01111 + \$0.201D/V. \qquad (12.18)$$

Note that these equations also involve the ratio D/V; in simple terms, they indicate that average delivery costs in rural areas are an inverse function of route delivery density.

It should be pointed out that the rural-area cost equations will tend to overestimate costs for large routes where total time requirements exceed seven hours per day. About 96 percent of all producer-dealers in Connecticut deliver less than 300 quarts daily, however, so errors involved in the use of these equations should be quite small.

Wholesale route time requirements and route volumes

The results of detailed studies of the time requirements on wholesale milk delivery routes were presented in Chapter 10. While time requirements were found to be a complex function involving many variables, the following equation may be accepted as a reasonable description under more or less typical urban conditions:

$$T = 111.32 + 2.640D + 3.958C + 0.346V + 1.531N, \qquad (10.26)$$

where T represents daily route time in minutes, D represents daily mileage, C represents the number of customers served, V represents the route volume in case equivalents, and N the total number of delivery trips from the truck to consumers' establishments.[6]

Under any given conditions, this equation may be used to estimate the time required to deliver a given quantity of milk or, conversely, the volume of milk that could be delivered in any given number of hours. Moreover, it is possible to convert this equation into simple functions defining either time or volume in

[6] Note, however, that this equation includes loading and unloading time as a constant 57 minutes per route. While our analysis failed to reveal any significant relations between route driver's loading and unloading time and such factors as route volume, it seems probable that marked increases in volume would be reflected in this item. As a consequence, time estimates for very large routes may be somewhat understated.

terms of market delivery densities. While these functions cannot be expected to represent conditions on particular routes with great accuracy, they may be used to approximate conditions for entire markets or for a number of routes operated by one dealer.

For purposes of illustration, consider the conditions that would apply to a market reorganization where all milk is to be handled on wholesale routes and where stores or depots will be evenly distributed over the market area so that no consumer will have to travel more than M miles to reach the nearest store. Under these conditions, average route mileage may be represented by the equation

$$D = 2M(C + 1), \tag{12.19}$$

for the average distance between stops will be approximately $2M$. In addition, we may define the number of customers (stores) as

$$C = V/S, \tag{12.20}$$

where V represents the route volume in cases and S the deliveries per customer in cases. Moreover, S may be expressed approximately in terms of the radius M of the area served by the store and K the density of total deliveries in cases per square mile:

$$S = 3.1416M^2K. \tag{12.21}$$

Substituting into the previous equation, we obtain:

$$C = \frac{V}{3.1416M^2K}, \tag{12.22}$$

$$D = \frac{2V}{3.1416MK} + 2M. \tag{12.23}$$

Finally, we may define N as

$$N = V/L, \tag{12.24}$$

where L represents the average number of cases per delivery trip.

If we substitute these in equation (10.26), we may redefine our time function in terms of the route volume V, the maximum distance M from households to nearest stores, the total density K in cases per square mile, and the number L of cases per delivery trip:

$$T = 111.32 + \frac{5.28V}{3.1416MK} + 5.28M + \frac{3.958V}{3.1416M^2K}$$

$$+ 0.346V + \frac{1.531V}{L}. \qquad (12.25)$$

This may be greatly simplified by substituting appropriate values for some of the variables. Previous sections have indicated that hand trucks are used to make deliveries at most large-volume stops; since the volume per stop will be large under the reorganization here discussed, we may reasonably assume that L will equal about 5 cases per trip. The decision as to the maximum distance that consumers will have to travel in order to reach the nearest store or depot is necessarily arbitrary, and we will use a value for M of 0.2 mile. This will mean that the average customer will travel about 700 feet to the nearest store. Finally, let us assume a working day of eight hours (excluding lunch stops) and derive an expression for route volumes. Such an equation is given below:

$$V = \frac{360.12}{39.891/K + 0.652}. \qquad (12.26)$$

This equation indicates that reasonable route volumes will increase at a decreasing rate with increases in delivery density. This tendency is represented graphically in Fig. 55. It may be noted that, with total market densities (as distinct from the delivery density for any single dealer) such as characterize Connecticut markets, reasonable route volumes would average about 110 cases for the typical secondary market and 340 cases for the average major market.

The pronounced increases in potential route volumes that accompany increases in delivery density per square mile reflect two main influences: (1) a decrease in the relative and absolute importance of distance and driving time; and (2) a pronounced increase in the volume per store under the conditions stated, and the accompanying decrease in the number of customer stops per route. With a delivery density of 20 cases per square mile, the average wholesale route could handle about 135 cases and would travel roughly 22 miles while serving 54 customers. With a den-

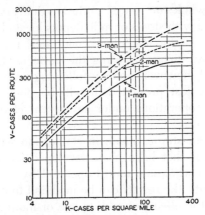

Fig. 55. Effect of delivery density on the volume of milk that can be delivered by wholesale routes in eight hours.

sity of 200 cases per square mile and with exclusive delivery areas, however, the typical route could deliver about 430 cases to 17 customers and would travel only about 7 miles per day. The effects of delivery density on the number of customers per route and the average volume per customer *under the conditions that have already been stated* are shown in Fig. 56.

It should be emphasized that these results are given as illustrations of the application of the route-time functions, and that they refer specifically to an assumed situation involving the delivery

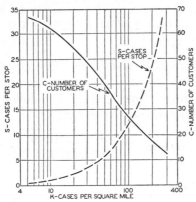

Fig. 56. Effects of delivery density on the number of customers per route and the volume per customer for one-man wholesale routes.

of all milk on wholesale routes, exclusive delivery territories for each dealer, and with stores or milk depots located approximately every 0.4 mile. Under any other conditions, the results would differ from those given. By using the basic relations that have been developed, however, and by following methods essentially similar to those just presented, it will be possible to describe wholesale-route operations under any given set of actual or assumed conditions.

While the field studies made in connection with this project and the relations that have been developed from these studies refer directly to wholesale routes operated by the delivery man without assistants, the results can be modified to indicate at least approximately the effects of adding one or more assistants. This may be done by considering the details of time requirements for the several operations and indicating how they might be expected to change under revised conditions. Certain elements, such as driving time per mile, will be unaffected by the addition of route assistants. On the other hand, such elements as the time required to carry the milk from the truck to the stores may be expected to vary inversely with the number of men.

Following this general procedure, equation (10.26) has been converted into expressions giving approximate time requirements for two- and three-man routes.[7]

Two-man: $T = 68.86 + 2.640D + 3.339C + 0.182V$
$$+ 1.146N, \qquad (12.27)$$

Three-man: $T = 55.04 + 2.640D + 3.223C + 0.093V$
$$+ 0.637N. \qquad (12.28)$$

These have in turn been transformed into equations describing potential or reasonable route volumes under the conditions assumed in the previous paragraphs. The following results are directly comparable with equation (12.23):

$$\text{Two-man:} \quad V = \frac{412.08}{34.996/K + 0.411}, \qquad (12.29)$$

$$\text{Three-man:} \quad V = \frac{425.90}{34.043/K + 0.220}. \qquad (12.30)$$

[7] See Appendix for details of time allocations.

Curves representing these relations have been included in Fig. 55, and indicate that both the absolute and the relative effects of adding route helpers increase with increases in delivery density. As a result, the two- and three-man curves show less tendency to flatten off in the high density ranges. Under conditions typical of secondary markets in Connecticut, potential daily volumes would be approximately 150 cases for two-man routes and 170 cases for three-man routes, as compared with 110 cases for one-man routes. In major markets, on the other hand, potential daily route volumes would be approximately 540 cases and 760 cases for two- and three-man routes respectively and 340 cases for one-man routes.

Wholesale delivery cost functions

In Chapter 9, simplified cost equations were developed for wholesale trucks with capacities varying from 3 to 10 tons. These equations are repeated below, where C represents daily truck costs assuming 300 days of operation annually, D the route mileage per day, and the subscripts refer to truck capacity in tons:

$$C_3 = \$2.979 + \$0.0368D, \qquad (9.9)$$
$$C_4 = \$3.159 + \$0.0450D, \qquad (9.10)$$
$$C_6 = \$4.287 + \$0.0588D, \qquad (9.11)$$
$$C_{10} = \$5.775 + \$0.0707D. \qquad (9.12)$$

In a similar way, Chapter 10 developed a simplified expression for wholesale route-time requirements, and converted this to a labor cost function by applying suitable wage rates:

$$C_1 = \$3.62 + \$0.086D + \$0.129V + \$0.050B, \quad (10.31)$$

where C_1 represents the daily labor cost, D the route miles, V the route volume in case equivalents, and B the number of delivery trips from the truck to delivery points in stores and other establishments.

Assuming that 70 percent of route loads are in paper containers and the balance in glass (the average for the routes studied), the maximum effective loads for the several truck sizes would be approximately: 3-ton trucks, 144 cases; 4-ton trucks, 192 cases; 6-ton trucks, 288 cases; and 10-ton trucks, 480 cases. With these limits, it will be possible to select the appropriate truck cost equation, combine it with the labor cost equation, and so obtain an expression for combined wholesale delivery costs. The four equations are given below, where the subscripts identify maximum route volumes in case equivalents:

$$C_{144} = \$6.599 + \$0.1228D + \$0.129V + \$0.050B, \quad (12.31)$$
$$C_{192} = \$6.779 + \$0.1310D + \$0.129V + \$0.050B, \quad (12.32)$$
$$C_{288} = \$7.907 + \$0.1448D + \$0.129V + \$0.050B, \quad (12.33)$$
$$C_{480} = \$9.395 + \$0.1567D + \$0.129V + \$0.050B. \quad (12.34)$$

Each of these may be converted to an average cost equation by dividing all terms by V, of course, and again these conversions will indicate that average delivery costs are — directly or indirectly — an inverse function of delivery density.

Optimum plant size

As was pointed out in Chapter 8, the optimum organization of distribution involves a balancing off of plant and delivery costs to determine the least-cost combination. In general, long-run plant costs per quart will decrease with increases in the volume handled. But increasing plant volume means an expanding delivery area, with consequent increases in average route miles, decreases in average route volume, and increases in average delivery costs. With the information now available, it is possible to state these relations as specific functions and so to indicate optimum plant volumes under various conditions.

In order to develop these functions, it is necessary to determine the relations between plant volume, size of delivery area, and average length of delivery route. While these relations will depend on the particular street and delivery patterns for any market, present purposes may be served by expressing the area as an approximate function of the volume and the delivery density per square mile, and then determining the appropriate relation between delivery density per square mile and per mile of street. The ideal delivery area served by a plant will be approximately circular, with radius given by the following formula:[8]

[8] Considering a number of plants in an area with constant delivery density, the plant delivery areas would be hexagonal. The derivations above would not be greatly changed, however, by this modification.

$$R = \frac{P^{\frac{1}{2}}}{(\pi S)^{\frac{1}{2}}}, \qquad (12.35)$$

where R represents the radius in miles, P the daily plant volume in quarts, and S the delivery density in quarts per square mile.

The average distance from the plant to customers in this area would be $2R/3$, and this may be used as the approximate one-way distance traveled by routes between the plant and the route delivery areas. The average length of route may then be represented by:

$$D = \frac{4R}{3} + \frac{HV}{M}, \qquad (12.36)$$

where D represents the distance traveled in miles, V the daily route volume in quarts, M the market delivery density in quarts per street mile, and H a ratio representing unavoidable route duplication.[9] Substituting for R, the equation giving the average length of route will be:

$$D = \frac{4P^{\frac{1}{2}}}{3(\pi S)^{\frac{1}{2}}} + \frac{HV}{M}. \qquad (12.37)$$

In an earlier section, average retail costs for daily delivery under present conditions were described as inverse functions of route volume and delivery densities per route mile:

$$c_d = \$2.722/V + \$0.0415 + \$0.1868D/V. \qquad (12.11)$$

Substituting for D, we obtain:

$$c_d = \$2.722/V + \$0.042 + \$0.14052P^{\frac{1}{2}}/VS$$
$$+ \$0.1868H/M. \qquad (12.38)$$

Long-run average plant costs, on the other hand, may be represented by:[10]

$$c_p = \$21.00/P + \$0.01743 - \$0.0000000388P, \qquad (11.1a)$$

[9] With daily delivery, this constant is $1.0 + h$, where h represents unavoidable route duplication in relative terms. Detailed studies in sample markets indicate that H would have values of approximately $1.40 - 0.001M$. With alternate-day delivery, values would be exactly half of the daily-delivery values.

[10] Based on equation (11.1). This function holds approximately for the range between 5,000 and 150,000 quarts per day. For smaller volumes, costs indicated by Fig. 54 should be used.

where P has been expressed in quarts rather than thousand quarts. Finally, these two may be added together to obtain an expression for combined costs per quart:

$$c_c = \$2.722/V + \$0.05893 + \$0.14052P^{0.5}/VS^{0.5}$$
$$+ \$0.186H/M - \$0.0000000388P + \$21.00/P. \quad (12.39)$$

This equation represents daily delivery; the alternate-day delivery equation would be identical except that the constant term would be reduced from \$0.05943 to \$0.04463. In this combined cost equation, all unknowns other than P have values that may be

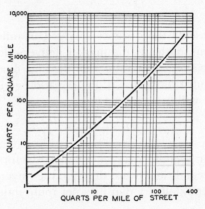

Fig. 57. Relation between delivery density per mile of street and per square mile, sample Connecticut markets.

determined in any particular case. If delivery density in quarts per street mile is known, a measure readily determined for any market, V may be approximated in a manner already described.[11] Figure 57 shows the approximate relation between delivery density per street mile and per square mile.[12] In short, for any given market with known delivery density, the combined costs per quart for plant and delivery operations may be expressed as a function of total plant volume.

It will be observed that the delivery cost function indicates that average costs increase with plant volume but at a decreasing

[11] See Figs. 54, 80, and 81.
[12] Based on data for the 24 sample markets. The standard error of estimate for this regression is about 26 percent.

rate. The rate of increase will be a function of density, with relatively rapid increases in costs in low-density areas and vice versa. Plant costs, on the other hand, decrease at a decreasing rate with increases in plant volume. As a consequence, combined costs will be nearly constant over wide volume ranges. This is illustrated for a low-density situation ($M = 10$ quarts per mile of street) in Fig. 58. Even with this low density, delivery costs under a consolidated system would not increase rapidly. Combined costs decline sharply with plant-volume increases in the ranges below 1,000 quarts, but then the cost curve flattens out and average costs

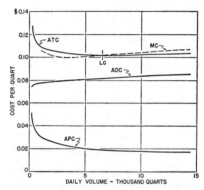

Fig. 58. Effect of volume on long-run plant and daily delivery costs when density averages 10 quarts per mile of street APC — average plant cost; ADC — average delivery cost; ATC — average total cost, the sum of plant plus delivery costs; MC — marginal combined cost; and LC — the least cost point.

are nearly constant over the range from 4,000 to 15,000 quarts per day. Corresponding to this flat average-cost curve, the long-run marginal-cost curve is not steeply inclined.[13] The minimum point on the average curve occurs at a volume of approximately 6,500 quarts, but as indicated above there are wide ranges above and below this point where combined costs would be only a small fraction of a cent above the minimum.

With higher densities, the delivery-cost curves would be even less steeply inclined and combined-cost curves would have less

[13] Note that the first derivatives of the average combined cost equations are complex functions that can only be solved by successive approximation to determine least-cost points.

clearly defined minimums. As a matter of fact, with densities as high as 30 quarts per street mile with daily delivery and 60 quarts per mile with alternate-day delivery, the combined average cost functions will have negative inclination throughout the entire range of observed volume. This is illustrated in Fig. 59, where the combined-cost equations summarized in Table 87 are shown graphically.

In considering these results, it should be remembered that rural markets have been defined as towns where less than 30 quarts of milk were delivered per mile of street, secondary markets as those with densities ranging from 30 to 119 quarts per mile, and major markets as those with densities of 120 quarts or more per mile of street. In Connecticut, rural markets typically had total volumes of less than 3,000 quarts per day in 1940, secondary markets ranged from 2,500 to 10,000 quarts daily, while major markets had volumes ranging up to 55,000 quarts. In all cases, then, these markets would fall within the range of decreasing average combined costs, indicating that retail milk distribution could be most advantageously carried on from a single consolidated plant. In fact, where a number of secondary and major markets form a contiguous area, the combined volume for the group of towns could most economically be handled by a single plant.

The above calculations have been based on urban rather than rural cost regressions for low-density markets. While the rural regressions that have been developed are appropriate for individual distributors that make only part-time use of nonspecialized labor and equipment, they do not seem appropriate under a consolidated or unified system and so the urban regressions have been used. With these regressions, the minimum-cost points on the average-combined-cost curves fall well beyond the actual volume handled in any of the rural Connecticut markets. The average delivery density for the 125 rural towns in Connecticut was only 10.3 quarts per street mile in 1940. According to Figs. 58 and 59, optimum volume with a density of 10 quarts per street mile would be about 6,500 quarts per day with daily delivery and nearly 10,000 quarts per day with alternate-day delivery. Since these towns averaged only 540 quarts per day, it is clear that a great many towns could be served from a single plant and that

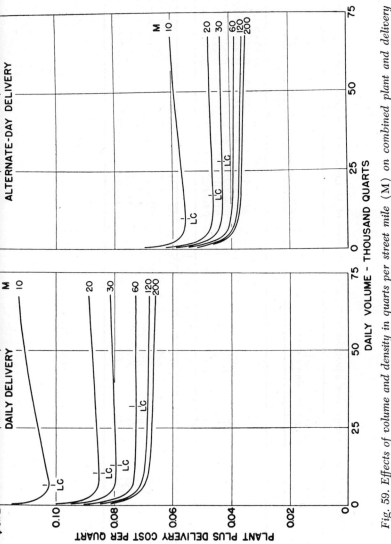

Fig. 59. Effects of volume and density in quarts per street mile (M) on combined plant and delivery costs.

TABLE 87. Combined average cost equations with indicated levels of M, the density in quarts per mile of street.

M (quarts per mile of street)	V* (quarts per route)	S† (quarts per square mile)	H‡ Duplication ratio	Combined average cost equations**
				Daily delivery
10	352	21	1.39	$C = \$0.092628 + \$0.0008709P^{1/4} + \$21.00/P - \$0.0000000388P$
20	393	55	1.38	$C = 0.078745 + 0.00004821P^{1/4} + 21.00/P - 0.0000000388P$
30	407	88	1.37	$C = 0.074149 + 0.00003680P^{1/4} + 21.00/P - 0.0000000388P$
60	427	240	1.34	$C = 0.069477 + 0.00002125P^{1/4} + 21.00/P - 0.0000000388P$
120	440	700	1.28	$C = 0.067109 + 0.00001207P^{1/4} + 21.00/P - 0.0000000388P$
200	448	1,620	1.20	$C = 0.066127 + 0.00000779P^{1/4} + 21.00/P - 0.0000000388P$
				Alternate-day delivery
10	600	21	0.695	$C = 0.050950 + 0.00005110P^{1/4} + 21.00/P - 0.0000000388P$
20	656	55	.690	$C = 0.044023 + 0.00002888P^{1/4} + 21.00/P - 0.0000000388P$
30	683	88	.685	$C = 0.041681 + 0.00002193P^{1/4} + 21.00/P - 0.0000000388P$
60	717	240	.670	$C = 0.039312 + 0.00001265P^{1/4} + 21.00/P - 0.0000000388P$
120	743	700	.640	$C = 0.038090 + 0.00000715P^{1/4} + 21.00/P - 0.0000000388P$
200	754	1,620	.600	$C = 0.037600 + 0.00000463P^{1/4} + 21.00/P - 0.0000000388P$

* Based on Fig. 54.
† Based on Fig. 57.
‡ $H = 1.40 - 0.001M$.
** Derived from equation (12.39) and the corresponding alternate-day delivery function.

not more than six or seven plants would be required to serve all of these towns with minimum costs under alternate-day delivery.

The logical solution in this case would be to have the rural areas served by routes originating at plants located in the secondary and major markets. If a municipal system were to be established in the typical rural town, combined costs with alternate-day delivery would average about $0.072 per quart. If a single central plant served 15 or 20 towns of this size, costs would average about $0.058 per quart and the area served would not exceed 15 miles in radius. The *added* or marginal cost of handling deliveries in these rural towns from plants located in nearby urban markets, however, would be approximately $0.055 at a distance of 5 miles, $0.058 at 10 miles, and $0.061 at 15 miles.[14] Comparing these added costs with the averages for systems based on rural plants, and remembering the wide geographic distribution of urban markets, there appear to be very few areas in Connecticut where rural plants would be as economical as distribution from nearby urban markets.

Some simplifications

The foregoing material may now be summarized into a relatively simple set of procedures to be followed in making synthetic studies of the effects of several types of milk-distribution reorganization on physical inputs and economic costs. Two general types of reorganization study will be made: (1) maintaining all existing dealers in business but allocating markets into areas within which a single dealer will have exclusive delivery rights; and (2) centralizing all milk distribution in the hands of a public or private agency. In the first type, the original step will be to allocate the market among the several dealers. From that point on, the procedures in both types of study will be essentially similar. The maximum route volumes developed in a previous section will be used to determine the number of routes required. Hypothetical delivery routes will then be mapped to determine mileage requirements. Delivery-route costs will be computed on the basis

---

[14] These cost levels could be further reduced by a system of distribution "substations," with large-volume transport from plant to substation and delivery routes originating at each substation.

of the number of routes, the average volume, and the number of miles required for daily and alternate-day delivery.

Potential plant costs will be estimated from the long-run cost curve presented in Chapter 11. In the case of exclusive territories, plant volumes will be equal to the volumes handled by the existing dealers. In reorganizations involving some form of municipal distribution, plant volumes will be equal to the entire volume of the market. Only one plant will be used in each market, since optimum volumes exceed the actual volumes of Connecticut markets by a considerable margin. Where sample towns constitute a single metropolitan district, one central plant will serve the entire district.

As a practical matter, some simplifications to the theoretical procedures will be made. Several of these have to do with the manner of allocating exclusive delivery territories. While all dealers should be included in this system of allocations, the problem of tracing through the interactions would become very complex as the number of dealers increased. As a consequence, the smaller dealers in each market have been assigned territories adjacent to their plants on an informal and fairly arbitrary basis. The remaining larger dealers have been included in a theoretical allocation, and the theoretical areas have then been modified slightly to conform with outstanding physical characteristics of the district.

In some markets a number of dealers' plants are located outside of the regular market area. In such cases, allocations have been based not on the location of the plants but on the points where routes originating at the several plants would normally enter the market. In most secondary markets, for example, these focal points are the main roads entering the town. Allocations will be based on these points, and the market divided into major segments. Within these major subdivisions, allocations will then be made to the individual dealers. These may follow more or less arbitrary lines as long as the areas are contiguous and include milk deliveries equal to the volumes actually handled by the dealers involved. Some savings in mileage and costs will result if the smaller dealers within these major subdivisions are assigned areas at the edge of the market while the larger dealers are allocated territories near the center of the market.

The procedures to be used in determining hypothetical route mileages may also be simplified. Detailed mapping may be confined to a sample area of the market. Within this area, the mapping will reveal the unavoidable duplication of the delivery sections of routes. This ratio may then be applied to the miles of streets to estimate total delivery miles, while average hauling miles may be estimated on the basis of the average distance from the plant to the route delivery areas. While estimates made in this way will fail to consider some of the local conditions that would result in larger or smaller amounts of route duplication, they will give very close approximations to the results of the more detailed procedures when a whole market is considered.

The essential theoretical and empirical groundwork is now complete. In Part Four the methods and relations developed will be applied to the sample Connecticut markets. Results of the sample studies will then be generalized to indicate the probable effects of reorganization programs in other markets.

PART FOUR ———

SYNTHETIC STUDIES OF
MILK DISTRIBUTION

13 —

EXCLUSIVE DELIVERY
TERRITORIES

Exclusive delivery territories

The duplication of delivery routes characteristic of fluid-milk markets was described in Part Two of this report. Part Three pointed out that such duplication could be reduced by an exchange of customers among distributors, and that the logical extension of such a program would be the systematic allocation of the market into delivery territories within which the most advantageously located distributor would have exclusive delivery rights. If such allocations are to maintain the present volume of business for all distributors and at the same time reduce route travel as much as possible, the exclusive territories must be assigned in a particular way. Chapter 8 developed the principles for such efficient allocations, and the present chapter applies them to milk delivery in the sample Connecticut markets.

Mileage and route requirements with exclusive territories in rural towns[1]

With only a few modifications, the allocation of exclusive delivery territories to dealers in rural areas has followed the general principles established in Part Three. In most cases dealers handling less than 100 quarts per day were assigned compact areas adjacent to their plants in a more or less arbitrary fashion, while

[1] The towns of Orange, Woodbridge, and North Haven have been included as part of the New Haven metropolitan market, and are not discussed in this section.

theoretical allocations similar to those discussed in Chapter 8 were made only for the larger dealers. In some of the sample towns, dealers delivering in the town but with plants located outside were not included in the allocation if it was feasible to indicate an exchange of volume between these dealers and dealers with plants located in the town. This was justified by the fact that town lines frequently do not conform with actual market boundaries, and was consistent with the allocations that would have been made if complete sections of the state had been studied in detail. Such exchanges reduced route duplication and, in some cases, reduced the number of dealers that would serve a particular town.

Within the allocated territories, revised routes were laid out on the basis of maximum loads of 325 quarts with daily delivery and 550 quarts with alternate-day delivery unless the existing routes were already operating with higher volumes. Only a few dealers in rural areas handled total volumes in excess of these levels. In the 14 towns studied in detail, 50 dealers handled volumes of less than 50 quarts per day, 19 dealers delivered between 50 and 99 quarts daily, 8 dealers ranged between 100 and 199 quarts, and 8 dealers between 200 and 325 quarts. Only three other dealers operated in these towns, and their daily volumes were 406 quarts, 641 quarts, and 703 quarts. In view of these volumes, it is clear that the preliminary reorganization studies based on maximum loads of 325 quarts with daily delivery and 450 quarts with alternate-day delivery will not differ significantly from the final reorganizations.[2] The preliminary results, therefore, have been used for the rural markets without further revision.

The nature of milk-route organization within the exclusive delivery territories may be illustrated by the details for the Chester–Essex–Saybrook area. Examination of the route map in Fig. 60 will indicate how a number of small dealers have been allocated areas around their plants that permit deliveries with very low route mileages. The areas for larger dealers will permit loop-type routes in the sparsely populated sections of the market or concentrated routes in districts where population and milk-delivery densities were relatively high. A comparison of this map

[2] See the Appendix to Chapter 12.

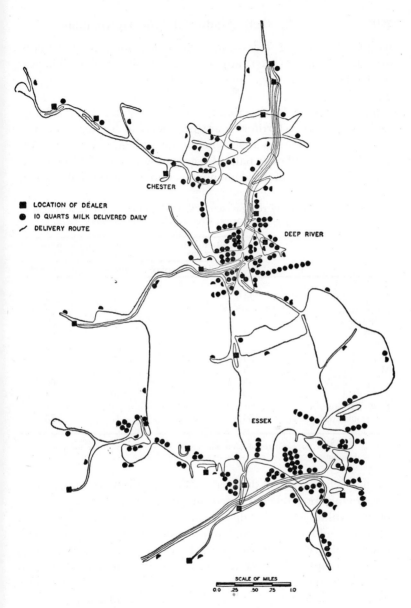

LOCATION OF DEALER
10 QUARTS MILK DELIVERED DAILY
DELIVERY ROUTE

CHESTER

DEEP RIVER

ESSEX

SCALE OF MILES
0.0   .25   .50   .75   1.0

Fig. 60. Reorganized routes in Saybrook area under exclusive territory system. Compare with Fig. 7.

with the map in Fig. 7 showing the system of milk routes actually operating in the Saybrook area in 1942 will give striking evidence of the potential savings inherent in such a reorganization program.

Summary statistics describing milk delivery under a system of exclusive delivery territories are presented in Table 88 for the sample rural towns. In areas where only a few quarts of milk are delivered per road mile, natural segregation has resulted in a considerable amount of local monopoly under the present system,

TABLE 88. Estimates of reorganized milk-route mileages under a system of exclusive delivery territories, Connecticut rural markets, 1942.

Town	Reorganized route miles per day		Percent reduction from present daily delivery*	
	Daily	Alternate-day	Daily	Alternate-day
Ashford............	5	3	0	40
Bridgewater.........	26	17	0	35
Harwinton..........	31	22	0	29
Willington..........	25	13	4	50
Brookfield..........	32	20	54	71
Ellington............	44	25	20	55
Somers..............	40	21	46	72
Mansfield...........	85	46	28	61
Old Saybrook.......	55	35	38	60
Ridgefield..........	86	44	50	74
East Windsor.......	81	44	47	71
Saybrook area......	136	70	47	73

* See Table 10 for estimates of route miles with daily delivery under the present system of distribution.

so that delivery routes duplicate little if at all. As a consequence, a reorganization scheme based on exclusive territories would be of little value. As market density increases, however, the potential effects would be more and more pronounced. Compared with daily delivery under the present system, exclusive territories would permit mileage reductions averaging about 50 percent with daily delivery and 75 percent with alternate-day delivery as market density approaches 30 quarts per road mile.

While exclusive territories would reduce route hours materially in most rural towns, the total number of routes would not be greatly affected. As has been pointed out, most dealers in these rural towns handle relatively small volumes, far less than a complete load for a delivery truck. Consequently, there will be very few opportunities for route consolidation in any program that maintains all dealers in business. For the sample towns, daily delivery under the present system involved 94 truck routes with an average daily volume of only 79 quarts per route. Daily delivery with a program of exclusive territories could reduce this number to 83, partially through reducing the number of dealers allotted to the sample areas, while alternate-day delivery would permit added consolidations in several cases so that the number of routes could be reduced to 81. In addition, "skip-day" operations could reduce the number of days that many routes operate, thus freeing manpower and equipment for alternative uses on the farms and in the plants of these dealers.

The Torrington market

To determine the effects of the elimination of all unnecessary duplication of delivery routes, the Torrington milk market was divided into 36 exclusive delivery territories corresponding to the 36 dealers included in the detailed study. The results of this allocation are illustrated in Fig. 61; each area contains a volume of milk equal to the present volume of the dealer in question. The market was first divided into five major areas corresponding to the four main roads by which producer-dealers entered the market and to one large plant that is centrally located. These theoretical allocations are indicated by the dotted lines in the diagram, while the focal points used in determining the allocations are indicated by five stars. Actual allocations of these five main areas deviated somewhat from the theoretical in order to follow such natural divisions as railroads, streams, parks, and the layout of streets. Within the main divisions, individual dealer areas were established as explained in Chapter 12. These dealer areas could be shifted within the main allocations without affecting delivery mileages greatly.

The allocations were based on all deliveries, both wholesale and retail. Hypothetical delivery routes with maximum volumes of approximately 400 quarts with daily delivery and 650 quarts with alternate-day delivery were then mapped in detail and necessary delivery distances determined. With daily delivery, 48 retail and mixed routes could serve the market by traveling 233 miles between plants and delivery areas and 110 miles within the exclusive delivery areas, or a total of 343 miles daily.[3] This would

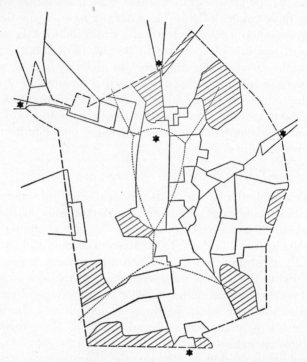

Fig. 61. Allocation of the Torrington urban market into exclusive delivery territories. Dotted lines represent the theoretical allocation into five major areas. Stars indicate focal points for the theoretical allocation. Solid lines represent modifications to the theoretical areas and the division of the major areas into delivery territories for individual dealers.

represent a reduction of 75 percent below daily-delivery mileages with the existing system. With alternate-day delivery, 42 routes would be adequate and would require roughly 224 miles per day hauling and 55 miles delivering, or a total of 279 miles per day.

[3] All routes were planned as retail or mixed routes. As a practical matter, one and possibly two of the dealers could (and do) use one or more fairly large wholesale routes. This explains why the number of routes with exclusive territories and daily delivery appears to be slightly larger than the number under the existing organization.

However, 29 dealers had total volumes small enough to operate on a "skip-day" schedule, whereby they would deliver to all customers on one day and make no deliveries on the following day. While this poses some problems in the plant and necessitates holding half of the milk at the plant for an extra 24-hour period, it has been adopted by many small dealers and producer-dealers in Connecticut. With "skip-day" operations for the 29 handlers already mentioned, alternate-day delivery would require about 135 miles daily in hauling, 55 miles in delivering, or a total of 190 miles per day. Compared with present alternate-day delivery mileages, this represents a potential saving of 78 percent. The

TABLE 89. Unavoidable delivery-route duplication in the exclusive areas described for the Torrington milk market.

Unavoidable duplication (percent)*	Number of areas
0– 19.....................	11
20– 39.....................	9
40– 59.....................	6
60– 79.....................	2
80–100.....................	8

* Miles traveled within area in excess of street mileage, expressed as percent of street mileage. Hauling distances have not been included.

over-all reduction from daily delivery under the present organization to alternate-day with exclusive delivery territories would be about 86 percent.

Because so many dealers are located outside the urban district, the mileage reduction in Torrington is smaller than would be the case for a market with more centrally located plants. With daily delivery, the exclusive areas would permit deliveries with 343 miles of truck travel on 82 miles of streets, or a ratio of more than four to one. If hauling mileages are disregarded, the actual delivery travel totals 110 miles, or about one-third more than the street mileage. This represents unavoidable duplication and backtracking of the routes. For individual areas (or dealers), this unavoidable duplication would range from zero to 100 percent, with two-thirds of the cases falling below 50 percent (Table 89).

The mileage reduction for any particular dealer would depend primarily on the location of his plant with reference to the urban market, on his volume per route, on the concentration of his present deliveries, and on the delivery density in the exclusive area assigned to him. Because of variations in these factors, mileage savings for individual dealers under the plan just described would range from 48 to 96 percent. Plant location is especially important in Torrington because most of the handlers are located outside of the urban district. In general, each added mile from market reduced potential mileage savings by about 4 percent, with some tendency for the effect to become less important as distance increased.[4]

The Willimantic market

To determine the minimum mileage necessary to deliver milk in Willimantic, the market was first divided into seven sections

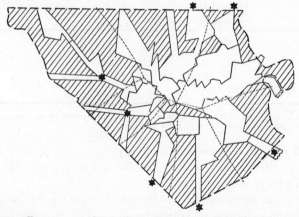

Fig. 62. *Allocation of the Willimantic urban market into exclusive delivery territories. Dotted lines represent the theoretical allocation into seven major areas. Stars indicate focal points for the theoretical allocation. Solid lines represent the suggested modifications of the theoretical areas and the division of the major areas into delivery territories for individual dealers. Shaded areas are districts where there are no milk deliveries.*

corresponding to the seven main roads by which dealers entered the city. In Fig. 62 the dotted lines indicate these seven theoretical areas. The stars indicate the points at which the dealers enter the city. After the theoretical areas were determined they were modified slightly so that natural barriers such as bridges, rail-

[4] See the Appendix for a more detailed analysis of the effects of location and other factors on potential mileage savings.

roads, and street layouts would not hinder the actual operation of milk routes. Within the seven main divisions 22 separate areas, indicated by the solid lines, were drawn giving each dealer an amount of milk equal to his total volume. Five dealers were allocated areas outside the city limits. The allocations of the individual areas within the main divisions were quite arbitrary and shifts could be made without materially affecting the mileage traveled. All allocations were based on both retail and wholesale deliveries, and routes were planned with maximum loads of 400 quarts with daily delivery and 650 quarts with alternate-day delivery.

In this study delivery routes for only a few dealers were laid out and actually measured. This was done to determine the amount of necessary duplication caused by one-way streets and street layout that would necessitate backtracking. The necessary duplication was found to be about 40 percent, or for every mile of street 1.4 miles had to be covered in making delivery. In determining delivery mileage, this percentage was then applied to the street mileage within each dealer's area. Hauling mileages to dealers' areas were actually measured.

With daily delivery in these exclusive territories, 33 retail and mixed routes would travel a total of 187 miles. This is a reduction of 73 percent from daily delivery under the present system. Of the 187 miles, 103 would be covered in hauling to and from areas and 84 represented delivery miles. With alternate-day delivery, 28 routes would be operated but they would travel 132 miles daily. Hauling would require 90 miles and delivery 42 miles daily.

Twenty dealers had enough excess truck and labor capacity to permit delivery on a "skip-day" basis. With these on "skip-day" delivery and other dealers on alternate-day delivery, 57 miles would be required in hauling and 42 miles in delivering for a total of 99 miles. This represents a reduction of 86 percent below daily delivery under present conditions, exactly the same as for the Torrington market.

The effects of exclusive territories on mileage reductions varied greatly from dealer to dealer depending on such factors as plant location, volume, and present and reorganized delivery densities. Comparing the mileages required for daily delivery, reductions resulting from exclusive territories would range from 25 to 92 percent. With many plants located beyond the limits of the urban market, plant location was especially important. Increased distance from market reduced mileage savings at a rate averaging about 6 percent per mile. This is somewhat more pronounced than in the Torrington market as a result of lower average volumes per route, lower revised densities, and higher densities under the present organization.[5]

The Hartford market

To illustrate the effects of exclusive delivery territories in a major market, the city of Hartford was allocated into dealer areas and reorganized milk-delivery requirements were calculated. Exclusive areas were not assigned, however, for all of the 149 dealers that were delivering milk in Hartford in 1940. Any program of this type would include suburban areas as well as the city, and most of the dealers located outside of the city limits would be allocated areas in their localities. Data were not available to make such a complete allocation for the greater Hartford market, but it so happened that the 20 merchant- and producer-dealers (and their sub-dealers) who had plants within the city limits handled a total Class I volume approximately equal to the total fluid-milk consumption in the city.[6] Only these plants have been included in the allocation, although it is recognized that a complete allocation for the metropolitan district would undoubtedly involve the extension of the areas for some Hartford plants into adjacent towns and a counterbalancing allocation of Hartford territory to some plants located beyond the city limits.

The results of this theoretical allocation are shown in Fig. 63. In determining these areas, 15 of the smaller plants were arbitrarily assigned compact territories in their immediate vicinities. The remaining five plants were used to determine theoretical boundaries that would minimize transportation requirements. Final allocations for these plants followed the theoretical patterns with minor variations to allow for such natural characteristics as parks, rivers, and main streets.

[5] See the Appendix.
[6] A total of 54,184 quarts daily as compared to the Board of Health total of 52,497 quarts.

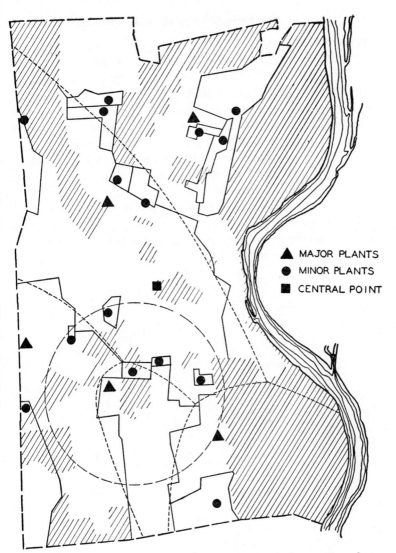

▲ MAJOR PLANTS

● MINOR PLANTS

■ CENTRAL POINT

Fig. 63. Theoretical allocation of the city of Hartford into 20 exclusive milk-delivery territories. The 15 small dealers represented by circles were arbitrarily assigned areas in their immediate vicinities. The remaining five large dealers, represented by triangles, were used as focal points for a theoretical allocation designed to reduce hauling distances to a minimum. This allocation is indicated by the smooth dashed lines. The final allocations for these handlers were modified to allow for such factors as parks, railroads, and major streets. The circular area in the southern part of the city represents the sample for which detailed route reorganizations were planned. Shading shows areas where there were no milk deliveries.

With maximum route loads of 450 quarts, total deliveries in
Hartford are roughly equivalent to 120 retail routes under daily-
delivery conditions. To plan in detail the organization of all of
these routes would be a complicated and unnecessary process. As
an alternative, theoretical routes were mapped for a sample area
and necessary route duplication was determined. Estimates of
total route requirements for the entire city were then based on
hauling distances from plants, miles of streets on which deliveries
were to be made, and the percentage of unavoidable duplication
as determined in the sample area.

A sample area for detailed mapping was selected in the southern half of the city. This area, 2 miles in diameter, was chosen because it contained a variety of street and density conditions and

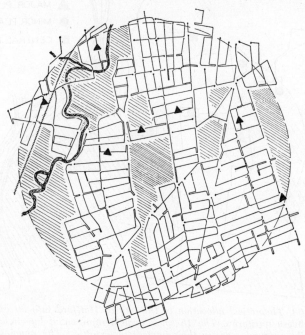

*Fig. 64. Detailed route organization in a sample area to show unavoidable
duplication under a system of exclusive delivery territories. Only the delivery
sections of the routes have been shown, it being assumed that the trucks
would travel to and from the plant by the most convenient streets. On 59
miles of streets included in this area, the delivery sections of the routes
would require 67 miles to make daily deliveries, or an unavoidable duplication of about 14 percent.*

included parts of the allocated territories for a number of large and small dealers. Route organizations are indicated in Fig. 64, where only delivery sections of the routes have been shown. It is clear that some duplication of the delivery sections of routes would be unavoidable even under these optimum conditions. This results from such factors as one-way and dead-end streets and the occasional paralleling of adjoining routes. For the sample area, embracing more than 50 routes, it would have required 67 miles of route delivery travel to serve customers on 59 miles of streets. This represents unavoidable duplication of the delivery portions of routes equivalent to 14 percent of the street mileage.

Estimates of reorganized delivery mileages for the entire market are given in Table 90. These are based on the assumption that all milk would be delivered by retail or mixed routes and that loads would average 450 quarts with daily delivery and 700 quarts with alternate-day operations. Daily delivery would require a total of 122 routes traveling a total of 437 miles per day.[7] With alternate-day delivery, distances on the delivery sections of routes would be reduced about 50 percent while miles traveled between plants and delivery sections would be reduced roughly in inverse proportion to the increase in load size or in direct proportion to the reduction in the number of routes. Under the stated load conditions, alternate-day delivery would require 82 routes traveling a total of 251 miles per day. Compared to daily deliveries under the present system, these would represent reductions of 91 and 95 percent respectively. Note that the reorganized mileages would be 2.4 times the total street mileage with daily delivery and 1.4 times the street mileage with alternate-day delivery.

Before leaving these estimates, it may be helpful to illustrate the estimating procedure by reference to the details for a single dealer. Consider the case of a dealer who delivered a total of 5,674 quarts of milk daily. With daily delivery and maximum loads of 450 quarts, he would require 13 routes. The exclusive delivery territory assigned to him included 17.1 miles of streets on which deliveries were to be made. With an allowance of 14 percent for unavoidable duplication, the delivery sections of his routes would thus total about 19.5 miles per day. The average

[7] Even the longest routes would travel only about 7 miles per day.

TABLE 90. Estimates of milk-delivery requirements with exclusive delivery territories and reorganized routes, Hartford.

Dealer volume (quarts per day)	Number of dealers	Total volume (quarts)	Daily delivery				Alternate-day delivery			
			Number of routes*	Daily route miles			Number of routes*	Daily route miles		
				Deliver	Haul	Total		Deliver	Haul	Total
0– 499........	10	2,851	10	20	3	23	10	10	3	13
500– 999........	3	1,937	6	5	2	7	4	2	1	3
1,000–1,999........	2	2,349	6	14	3	17	4	7	2	9
2,000–7,999........	3	14,594	33	63	54	117	21	32	34	66
8,000 and over....	2	30,153†	67	106	167	273	43	53	107	160
Total........	20	51,884‡	122	208	229	437	82	104	147	251

* This reorganization was based on the assumption that all milk would be delivered on retail or mixed routes, with maximum loads of 450 quarts with daily delivery and 700 quarts with alternate-day delivery.

† In addition to this volume of milk in Hartford, the area for one of these dealers would include 2,300 quarts of milk in an adjacent town, probably East Hartford.

‡ Does not include 613 quarts handled through chain stores. This was eliminated because the handler made no retail deliveries and would be in no position to make retail deliveries in an exclusive territory.

one-way length of haul from his plant to the delivery sections of the routes was just under 1 mile, and the total round-trip hauling distance for 13 routes amounted to 25.7 miles. Adding together the delivery and hauling distances, it is estimated that the total would be 45.2 miles, or an average of 3.5 miles per route. With alternate-day delivery and 700-quart loads, he would require about 8 routes. Covering any street only every other day would reduce the length of delivery sections by 50 percent to 9.8 miles. With 8 routes, hauling distances would be reduced to 15.8 miles per day. The alternate-day total would then be estimated at 25.6 miles daily.

The New Haven metropolitan market

The process of allocation for the New Haven market was complicated by the fact that a number of plants are located to the north and east of the major consuming areas, with the result that territories for these plants must crowd to the south and west in order to include adequate volumes. Furthermore, the area includes a bay and several rivers and steep ridges that distort the allocations. These factors have been taken into account in establishing the areas shown in Fig. 65. Allocations have been made for 35 plants operated by 16 merchant-dealers, 16 producer-dealers, and three sub-dealers. In most cases, sub-dealers were not included separately in the computations but were included with the dealers who processed the milk for them. In the three cases mentioned above, sub-dealers were included because data had not been obtained from the merchant- and producer-dealers involved.

Estimates of the route mileages that would be required for milk deliveries within these exclusive territories are summarized in Table 91. For the entire group of dealers, daily delivery would be possible with only 1,401 miles of truck travel per day. This estimate is based on routes with maximum loads of about 450 quarts, and with all milk delivered by either retail or mixed routes. With alternate-day delivery and 700-quart loads, exclusive territories would permit deliveries with 829 miles of truck travel. Compared with daily delivery under the existing system, these mileages correspond to reductions of 85 and 91 percent respectively.

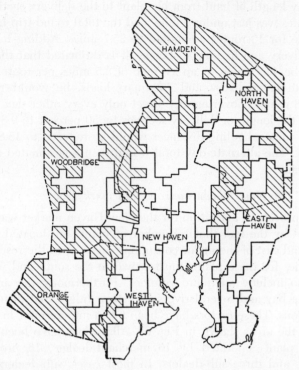

Fig. 65. *Allocation of the New Haven metropolitan market into exclusive delivery territories.*

No consistent relation was apparent between potential mileage reductions and dealer volume. Individual dealers would experience reductions differing from the average, however, as a result of their locations, relative efficiencies under the present system, and the characteristics of the particular areas assigned to them by the allocation procedures. With daily delivery in both cases, potential mileage reductions for individual dealers would range from 21 to 97 percent, but only in six cases would these reductions be less than 70 percent (Table 92). These included several dealers whose plants were located at a distance from the market and who would have relatively long hauling distances under any system that permitted them to deliver milk in the New Haven area. In several other cases, low potential mileage reductions re-

TABLE 91. Estimates of milk-delivery requirements with exclusive delivery territories and reorganized routes, New Haven metropolitan market.*

Dealer volume (quarts per day)	Number of dealers†	Total volume (quarts)	Daily delivery				Alternate-day delivery			
			Number of routes‡	Daily route miles			Number of routes‡	Daily route miles		
				Deliver**	Haul	Total		Deliver**	Haul	Total
0- 499.........	16	3,453	16	165	81	246	16	83	81	164
500- 999.........	7	4,630	14	69	47	116	9	34	25	59
1,000-1,999.........	4	5,196	13	109	58	167	9	54	41	95
2,000-2,999.........	3	7,762	19	78	34	112	12	39	22	61
3,000-5,999.........	2	10,684	25	129	128	257	16	65	82	147
6,000 and over....	3	41,211	93	170	333	503	61	85	218	303
Total..........	35	72,936	180	720	681	1,401	123	360	469	829

* Based on a sample of approximately 94 percent of the total milk now distributed in the seven-town metropolitan area, including both wholesale and retail milk.

† Sub-dealers are included with the handlers who process the milk for them. The total of 35 represents the number of separate areas included in the allocation.

‡ This reorganization was based on the assumption that all milk would be delivered on retail or mixed routes, with maximum loads of 450 quarts with daily delivery and 700 quarts with alternate-day delivery.

** Necessary duplication of delivery sections of routes figured at 20 percent for the entire metropolitan district. This is higher than the unavoidable duplication found in the Hartford study, but lower than the rates found in the secondary-market studies made in Torrington and Willimantic.

TABLE 92. Distribution of milk dealers according to potential delivery-mileage reductions from exclusive territories, daily delivery, New Haven metropolitan market.*

Percent reduction in mileage	Number of dealers
Less than 70	6
70–74	5
75–79	4
80–84	7
85–89	4
90–94	4
95–99	5
Total	35
Weighted average percent reduction†	85

* Daily delivery under exclusive territory system compared to daily delivery under present system.
† Weighted by dealer volumes.

flected unusually efficient and compact routes under the present system. If all sub-dealers had been considered separately in these computations, a number of them would have fallen into this last classification because their delivery operations tended to be confined to relatively small sections of the market.

Allocations involving more than one dealer per area

While exclusive delivery territories would minimize delivery-route mileages for existing dealers, the complete monopoly granted to each dealer within his territory might create serious problems. Two possible disadvantages that have been pointed out are: (1) that the monopoly position would be used to exploit consumers with respect to quality of the product and of the associated services; and (2) that consumers would be forced to accept the product of the dealer assigned to their section. The second of these has usually been mentioned in connection with pasteurized milk and premium qualities. Under the present system, consumers are free to choose between dealers and to shift to a new dealer if the product or service becomes unsatisfactory.

Some of the advantages of both the present and the exclusive-territory systems may be had through a system of market allocations that would permit two or more dealers to serve each area.

Studies have been made of the potential effects of three general systems of this type: (1) exclusive territories for retail deliveries but with wholesale routes free to serve stores in any section of the market; (2) allocations based on limited groups of dealers; and (3) double or triple allocations with overlapping areas (semiexclusive territories) so that every customer could choose between two or three dealers. The results of these are presented briefly in the following pages. For the most part, they refer specifically to the New Haven market, but mileage and route requirements with semiexclusive territories have been computed for several other markets.

Since such delivery systems would emphasize the competition between dealers for customers, the advantages would not be gained without some disadvantages. Soliciting and other competitive sales activities on the part of the routeman would not be eliminated, and might even be intensified by the direct impact of the actions of one dealer on another. As a consequence, potential route volumes would be smaller than under a system of exclusive territories. The following computations have been made on the basis of maximum loads of 350 quarts per day with daily delivery and 500 quarts per day with alternate-day operations, as suggested by Fig. 54.

The New Haven area has been allocated into a system of exclusive retail-delivery areas. Routes organized within these areas would permit the daily delivery of some 51,000 quarts of retail milk with 1,260 miles of route travel, or 810 miles per day with alternate-day delivery (Table 93). Only approximate comparisons with the present system are possible for this allocation, for many existing routes carry both wholesale and retail milk. Estimates of present retail delivery mileages have been made by allocating the total miles traveled by mixed routes on the assumption that wholesale deliveries on these routes involve route densities comparable with those achieved by existing specialized wholesale routes. In other words, wholesale miles have been estimated by dividing the wholesale volume on a mixed route by the number of quarts delivered per route mile on specialized wholesale routes, and these estimates were subtracted from total route miles to obtain an estimate of the retail mileage. While these procedures

TABLE 93. Summary of route and mileage requirements under present and reorganized systems of milk delivery, New Haven metropolitan milk market.

Delivery system*	Daily quarts	Daily delivery		Alternate-day delivery	
		Routes†	Miles‡	Routes†	Miles‡
All Dealers					
All milk					
Present..........	72,936	234	9,045	217	5,284
Exclusive areas...	72,936	180	1,401	123	829
Semi-exclusive areas	72,936	218	2,656	174	1,756
Retail milk only					
Present..........	50,894	164	8,490	139	4,730
Exclusive areas...	50,894	155	1,260	123	810
Nine Dealers					
All milk					
Present..........	57,724	160	6,354	138	3,659
Allocated areas...	57,724	167	1,354	128	850
Retail milk only					
Present..........	39,776	128	5,900	108	3,210
Allocated areas...	39,776	116	1,202	88	733
Three Dealers					
All milk					
Present...........	3,183	14	430	12	242
Allocated areas...	3,183	11	249	8	134

* See text for explanation of the several systems of reorganization.

† Present routes include 23 wholesale routes. Present routes for retail milk represent only the number that would have been required at average volumes. Since many actual routes carried wholesale as well as retail milk, it was impossible to determine retail route numbers directly. Reorganized routes calculated on basis of loads averaging 350 quarts with daily delivery and 500 quarts with alternate-day delivery except in the case of exclusive areas, where load limits were 450 and 700 quarts.

‡ Present retail miles represent equivalent miles for retail milk, which were obtained by estimating wholesale quarts per mile and using this factor to adjust total miles. As explained above, the prevalence of mixed routes made it impossible to obtain a retail figure directly.

are necessarily arbitrary, they may be used to provide an approximate basis for comparison.

With these limitations in mind, it appears that retail deliveries alone required the equivalent of 164 daily-delivery routes traveling 8,490 miles or 139 alternate-day routes traveling 4,730 miles per day. If retail deliveries were zoned into exclusive territories, the number of routes could be reduced to some 155 with daily delivery and 123 with alternate-day delivery, while route miles could be reduced to the above-mentioned levels of 1,260 and 810 per day. In relative terms and with present daily delivery as a base, the potential reductions would be 85 percent with daily delivery and 90 percent with alternate-day delivery.

It is well recognized that many dealers and probably some consumers would accept exclusive delivery territories only with the greatest reluctance. On the other hand, there may be a few dealers in any market who would be willing to try out such a program. To illustrate the conservation possibilities available to such limited groups of dealers, two additional allocations have been made for the New Haven market: (1) allocated territories based on the operations of nine dealers of widely varying size who accounted for nearly 80 percent of all milk in the market; and (2) an allocation or exchange of customers for three small dealers whose combined volume represented less than 5 percent of the market total. These allocations have been made on the assumption that it would be possible for the dealers to exchange customers without serious loss of business to noncoöperating dealers. The history of customer transfers in normal times suggests that this assumption may be unrealistic and that there might well be significant decreases in volumes for some of the participating dealers. Whether or not this tendency could be counteracted by passing some of the cost reductions on to the consumer in the form of lowered prices is a question.

Since the nine dealers selected for the first allocation handled nearly 80 percent of all milk in the market, it is not surprising to find that their present operations duplicate and overlap and that allocated delivery territories would result in marked mileage reduction. If all deliveries were made on mixed routes, it is estimated that these dealers could reduce their daily-delivery mileage from 6,354 to 1,354 miles. Alternate-day delivery has already reduced the distances traveled by the routes of these dealers to 3,659 miles per day, but the addition of allocated territories to alternate-day delivery would result in a total of only 850 route miles (Table 93). If the allocations included only retail delivery, the daily-delivery requirements would be about 1,200 miles and the alternate-day delivery requirements about 730 miles.

Many dealers have had some experience in exchanging customers, especially when war shortages forced route-mileage reductions. If several small dealers in the New Haven area decided on an extensive exchange of customers among themselves, the result would be similar to an allocation of delivery territory. Three small dealers with volumes ranging between 700 and 1,250 quarts daily have been selected to illustrate this situation. The locations of their plants and the approximate areas in which they were making deliveries are given in the first map in Fig. 66. These dealers were located in different sections of the market and most of their operations were confined to the area between their plants

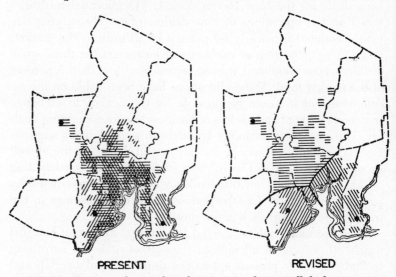

PRESENT   REVISED

Fig. 66. Present and revised market areas for three small dealers operating in the New Haven metropolitan milk market.

and the central district of New Haven. In spite of this natural segregation, however, delivery territories overlapped to a considerable extent.

The three-dealer allocation to prevent the overlapping and duplication of delivery routes is shown in the second part of Fig. 66. The indicated margins would permit deliveries with a minimum of route travel. The three dealers already handle 56, 65, and 83 percent of the milk in their allocated territories so that only 962 quarts out of the total of 3,183 quarts of deliveries would need to be exchanged. As a result of this exchange, routes would need to travel only 249 miles as compared with the present 430 with daily delivery, or only 134 miles compared with the present 242 miles with alternate-day delivery. In spite of the small proportion of the total market deliveries involved, these three dealers could reduce their present route mileages by more than 40 percent.

The third type of allocation system with more than one dealer per area involves dividing the dealers into two or more groups and establishing market-wide allocations for each group. The overlapping areas that result will permit consumers to choose between two or more dealers. Semiexclusive allocations of this type were used in Great Britain during the war.[8] Milk markets were frequently zoned so that consumers were limited to a choice between one proprietary company and one consumer coöperative, while occasionally a third allocation and choice was made on the basis of some special grade of milk.

As compared to exclusive delivery territories, semiexclusive allocations will affect mileage and route requirements in three ways: (1) the competitive aspects will reduce average load size and increase the number of routes while route hauling mileage will increase in direct proportion to the number of routes; (2) delivery miles will increase more or less in direct proportion to the number of handlers, provided the number permitted to serve any one area is small and each covers the entire area allocated to him; and (3) dealer delivery densities will be reduced and the size of the area served by a given dealer increased, so that average hauling miles will increase roughly as the square root of the number of dealers assigned to each area. On this basis, rough estimates of the route and mileage requirements for the Torrington, Willimantic, and New Haven markets have been made and are summarized in Table 94. Permitting two dealers to serve each area in the two secondary markets would increase daily delivery mileage about 65 percent above exclusive territory requirements. With alternate-day delivery the increase over exclusive-territory

[8] "The 'Rationalization' of Retail Distribution of Milk in Great Britain," mimeographed report of the New England Research Council in coöperation with the Storrs Agricultural Experiment Station and the U. S. Department of Agriculture (April 1944).

mileages would be about 95 percent. Since relatively few dealers in these markets have large enough volumes to justify more than one route, the number of routes would not be greatly affected by the semiexclusive delivery system. In the New Haven market, on the other hand, semiexclusive areas would involve about 20 percent more daily-delivery routes and 40 percent more alternate-day routes than would the exclusive delivery system. Route mile-

TABLE 94. Estimates of route and mileage requirements with the present system, exclusive territories, and semiexclusive areas, selected Connecticut markets.

	Daily delivery		Alternate-day delivery	
Market and system	Routes*	Miles	Routes*	Miles
Torrington				
Present..............	48	1,384	46	853
Exclusive territories....	48	343	42	190†
Semiexclusive areas.....	48	550	46	370†
Willimantic				
Present..............	33	703	32	508
Exclusive territories....	33	187	28	99†
Semiexclusive areas.....	33	310	32	190†
New Haven area				
Present..............	234	9,045	217	5,284
Exclusive territories....	180	1,401	123	829†
Semiexclusive areas.....	218	2,656	174	1,756†

* Maximum route volumes for Willimantic and Torrington: with exclusive territories, 400 quarts with daily delivery and 650 quarts with alternate-day delivery; with semiexclusive areas, 350 quarts with daily delivery and 500 quarts with alternate-day delivery. In the New Haven area, the maximum loads were 450 and 700 quarts with exclusive territories and 350 and 500 quarts with semiexclusive areas.

† Including mileage reductions due to "skip-day" operation of small routes.

ages would be increased 90 percent with daily delivery and about 110 percent with alternate-day delivery.

The data in Table 94 make it quite clear that semiexclusive areas would permit milk delivery with route mileages substantially lower than under the present system. Both the number of routes and delivery mileages would be larger than would be possible under a complete allocation involving exclusive territories, however, especially in the larger markets. The effects of these changes on potential delivery costs will be discussed in the following section.

Estimated costs and potential savings

With the physical requirements for milk delivery under a system of exclusive territories and the previously developed cost functions, it should be a relatively simple matter to estimate milk delivery costs. One important point must be clarified, however, before satisfactory estimates can be made. In discussing delivery costs in rural areas, it was pointed out that milk distribution is a supplementary enterprise for many small dealers, involving the part-time use of unspecialized labor and equipment to a considerable extent. Cost functions were developed for these areas with this in mind, and involved the allocation of fixed truck costs and labor costs to milk distribution in proportion to the time devoted to this enterprise.

Even in urban markets, many dealers operate on a part-time basis. In Torrington and Willimantic, for example, most handlers were small producer-dealers and only one-third of the routes were operated by handlers with sufficient volume to justify more than one route. While less pronounced in the major markets, this same situation is found in all Connecticut markets. If costs were computed for these markets on the basis of the average route volumes and the urban cost equations that assume full-time utilization in milk delivery, the results would be quite misleading. Cost estimates for the urban markets, therefore, have been based on potential route volumes rather than actual averages. These volumes will be representative of the situation for dealers with sufficient volume to operate a number of routes and to permit route consolidations in order to exploit the potentialities of the several delivery systems. For smaller operators, such estimates are equivalent to an assumption that fixed daily truck and route labor costs will be allocated to milk delivery in proportion to the ratio of actual route volumes to potential route volumes. This is necessarily arbitrary, but it may be supported by the same general arguments presented in the case of rural routes. If potential route volumes are about 700 quarts with exclusive territories and alternate-day delivery, a 200-quart route will not provide full-time employment for a deliveryman or for a truck, and returns to these factors on a daily basis cannot be expected to equal the returns on a route approximating the 700-quart level. Moreover, this particular method of allocation has some precedent in the existing methods of labor payments where earnings are entirely or at least in part a function of daily volume.

With this modification, cost estimates have been made and are summarized in Table 95. Potential urban route volumes were the previously determined maximum loads of 400 and 650 quarts with daily and alternate-day delivery in secondary markets and 450 and 700 quarts in major markets. For the present system, loads were taken at 300 quarts with daily delivery and 450 quarts with alternate-day delivery; these are in line with typical performances of larger dealers who have taken advantage of the opportunities afforded by alternate-day delivery to consolidate routes. Under these limits, the costs for alternate-day delivery under the present system are potential costs comparable to the estimates for other reorganized systems.

These estimates indicate that, with 1947 levels of wages and costs, the program of alternate-day delivery would have reduced milk delivery costs about 1.8 cents per quart in rural areas and 2.3 to 2.7 cents in the secondary and major markets. The addition of exclusive delivery territories to alternate-day delivery would involve potential cost reductions of about 0.7 cent per quart below alternate-day delivery costs under the present system in rural areas. In the secondary markets the added potential savings would range between 1.9 and 2.0 cents per quart. These potential savings, as indicated above, are in addition to the savings from alternate-day delivery under the present system of distribution.

Because of competitive sales activities and consequently lower daily route volumes, potential savings from systems involving limited market allocations would not be as great as under a system of exclusive territories. Computations for the New Haven metropolitan market indicate that an allocation based only on retail milk would result in savings of about 1.5 cents per quart as compared to alternate-day delivery under 1947 conditions. If

TABLE 95. Estimated costs of milk delivery under the present and exclusive territory systems, Connecticut markets.

Market and delivery system	Total quarts per day	Route miles per day	Estimated average delivery* costs per quart
14 Rural Areas			
Daily delivery			
Present system........	7,404	1,077	$0.046
Exclusive territories...	7,404	634	.034
Alternate-day			
Present system........	7,404	610	.028
Exclusive territories...	7,404	360	.021
Torrington			
Daily delivery			
Present system........	11,685	1,384	.073
Exclusive territories...	11,685	343	.047
Alternate-day			
Present system........	11,685	853	.047
Exclusive territories...	11,685	190	.028
Willimantic			
Daily delivery			
Present system........	6,744	703	.070
Exclusive territories...	6,744	187	.047
Alternate-day			
Present system........	6,744	508	.047
Exclusive territories...	6,744	99	.028
Hartford			
Daily delivery			
Present system........	52,497	5,000	.069
Exclusive territories...	51,884	437	.043
Alternate-day			
Present system........	52,497	3,000	.044
Exclusive territories...	51,884	251	.025
New Haven Area			
Daily delivery			
Present system........	72,936	9,045	.074
Exclusive territories...	72,936	1,401	.045
Alternate-day			
Present system..........	72,936	5,284	.047
Exclusive territories...	72,936	829	.027

* Delivery costs estimated on the basis of the cost equations given in Chapter 12, with route volumes assumed to equal the potential levels in secondary and major markets.

nine dealers handling about 80 percent of the milk in the market agreed to allocate among themselves, potential savings would be about 1.0 cent per quart. Even in the case of three small dealers, a complete exchange of customers to eliminate overlapping delivery routes would reduce alternate-day delivery route mileage more than 40 percent and would result in potential savings of 0.7 cent per quart from the mileage factor plus 0.3 cent from further route consolidations. Semiexclusive territories for all dealers in secondary and major markets would permit savings of about 0.9 cent per quart with alternate-day delivery. In general, the potential savings from semiexclusive territories would be about half the savings from a complete allocation of exclusive territories.

14 —

MUNICIPAL MILK
DISTRIBUTION

Potential advantages of market-wide operations

Even under the best of delivery conditions, the presence of a relatively large number of relatively small dealers in most markets will make some plant and route inefficiencies unavoidable. In such markets, the milk-distribution system with the greatest potentialities involves complete monopoly. This could take various forms, including coöperative amalgamation of all handlers, privately operated monopoly with public-utility status and regulation, or outright municipal ownership and operation.

The advantages of such a system fall into three main categories: (1) the elimination of delivery-route duplication; (2) the elimination of excess route capacity that is always present where many dealers have total volumes too small to permit effective route organization; and (3) the concentration of plant operations so as to eliminate the many small and uneconomical units that characterize most markets. Mileage requirements will frequently be higher under such a program than under exclusive territories because of the longer distances involved in traveling from one or two central plants to the delivery areas. But these mileage increases will be insignificant when compared to the potential gains in the use of plant and route labor and equipment.

While some form of complete market monopoly of milk distribution has frequently been suggested, and despite the fact that a very small group of dealers handles the vast bulk of deliveries in most cities, the little town of Tarboro, North Carolina, is the only place in the United States known to the author where milk distribution is handled under such a system. In spite of a delivery system involving twice-a-day delivery, special deliveries on call, and a total volume of bottled milk averaging less than 600 quarts daily, municipal milk distribution in that town appeared to be relatively efficient in 1936. "All things considered, it appears that the citizens of Tarboro believe their milk plant to be a good investment and that under no circumstances should it pass into private hands. This position seems to be justified on the basis of survey data: Products of high quality are obtainable at reasonable cost, the service appears to be excellent, and no evidence was found indicating any of the oft-alleged wastes of public enterprise." [1]

The city of Wellington in New Zealand has a municipally owned and operated milk-distribution system that handles about 80 percent of the volume in the market, the balance being in the hands of nearby farmers who deliver bulk raw milk. Reports indicate that route volumes under this system are larger than in any other city in New Zealand, averaging 120 gallons per man with daily delivery, and that delivery costs are from 16 to 38 percent lower than the costs of distributors in other cities. [2]

Outside of the field of milk distribution the United States has had some experience in public operation of the mail system and municipal power companies, as well as a fairly widespread system of public-utility regulation. These indicate a wide variation in performance and success; the field of regulation especially leaves much to be desired from the standpoint of efficiency and low costs.

With actual experience so limited and inconclusive, studies of the potentialities of municipal milk distribution can only be based on a synthetic approach similar to that used in the studies of exclusive territories. The results of such studies in Connecticut markets are reported in the pages that follow. Based on the find-

---

[1] A. J. Nixon and O. M. Reed, *Municipal Milk Distribution in Tarboro, North Carolina* (Dairy Section, Agricultural Adjustment Administration, U. S. Department of Agriculture, Bulletin DM-5, 1938), 3–15.

[2] *Milk Commission Report on the Supply of Milk to the Four Metropolitan Areas of Auckland, Wellington, Christchurch, and Dunedin* (New Zealand, 1944).

ings of Chapter 12, the studies show the effects on routes, route mileages, and distribution costs of delivering all milk in a given market from a centrally located plant.

Municipal distribution in rural markets

Hypothetical routes were mapped for the sample rural markets to illustrate the potential effects of deliveries from a single plant. The results may be illustrated by the map for the Saybrook area, reproduced in Fig. 67. These routes were outlined without regard for present dealers' operations, on the assumption that all commercially distributed milk in the area would be sold by a single agency operating a centrally located plant. Separate systems were laid out for daily delivery routes with maximum volumes of 325 quarts and for alternate-day routes with maximum loads of 550 quarts per day. Confining operations within town lines was arbitrary and unrealistic, of course, but the results indicate the general levels of performance that could be expected from some form of municipal distribution. In most rural areas, the optimum organization would involve either one plant for a number of towns or service from a plant located in some nearby urban market.

The results of these studies are summarized in Table 96. As is to be expected, municipal distribution in rural areas would not reduce mileage requirements much below the exclusive-territory levels, but very important reductions in the number of delivery routes could be made in all markets except Ashford (where only one dealer operates under the existing system). On a daily delivery basis and compared to exclusive-territory requirements, mileage reductions would average 15 percent while the number of routes could be reduced 65 percent. Potential reductions with alternate-day delivery for both systems would be about the same, averaging 12 percent in route miles and 70 percent in the number of routes. Reductions below the requirements for daily delivery under the present system would average 49 and 70 percent in daily and alternate-day route mileages and 69 and 74 percent respectively in the number of daily and alternate-day delivery routes.

The extent to which distribution from a central plant would

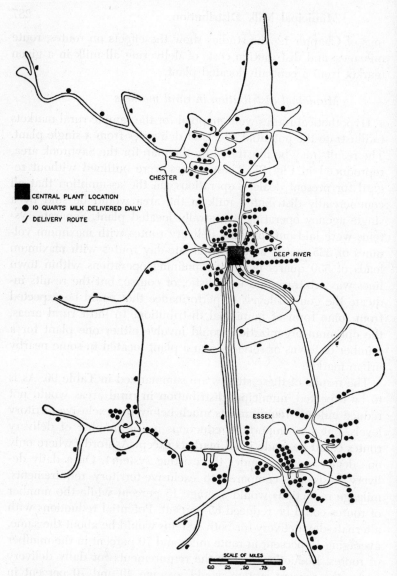

CENTRAL PLANT LOCATION
10 QUARTS MILK DELIVERED DAILY
DELIVERY ROUTE

CHESTER

DEEP RIVER

ESSEX

SCALE OF MILES
0.0 .25 .50 .75 1.0

Fig. 67. Delivery routes in Saybrook Area if milk were distributed from a central plant located so as to minimize delivery distance. Compare with Figs. 7 and 60.

involve unavoidable duplication of mileage can be estimated by measuring the total mileage of roads along which milk is distributed and expressing the total route mileage under a central-plant system as a percentage of the road miles. In the 14 towns studied, the average unavoidable duplication was 37 percent.

TABLE 96. Milk delivery route and mileage requirements if deliveries were made from a central plant in each sample rural market.

Rural town	Quarts per day	Daily delivery		Alternate-day	
		Routes*	Miles	Routes*	Miles
Ashford................	9	1	5	1	3
Bridgewater............	65	1	17	1	8
Harwinton.............	98	1	23	1	12
Willington..............	113	1	23	1	11
Brookfield..............	263	1	24	1	11
Ellington..............	363	2	36	1	18
Somers................	488	2	38	1	19
Mansfield..............	583	2	55	2	31
Old Saybrook..........	782	3	28	2	15
Ridgefield.............	1,155	4	68	3	35
East Windsor..........	1,214	4	56	3	36
Saybrook Area.........	2,271	7	88	5	50

* Based on maximum route volumes of 325 quarts with daily delivery and 550 quarts with alternate-day delivery.

Percentages ranged from more than 50 in some of the smaller markets to less than 30 in Somers, Ellington, and Mansfield. These estimates, when compared with conditions in some of the larger cities under exclusive territories, indicate that distribution in all except the smallest rural markets does not necessarily involve more unavoidable duplication of mileage than would be characteristic of some of the urban markets.

Secondary markets

To test the possibilities of centralized operations, the approximate centers of milk distribution were determined for the five sample secondary markets and hypothetical delivery routes set up around these points. The number of delivery routes and the required mileages were computed and are summarized in Table 97. In all markets, the distribution mileage requirements with deliveries from a central plant were found to be somewhat lower than those for exclusive territories. This was the result of two main factors: (1) many of the existing plants were not strategically located but were outside of the area; and (2) the small volumes handled by many dealers resulted in an excessive number of routes while with a central plant all routes would operate approximately at capacity, the total number would be lower, and total hauling miles would thereby be reduced.

If central-plant operations were adopted, it would be necessary

TABLE 97. Milk-delivery routes and mileages with municipal distribution, urban markets.

Market	Daily delivery			Alternate-day	
	Quarts per day	Number of routes*	Miles per day	Number of routes*	Miles per day
Secondary Markets					
Torrington............	11,685	29	146	18	77
Willimantic...........	6,744	17	104	11	55
Hamden..............	9,328	24	207	15	112
West Haven..........	9,003	23	161	14	85
East Haven..........	3,115	8	86	5	46
Major Markets					
Hartford.............	52,497	117	505	75	294
New Haven†.........	48,754	109	590	70	342
New Haven Area‡.....	72,936	162	1,365	104	774

* On the basis of average loads of approximately 400 quarts with daily delivery and 650 quarts with alternate-day delivery for secondary markets, and 450 and 700 quarts for major markets.
† New Haven only.
‡ Seven-town metropolitan market.

to collect the milk from present sources and deliver it to the central plant. In many cases this would merely mean a new destination for the collection routes and would not have a great effect on collection mileages. In others, it would be possible to add the milk of present producer-dealers to existing collection routes, again with little change in collection miles. If these possibilities are disregarded and new collection routes organized to pick up the milk at the farms of producer-dealers, some additional travel would be involved. This has been studied for the Torrington market, with an indicated additional collection travel of about

90 miles per day. As already noted, the integration of existing collection routes would reduce this distance.

Major markets

The geographic center of milk distribution for the city of Hartford is approximately at the location of the State Armory (Fig. 63). This was used as a center for delivery calculations, although it was realized that property limitations would prevent the location of an actual plant on this site. Table 98 shows the distribution of milk around this point by zones of 2,000-foot intervals

TABLE 98. Deliveries of milk by zones around a central point, Hartford.

Zone (1,000 feet)	Daily milk deliveries (quarts)	Length of streets (1,000 feet)	Average density (quarts per 1,000 feet)	Average distance from central point* (1,000 feet)
0– 1.9	3,624	45.8	79	0.6
2.0– 3.9	9,662	117.9	82	3.0
4.0– 5.9	9,901	134.8	73	4.9
6.0– 7.9	10,857	170.3	64	6.8
8.0– 9.9	7,732	141.2	55	8.6
10.0–11.9	5,244	133.3	39	10.6
12.0–13.9	3,500	113.8	31	12.7
14.0–15.9	1,012	58.7	17	14.3
16.0–17.9	468	26.5	18	17.2
18.0–19.9	497	24.5	20	19.0
All	52,497	966.8	54	6.7

* Distances by street from a central point located at the present site of the State Armory.

(actual street distances). The amount of milk per zone increased rapidly with the expansion of the area in the first zones, but then declined as a result of decreasing density and the pinching off of some of the zones at the city limits. This table also indicates that milk was delivered on 183 miles of streets with an average delivery density of 285 quarts per mile. Individual milk deliveries were located as much as 3.8 miles from the central-plant site, but the average distance was only 1.27 miles.

With daily delivery and average loads of 450 quarts for retail and mixed routes, it would require 117 routes to deliver the 52,497 quarts of milk included in the tabulation. On the average these routes would travel 1.27 miles between the central plant and the delivery area, or a round trip of 2.54 miles. Hauling distances would thus total about 296 miles. Distances traveled on the delivery sections of routes would be 14 percent higher than street mileages for a total of 209 miles. Combining these two elements, it would appear that daily delivery from a central plant would require about 505 miles.[3]

If deliveries were made on alternate days and loads averaged 700 quarts, central-plant operations would require only 75 routes.

TABLE 99. Percentage distribution of milk by distance from plants for exclusive delivery areas and for a single central plant, New Haven metropolitan market.

Miles from plant*	Percent of milk	
	Exclusive	Central
0.0– 0.9....................................	30.8	33.2
1.0– 1.9....................................	28.0	31.6
2.0– 2.9....................................	17.9	12.8
3.0– 3.9....................................	13.9	8.0
4.0– 4.9....................................	7.3	7.4
5.0– 5.9....................................	1.2	4.5
6.0– 6.9....................................	0.8	1.6
7.0 –7.9....................................	.1	0.6
8.0– 8.9....................................	—	.2
9.0 –9.9....................................	—	.1
10.0–10.9....................................	—	†
Weighted average miles.....................	1.86	1.99

* Actual street distances.
† Less than 0.05 percent.

Hauling distances would be 190 miles, delivery distances 104 miles, and the total route travel 294 miles. These central-plant totals are somewhat higher than the previously discussed requirements for exclusive territories. This is to be expected where existing plants are well distributed throughout the market. The additional mileage would represent a very small increase in unit

[3] If the total volume corresponded to the 51,884 quarts handled by the 20 dealers described in Table 90, central-plant organization with daily delivery would require 115 routes traveling a total of 501 miles. With alternate-day delivery, the requirements would be 74 routes and 292 miles.

costs, however, and probably would be insignificant when balanced against savings in plant operation.

The percentage distribution of milk deliveries by zones around a central point in New Haven is given in Table 99, together with a similar distribution for the system of exclusive delivery territories. Because the central point was found to coincide approximately with the densest delivery areas, the proportion of the total milk included in the nearby zones is greater than for the exclusive territories. The location of plants on the outskirts of the market, however, reduced the volume of milk in the more distant zones for the system of exclusive territories. The weighted-average distances from plants was 1.86 miles for exclusive areas and 1.99 for the central-plant organization.

With the elimination of small dealers who operated routes at less than capacity, the number of routes under a central system would be about 162 with daily delivery and 104 with alternate-day delivery. This reduction would offset the increase in the average hauling distance, so that daily delivery would require 1,365 miles and alternate-day delivery 774 miles of route travel.

Estimated costs and potential savings

The methods used to estimate delivery costs have already been described, and need not be discussed at this point. In the case of municipal distribution, however, plant as well as route operations are involved and the effects on plant costs must be estimated. These have been determined from the plant-cost relations developed in Chapters 11 and 12 with one modification: costs for plants with daily volumes less than 228 quarts have been estimated at the 228-quart rate of $0.0523 per quart, corresponding to plant A in Chapter 11. This maximum was established for two reasons: (1) small plants use nonspecialized labor and equipment to a considerable extent and so are able to write off excessive costs or to allocate part of the costs to other enterprises; and (2) most small plants do not pasteurize, and costs for raw-milk plants are lower than for the pasteurizing plants used as the basis for comparisons.

Costs have been estimated for the present and the reorganized systems by applying appropriate volume data to these relations.

For the present system, weighted-average costs have been estimated for all plants serving the market in question. For the municipal system, costs have been estimated for a single plant large enough to serve the entire market.

The results of these procedures are summarized in Table 100. In a typical rural town, a combination of municipal distribution and alternate-day delivery apparently would reduce milk-distribution costs about 2.3 cents per quart below the levels of alternate-day delivery costs under the present system. In the secondary markets, potential savings would average about 4.0 cents per quart if wages and other cost rates were held at 1947 levels. The number of relatively small dealers in these markets would make plant-cost savings especially important. In Hartford, the potential savings would average 3.0 cents per quart, while in the New Haven metropolitan area they would average about 2.7 cents. Larger potential savings in the Hartford market are due to higher present costs rather than to lower potential costs, for roughly three times as many dealers serve the Hartford area as deliver milk in the New Haven district.

Comparison of these results with the estimates given in Table 95 for deliveries under a system of exclusive territories indicates that delivery costs for the two systems are nearly identical and that the added savings from municipal distribution come from reductions in plant costs. While this is generally true, it should be emphasized that route volumes under municipal distribution will approach the theoretical limits very closely and that the indicated reductions in delivery costs are real savings. It will be recalled that average route volumes fell below these limits in the case of exclusive territories, because many dealers handled volumes too small to realize the full advantages of the system. In these cases, route hours would be reduced and so costs were estimated on the basis of the full-time equivalents. If route labor and equipment could not be used for other purposes, however, real costs would be somewhat higher than was indicated, and the potential advantages of municipal distribution over exclusive territories would be greater than has been indicated.

Since the basic plant-cost relations are long-run curves, they describe situations where plant capacities are adjusted to the

TABLE 100. Estimated plant and delivery costs under the present and municipal milk-distribution systems, Connecticut markets.

Market and distribution system	Estimated average costs per quart*		
	Plant	Delivery	Total
14 Rural Towns			
Daily delivery			
Present system............	$0.046	$0.046	$0.092
Municipal system.........	.033	.029	.062
Alternate-day			
Present system............	.046	.028	.074
Municipal system.........	.033	.018	.051
Torrington			
Daily delivery			
Present system............	.038	.073	.111
Municipal system.........	.019	.044	.063
Alternate-day			
Present system............	.038	.047	.085
Municipal system.........	.019	.026	.045
Willimantic			
Daily delivery			
Present system............	.041	.070	.111
Municipal system.........	.020	.045	.065
Alternate-day			
Present system............	.041	.047	.088
Municipal system.........	.020	.026	.046
Hartford			
Daily delivery			
Present system.............	.028†	.069	.097
Municipal system.........	.016	.043	.059
Alternate-day			
Present system............	.028†	.044	.072
Municipal system.........	.016	.026	.042
New Haven Area			
Daily delivery			
Present system............	.022	.074	.096
Municipal system.........	.015	.045	.060
Alternate-day			
Present system............	.022	.047	.069
Municipal system.........	.015	.027	.042

* Based on cost relations developed in Part III and the physical data presented in previous sections of this chapter.

† Based on total plant volumes, and not the volumes distributed in the city of Hartford. Total volumes averaged 64 percent higher than the Hartford sales.

volumes to be handled. This is not true of many existing dairy plants, and so the estimates represent potential rather than actual costs. This parallels the situation with respect to delivery routes; in all cases the costs reported are potential costs for the present system, with excessive costs due to unutilized capacity either written off or allocated to other enterprises. It seems unnecessary to add that real costs may exceed this level, and that the perpetuation of such inefficiencies would represent a malallocation of resources with costs to society at higher levels than have been indicated. In short, the indicated savings from municipal distribution are conservative in that costs for the present system have been estimated on as favorable a basis as possible.

Geographic variations in costs within a single market

The foregoing estimates are averages for entire markets. Within any market, delivery costs would vary as a result of such factors as the distance from the central plant and the density of deliveries. Some indication of these effects is given in Table 101 for the New Haven area. With a plant located near the center of consumption, routes would become longer and delivery densities lower as distance from the plant increased. For both of these reasons, potential route volumes would decrease and delivery costs would increase. While combined plant and route costs for alternate-day delivery under a municipal system would average about 4.2 cents per quart for the whole market, the *additional* costs of operating routes serving areas from 6.5 to 10.5 miles from the plant would be about 4.8 cents, while areas from 1.5 to 2.5 miles from the plant would have an additional cost of about 4.0 cents.

The relatively rapid increase in additional costs for zones distant from the central plant might suggest that the optimum arrangement would involve more than one plant. As a matter of fact, these cost increases are influenced more by decreases in density than by the increases in the distance from the plant. In the area 6.5 miles or more from the central-plant location, routes would average only 570 quarts per day with alternate-day delivery. Daily route travel would amount to about 34 miles, of which 15 miles would represent the travel between the plant and the delivery area and the balance of 19 miles would be covered while making deliveries. If densities were as high in this zone as at the center of the market, route travel would average only 17 miles, and delivery costs about 3.0 cents. Distance from plant, then, would have the effect in this case of increasing delivery costs about 0.5 cent per quart, while low density of deliveries within the zone would be reflected in an increase of approxi-

TABLE 101. Delivery conditions and estimated costs by zones
for municipal distribution on an alternate-day basis,
New Haven Area.

Miles from central plant	Quarts of milk per day	Quarts per route mile*	Quarts per route†	Estimated costs per quart			
				Delivery	Marginal plant cost‡	Total	Cumulative average combined costs**
0–0.49	10,362	300	770	$0.0248	$0.0166	$0.0414	$0.0439
0.50–0.99	13,824	227	760	.0251	.0156	.0407	.0423
1.00–1.49	12,877	139	750	.0256	.0146	.0402	.0418
1.50–1.99	10,150	111	740	.0261	.0138	.0399	.0414
2.00–2.49	5,367	80	730	.0267	.0133	.0400	.0413
2.50–2.99	3,959	62	715	.0275	.0130	.0405	.0413
3.00–3.49	3,043	57	705	.0279	.0128	.0407	.0412
3.50–3.99	2,803	50	695	.0283	.0126	.0409	.0412
4.00–4.49	4,408	38	675	.0296	.0122	.0418	.0413
4.50–4.99	968	36	660	.0300	.0122	.0422	.0413
5.00–5.49	2,556	30	645	.0311	.0120	.0431	.0414
5.50–5.99	846	26	630	.0323	.0119	.0442	.0414
6.00–6.49	697	21	600	.0342	.0119	.0461	.0414
6.50 and over	1,076	17	570	.0367	.0118	.0485	.0416

* Smoothed in the more distant zones to eliminate random fluctuations.
† Estimated from Fig. 54.
‡ Marginal to the long-run plant-cost curve: $MC = \$0.01743 - \$0.0000000776P$.
** Cumulative average delivery cost plus average plant costs.

mately 0.7 cent. Moreover, the increase in costs due to low density could not be avoided by adding plants, but would persist under any organization. If deliveries are to be made in such areas, costs will be high because of the scattered population and the small number of quarts delivered per mile.

This leads to an interesting but difficult problem. How should charges for milk distribution vary within a market? Because plant costs are in part joint costs for all milk handled, there can be no exact and scientific answer to this question. The additional plant and delivery costs, however, provide a lower limit below which charges should not go. These represent the direct costs per quart that must be incurred if the market area is to be expanded and additional plant capacity provided. To these must be added the overhead and joint plant costs if total costs are to be covered, and this can only be done in an arbitrary manner. In this respect milk distribution involves rate-making problems similar to those that are involved in the public-utility field. In spite of these difficulties, it is clear that additional costs in sections of low delivery density will be well above the average costs for the market even under completely consolidated deliveries, and that a flat price over the entire market means that consumers in high-density areas are subsidizing delivery to sparsely populated sections.

15 —

SOME ASPECTS OF
WHOLESALE MILK DELIVERY

The proposal to eliminate retail milk delivery

In many markets consumers pay less for milk purchased from stores than they do to have it delivered to their homes. According to the data summarized in Table 4 and discussed in Chapter 1, the margins or spreads between producer prices and the wholesale prices charged to stores ranged from 4.5 to 9.9 cents and averaged 6.8 cents per quart in the major milk markets of the United States during January 1950. The price spread to cover store operations ranged from 0.5 to 3.9 cents and averaged about 2.0 cents. The combined margin to cover wholesale delivery and store operations ranged from 6.5 to 12.4 cents, and averaged 8.8 cents per quart. During the same period, the price spread for retail milk distribution in these markets ranged from 6.5 to 13.4 cents and averaged 9.3 cents per quart. The difference between the store and home-delivered prices, or the "store differential," then, ranged from less than zero to 2.9 cents per quart, and averaged 0.5 cent. In nearly half of the reported markets, however, customers paid as much for milk at stores as they did to have it delivered to their homes, while several markets actually reported store prices higher than home-delivered prices.

The fact that consumer prices for milk sold through stores are lower than home-delivered prices in many markets has sometimes led to the suggestion that milk-market reorganization should take the form of the complete elimination of home delivery. Under such a scheme, wholesale routes would service regular stores and special milk depots scattered throughout the market area, and consumers would obtain all of their milk supplies from these outlets. The following pages consider various aspects of such proposals, but the analysis is admittedly less rigorous than the foregoing studies of retail distribution.

Wholesale delivery without restriction

If milk-marketing reorganization took this form and retail deliveries were eliminated without placing any restrictions on wholesale deliveries, it seems quite probable that many of the inefficiencies that now characterize retail routes would flourish in the wholesale field. As a matter of fact, duplication of wholesale routes and services has already become an important factor in many markets. In describing wholesale operations in New York City, President Fred Sexauer of the Dairymen's League wrote:

> We know, for example, that 3 to 14 wholesale milk routes travel each street in the business and retail sections of New York City every day. We know that most stores, hotels, and many restaurants are served by from 2 to 7 separate dealers.[1]

Similar results have been reported for California markets.[2] Studies in Los Angeles, San Francisco, and Stockton during 1950 indicated that most stores were being served by more than one milk distributor and that the number of distributors per store tended to increase with increases in store volume. The major exceptions to this resulted from the development of "captive creameries," whereby some chain stores and supermarkets operated their own processing and distribution facilities. The resulting large volume per delivery stop and streamlined service made possible by the elimination of sales activities were reflected in increased route volumes and significantly lower costs.

There appears to be no reliable basis for forecasting exactly how wholesale milk distribution would develop under these con-

---

[1] F. H. Sexauer, "Survey Would Show How Men, Materials Could Be Conserved to Speed War Work," *Dairymen's League News* (The Dairymen's League Coöperative Association, Inc.), XXVI, No. 20 (1942).

[2] David A. Clarke, Jr., "Wholesale Milk Delivery," unpublished thesis, University of California (1951), pp. 57–58.

ditions. The four- or fivefold increase in wholesale trade that would accompany the elimination of retail delivery in major Connecticut markets, however, would almost certainly result in some increase in route densities and volume per delivery stop, even with substantial increases in wholesale duplication. The large increase in volume per store should also permit some reduction in the store margin, although specific cost findings would be difficult to obtain owing to the problems of joint and overhead cost allocations.[3]

For lack of more precise information, suppose we assume that the deliveries per store for individual distributors were to increase from the present average of about 1.5 cases to 3.0 cases.[4] Assume further that wholesale routes operate for eight hours daily, and that daily truck travel averages 30 miles per route. These values may be substituted in the wholesale delivery-time equation (10.26), and estimates may then be made of the volume that could be delivered in an eight-hour day. These calculations result in an estimate of about 72 cases with deliveries of 1.5 cases per customer. Converted to a quart basis, the estimate of 1,440 quarts per day compares favorably with the present average of about 1,375 quarts for major Connecticut markets. With deliveries averaging 3.0 cases per customer, on the other hand, route volumes could average about 133 cases or 2,660 quarts per day.

To convert these volume estimates to estimates of costs, we need to refer to the truck and labor cost information given in Chapters 9 and 10. The daily costs of operating a 3-ton wholesale truck were given as

$$C_3 = \$2.979 + \$0.0368D. \tag{9.9}$$

With D equal to 30 miles, truck costs would be about $4.08 per day. In Chapter 10 we discussed labor costs for wholesale delivery routes and established $15.62 per day as appropriate for postwar conditions. Combining these, the total costs of wholesale

[3] See the Appendix for a brief discussion of the costs of handling milk through stores and depots.

[4] With 30 percent of the volume in glass bottles (12 quarts to the case) and 70 percent in fiber (20 to 24 quarts to the case), the quart equivalent of a case will average about 20 quarts. This conversion ratio has been used throughout the wholesale studies.

delivery would be about $19.70 per day. If daily route volumes increased from 1,440 to 2,660 quarts, then, delivery costs would be reduced from about 1.36 cents to 0.74 cent per quart, or a saving of about 0.6 cent per quart in delivery alone. Plant costs would probably be unaffected, although some exclusively wholesale plants do carry on streamlined operations at low costs.[5] As indicated above, store margins might be narrowed as a result of the great increase in the volume of milk sold, but estimates of the savings possible are difficult or impossible to make.

Perhaps the over-all effect of such a program would be to permit the out-of-store price to decrease about 1 cent per quart, with approximately two-thirds of the decrease representing savings in delivery costs and the balance, the narrowing of store margins. Since the store differential in Connecticut markets is now 1 cent, this would mean a total saving of 2 cents as compared to the existing levels of home-delivered prices.

It need not be emphasized that this estimate is subject to wide variation depending on the particular ways in which wholesale distribution might develop if retail were eliminated and all dealers permitted to enter the wholesale trade on an unrestricted basis. It is quite conceivable that a number of the smaller distributors who now have little if any wholesale contacts would be forced out of business; or a system of price discounts might develop that would encourage each store manager to buy from a single distributor, with the result that the growth of delivery duplication would be limited and savings might be greater than those indicated. As a consequence, the estimate of savings of 1 cent per quart below present wholesale and store margins must be viewed simply as a rough guess based on the premise that *some* savings would almost certainly accompany such a program.

Zoned wholesale deliveries

Even if wholesale deliveries were to be zoned, and each distributor allocated an exclusive delivery territory, it would be difficult to make an accurate prediction of the potential level of costs. In the foregoing retail studies, it was assumed that the

[5] See, for example, the plant costs reported by R. W. Bartlett, *The Milk Industry.*

existing geographic pattern of homes and customers would be unaffected by the reorganization proposals, and delivery routes were planned to serve these customers. With all milk sales through stores, however, there would be marked increases both in the number of stores handling milk and in the volume per store. As a consequence, the existing geographic pattern of customers (stores) has little significance, and cost calculations can only be made on the basis of some assumption as to the geographic distribution of wholesale customers.

It will be recalled that such a hypothetical situation was developed in Chapter 12, on the assumption that stores or milk depots would be scattered throughout a market in such a manner that no customer would be forced to travel more than 0.2 mile in order to obtain milk supplies. While this situation is obviously arbitrary, it will serve to indicate the general potentials of a milk-market reorganization based on wholesale delivery without duplication of routes and sales efforts.

The effects of density on potential route volumes under such a system were indicated in Fig. 55. Using this and the labor and truck cost information given in Chapters 9, 10, and 12, the effects of density on wholesale delivery costs have been computed and are presented in Fig. 68. Labor costs per case decrease with increases in market density, representing the allocation of the fixed $15.62 per day over an increasing route volume. Truck costs also decrease, but the cost function is discontinuous because of the necessary shifting to larger trucks as route volume increases. Combined costs for wholesale delivery would average about $0.184 per case or 0.92 cent per quart with density of 15 cases per square mile — approximately the average density for secondary markets in Connecticut. At a density of 100 cases — the average for major markets — costs would average about $0.070 per case or 0.35 cent per quart.

Limiting our comparisons to the major markets, since most wholesale operations of any size are now found in these markets, it would appear that delivery costs might be reduced from the present level of about 1.37 cents to 0.35 cent per quart. This saving of more that 1 cent would be added to any reduction in the store margin to obtain an estimate of total savings. As in the

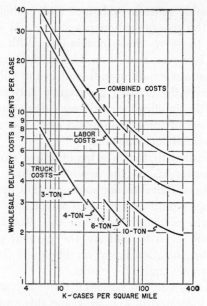

Fig. 68. Effects of delivery density on the costs of operating wholesale milk-delivery routes.

previous section, the potential narrowing of the store margin may be assumed to average about 0.4 cent per quart, which would make the total savings amount to some 1.4 cents per quart. When the present store differential of 1 cent is added, it would appear that a system of zoned wholesale deliveries might permit savings of about 2.4 cents per quart below the current level of retail delivered prices with alternate-day delivery.

The effects of volume per customer on wholesale delivery costs

Mention has been made of the possibility of reducing wholesale delivery duplication through a system of volume discounts. Under such a plan, milk would be priced to the store at different levels depending on the quantity purchased from a single distributor. This would give the store manager an incentive to consolidate his purchases, and so would tend to reduce wholesale-delivery duplication. Such a program might have considerable merit without any further type of reorganization, and has been the subject of considerable interest with the growth of mass food-distributing agencies and the "captive" creamery.[6]

As in the previous sections, accurate estimates of costs must be based on the particular conditions in any market, but the use of the cost relations and the general nature of the results may be illustrated by application to a hypothetical case. Suppose we again assume that wholesale deliveries are made by one-man routes traveling an average of 30 miles per day, and that the daily route time is eight hours.[7] Substituting these values in equation (10.26), we obtain the following formula:

$$289.48 = 3.958C + 0.346V + 1.531N, \qquad (15.1)$$

where as before C represents the number of customers served, V the daily route volume in case equivalents, and N the total number of delivery trips from the truck to consumers' establishments. Using S to represent the case equivalents per customer (store), and assuming a maximum of five cases per delivery trip using hand trucks or dollies, this may be further reduced to:

$$291.48 = \frac{3.958V}{S} + 0.346V + \frac{1.531V}{S}(S/5), \qquad (15.2)$$

where the final term $(S/5)$ must always be rounded upward to the nearest whole number, since it is impossible to make fractional delivery trips. From this equation it is clear that, if we specify the average volume per store S, it will be possible to calculate the corresponding route volume that could be handled in an eight-hour day. It will then be possible to work back from this volume to define the corresponding number of customer stops, time requirements per stop, and time requirements per case of milk delivered.

The results of such calculations are summarized in Table 102 and in Fig. 69 through 72. In Fig. 69, we show the effects of in-

[6] D. A. Clarke, Jr., "Wholesale Milk Delivery."
[7] Note that the constant mileage is a simplification, and that increases in route volume would ordinarily require increases in mileage. Drastic reduction in the number of stores that would be served with increases in volume per store, however, will tend to offset this and the assumption should not distort the results materially.

TABLE 102. The effects of volume per customer stop on wholesale delivery route volume and truck costs.*

Number of cases	S/5†	$\frac{3.958}{S}$	$\frac{1.531}{S}\left(\frac{S}{5}\right)$	Daily route volume (cases)	Number of customers served	Route minutes Per case	Route minutes Per stop	Truck costs (cents) Per case	Truck costs (cents) Per stop
1	1	3.958	1.531	50	50.0	9.60	9.6	8.16	8.2
2	1	1.979	.766	94	47.0	5.11	10.2	4.34	8.7
3	1	1.319	.510	134	44.7	3.58	10.7	3.04	9.1
4	1	.990	.383	170	42.5	2.82	11.3	2.65	10.6
5	1	.792	.306	202	40.5	2.38	11.9	3.00	15.0
5	2	.792	.612	167	33.4	2.87	14.4	2.70	13.5
6	2	.660	.510	192	32.0	2.50	15.0	2.35	14.1
7	2	.565	.437	216	30.9	2.22	15.5	2.80	19.6
10	2	.396	.306	278	27.8	1.73	17.3	2.18	21.8
10	3	.396	.459	243	24.3	1.98	19.8	2.50	25.0
12	3	.330	.383	275	22.9	1.75	21.0	2.21	26.5
13	3	. 304	.353	291	22.4	1.65	21.4	2.72	35.4
15	3	.264	.306	318	21.2	1.51	22.6	2.49	37.4
15	4	.264	.408	286	19.1	1.68	25.2	2.12	31.8
16	4	.247	.383	299	18.7	1.61	25.8	2.65	42.4
20	4	.198	.306	343	17.2	1.40	28.0	2.30	46.0
20	5	.198	.383	314	15.7	1.53	30.6	2.52	50.4
25	5	.158	.306	360	14.4	1.33	33.2	2.19	54.8
25	6	.158	.367	335	13.4	1.43	35.8	2.35	58.8
30	6	.132	.306	372	12.4	1.29	3.87	2.12	63.6
30	7	.132	.357	349	11.6	1.38	41.4	2.27	68.1
50	10	.079	.306	399	8.0	1.20	60.0	1.97	98.5
50	11	.079	.337	382	7.6	1.26	63.0	2.07	103.5

* See equations (15.1) and (15.2) for explanation of symbols.
† Rounded upward to nearest whole number—this represents the number of delivery trips per customer.

creases in the volume per customer stop on the total number of cases per route and on the number of customers served by a single route. Route volumes will increase with increases in volume per stop but at a decreasing rate, from 50 cases where deliveries average only one case per store to nearly 400 cases as deliveries increase to more than 30 cases per store. At the same time, the number of stores served would decrease from 50 with one case per store to 12 with 30 cases per store. The discontinuities in these diagrams are a reflection of the number of delivery trips per store — the range up to five cases being handled by one trip, from 6 to 10 cases by two trips, and so on.

Figure 70 shows the progression of time per customer stop as the volume per stop increases. Again there is a step-type rate of increase reflecting the discontinuities of individual delivery trips, but the entire relation may be represented quite accurately by the following equation:

$$t = 8 + 1.07S, \qquad (15.3)$$

where t represents the time per stop in minutes and S the number of case equivalents per customer store. This time equation can

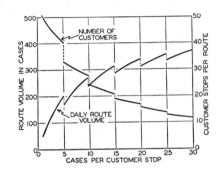

Fig. 69. Effects of volume per customer stop on wholesale delivery-route volumes and number of customers per route.

be converted into the following labor cost function by applying the rate of $0.0325 per minute developed in Chapter 10:

$$c_1 = \$0.26 + \$0.0348S, \qquad (15.4)$$

where c_1 represents the labor cost per customer (store) and S the number of cases per store. This function is appropriate for Connecticut conditions; equations for other markets can be obtained by applying suitable labor rates to equation (15.3).

Turning now to truck costs, equations (9.9) through (9.12) provide us with the basis for our present calculations. Remembering that we have held route mileage constant at 30 miles per day, these indicate daily costs of $4.08 for 3-ton trucks, $4.51 for 4-ton trucks, $6.05 for 6-ton trucks, and $7.90 for 10-ton wholesale trucks.[8] Together with the previously presented route volume and number of customer regressions, these permit us to estimate

[8] Based on 300 days of operation per year.

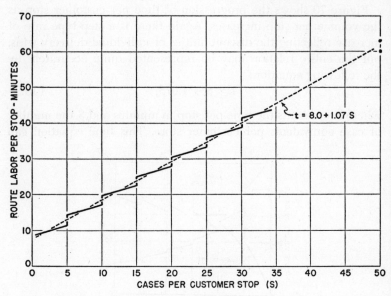

Fig. 70. *Effect of volume per customer stop on route labor time per stop.*

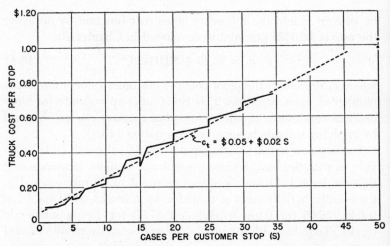

Fig. 71. *Effect of volume per customer stop on wholesale truck costs per customer stop.*

delivery-truck costs per case or per customer stop. Such estimates are given in Fig. 71 and show costs per customer increasing in a discontinuous but rather regular pattern with increase in number of cases per customer. The discontinuities here include not only the delivery trip breaks important in the time regressions but also the increases in truck size. The diagram also shows a smoothed regression that may be used as a more convenient approximation to the irregular progression. This regression corresponds to the equation

$$c_t = \$0.05 + \$0.02S, \qquad (15.5)$$

where c_t represents the truck costs per customer and S the number of cases delivered per customer.

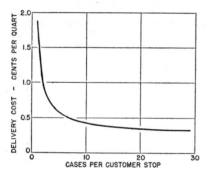

Fig. 72. *Effect of volume per customer stop on wholesale delivery costs per quart.*

To obtain an expression for wholesale delivery costs per customer simply requires the addition of equations (15.4) and (15.5):

$$c_d = \$0.31 + \$0.0548S. \qquad (15.6)$$

According to this equation, the cost of making a wholesale delivery can be approximated by a constant cost of $0.31 per delivery plus a variable charge of about $0.055 per case. Using 20 quarts as the equivalent of one case, this cost-per-delivery relation has been converted to the cost-per-quart regression shown in Fig. 72. With volume per delivery of only one case, wholesale delivery costs would average about 1.8 cents per quart. Increases in volume are associated with rapid decreases in delivery costs, with costs per quart averaging less than 0.6 cent with a volume of five cases and about 0.43 cent with a volume of 10 cases. Beyond 10 cases, unit costs decrease slowly, and would average about 0.3 cent per quart for 50-case deliveries.

Any of a number of price-discount plans could be used to approximate this cost pattern. Perhaps the most convenient would be to fix a service charge of $0.31 per delivery, plus an additional charge of about $0.055 per case.[9] These charges would cover only the delivery operation, and the price schedule would need to reflect the producer price for the raw product and an allowance to cover bottling and processing costs. Since these types of cost are not related to volume per delivery, however, only the delivery costs would influence the volume-discount schedule.

[9] For a discussion of the use of service charges in pricing milk, see "The Elwell Plan of Pricing Milk," *American Milk Review*, XII, *No. 11* (November 1950).

16 —

SUMMARY OF FINDINGS

Route mileages and route volumes

The duplication of delivery routes under the present system of milk distribution was described in Part Two, while Part Three provided the basis for reorganization studies. Retail delivery route mileages and volumes were shown to be functions of delivery densities, and two general methods of increasing effective densities were noted: (1) by reducing the duplication of routes operated by competing dealers; and (2) by lengthening the time span between deliveries. Part Four has applied these methods to 17 rural towns, five secondary markets, and two major markets in Connecticut, and estimates have been made of the physical and economic requirements under reorganized conditions.

Route mileage requirements under a system of exclusive delivery territories are generalized in curves I and III of Fig. 73, while curves II and IV show similar relations for municipal distribution. These regressions, based on the results for the sample markets, show delivery mileage requirements as inverse functions of market densities M. Disregarding curvilinearity, average route mileage requirements where total delivery densities range between 10 and 100 quarts per street mile are approximately functions of $M^{-0.75}$ in the case of daily delivery with exclusive territories, $M^{-0.72}$ for alternate-day exclusive territories, $M^{-0.66}$ for daily delivery with municipal distribution, and $M^{-0.60}$ for alternate-day municipal delivery. These exponents differ from -1.0 (representing a perfect inverse relation) for several reasons: (1) in low-density ranges, the ratio of total volume to road miles is not a good indicator of market density, for all roads in rural towns will not be covered by delivery routes; (2) some route duplication will be unavoidable under any system of delivery in most markets; and (3) and most important, route requirements include traveling between plants and delivery areas, and these "hauling" mileages will become more important as market density increases, especially in the case of municipal distribution.

Since mileage requirements are influenced by such factors as the number of dealers serving a market, present and potential plant locations, and the peculiar network of streets, the above regressions do not describe the results of the sample market studies with perfect accuracy. The standard errors of an individual estimate for both of the exclusive-territory regressions are

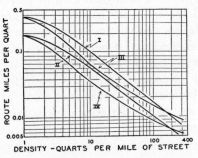

Fig. 73. *Relations between total delivery density and milk delivery mileage requirements under reorganized systems of distribution: I, exclusive territories, daily delivery; II, exclusive territories, alternate-day delivery; III, municipal distribution, daily delivery; IV, municipal distribution, alternate-day delivery. Compare with requirements for the present system, Fig. 22.*

about 30 percent, while for the municipal-distribution curves they average 18 percent. In spite of these ranges, however, the regressions provide useful bases for making tentative estimates for other markets. Moreover, milk-delivery mileage requirements are given as functions of total deliveries and total street miles — measures readily obtainable for most markets.

Using these regressions, estimates have been made for all Connecticut towns, with the results given in Table 103. These group estimates are considerably more reliable than would be any single market estimate, for there is a tendency for high and low estimates to average out. The standard errors of the exclusive-territory group estimates are about 3 percent for the rural towns,

5 percent for the secondary markets, 10 percent for the major markets, and about 2.3 percent for the state totals. With municipal distribution, the standard errors of estimate are approximately 2 percent for the rural-town group, 3 percent for secondary markets, 6 percent for major markets, and 1.4 percent for the state totals.

Using daily delivery under the present system as a base, the

TABLE 103. Estimates of milk-delivery mileages under the present and reorganized distribution systems, Connecticut markets.

Type of market and distribution system	Daily Number of towns	Daily volume (quarts)*	Estimated miles per day†	
			Daily delivery	Alternate-day delivery
Rural towns................	125	67,633		
Present system...........			9,600	5,300
Exclusive territories......			5,900	3,600
Municipal distribution....			4,500	2,300
Secondary markets.........	36	209,663		
Present system...........			25,700	15,400
Exclusive territories......			5,300	3,500
Municipal distribution....			4,300	2,400
Major markets.............	8	238,363		
Present system...........			25,700	16,200
Exclusive territories......			2,400	1,500
Municipal distribution....			2,500	1,500
Entire State..............	169	515,659		
Present system...........			61,100	37,000
Exclusive territories......			13,600	8,700
Municipal distribution....			11,400	6,300

* Based on 1940 records of the Connecticut Milk Administrator.
† Estimated from the regressions given in Figs. 22 and 73.

estimates indicate that alternate-day operations reduced milk-delivery route mileages about 40 percent in Connecticut, with savings slightly higher in rural markets and lower in major markets. Exclusive territories would permit average reductions of 78 percent with daily delivery and 86 percent with alternate-day delivery, while municipal distribution would increase these to 81 and 90 percent respectively. With both types of delivery reorganization, potential savings would be greatest in the high-density markets and would decrease as density decreases.

Potential route volumes are also functions of delivery density, and appropriate values may be determined from the above regressions and the relations between route density and potential route volumes given in Fig. 54. With exclusive delivery territories and daily delivery, potential volumes would increase rapidly from appoximately 190 quarts with a density of 1 quart per street mile to 400 quarts with a density of 30 quarts per street mile, and then more slowly to 450 quarts with density of 300 quarts per mile. Alternate-day delivery would permit loads of 350 quarts with total deliveries of 1 quart per street mile, 670 quarts with a density of 30 quarts per mile, and about 750 quarts per day with a density of 300 quarts per street mile. Potential volumes with municipal distribution would not differ significantly from the above in the very low and very high density ranges, but would be somewhat higher in the intermediate ranges. With a density of 30 quarts per street mile, for example, municipal distribution would permit route volumes of approximately 410 quarts with daily delivery and 700 quarts per day with alternate-day delivery.

In presenting these general relations between market densities and milk-delivery requirements, it is not contended that they provide complete and satisfactory bases on which to inaugurate reorganization programs in any milk market. Rather, they may be used to indicate the approximate levels of performance that can be expected from such programs. If such a program were to be adopted in any market, it would have to be preceded by detailed studies similar to those made in the sample markets and specific requirements estimated for the particular market in question.

Estimated costs and potential savings

Estimates of combined plant and delivery costs under several systems of milk distribution have been made in the foregoing chapters, and these are summarized in Table 104. It should be emphasized that these estimates represent potential rather than actual costs, in that they are based on cost rates and wages that appear appropriate for Connecticut conditions in the postwar (1947) period. In addition, and especially in the rural markets, these cost estimates reflect assumptions about the use of non-

TABLE 104. Estimated milk-distribution costs under present and reorganized delivery systems, Connecticut markets.

Type of market and distribution system	Estimated distribution costs per quart*	Potential savings per quart†
Rural towns		
Present system		
Daily delivery...............	$0.092	$0.018‡
Alternate-day...............	.074	—
Exclusive territories		
Daily delivery...............	.080	.006‡
Alternate-day...............	.067	.007
Municipal distribution		
Daily delivery...............	.062	.012
Alternate-day...............	.051	.023
Secondary markets		
Present system		
Daily delivery...............	.111	.025‡
Alternate-day...............	.086	—
Exclusive territories		
Daily delivery...............	.086	.00
Alternate-day...............	.068	.018
Municipal distribution		
Daily delivery...............	.064	.022
Alternate-day...............	.046	.040
Major markets		
Present system		
Daily delivery...............	.096	.026‡
Alternate-day...............	.070	—
Exclusive territories		
Daily delivery...............	.069	.001
Alternate-day...............	.051	.019
Municipal distribution		
Daily delivery...............	.060	.010
Alternate-day...............	.042	.028
Wholesale deliveries**............	—	.024

* Averages for sample markets, plant and delivery operations, as reported in Tables 95 and 100.

† Savings relative to the estimated costs for the present system with alternate-day delivery.

‡ Costs higher than present alternate-day delivery.

** Zoned wholesale deliveries, as reported in Chapter 15.

specialized labor and equipment that may or may not correspond to actual conditions for particular distributors. For these reasons, the *differences* in estimated costs given in the last column of the table are probably of more significance than the absolute levels of costs.

Cost differences have been calculated using the present system of alternate-day delivery as a base. These indicate that, with 1947 wages and cost rates, a return to daily delivery would increase costs by about 1.8 cents per quart in rural markets and about 2.5 cents in secondary and urban markets. The reorganization of milk distribution with alternate-day delivery and exclusive delivery territories for each distributor would permit an average reduction of about 0.7 cent per quart in rural markets and of nearly 2.0 cents per quart in secondary and major markets. Municipal milk distribution on an alternate-day basis would make possible average savings of about 2.3 cents per quart in rural markets, 4.0 cents in secondary markets, and 2.8 cents in major markets. The larger savings indicated for secondary markets under this system stem from the fact that plant-cost reduction potentials are greatest when relatively small operations are consolidated, since the economy-of-scale curve declines most rapidly in the lower volume ranges.

Finally, Table 104 includes an estimate of the cost reduction that would accompany the complete elimination of retail distribution. If wholesale deliveries were based on a system of zoned or exclusive territories, it is estimated that costs would be about 2.4 cents per quart below present levels for alternate-day retail distribution. This estimate is admittedly weak, however, and larger savings in both delivery and store operations would be possible if the number of stores or milk depots were limited.

These brief statements represent the end products of the detailed studies of city milk distribution. They are based entirely on the physical and economic potentialities, however, and take no account of the economic desirability of such adjustments. Before final conclusions can be drawn, some attention must be paid to the consumption and demand side of milk distribution. This will be the subject of Part Five.

PART FIVE ———

*THE CONSUMER AND MILK
DISTRIBUTION*

17 —

CONSUMER DEMANDS
AND PREFERENCES

The problem of determining consumer demands

The studies reported in Part Four have indicated that various methods of reorganizing milk distribution might result in cost reductions ranging from 0.7 to 4.0 cents per quart. Now, if minimum direct costs were the sole consideration it would be a simple matter to conclude that some form of municipal distribution is the most desirable type of milk marketing, or, better yet, that all consumers should be forced to obtain their supplies directly from dealers' plants. But this is not the case.

In an economy such as ours, consumers frequently do not want the cheapest hat or car or bottle of milk, but are willing to pay more for a better product or for more or better service. When a housewife buys a bottle of milk, she buys all of the associated services of processing and delivery that go with it. Her demand is a joint demand for the physical product, the brand, and the service, and any change in the service or the conditions of delivery may be as significant to her as a change in butterfat test or bacterial content.

In most situations, consumer demands for brands and service are expressed in exactly the same manner as are demands for products — by bidding on the market. Demands for and supplies of alternative services are brought into equilibrium through the market and pricing mechanism. Unfortunately, this market mechanism operates only imperfectly, if at all, in the present case. Prices (margins) for services such as home or store delivery are frequently set administratively or by "general consent" of the dealers in a given market.

Many of the methods in question are mutually exclusive, so that they cannot exist side by side as alternatives between which consumers are free to choose. While we can have home and store delivery at the same time, although usually with some diseconomies in both, it is impossible to offer both the present system and a system of exclusive territories on the market so that consumers can select one or the other. Finally, the whole problem is complicated by the already-mentioned fact that the demands for products and services are joint demands, and as such are difficult to separate into component parts. The demand for milk is usually taken to be fairly inelastic; if dealers elect to widen their margins, the reactions of consumers are not based on their demands for delivery services alone but on their demands for milk plus the services.

Under these conditions, it is useless to expect that marketing reorganizations will take place more or less automatically and lead easily to the most desirable organization. The nature of the alternatives and of the market precludes this direct solution. It would be possible to try out such programs experimentally, but social experiments of this type are difficult to inaugurate. Some indications of consumer reactions and preferences may be had by considering markets where such programs have been adopted, but such cases are almost nonexistent in the United States. The last remaining alternative, and it is admittedly a poor one, is to question groups of consumers in an effort to determine how they *would* react under the several situations.

The consumer studies

In view of the above, consumer surveys were made in two Connecticut markets in 1946 to determine consumer reactions to alternate-day delivery, exclusive delivery territories, municipal distribution, and the complete elimination of retail milk delivery. In addition, several statistical analyses were made of the influence of store price differentials on the proportion of store milk sales in a number of markets scattered throughout the United States.

The procedure used in the consumer surveys was essentially

one of drawing random samples of areas to be visited in Willimantic, a secondary market with a population of 14,000, and in
metropolitan Hartford, a seven-town district comprising one of
the largest milk markets in the state and with a combined population of about 250,000.[1] The number of households to be visited in
each small area was established in proportion to the milk consumption of the area, and personal visits were made to obtain the
desired information. Each householder was questioned to obtain
the composition and income of the family, the volume of milk
delivered to the home and purchased at stores, and the reaction
to alternate-day delivery and the other proposals. In the latter
cases, the householder was asked to estimate the monetary savings
that would be necessary to induce her to accept the program in
question.

A total of 152 records were obtained in Willimantic, representing about 5 percent of the milk consumption of the market. A
sample of only about 1 percent in the Hartford area yielded 449
records. These questionnaires were tabulated, and the results are
presented in the following pages. For comparison, summaries of
the results of a number of studies in other states have also been
presented.

Consumer reactions to alternate-day delivery

Alternate-day milk delivery was introduced in many Connecticut markets early in 1942. In June of that year the Connecticut
Milk Administrator outlawed daily deliveries in the major markets of the state for the war period, while the Office of Defense
Transportation later gave national status to the program. These
orders were terminated with the end of the emergency period,
but the alternate-day delivery program has been retained almost
without exception. Most Connecticut consumers, then, had had
four years of experience with this form of delivery when the
present survey was made.

In a surprisingly large number of homes, alternate-day delivery
proved to be more convenient and acceptable than daily delivery;
14 percent of the consumers interviewed in Willimantic and 38

[1] See the Appendix for details of the sampling procedure and the questionnaire.

percent in Hartford actually preferred alternate-day to daily delivery at the same price (Table 105). Including these groups, 68 percent of the Willimantic consumers and 79 percent of the Hartford consumers were so well satisfied with the program that they expressed themselves as unwilling to pay a higher price in order to have daily delivery. Most of those indicating a willingness to pay for daily service limited the price increase to 1 cent or less per quart.

TABLE 105. Consumer reactions to alternate-day milk delivery in two Connecticut markets, 1946.

Consumer reaction	Price differential (cents per quart)	Households in			
		Willimantic		Hartford	
		Number	Percent*	Number	Percent*
Prefer alternate-day delivery.........	0	20	14	172	38
Indifferent........	0	47	32	104	23
Prefer daily.......	0	32	22	81	18
	+½	9	6	20	4
	+1	27	19	51	11
	+2	9	6	14	3
	+3	—	—	2	1
	+4	—	—	1	†
	+5‡	1	1	2	1
Uncertain.........	—	7		2	
Total.........	—	152		449	

* Based on totals less those "uncertain." May not add to 100 percent because of rounding.
† Less than 0.5 percent.
‡ Including those who would have been willing to pay more than 5 cents per quart and those completely unsatisfied with alternate-day delivery.

Seven percent of the Willimantic householders and about 1 percent of those in the Hartford area indicated that space-saving square bottles would reduce or eliminate their dissatisfaction with alternate-day delivery. This group included 27 percent of the Willimantic consumers who were willing to pay 1 cent or more to have daily delivery, but only 4 percent of the comparable group in Hartford. Many others admitted that this type of bottle would be a convenience, but that it would not be important enough to affect their price estimates.

Alternate-day delivery results in crowding of home refrigerators, so it is to be expected that customers buying large volumes of milk would be less willing to have the program continued than those using small volumes. The tabulations given in Table 106 indicate that this was true in Connecticut; 81 percent of the households receiving one quart or less per day were unwilling to pay more for daily delivery while only 68 percent of those receiving more than three quarts fell in this category. Less than 10 percent of the consumers in each volume class, however, expressed them-

TABLE 106. Effect of volume of milk purchased on willingness to pay for daily delivery service, Connecticut markets, 1946.

Price differential (cents per quart)	Percent of households*			
	Quarts of milk per day			
	0.5–1.0	1.5–2.0	2.5–3.0	3.5 and over
0.................	81	74	69	68
0.5................	2	6	8	2
1.0................	10	15	15	27
2.0................	6	4	6	3
3.0................	—	†	1	—
4.0................	—	†	—	—
5.0 or more..........	1	—	1	—

* Simple average of the two Connecticut markets. The simple average was used in this and following tabulations because the total sales in Connecticut major markets (such as Hartford) and in secondary markets (such as Willimantic) are approximately equal.
† 0.5 percent or less.

selves as willing to pay more than 1 cent per quart for the return of daily delivery.

Table 107 indicates that per capita income had some effect on the willingness of consumers to pay for daily delivery, but that the relation tended to be negative. Thus 34 percent of households with per capita incomes between $5 and $14 per week were willing to pay 0.5 cent or more per quart for daily delivery while only 20 percent of the households with per capita incomes of $25 or more would pay for this service. Such a relation is logically unacceptable as a true description of the "net" effect of income on the demand for delivery service. It probably reflects the influence of some factor associated with income, possibly the absence of mechanical refrigerators in some low-income homes.

The results of several other surveys of consumer attitudes

TABLE 107. Effect of per capita income on willingness to pay for daily delivery service, Connecticut markets, 1946.

Price differential (cents per quart)	Percent of households*		
	Weekly per capita income		
	$5–$14	$15–$24	$25 and over
0..............................	66	77	80
0.5............................	9	2	2
1.0............................	19	14	7
2.0............................	4	9	10
3.0............................	†	—	—
4.0............................	—	†	—
5.0 or more....................	—	—	†

* Simple average of the two Connecticut surveys; may not add to 100 percent because of rounding. Income data were obtained for 64 percent of the Willimantic households and 59 percent of the Hartford households.

† 0.5 percent or less.

TABLE 108. Summary of the proportion of consumers willing to accept alternate-day milk delivery for indicated savings as reported in several studies.

Price differential cents per quart	Cumulative percent of households*				
	Connecticut markets†	Burlington Vermont‡	Essex Junction Vermont‡	New York City New York**	Ithaca New York††
0.........	74	58	51		
−0.5.......	78	66	79		19
−1.0.......	93	78	86	76	31
−2.0.......	98				44
−3.0.......	99				48
−4.0 or more‡‡	100	100	100	100	100

* Not including consumers who were uncertain or unable to give specific answers.

† Simple average of the two Connecticut surveys.

‡ T. M. Adams, *Wartime Changes in Milk Distribution and in the Consumption of Milk, Cream, Butter, and Oleomargarine in Vermont* (University of Vermont, Agricultural Experiment Station, Bulletin 527, Burlington, Vermont, October 1945).

** Crosley Survey, "E. O. D. Satisfaction," *American Milk Review*, VII, No. 10 (October 1945). This survey questioned consumers as to their willingness to pay 1.3 cents per quart more for the return of daily delivery; 76 percent were unwilling.

†† M. V. Rockwell, "Consumers' Attitudes Toward Proposed Changes in Milk-Delivery Service," *Farm Economics*, No. 127 (Cornell University, November 1941). The details given above are from unpublished tables obtained through the courtesy of Leland Spencer, Department of Agricultural Economics, Cornell University.

‡‡ Including those who were unwilling to accept the program regardless of savings.

toward alternate-day delivery are summarized in Table 108. Some of these results originally were given in terms of the savings required to accept alternate-day delivery, while others were in terms of the price increases that consumers would be willing to pay in order to have the return of daily delivery. In spite of the fact that psychological and other factors may prevent these from being exactly comparable, all have been expressed in terms of savings. In all cases, percentages refer to the group answering the question and do not include those that refused to answer or were uncertain.

In general, Connecticut consumers seemed slightly more satisfied with alternate-day delivery than were consumers in Vermont

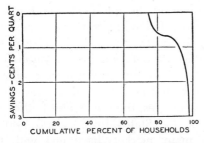

Fig. 74. *Effect of monetary savings on the willingness of Connecticut consumers to accept alternate-day milk delivery.*

and New York City, although the results compare reasonably well. The results of the Ithaca survey, however, differ markedly from the others in that a large proportion of consumers either indicated an unwillingness to accept the program or would accept it only with relatively large savings. This difference probably stems from the fact that the Ithaca survey was made in 1940, before alternate-day operations were in widespread use. The other surveys, including those in Connecticut, were made after the program had been in effect for some time. This reaction against new and untried programs illustrates the difference between consumer forecasts and their subsequent reactions, and must be counted as one of the most serious limitations of the survey method.

The Connecticut results, plotted in Fig. 74, make it clear that the vast majority of consumers would prefer to have alternate-day delivery in order to make the potential savings or to avoid the required price increases. Formal and informal reports from various sections of the country indicate that this reaction is almost universal.

It is significant that consumers' attitudes toward alternate-day delivery are paralleled by the reactions of many milk dealers. In Vermont, 53 percent of the dealers reporting wanted to continue alternate-day operations, 43 percent were opposed, and 9 percent were undecided.[2] In general, the larger dealers and those in the larger markets were more favorable to the program than small dealers and dealers operating in the smaller communities. In the New York City area, 89 percent of the dealers who took a position were in favor of continuing alternate-day service.[3] Of the dealers in this area answering the question, two-thirds suggested that some form of state or federal regulation was desirable to continue the program in the postwar period. "It appears to be conceded very generally that without some form of public regulation, competition would force a return to the more expensive methods of distribution which prevailed before the war, including every-day service, special deliveries, the use of pint bottles, and the like." [4]

In Connecticut, the State Milk Dealers' Association and the Associations in many markets have met with their members, public-health officials, and representatives of consumers and milk routemen in order to continue alternate-day delivery on a voluntary basis. They have also explored the possibility of continuing the program through public action, but such regulatory action has not been necessary up to the present time.

Exclusive delivery territories

In order to check the growth of competitive sales activities and to reduce the duplication of delivery routes that have characterized retail milk distribution, it has been suggested that

[2] T. M. Adams, *Wartime Changes in Milk Distribution and in the Consumption of Milk, Cream, Butter, and Oleomargarine in Vermont* (University of Vermont, Agricultural Experiment Station, Bulletin 527, Burlington, Vermont, October 1945).

[3] Leland Spencer, "Views of New York Milk Distributors Concerning Continuation of Wartime Limitations on Delivery Services After the War Ends," New York State College of Agriculture Mimeograph A. E. 508 (1945).

[4] *Ibid.*, 11.

milk markets be allocated or zoned into exclusive delivery territories. Within each of these territories or areas a single dealer
would have a complete monopoly of retail delivery. Areas would
be assigned to every dealer serving the market, and would be so
arranged as to minimize route mileages while retaining for each
dealer his approximate share of the market. In essence, dealers
would exchange customers until each had his business concentrated in a solid block.

It is clear that such a system would increase the possibilities
for consumer exploitation with respect to service, quality, and

TABLE 109. Savings necessary to induce consumers to accept exclusive
milk delivery territories, two Connecticut markets, 1946.

Price differential (cents per quart)	Households in			
	Willimantic		Hartford	
	Number	Percent*	Number	Percent*
0.................	36	27	212	48
−0.5..............	16	12	23	5
−1.0..............	10	6	24	5
−2.0..............	18	14	25	6
−3.0..............	8	6	19	4
−4.0..............	—	—	6	1
−5.0 or more........	43	33	132	30
Uncertain..........	21		8	
Total..........	152		449	

* Not including consumers who were uncertain or unable to give specific answers.

price unless it were accompanied by some form of public super-
vision and regulation. To test the acceptability of such an arrangement, consumers were asked to indicate the savings that
would induce them to accept it, *provided that services and quality
were satisfactory.*[5] Their responses are summarized in Table 109.

[5] It was not the object of the survey to test consumers' opinions as to the
quality and service that would be associated with exclusive territories; such
nontechnical opinions might be of interest in explaining consumer reluctance
to accept the program but they could not be accepted as significant indications of conditions that would characterize the actual operation of the plan.
A petition widely circulated among Connecticut women's groups a few years
ago attempted to prevent the adoption of a milk-delivery program "endanger-
ing the health and happiness of every mother and child in the State"; the
program referred to was alternate-day delivery.

It is interesting to note that monetary savings were not especially important in this connection; the bulk of consumers expressed themselves as either willing to accept the program without savings or unwilling to accept even with savings of 5 cents or more per quart. In Willimantic, the cumulative percent in favor of the proposal increased from 27 percent with zero savings to 67 percent with savings of 3 cents or less. One-third of the sample in this market were either unwilling to accept the program regardless of savings or would have required savings of 5 cents or more per quart. In Hartford, the proportion increased

TABLE 110. Effect of per capita income on willingness to accept exclusive delivery territories, Connecticut, 1946.

Price differential (cents per quart)	Percent of households*		
	Weekly per capita income		
	$5-$14	$15-$24	$25 and over
0...........................	38	51	35
−0.5.........................	16	8	9
−1.0.........................	6	9	7
−2.0.........................	12	8	9
−3.0.........................	4	4	2
−4.0.........................	1	†	—
−5.0 or more.................	24	21	37

* Simple average of the Connecticut surveys; may not total to 100 percent because of rounding, and not strictly comparable with Table 109 because of the smaller number of records from which income data were obtained.

† 0.5 percent or less.

more slowly from 48 percent at zero savings to 69 percent with savings of 4 cents or less, leaving some 30 percent in the unwilling classification.

Some of the disadvantages (and of the advantages) of exclusive delivery territories would be reduced by permitting several dealers to serve each area. In spite of the wider choice and the possible benefits from the limited form of competition, Connecticut consumers indicated that two dealers per area would not change their replies very materially. In Willimantic, 20 percent of the households (about 33 percent of those who would require savings of 1 cent or more) would have lowered their previous replies by 1 cent per quart. In Hartford, only 5 percent changed

TABLE 111. Savings necessary to induce consumers to give up their choice of milk dealer, Connecticut and New York markets.

Price differential (cents per quart)	Cumulative percent of households*		
	Connecticut markets†	Ithaca New York‡	Jamestown New York**
0.....................	38		3
−0.5....................	46	29	40
−1.0....................	52	45	51
−2.0....................	62	52	61
−3.0....................	68	60	75
−4.0 or more††...........	100	100	100

* Not including consumers who were uncertain or unable to give specific answers.
† Simple average of the two Connecticut surveys.
‡ T. M. Adams, *Wartime Changes in Milk Distribution and in the Consumption of Milk, Cream, Butter, and Oleomargarine in Vermont.*
** Leland Spencer and H. A. Luke, "Consumers' Attitudes Toward Unified Delivery of Milk and the Proposal for a Municipal Milk Plant in Jamestown, New York," New York State College of Agriculture Mimeograph A. E. 404 (September, 1942). Details from unpublished material through the courtesy of the authors.
†† Including those who were unwilling to accept the proposal regardless of savings.

their estimates (about 10 percent of those requiring savings of 1 cent or more).

There was some tendency for consumer reaction to the exclusive-territory proposal to vary with per capita income, although the income effects were irregular and not pronounced (Table 110). Of the families with per capita incomes between $5 and $14 per week, some 60 percent were willing to accept the program for savings of 1 cent or less while only 24 percent were unwilling to consider it unless savings were 5 cents or more. With per capita

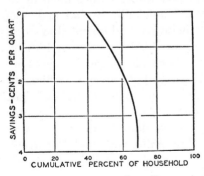

Fig. 75. *Effect of monetary savings on the willingness of Connecticut consumers to accept exclusive milk delivery territories.*

incomes of $25 or more per week, the proportions were 51 and 37 percent respectively.

The Connecticut results have been averaged and accumulated in Table 111, together with similar results for two markets in New York. With savings of 1 cent or more per quart, the findings of these studies are remarkably consistent. These data and the material in Fig. 75 suggest that, while the demand for such a program is far from unanimous, a majority of consumers would be willing to give exclusive territories a trial. Many consumers would be reluctant to give up their present dealer, but the choice of a dealer is more of a chance affair that has sometimes been supposed. With the standardization of methods, products, and services that applies to much of modern milk distribution, this chance element must be viewed as highly rational consumer reaction.

Municipal milk distribution

While some form of complete monopoly in milk distribution under public ownership or public utility control has frequently been suggested, the town of Tarboro, North Carolina, is the only place in the United States known to the author where milk distribution is handled under such a system.[6] The potential cost advantages in delivery and in plant operation of such a plan are so great, however, that questions regarding it were included in the Connecticut surveys. Consumers were asked to estimate the monetary savings that would induce them to accept milk distribution through a municipally owned and operated system or through a privately owned and operated monopoly under public-utility regulation, provided that the equities of present dealers were liquidated at fair and reasonable valuations.

As the data in Table 112 indicate, Willimantic consumers appeared to be slightly more reluctant and Hartford consumers considerably more reluctant to accept such a plan than they were in the case of exclusive delivery territories. About 24 percent of those interviewed in Willimantic and 31 percent of the Hartford group expressed themselves as willing to accept the program

[6] A. J. Nixon and O. M. Reed, *Municipal Milk Distribution in Tarboro, North Carolina.*

without savings, but 40 percent in Willimantic and 51 percent in Hartford would have been unwilling to accept unless savings amounted to 5 cents or more per quart.

Some of this reluctance was attributed to dissatisfaction with municipal operations in garbage disposal, snow removal, and the like or to a feeling that public-utility regulation was not working in the interest of consumers. In short, there was a tendency to reject the proposal both by those who would object to public ownership and those who would object to private monopoly under public regulation. It is possible, therefore, that a clearly

TABLE 112. Savings necessary to induce consumers to accept milk delivery through a centralized plant and delivery system under public or private operation, two Connecticut markets, 1946.

Price differential (cents per quart)	Households in			
	Willimantic		Hartford	
	Number	Percent*	Number	Percent*
0................	30	24	129	31
−0.5.............	10	8	21	5
−1.0.............	15	12	16	4
−2.0.............	13	10	17	4
−3.0.............	6	5	13	3
−4.0.............	1	1	11	3
−5.0 or more........	51	40	214	51
Uncertain...........	26		28	
Total..........	152		449	

* Not including consumers who were uncertain or unable to give specific answers.

stated proposal along either line might have been more acceptable than the mixed proposal as stated and explained in the survey.

Consumers with relatively high incomes were less willing to accept this proposal than were those with low incomes (Table 113). Only 30 percent of the high-income group expressed themselves as willing to accept municipal distribution with savings of 1 cent per quart or less, as compared to 49 percent for the low-income group; 56 percent of the high-income households were either completely unwilling to consider the plan or indicated necessary savings of at least 5 cents per quart as compared to 34 percent of the low-income households. Corresponding to these figures, the proportion of low-income consumers willing to accept the program increased by about 10 percent for each 1-cent increase in savings while the proportion of high-income consumers increased only 5 percent.

The 1942 consumer survey in Jamestown, New York, included questions on the desirability of a municipal milk-delivery system.[7] This proposal had been seriously discussed in Jamestown, and had received considerable publicity in local newspapers prior to the survey. On the basis of more than a thousand replies, it appeared that 62 percent of the families favored the proposal, 25 percent were uncertain, and only 13 percent were definitely

TABLE 113. Effect of per capita income on willingness to accept municipal milk distribution, Connecticut, 1946.

Price differential (cents per quart)	Percent of households*		
	Weekly per capita income		
	$5–$14	$15–$24	$25 and over
0	28	36	26
−0.5	12	4	2
−1.0	9	9	2
−2.0	10	8	10
−3.0	6	5	2
−4.0	2	2	4
−5.0 or more	34	38	56

* Simple average of the Connecticut surveys; may not total to 100 percent because of rounding, and not strictly comparable with Table 112 because of smaller number of records from which income data were obtained.

opposed. Lower prices were cited as the most common reason for favoring the program, while such items as savings in manpower and equipment, improved quality, and improved service were frequently listed. Interestingly enough, increased prices and decreased quality and service were sometimes suggested as possible disadvantages, together with unfair treatment of present dealers.

The average of the Connecticut survey results is given in Fig.

[7] Leland Spencer and H. A. Luke, "Consumers' Attitudes Toward Unified Delivery of Milk and the Proposal for a Municipal Milk Plant in Jamestown, New York," New York State College of Agriculture Mimeograph A. E. 404 (September 1942). Details from unpublished material through the courtesy of the authors.

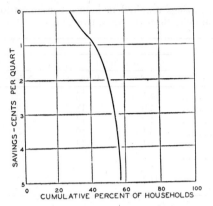

Fig. 76. Effect of monetary savings on the willingness of Connecticut consumers to accept municipal milk distribution.

76. This curve indicates that about half of Connecticut consumers would be willing to try municipal milk operations at the probable levels of savings. The Jamestown results summarized above suggest that the proportion favoring such a program would increase after discussion and publicity had removed some of the newness of the proposal.

Milk sales through stores

While the differential between store and home-delivered milk prices has not been fixed by the Connecticut Milk Administration for some years, 1 cent per quart has been quite typical throughout the state. Perhaps as a consequence, very few consumers purchase their supplies exclusively through stores and the proportion of store sales to total home consumption is relatively low. The surveys here reported found only 7 percent of the homes in Willimantic and 3 percent in metropolitan Hartford using stores as their sole sources of milk supply. Many others supplemented home delivery with regular or occasional store purchases, however, so that store sales accounted for 16 and 9 percent respectively of total home consumption in the two markets.

As is indicated in Table 114 and Fig. 77, most Connecticut consumers would be very reluctant to give up the convenience of home delivery. In Willimantic, 44 percent of those interviewed

TABLE 114. Savings required to induce consumers to obtain all of
their milk supplies through stores, two Connecticut markets, 1946.

Price differential (cents per quart)	Households in			
	Willimantic		Hartford	
	Number	Percent*	Number	Percent*
−1.0 or less†........	21	15	27	6
−2.0..............	26	18	46	10
−3.0..............	20	14	54	12
−4.0..............	14	10	39	9
−5.0 or more........	64	44	277	63
Uncertain...........	7		6	
Total...........	152		449	

* Not including consumers who were uncertain or unable to give specific answers.

† With typical store differentials of 1 cent per quart in these markets, only 7 percent
of the Willimantic and 3 percent of the Hartford consumers interviewed were buying all
of their milk supplies through stores. Some were surprised to learn that the store price
was lower.

stated that they were either completely unwilling to give up home
delivery or that the change would require savings of at least 5
cents per quart. Consumers in the Hartford area were even less
"price conscious" in this connection, with 63 percent falling in
this class. As the data in Table 115 indicate, low-income consumers were nearly as reluctant to give up home delivery as were
those with relatively high incomes.

While many mentioned such factors as bulkiness, bottle de-
posits, and bottle returns as disadvantages of store purchases, only

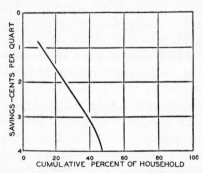

Fig. 77. *Effect of monetary savings on the willingness of Connecticut consumers to give up retail milk delivery and obtain all of their milk supplies
through stores.*

TABLE 115. Effect of per capita income on willingness to obtain all milk supplies through stores, Connecticut, 1946.

Price differential (cents per quart)	Percent of households*		
	Weekly per capita income		
	$5–$14	$15–$24	$25 and over
−1.0 or less...............	12	12	3
−2.0.....................	18	10	12
−3.0.....................	12	16	16
−4.0.....................	10	10	18
−5.0 or more.............	48	57	50

* Simple average of the Connecticut surveys. May not total to 100 percent because of rounding, and not strictly comparable with Table 114 because of smaller numbers of records from which income data were obtained.

9 percent in Willimantic and 2 percent in Hartford would have reduced their estimates of necessary savings if no-deposit, no-return paper containers were available in all stores. Even in these cases the reductions would not have exceeded 1 cent per quart. It is quite clear, then, that home delivery is a service for which most Connecticut milk consumers are more than willing to pay.

Comparable survey results are not available for other markets, but Fig. 78 shows the percent store sales and the actual store price differentials for a number of markets in recent years. While there is some tendency for store sales to be relatively large in markets where the home-delivered price of milk exceeded the price through stores, the relation is far from clear-cut. Such factors as the type of the area, the accessibility of stores, the racial

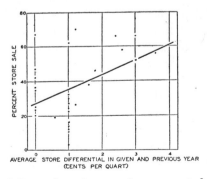

Fig. 78. Store differentials and store sales as reported for a number of milk markets since 1940.

characteristics of the population, the levels of consumer incomes, and the levels of milk prices all contribute to the importance of milk sales through stores. Nevertheless, these data suggest that store sales increase about 8 percent for each 1 cent per quart increase in the store price differential. Only 16 percent of the variance in relative store sales, however, was associated with variations in the differential.[8]

The effects of some of these other factors may be eliminated or reduced by comparing store sales and store differentials in identical markets over a period of time. Paired observations of this

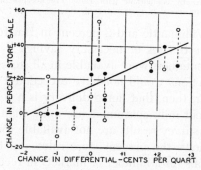

Fig. 79. *Effect of changes in store differential on the percent of milk sold through stores. Based on "paired" observations in identical markets over periods ranging from 5 to 14 years. The original data are represented by the small circles, while the solid dots represent corrections for the variations in time.*

type were available for 11 markets: six comparing changes in sales and differentials in 1935 and 1940; two comparing 1930 and 1940; and three comparing 1926 and 1940. While the nature and size of this sample preclude anything but a preliminary analysis, more than 80 percent of the changes in percent store sales appeared to be associated with changes in the store differential and with the time periods involved. In general, store sales tended to increase nearly 4 percent per year in these markets and to change more than 9 percent with an increase or decrease of 1 cent in the differential. The relation between change in store sales

[8] See the Appendix for basic data and for details of correlation analyses.

and change in store differentials, corrected for trend, is given in Fig. 79.

While these results are in terms of the proportion of milk sold through stores, not in terms of the proportion of consumers that would be willing to give up home delivery completely, they may be accepted as approximately comparable with the consumer-survey results. Comparing the two sets of information, it may be seen that Connecticut consumers expressed themselves as slightly more willing to give up home delivery in response to lower milk prices through stores than would be expected from the actual experience in the sample of relatively large markets. The survey material indicated that an average of 12 percent of the consumers interviewed would shift to store purchases with each 1-cent increase in the differential, while the correlation studies suggested only 8 or 9 percent. Whatever the exact regression, these results lead to the conclusion that the demand for home-delivery service is fairly inelastic and that many factors in addition to price are important to consumers in this connection.

Summary

From the foregoing material, it is apparent that most Connecticut consumers would be interested in programs to reorganize milk distribution with the intent of lowering milk prices. The vast majority of householders interviewed were not willing to pay higher milk prices in order to have their milk delivered every day. About 60 percent of the families would be willing to accept a program involving exclusive delivery territories if consumer savings amounted to 1.8 cents per quart, and about half would favor some form of municipal distribution with savings ranging from 2.8 to 4.0 cents per quart. While considerable amounts of milk are sold through stores in Connecticut markets, much of this supplements regular home delivery and only about one-quarter of the consumers surveyed indicated a willingness to give up home delivery completely in order to save 2.4 cents or less per quart.

While these proportions have been based on careful estimates of the potential savings that would result from milk-distribution reorganization, there is no assurance that savings of this magnitude would be passed on to consumers. Certainly producers and middlemen would want to retain some of the savings in the form of higher producer milk prices, higher wages, and wider margins. As a result, it may be argued that these estimates are too optimistic, even though it is admitted that most of the savings would normally be passed on to consumers through lower prices over a long-run period.

On the other hand, there is evidence that consumers as a group are overconservative in forecasting their reactions to new and changed conditions. This was illustrated by the reported reluc-

TABLE 116. Effect of potential savings on the willingness of Connecticut consumers to consider some form or reorganization of the milk industry.

Potential savings (cents per quart)	Cumulative percent of households*
0.	42
1.0.	60
2.0.	69
3.0.	74
4.0.	77
5.0 or more.	99
Uncertain.	100

* Simple average of Connecticut surveys. This combines consumer replies on exclusive delivery territories, municipal distribution, and the elimination of home delivery, tabulating the lowest savings required to induce the customer to accept any of the three proposals.

tance of consumers in Ithaca, New York, to consider alternate-day delivery in 1940 and the almost universal satisfaction with the program that characterizes consumer reactions in markets where the program has been in effect for some time.

Aside from the reaction to any specific proposal for reorganization, the survey results suggest that most consumers are favorably disposed toward milk-marketing reorganization. It is frequently implied that consumers are perfectly content with the existing system of distribution. The results reported in this study give little support to this contention or little cause for satisfaction on the part of those who have advanced it. Excluding the alternate-day delivery program that already is in effect, more than 40 percent of Connecticut consumers appear willing to have some fairly drastic form of milk-delivery reorganization *without any promise of price reductions* while 60 percent would be interested with savings of 1 cent or less (Table 116). In contrast, only 22 percent are so satisfied with the present system or so distrustful of new proposals that they either would be completely unwilling to change or would require price reductions of 5 cents or more per quart. Such factors as brand names and personal relations with handlers are important in this field as in others, but not so important as to prevent most consumers from giving favorable consideration to new forms of milk distribution.

18 ——

CONCLUSIONS

The Connecticut studies of city milk distribution

The Connecticut studies of city milk distribution have attempted a coördinated attack on the problem of inefficiency in marketing. Preliminary studies described conditions under the present system of distribution, indicating how the combination of competitive and monopolistic elements had resulted in the duplication of routes, excess route and plant capacity, and the multiplication of agencies and "competitive" services. Following this, the theory of efficient and economical distribution was developed. Basic elements in the theory were replaced by empirical relations through studies of route and plant operations, and these were used to develop criteria for reorganization studies. Reorganization studies were then made by combining the fundamental elements into new syntheses and checking the estimated physical and economic requirements for the new organizations against the requirements for the present system. Finally, potential savings were balanced against the expressed demands and preferences of consumers for various types of marketing services.

This procedure has revealed important potential savings in milk distribution. Zoning or allocating cities into exclusive delivery territories for each dealer would permit cost reductions ranging from 0.7 to 1.9 cents per quart. The consolidation of all milk distribution in a single public or private agency would bring important additional savings in plant costs, so that total distribution costs might be reduced 2.3 to 4.0 cents per quart. Total costs under such a system would be about half as high as characterized daily delivery under the present system. Savings estimated at 2.4

cents per quart would result from the complete elimination of retail delivery, but this would actually transfer some of the costs to the consumer by forcing him to carry his own milk supplies from a local store or milk depot.

While demands for marketing services are difficult to approximate, reactions in Connecticut as well as in other states indicate that most consumers would prefer the reorganized systems to the present system if the potential savings materialized in the form of lower milk prices. This conclusion does not extend to the proposal to eliminate home deliveries completely, however, for most consumers expressed themselves as willing to pay 4 cents per quart or more for the convenience of retail delivery.

In addition to the specific results, the studies provide the basis for reorganization studies in other areas. While it is certainly true that milk-marketing conditions differ in every market, reports from all sections of the United States indicate that the general circumstances are essentially similar to those found in Connecticut. Certainly there is little reason to expect pronounced differences in the basic "production" functions, although many cost rates will vary geographically and historically. Such changes may be incorporated in the economic relations given, and the revised functions used to make meaningful estimates of the costs and savings that could be expected from reorganizations of the type discussed.[1]

These studies do not exhaust the possibilities for improved efficiency and economy in milk distribution. As explained above, the approach has been one of synthesizing the basic relations for the existing system into new and different organizations. A host of unexplored possibilities remain that would involve fundamental changes in the nature of the distribution problem. The Connecticut studies have taken as given that fresh, whole milk will be delivered in bottles or containers. What of the possibilities of bulk deliveries — a system that was discarded long ago for sanitary reasons but that might offer possibilities under present techniques? What about unsterilized condensed milk? Preliminary reports from Michigan indicate that a product condensed to

---

[1] In this connection it should be emphasized that the cost estimates are more stable and reliable than the mileage estimates discussed in Chapter 16.

one-third or one-half of its original volume but without the characteristic caramelized flavor of canned condensed or evaporated milk is meeting with favorable consumer reaction and that it may be kept in the ordinary home refrigerator for several weeks without deterioration of quality.[2] Such a product could revolutionize the milk-distribution industry. Many other possibilities might be mentioned, but these few should indicate that the field is far from exhausted.

Some difficulties in market reorganization[3]

The foregoing discussion has stressed the advantages that could be expected from milk-distribution reorganizations. What are the disadvantages? For the most part, they stem from the high degree of monopoly that would be involved. In the case of exclusive delivery territories the granting of delivery monopolies would, unless regulated, open a wide range of possibilities for consumer exploitation through manipulation of prices and margins or through the deterioration of products and services. At present the consumer is afforded a measure of protection through his freedom to choose a milk dealer and to shift to another if the first proves to be unsatisfactory. This provides a competitive incentive to dealers that prevents the development of excessive abuses. At the same time, competition is supposed to insure the elimination of inefficient firms and the rapid adoption of new and improved techniques. In the case of municipal distribution, these difficulties would be augmented by the problems of the equities of concerns now in business and the oft-discussed possibilities of public or public-utility inefficiency.

It is difficult to appraise the true value of these disadvantages. One thing is certain — such programs would necessarily involve public regulation to prevent abuse, and the regulatory agencies would represent an overhead cost tending to offset some of the advantages of the reorganization. It would be a mistake, however,

---

[2] Based on preliminary results of experiments in Michigan cities as reported to the author by C. M. Hardin, Department of Economics, Michigan State College.

[3] This section has drawn heavily on R. G. Bressler, Jr., and Alan MacLeod, "Connecticut Studies Milk Delivery," *Journal of Marketing*, XXII (1947), 211–219.

to assume that such costs apply only to reorganized distribution systems. Public regulation of the milk industry has long been deemed necessary, not only with respect to prices and margins but also for many business practices. The regulation needed for reorganized systems would not differ greatly from that already in effect in many markets, and added costs would probably be quite small.

The value of competition in forcing marketing efficiencies may easily be exaggerated. The major burden of the foregoing pages has been to indicate how drastically the "free" development of milk marketing has failed in this respect. In most cases competition has taken the form of increased services and sales promotion rather than the lowering of costs and prices. Instead of efficiency and costs as low as possible, the limited type of competition has tended to average out costs at levels higher than would be necessary with more rational systems. Under these conditions, it does not seem unreasonable to believe that incentives to efficiency might better be provided by the narrowing of price margins under public control, although the history of public-utility and price regulation is not too reassuring from this standpoint.

The problem of present equities of private concerns and of the responsibility of the public with respect to these equities is a real stumbling block in the path of municipal milk distribution. Perhaps the greatest advantage of the existing system has been that such equities are solely the responsibility of the individual operator, and so the inefficient may be eliminated automatically without direct public expense. Actually, this virtue attaches only to the "accounting" problem, for society loses just as much from the poor allocation of resources in one case as in the other. Nevertheless, the generally accepted procedure in the case of public acquisition seems to involve reimbursing present owners on the basis of reasonable valuations. If this were done, a large part of the properties and equipment so acquired could undoubtedly be utilized in the new organization or sold for other uses, but some net loss would have to be counted as part of the cost of the public venture.

In the last analysis there is no way to evaluate objectively all of these pros and cons except through actual experience. The studies here reported have provided information as specific as possible on certain aspects of the problem — aspects that heretofore have more often been the subject of speculation than of real knowledge. Many other aspects remain unanswered and probably must remain so until actual experience is available to serve as a guide. Public action, if undertaken, can only be based on subjective evaluations of many of these other factors.

The challenge of improved marketing efficiency

While this study has dealt specifically with milk distribution, there can be little doubt that similar imperfections and potential economies characterize many other lines of marketing. Even the most casual survey suggests that too many resources have been drawn into many branches of transportation and of wholesale and retail trade, and that excess capacity and duplication of effort are the rule rather than the exception. While it is true that the rate of business mortality is high in these fields, new resources continue to replace the old and price margins typically widen to cover the costs of inefficient operation or to promote the sales of particular products. This trend has been strengthened by such developments as the unfair-trade-practices legislation that permits the freezing of margins at high levels. In most of these fields, inefficiency will persist until and unless a considerable degree of local monopoly is established, for the underlying factors are similar to those in milk distribution. The American economy faces a dilemma with respect to economy in marketing — "free" but inefficient markets on one hand or efficient monopolies with necessary controls and regulations on the other. Strange as it may seem, the controlled and regulated system will usually give a closer approximation to the competitive allocation of resources.

The increase in living standards in the United States has followed technological improvements and economic specialization. Output per worker in production has more than doubled since 1870, but specialization in production forced an increasing burden on the marketing process. The volume of goods distributed per worker in marketing has remained relatively constant, while marketing has become an increasingly important part of economic activity and today equals production in the national bill for commodities. In spite of these good reasons for the growth in marketing, technological and organizational efficiencies have not been fully exploited in this field. Continued failure to develop such economies will necessarily mean a lag in living standards below potential levels. This is the challenge to commodity distribution — a challenge that must be met by solutions that differ significantly from those that have been provided by the relatively free and unregulated evolution of the past.

APPENDIXES

APPENDIXES

Appendix to Chapter 8

Minimizing transportation costs[1]

In Chapter 8, the methods of determining the most efficient allocation of milk markets among dealers were discussed. In general the areas so determined were the same as those that would have occurred under competitive conditions. The consumers in each area would buy from the designated dealer because the price at the plant plus the costs of transportation represented lower net prices to the consumer than could be realized by buying from any other dealer. The margin (boundary) between competitive areas represents the locus of points where the net consumer prices would be equal regardless of which dealer the consumer patronized. It may be demonstrated that these "consumer-response" boundaries must also form the minimum-transportation-cost boundaries for the several areas and that the theoretical areas therefore represent the most efficient allocation of the market among dealers.

Suppose the entire consuming area contains K plants M_1, M_2, . . . , M_k, and that the competitive prices at these plants are P_1, P_2, . . . , P_k. Let the transfer cost per unit of product over a distance d from any of these plants be $t(d)$, a function of d not necessarily linear but quite general in form. Then, at any point A the consumer price from alternative dealers will be:

[1] This analysis has been paraphrased from a similar producer analysis given in D. O. Hammerberg, L. W. Parker, and R. G. Bressler, Jr., *The Efficiency of Milk Marketing in Connecticut, 1. Supply and Price Interrelationships for Fluid Markets,* Appendix A, 37–39. The original formulation of the problem was largely the work of R. O. Been.

$$P_{1A} = P_1 + t(d_{1A}),$$
$$P_{2A} = P_2 + t(d_{2A}),$$
$$\cdot \quad \cdot \quad \cdot \quad \cdot \quad \cdot \quad \cdot \quad \cdot$$
$$P_{kA} = P_k + t(d_{kA}),$$

where d_{1A} is the distance from A to M_1, etc. In short, the alternative consumer prices are the alternative plant prices plus the appropriate transfer costs.

Each consumer acting freely will consider these alternatives and select that particular dealer whose delivered price will be the lowest. Consider any two dealers, say M_1 and M_2, and disregard the others. The consumer at A, acting freely, will buy from M_1 and will be located in the sales area for M_1 if the delivered price P_{1A} is less than P_{2A}. Thus the property that A lie in the M_1 area is defined by

$$P_1 + t(d_{1A}) < P_2 + t(d_{2A});$$

or alternatively, by transposing terms,

$$t(d_{2A}) - t(d_{1A}) > P_1 - P_2;$$

and similarly if A lies in the M_2 area, then,

$$t(d_{1A}) - t(d_{2A}) > P_2 - P_1.$$

Repeating the comparison by pairs of dealers or plants will allocate all consumption to specific dealers and will define an equilibrium system of boundaries between dealer areas. This competitive equilibrium will involve plant prices so adjusted that each dealer will sell the quantity of milk that he is willing to supply.

To demonstrate that these "free-choice" areas involve the minimum transfer cost (pooled for all plants), first consider any two plants M_1 and M_2. Any possible reduction of transfer cost by changing sales areas must be brought about by shifting consumers from the M_1 area to M_2 and replacing them by consumers shifted to M_1 from M_2 to maintain the former total sales of each plant. Consider the exchange of one unit at A_1 in M_1 for a unit at A_2 in M_2. The decreases in transfer cost resulting from withdrawing the unit at A_1 from M_1 is $- t(d_{1A1})$, while the increase in transfer due to adding that unit to the sales of M_2 is $+ t(d_{2A1})$. The increment of transfer cost associated with shifting the A_1 unit then will be

$$\Delta t_1 = t(d_{2A1}) - t(d_{1A1}) > P_1 - P_2.$$

Similarly, the increment of transfer cost due to the offsetting shift of a unit at A_2 from M_2 to M_1 will be

$$\Delta t_2 = t(d_{1A2}) - t(d_{2A2}) > P_2 - P_1.$$

Adding these inequalities, the total increment in transfer cost resulting from compensating deliveries across competitive boundaries will be

$$\Delta t = \Delta t_1 + \Delta t_2 > 0;$$

Δt is always positive. So between any pair of dealers the competitive allocation gives the minimum total transfer costs if dealer volumes are to be maintained unchanged.

There remains the question whether by some more intricate system of exchanges among several dealers the total transfer cost might be reduced, even though a cost reduction is impossible between any pair of dealers. It may be shown that this is impossible by an extension of the use of the area inequalities given above, the result demonstrating that the increment of transfer cost is positive for any system of exchanges that maintains each dealer's volume unchanged. For, in the expressions for transfer-cost increments, each removal of a unit from the M_i area will contribute $- t(d_{iAi})$ on the left of the inequality and $+ P_i$ on the right, while each addition to the M_j area will contribute $+ t(d_{jAi})$ on the left of the inequality and $- P_j$ on the right. The number of units removed must equal the number added for each area in order to maintain dealer volume; so each P_i will occur the same number of times with a positive sign as with a negative sign to the right of the inequality. Therefore, in adding all transfer increments, the total cost increment will be greater than zero just as in the case involving only two dealers. Since any system of unit exchanges among dealers increases total transfer cost, the competitive allocation of areas originally defined must give the minimum transfer cost for the entire market.

Appendix to Chapter 9

Tire size and truck capacity

In July 1942, the Office of Defense Transportation issued Order No. 17 controlling the operations of motor trucks. City delivery trucks were required to eliminate special deliveries and call-backs and to reduce mileage by 25 percent. Intercity trucks and those engaged in over-the-road hauling were ordered to operate with full loads as determined either by the tire sizes or by

TABLE 117. Maximum and minimum loads based on tire sizes for common types of trucks used in milk delivery.

Tire size	Number of tires	Percent of trucks	Minimum pounds per tire*	Minimum net loads		Maximum net loads†	
				Pounds	Quarts‡	Pounds	Quarts‡
*½-ton pickup trucks; light weight, 2,500 lbs.; visible capacity, 300 quarts***							
6.00–16	4	87	1,130	2,020	404	2,924	585
6.25–16	4	13	1,210	2,340	468	3,308	662
Retail Make A; light weight, 3,200 lbs.; visible capacity, 500 quarts††							
6.00–16	4	32	1,130	1,320	264	2,224	444
6.25–16	4	23	1,210	1,640	328	2,608	522
6.50–16	4	45	1,290	1,960	392	2,992	598
Retail Make B; light weight, 4,200 lbs.; visible capacity, 500 quarts††							
6.00–20	4	8	1,350	1,200	240	2,280	456
7.00–16	4	18	1,395	1,380	276	2,496	499
7.50–16	4	43	1,560	2,040	408	3,288	658
6.50–20	4	23	1,600	2,200	440	3,480	696
Larger	4	8	—	—	—	—	—
Retail Make C; light weight, 4,300 lbs.; visible capacity, 500 quarts††							
7.00–18	4	97	1,525	1,800	360	3,020	604
Larger	4	3	—	—	—	—	—
Wholesale trucks: light weight, 7,200 lbs.; visible capacity, 1,200 quarts‡‡							
6.50–20	2	100	1,700	3,900	780	6,140	1,228
32 × 6	4		1,950				

* Taken from Office of Defense Transportation Order no. 17.
† Minimum net load plus 20 percent of minimum gross load.
‡ Based on weight of cases, bottles, and contents of 5 pounds per quart.
°° Approximately two tiers of quart cases.
†† Capacity of 42 cases
‡‡ Actual capacity of 120 cases, but with the last tier of 20 cases left open for empties and to facilitate handling.

visible truck capacity. While these load requirements have not been applied to city trucks they provide a widely accepted and fairly objective measure of truck capacity and may be much more useful than the commonly available measures such as registered capacity or manufacturers' ratings.

To indicate the approximate minimum and maximum tire loads permissible under the Office of Defense Transportation Order, calculations were made for several types of milk trucks and for the tire sizes commonly used in Connecticut. In accordance with the Order, the number of tires was multiplied by tire rating to determine the minimum gross load. Subtracting the light weight of the truck from this figure indicates the minimum net load. The maximum load is determined by increasing the minimum gross load by 20 percent. Finally, net loads have been converted into quarts of milk by dividing by 5 pounds per quart, as a full case of 12 quart bottles weighs approximately 60 pounds including the case. The results of these computations are given in Table 117. It will be noted that in the majority of cases the maximum allowable loads are in excess of the visible truck capacities.

Appendix to Chapter 10

Labor units and details of wholesale route-time correlations

TABLE 118. Labor units for various packages handled by milk distributors. *

Container size	Labor units, wholesale
10 gallon	12
5 gallon	6
3 gallon	4
2 gallon	3
1 gallon	2.4
½ gallon, glass	1.5
½ gallon, fiber	1
Quart, glass	1
Quart, conical fiber	1
Quart, Canco fiber–24	0.5
Quart, Canco fiber–12	1
Quart, Pure-pak fiber–24	0.5
Quart, Pure-pak fiber–20	.6
Pint, glass–24	.5
Pint, glass–20	.6
Pint, conical fiber–24	.5
Pint, conical fiber–12	1
Pint, Canco fiber–24	0.5
Pint, Canco fiber–20	.6
Pint, Pure-pak–24	.5
Pint, Pure-pak–20	.6
⅓ quart, glass–24	.5
⅓ quart, conical fiber–24	.5
½ pint, glass–24	.5
½ pint, fiber–24	.5
Quarter-pint, glass–24	.5
Butter, 60's	.2
Butter, 30's	.4
Butter, lbs	.5
Cheese, 8, 10, 12 oz	.6
Eggs, dozen, carton	1
Cheese, 40 lb	6
Cheese, 10 lb	2.4
Cheese, 5 lb	1.5
Cheese, 3 lb	1
Cheese, 1 lb	1
Evaporated milk, tall case–48	12
Evaporated milk, small case–96	12

* Report by the Bureau of Markets to the Director of Agriculture Pertaining to the Costs of Distributing Fluid Milk for the Los Angeles County Marketing Area For the Year 1939, Department of Agriculture, State of California (June 8, 1940).

TABLE 119. Effect of distance traveled and volume carried on time per delivery trip, twelve wholesale routes.

Routes	Number of Observations	Fixed time per trip (minutes)	Time (minutes) Foot	Time (minutes) Case	r	$\bar{R}$	Average Distance Traveled (feet)	Average Number of Cases	Average Time per trip (minutes)
1	34	0.20	0.0053	—	0.821	—	109	—	0.78
		.18	.0042	0.0500	—	0.840	—	2.6	
2	45	.10	.0046	—	.817	—	76	—	.45
		.09	.0045	.0042	—	.811	—	3.5	
3	41	.16	.0035	—	.637	—	95	—	.50
		-.03	.0036	.0467	—	.711	—	4.1	
4	59	.07	.0038	—	.870	—	63	—	.31
		.07	.0035	.0083	—	.870	—	1.7	
5	81	.12	.0031	—	.738	—	40	—	.24
		.08	.0029	.0269	—	.747	—	1.5	
6	44	.08	.0028	—	.893	—	42	—	.19
		.07	.0028	.028	—	.892	—	1.6	
7	37	.05	.0039	—	.906	—	44	—	.22
		.02	.0038	.0320	—	.906	—	1.1	
8	9	.02	.0047	—	.965	—	59	—	.30
		-.06	.0049	.0293	—	.974	—	2.2	
9	29	.31	.0030	—	.510	—	60	—	.49
		.15	.0022	.0701	—	.563	—	2.9	
10	47	.13	.0040	—	.839	—	75	—	.43
		.03	.0023	.0865	—	.892	—	.26	
11	38	.18	.0036	—	.473	—	51	—	.36
		-.001	.0041	.1000	—	.834	—	1.6	
12	36	.04	.0054	—	.945	—	56	—	.34
		.01	.0055	.0154	—	.945	—	1.5	
12 routes combined	500	.08	.0047	—	.811	—	62	—	.37
		.05	.0041	.0305	—	.828	—	2.2	

Appendix to Chapter 11

Details of plant-cost estimates under prewar conditions

Tables 120 to 128 parallel those given in Chapter 11, but are based on prewar rather than postwar prices and cost rates.

TABLE 120. Building investments for six hypothetical milk pasteurizing and bottling plants, based on prewar estimates.

| | Building investment in plant | | | | | |
| | Plant capacity (quarts per day) | | | | | |
Item	A 240	B 400	C 800	D 1,600	E 2,400	F 4,800
Concrete work...........	$ 220	$ 250	$ 370	$ 640	$ 805	$1,090
Walls and partitions......	445	490	690	990	1,220	1,530
Roof...................	115	145	260	515	740	1,130
Doors and windows......	250	250	320	545	580	650
Plant..................	370	390	530	645	790	1,090
Electrical work..........	30	30	35	55	60	65
Storage cooler...........	185	240	340	520	690	990
Total..............	$1,615	$1,795	$2,545	$3,910	$4,885	$6,545
Estimated Investment*...	$1,950	$2,150	$3,050	$4,700	$5,850	$7,850
Investment per quart of daily capacity.........	$ 8.12	$ 5.38	$ 3.81	$ 2.94	$ 2.44	$ 1.64

* Including approximately 20 percent to cover contractor's overhead costs and profits.

TABLE 121. Detailed equipment cost for plant *D*.

Item	Size, number, or capacity	Price
Weight can	1 unit	$ 360.00
Can washer	2–3 cans per minute	400.00
Pipe-line filter	2,500 pounds per hour	83.00
Pasteurizers	2–100 gallons	870.00
Recording thermometer	3 units	120.00
Indicating thermometer	2 units	25.00
Sanitary fittings		125.00
Tubular cooler	1,800 pounds per hour	325.00
Bottle filler	20 per minute	1,170.00
Milk pump	1 unit	85.00
Case trucks	27 single	324.00
Bottle washer	20 per minute	2,000.00
Bottle conveyor	9 feet	200.00
Wash tanks	3 units	285.00
Boiler	9 horsepower	598.00
Oil burner	1 unit	280.00
Compressor	1.5 tons	525.00
Brine tank and coils	1 unit	750.00
Brine pump	6 gallons per minute	75.00
Unit cooler	1 unit	250.00
Bottles	3,600	180.00
Cases	295	825.00
Separator	1 unit	150.00
Total		$11,140.00
Estimated investment, shipping, and installation charges		$13,350.00
Estimated investment per gallon		$8.34

TABLE 122. Investment in equipment for six hypothetical milk pasturizing and bottling plants, based on prewar estimates.

Item	Equipment investment in plant Plant capacity (quarts per day)					
	A 240	B 400	C 800	D 1,600	E 2,400	F 4,800
Receiving	$ 35	$ 35	$ 255	$ 515	$ 515	$ 900
Pasteurizing	660	710	860	1,695	1,985	2,615
Cooling*	585	780	925	1,230	1,700	2,300
Bottle filling	120	150	220	565	900	1,500
Bottle washing	165	205	595	1,380	1,700	2,300
Boiler	385	405	535	560	665	905
Bottles, cases	100	170	330	610	990	1,980
Miscellaneous	80	100	134	200	270	480
Total	$2,130	$2,555	$3,855	$6,755	$ 8,725	$12,980
Estimated Investment†	$2,550	$3,050	$4,650	$8,100	$10,450	$15,600
Investment per quart of daily capacity	$10.62	$ 7.62	$ 5.81	$ 5.06	$ 4.35	$ 3.25

* Including the costs of brine tanks and refrigerating coils.
† Including approximately 20 percent to cover shipping and installation charges.

TABLE 123. Total investments for six hypothetical milk pasteurizing and bottling plants, based on prewar estimates.

Item	Total investment for plant Plant capacity (quarts per day)					
	A 240	B 400	C 800	D 1,600	E 2,400	F 4,800
Building	$1,950	$2,150	$3,050	$ 4,700	$ 5,850	$ 7,850
Equipment	2,550	3,050	4,650	8,100	10,450	15,600
Land	410	440	510	600	680	1,020
Total	$4,910	$5,640	$8,210	$13,400	$16,980	$24,470
Total investment per quart of daily capacity	$20.46	$14.10	$10.26	$ 8.38	$ 7.08	$ 5.10

TABLE 124. Fixed costs for six hypothetical milk pasteurizing and bottling plants, based on prewar estimates.

	Annual fixed costs in plant					
	Plant capacity (quarts per day)					
Item	A 240	B 400	C 800	D 1,600	E 2,400	F 4,800
Depreciation*......... $	252 $	287 $	428 $	736 $	912 $	1,283
Interest†.............	147	169	246	402	509	734
Repairs*.............	225	260	385	640	815	1,172
Insurance*..........	22	26	38	64	82	172
Taxes†..............	59	68	98	161	204	294
Total........... $	705 $	810 $	1.195 $	2,003 $	2,522 $	3,655
Fixed costs per day.... $	1.93 $	2.22 $	3.27 $	5.49 $	6.91 $	10.01
Fixed costs per quart of daily capacity......	$0.0080	$0.0056	$0.0041	$0.0034	$0.0029	$0.0021

* Based only on investments in buildings and equipment.
† Based on total investment in land, buildings, and equipment.

TABLE 125. Estimates of labor costs under two wage rates for six hypothetical milk pasteurizing and bottling plants.

			Estimated costs for plant labor at*			
	Hours of labor		$0.70 per hour		$1.50 per hour	
Plant	Per day	Per quart	Per day	Per quart	Per day	Per quart
A	5.5	0.0229	$ 3.85	$0.0160	$ 8.25	$0.0344
B	7.0	.0175	4.90	.0122	10.50	.0262
C	10.0	.0125	7.00	.0088	15.00	.0188
D	18.0	.0112	12.60	.0079	27.00	.0169
E	25.0	.0104	17.50	.0073	37.50	.0156
F	40.0	.0083	28.00	.0058	60.00	.0125

* Hourly rates cover wages, Social Security taxes, workman's unemployment insurance, and the allocated costs of vacations with pay.

TABLE 126. Summary of costs for six hypothetical milk pasteurizing and bottling plants, based on prewar estimates.

	Operating costs in plant					
	Plant capacity (quarts per day)					
Item	A 240	B 400	C 800	D 1,600	E 2,400	F 4,800
Fixed costs per year						
Depreciation........$	252 $	287 $	428 $	736 $	912 $	1,283
Interest............	147	169	246	402	509	734
Repairs............	225	260	385	640	815	1,172
Insurance..........	22	26	38	64	82	172
Taxes..............	59	68	98	161	204	294
Subtotal.........$	705 $	810 $	1,195 $	2,003 $	2,522 $	3,655
Fixed costs per day....$	1.93 $	2.22 $	3.27 $	5.49 $	6.91 $	10.01
Fixed costs per quart..	$0.0080	$0.0056	$0.0041	$0.0034	$0.0029	$0.0021
Labor costs per day*.. $	3.85 $	4.90 $	7.00 $	12.60 $	17.50 $	28.00
Labor costs per quart..	$0.0160	$0.0122	$0.0088	$0.0079	$0.0073	$0.0058
Variable costs per qt.						
Electricity..........	$0.0030	$0.0023	$0.0020	$0.0014	$0.0012	$0.0009
Fuel†..............	.0011	.0009	.0007	.0006	.0006	.0005
Supplies‡...........	.0024	.0024	.0024	.0024	.0024	.0024
Plant loss**........	.0004	.0004	.0004	.0004	.0004	.0004
Subtotal........	$0.0069	$0.0060	$0.0055	$0.0048	$0.0046	$0.0042
Combined cost at full capacity..........	$0.0309	$0.0238	$0.0184	$0.0161	$0.0148	$0.0121

* Assuming operation at full capacity and labor rates averaging $0.70 per hour; if plant volumes were reduced enough to reduce the number of batches of milk to be pasteurized, hours of labor and labor costs would be reduced accordingly.

† Assuming a prewar price of $0.06 per gallon for number 2 fuel oil.

‡ With plug-type caps; if crown-type caps are used, supply costs will average about $0.0041 per quart; bottles priced at $37.50 per thousand.

** On the basis of the prewar Class II average of $1.71 per hundred-weight.

TABLE 127. Estimates of labor costs for bookkeepers and clerks under two wage rates, six hypothetical milk pasteurizing and bottling plants.

Plant	Daily volume (quarts)	Hours of office labor per week*			Hours per 100 quarts	Office labor costs†		Office labor costs‡	
		Bookkeeper	Clerks	Total		Per week	Per quart	Per week	Per quart
A	240	—	—	8**	0.48	$ 5.60	$0.0033	$ 12.00	$0.0071
B	400	—	—	13**	.46	9.10	.0032	19.50	.0070
C	800	24	—	24	.43	16.80	.0030	28.80	.0051
D	1,600	44	—	44	.39	30.80	.0028	52.80	.0047
E	2,400	44	20	64	.38	40.80	.0024	68.80	.0041
F	4,800	44	68	112	.33	64.80	.0019	107.20	.0032

* Based on information from the Connecticut Milk Administrator.

† With prewar wage rates averaging $0.70 per hour for plant workers and bookkeepers and $0.50 per hour for clerks. These rates are assumed to cover Social Security taxes, workman's unemployment insurance, and the allocated costs of vacations with pay.

‡ With possible postwar wage increases amounting to $1.20 per hour for bookkeepers and $0.80 per hour for clerks. Plant workers, under these conditions, will be paid at the rate of $1.50 per hour.

** Records kept by the plant manager or owner, and assuming that the records will be comparable to those kept by the larger plants.

TABLE 128. Summary of costs including bookkeeping and laboratory costs for plants operating at 95 percent capacity.

Item	Operating costs per quart in plant					
	Daily plant volume (quarts)					
	A 228	B 380	C 760	D 1,520	E 2,280	F 4,560
Laboratory*.......	$0.0006	$0.0006	$0.0006	$0.0006	$0.0006	$0.0006
Bookkeeping†.....	.0033	.0032	.0030	.0028	.0024	.0019
Subtotal......	$0.0039	$0.0038	$0.0036	$0.0034	$0.0030	$0.0025
Plant costs‡.......	$0.0322	$0.0247	$0.0190	$0.0167	$0.0153	$0.0125
Total.........	$0.0361	$0.0285	$0.0226	$0.0201	$0.0183	$0.0150

* Assuming laboratory costs amount to $1.00 per test per producer.
† Obtained from Table 127.
‡ Computed from data in Table 126, assuming plants operate at 95 percent of full capacity.

Appendix to Chapter 12

Results of preliminary reorganization studies

Since the procedures to be followed in making reorganization studies have been discussed in Chapters 8 and 12 and illustrated in Chapters 13 and 14, this appendix is limited to a summary of the results of the preliminary reorganization studies. As explained in Chapter 12, approximate values for delivery densities per route mile are basic to the determination of the maximum route volumes appropriate for any type of delivery system. Such approximate values have been determined by making preliminary reorganization studies in the sample markets, with the assumption that maximum route volumes would be 350 quarts with daily delivery and 450 quarts with alternate-day delivery.

The results of these studies have been summarized in Table 129. When converted into route miles per quart, the reciprocal of route density, and related to total delivery density per mile of street, the regressions given in Figs. 80 and 81 were obtained.[1] Many factors other than market density affect the efficiency of milk delivery, so these regressions are far from exact representations of the results of the sample studies. The standard error of estimating exclusive-territory mileages for an individual market

[1] Compare these regressions with Fig. 22.

TABLE 129. Preliminary estimates of milk-delivery mileages under reorganized systems of distribution, sample Connecticut markets.*

Market	Total quarts per day	Estimated delivery miles per day			
		Exclusive territories		Municipal districts	
		Daily delivery	Alternate-day	Daily delivery	Alternate-day
Ashford..........	9	5	3	5	3
Bridgewater......	65	26	17	23	14
Harwinton.......	98	31	22	31	22
Willington........	113	25	13	24	12
Brookfield........	263	32	20	25	15
Ellington.........	363	44	25	42	24
Somers...........	488	40	21	38	19
Mansfield........	583	85	46	65	39
Old Saybrook.....	782	55	35	36	23
Ridgefield........	1,155	86	44	79	40
East Windsor.....	1,214	81	44	70	44
Saybrook area....	2,271	136	70	112	63
Willimantic.......	6,744	185	121	106	59
Torrington.......	11,685	345	241	151	86
Hartford.........	52,497	500	334	590	401
New Haven area†.	72,936	1,547	1,074	1,556	1,009

* Based on assumed maximum route volumes of 350 quarts with daily delivery and 450 quarts with alternate-day delivery. In rural areas, daily route volumes were limited to 325 quarts.
† Separate estimates were made for each of the seven towns in the metropolitan district; the separate estimates were used in determining the regressions in Figs. 80 and 81.

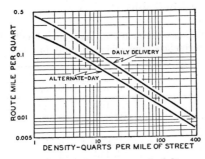

Fig. 80. Preliminary relations between total delivery density and milk-delivery mileage requirements with exclusive delivery territories. Based on maximum route volumes of 350 quarts with daily delivery and 450 quarts with alternate-day delivery.

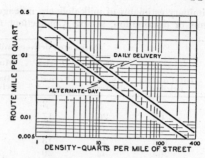

Fig. 81. Preliminary relations between total delivery density and milk-delivery mileage requirements with municipal distribution. Based on maximum route volumes of 350 quarts with daily delivery and 450 quarts with alternate-day delivery.

is 24 percent in the case of daily delivery and 32 percent for alternate-day delivery. With municipal distribution, the standard error of estimate is 22 percent for daily delivery and 28 percent for alternate-day delivery.

In spite of these relatively large errors for individual estimates, the regressions may be used with some assurance to estimate the mileage requirements for groups of markets, for individual errors will then compensate to a considerable extent. The regressions have been used to make estimates for all the rural, secondary, and major markets in Connecticut, with the results shown in Table 130. These group estimates, which should be accurate within 2 or 3 percent, were used to compute the preliminary route delivery densities presented in Table 54.

TABLE 130. Preliminary estimates of reorganized milk-delivery miles for rural, secondary, and major markets in Connecticut.

Item	Type of market			
	Rural	Secondary	Major	All
Number of towns............	125	36	8	169
Daily quarts delivered........	67,633	209,663	238,383	515,659
Exclusive territories				
Daily delivery miles........	5,836	6,711	3,420	15,967
Alternate-day miles.........	3,446	4,577	2,360	10,383
Municipal distribution				
Daily delivery miles........	5,408	5,364	2,611	13,383
Alternate-day miles.........	3,105	3,229	1,655	7,978

Appendix to Chapter 12

Time allocations for two- and three-man wholesale routes

TABLE 131. Details of the allocations of wholesale route time in order to estimate elapsed time requirements for two-man route operations.

Operation	Elapsed-time requirements (minutes)				
	Per day	Per mile	Per customer	Per case	Per trip
Driving*...............	23.40	2.640	1.027		
Arranging load†........			0.225	0.171	
Delivering‡............					0.386
Loading dolly**........			.011	.011	
Handling empties††.....					.760
Other operations‡‡......	73.46		2.076		
Total..............	96.86	2.640	3.339	0.182	1.146

* Based on equation (10.11), with allowance for the fact that there were 7 percent more customer stops than customers on the sample routes.

† Based on equation (10.20), with 87 percent of the volume in terms of cases of milk and 13 percent in terms of cases of miscellaneous products, and with 7 percent more stops than customers. This operation is performed by the assistant.

‡ Based on equation (10.21) and an average distance from truck to store of 65 feet, and including the time to deliver and to return. With two men, the elapsed time for delivering is estimated at one-half of the time required for a one-man route.

** Based on equation (10.24), with allowance for the fact that the dolly was used on only 20 percent of the stops and that there were 7 percent more stops than customers. With two men, the elapsed time is estimated at about one-half of the one-man requirement.

†† Taken from Table 57; this operation is performed by the assistant.

‡‡ Driver gets order while assistant walks from the cab and arranges the load, with no addition to elapsed time; driver bills and collects while assistant services the refrigerator, the average time amounting to 1.37 minutes times 107 percent; walking from cab, 0.57 minute times 107 percent; loading and unloading, 29 minutes per day, approximately half of the time required with one man; miscellaneous time, 30 minutes per day for lunch stops plus one-half of 28.92 minutes.

TABLE 132. Details of the allocations of wholesale route time in order to estimate elapsed time requirements for three-man route operations.

Operation	Elapsed-time requirements (minutes)				
	Per day	Per mile	Per customer	Per case	Per trip
Driving*...............	23.40	2.640	1.027		
Arranging load†.........			0.113	0.086	
Delivering‡.............					0.257
Loading dolly**.........			.007	.007	
Handling empties††.....					.380
Other operations‡‡......	59.64		2.076		
Total..............	83.04	2.640	3.223	0.093	0.637

* Based on equation (10.11), with allowance for the fact that there were 7 percent more customer stops than customers on the sample routes.

† Based on equation (10.20), with 87 percent of the volume in terms of cases of milk and 13 percent in terms of cases of miscellaneous products, and with 7 percent more stops than customers. This operation is performed by the assistants and requires about one-half of the time required by the one-man route.

‡ Based on equation (10.21) and an average distance from truck to store of 65 feet, and including the time to deliver and to return. With three men, the elapsed time for delivering is estimated at one-third of the time required for a one-man route.

** Based on equation (10.24), with allowance for the fact that the dolly was used on only 20 percent of the stops and that there were 7 percent more stops than customers. With three men, the elapsed time is estimated at about one-third of the one-man requirement.

†† Taken from Table 57; this operation is performed by the assistants, and requires about one-half of the time required by the one-man route.

‡‡ Driver gets order while assistants walk from the cab and arrange the load, with no addition to elapsed time; driver bills and collects while assistants service the refrigerator, the average time amounting to 1.37 minutes times 107 percent; walking from cab, 0.57 minute times 107 percent; loading and unloading, 20 minutes per day, approximately one-third of the time required with one man; miscellaneous time, 30 minutes per day for lunch stops plus one-third of 28.92 minutes.

Appendix to Chapter 13

The effects of plant location, dealer volume, and delivery density on potential mileage reductions

The general effects of such factors as plant location and delivery density on mileage requirements and on the percentage reduction in mileage that would accompany such reorganizations as exclusive delivery territory are not difficult to determine. It is clear that relatively low delivery densities under the existing system would result in unusually high present mileages and so in potentially large percentage reductions. If delivery densities in the assigned exclusive territory are unusually low, on the other hand, the revised mileages will be high and the potential mileage reductions relatively small. Routes originating at plants that are distant from market will have long hauling distances and these distances will persist even under reorganized delivery systems. As a result, the potential percentage reduction in mileage will decrease as distance from market increases. While these general relations are valuable, it is desirable to have more exact and specific descriptions of the relations.

The miles traveled by a delivery route may be divided into two parts: (1) hauling distance — the miles traveled from the plant to the delivery area and return; and (2) delivery distance — the miles traveled within the delivery area. Based on this division and in terms of the above-mentioned factors, equations for present and reorganized miles traveled by delivery trucks are given below. In these equations the following symbols have been used:

T, total daily miles traveled by delivery trucks;
L, miles from plant to urban market;
Q, average delivery miles within urban market;
V, average quarts delivered per route;
N, number of routes;
K, delivery density in quarts per route mile;
M, delivery density in quarts per street mile;
S, hauling miles from limits of urban market to exclusive territory;
H, ratio of reorganized delivery miles to miles of streets;
p, subscript representing present delivery system;
r, subscript representing reorganized delivery system.

Under actual conditions it is usually difficult to define delivery and hauling distances exactly. In some studies the distance traveled between the first and last customer has been called the delivery distance and the remainder the hauling distance. Many routes serve a few scattered customers as they travel to and from the primary delivery areas, however, so that the above definition may include a considerable amount of hauling mileage under the delivery-mileage classification. To avoid this and to focus attention on the distance from plant to market, hauling mileage has been defined in terms of the distance from plant to urban market for the Torrington and Willimantic markets. Distances within the urban market were then called delivery miles and delivery density was defined in terms of the ratio of total quarts delivered to the delivery mileage. Present mileage requirements could then be represented by the equation

$$T_p = N(2L + Q) = N(2H + V/K_p).$$

Under reorganized conditions and defining delivery density in terms of quarts per mile of street, distance requirements would be

$$T_r = N(2L + 2S + HV/M_r).$$

Mileage reductions through exclusive territories would then be

$$T_p - T_r = N(2L + V/K_p) - N(2L + 2S + HV/M_r)$$
$$= N(V/K_p - 2S - HV/M_r),$$

and the percentage mileage reduction[1] would be

$$\frac{T_p - T_r}{T_p} = \frac{V/K_p - 2S - HV/M_r}{V/K_p + 2L}.$$

This may be converted into other forms more useful in emphasizing the nature and importance of the several factors. Such transformations are given below:

$$\text{Percentage reduction} = \frac{VM_r - 2SM_rK_p - HVK_p}{VM_r + 2LM_rK_p},$$

$$\text{Percentage reduction} = \frac{V - 2SK_p - HVK_p/M_r}{V + 2LK_p},$$

$$\text{Percentage reduction} = \frac{VM_r/K_p - 2SM_r - HV}{VM_r/K_p + 2LM_r}.$$

[1] Assuming that the number of routes and average route volumes would be unchanged. The equations could be carried out in terms of differing numbers and volumes, but this assumption greatly simplifies the final equations and appears to be accurate enough for present purposes.

To indicate the accuracy of these descriptions, the equations have been used to estimate percent mileage reductions for all dealers included in the Torrington and Willimantic studies. Estimates made by this method corresponded closely to the estimates made through the detailed reorganization studies. In Torrington this correspondence resulted in a coefficient of correlation of 0.941 while in Willimantic the coefficient was 0.945.

The above equations indicate the complex nature of the relations between mileage reductions and the independent factors of route volume, present and revised delivery densities, and distance from plant to market. They show that the effect of any one factor is not independent but depends on the values of the other factors. In short, these are joint relations. In so far as each dealer has unique values for the several factors, the effects of the factors will differ from the effects experienced by other dealers. In order to indicate the general nature of the relations, however, average values for the variables have been determined and percentage mileage reductions calculated by varying one factor at a time while holding all others constant at their averages. The results are summarized in Tables 133 to 136 for the Torrington and Willimantic markets.

TABLE 133. Effects of changes in route volume on mileage reductions when other factors are held constant at their averages.*

V Route volume (quarts)	Mileage reduction (percent)	
	Torrington	Willimantic
25	31	44
50	49	58
100	65	70
150	72	75
200	77	78
400	85	83
600	88	85

* These computations refer to the mileage reductions that would result from daily delivery with exclusive territories as compared to daily delivery under the present conditions. Average values—Torrington: $K_p = 7.7$ quarts per mile; $M_r = 180$ quarts per mile; $L = 2.6$ miles; $S = 0.2$ mile; and $H = 1.42$. Average values—Willimantic: $K_p = 9.5$ quarts per mile; $M_r = 129$ quarts per mile; $L = 1.8$ miles; $S = 0.2$ mile; $H = 1.42$. The negative value of S for Willimantic results from the fact that some of the exclusive delivery areas were entirely outside of the limits of the city.

TABLE 134. Effects of changes in present delivery density on mileage reductions when other factors are held constant at their averages.*

K_p Present delivery density (quarts per mile)	Mileage reduction (percent)	
	Torrington	Willimantic
2	95	95
4	91	90
8	83	82
12	76	74
20	64	61
30	51	48
40	42	38

* These computations refer to the mileage reductions that would result from daily delivery with exclusive territories as compared to daily delivery under the present conditions. Average values—Torrington: $V = 325$ quarts; $M_r = 180$ quarts per mile; $L = 2.6$ miles; $S = 0.2$ mile; $H = 1.42$. Average values—Willimantic: $V = 211$ quarts; $M_r = 129$ quarts per mile; $L = 1.8$ miles; $S = 0.2$ mile; $H = 1.42$. The negative value of S for Willimantic results from the fact that some of the exclusive delivery areas were entirely outside of the limits of the city.

TABLE 135. Effects of changes in reorganized delivery density on mileage reductions when other factors are held constant at their averages.*

M_r Reorganized delivery density (quarts per mile)	Mileage reduction (percent)	
	Torrington	Willimantic
25	49	41
50	69	64
100	78	76
150	82	80
200	83	82
300	85	84
500	86	85

* These computations refer to the mileage reductions that would result from daily delivery with exclusive territories as compared to daily delivery under the present conditions. Average values—Torrington: $V = 325$ quarts; $K_p = 7.7$ quarts per mile; $L = 2.6$ miles; $S = 0.2$ mile; $H = 1.42$. Average values—Willimantic: $V = 211$ quarts; $K_p = 9.5$ quarts per mile; $L = 1.8$ miles; $S = 0.2$ mile; $H = 1.42$. The negative value of S for Willimantic results from the fact that some of the exclusive delivery areas were entirely outside of the limits of the city.

TABLE 136. Effects of changes in distance from market on mileage reductions when other factors are held constant at their averages.*

L Distance from market (miles)	Mileage reduction (percent)	
	Torrington	Willimantic
0	93	91
1	89	84
2	85	77
4	78	67
6	72	59
8	67	53
10	63	48

* These computations refer to the mileage reductions that would result from daily delivery with exclusive territories as compared to daily delivery under the present conditions. Average values—Torrington: $V = 325$ quarts; $K_p = 7.7$ quarts per mile; $M_r = 180$ quarts per mile; $S = 0.2$ mile; $H = 1.42$. Average values—Willimantic: $V = 211$ quarts; $K_p = 9.5$ quarts per mile; $M_r = 129$ quarts per mile; $S = -0.2$ mile; $H = 1.42$. The negative value of S for Willimantic results from the fact that some of the exclusive delivery areas were entirely outside of the limits of the city.

Appendix to Chapter 15

The costs of handling milk through stores and depots

Because of the problems of joint and overhead cost allocations, it is difficult to arrive at meaningful estimates of the costs of handling milk through stores or of the effects of volume changes on these costs. A study made in Boston in 1936 placed store costs at 1.35 cents per quart,[1] while similar studies in California in 1942 reported results ranging from 1.26 to 1.32 cents per quart in fiber and from 1.57 to 1.74 cents per quart in glass.[2] In these studies, costs were allocated between milk and other store items on the basis of careful studies of the proportions of store space and labor used for milk. Nevertheless, the allocations were necessarily arbitrary and other (and just as "reasonable") methods could have been used with significantly different results.

[1] C. F. Rittenhouse, *Summary Report.*
[2] "Report by the Bureau of Markets to the Director of Agriculture Pertaining to the Method Used to Determine the Cost of Handling Fluid Milk by Retail Food Stores for the Alameda County and San Francisco Marketing Areas," Department of Agriculture, State of California, Mimeograph (1942).

One method of avoiding these allocation problems is to study the operation of stores or depots where milk is the only product sold. The costs appropriate for such specialized operations do not define the levels of costs and margins for regular food stores, however, and can only be accepted as an upper limit to costs in the diversified operations. Preliminary and unpublished results of a Connecticut study of milk depots indicate that costs in the prewar period averaged about 1.9 cents per quart with daily volumes of 300 quarts, and declined to 0.5 cent per quart with volumes of 2,000 or more quarts daily.[3] Costs averaging about one

TABLE 137. Estimated costs of operating five hypothetical milk depots, 1947.

| | Average cost per quart | | | | |
| | Daily volume (quarts) | | | | |
Item	300	900	1500	2100	2700
Fixed costs	$0.0038	$0.0015	$0.0011	$0.0009	$0.0008
Labor	.0133	.0089	.0073	.0067	.0063
Fuel	.0007	.0003	.0002	.0002	.0002
Ice	.0025	.0025	.0025	.0025	.0025
Electricity	.0003	.0001	.0001	.0001	*
Supplies	.0020	.0020	.0020	.0020	.0020
Breakage loss	.0004	.0004	.0004	.0004	.0004
Total	$0.0230	$0.0157	$0.0136	$0.0128	$0.0122

* Less than $0.00005.

cent per quart would have been possible in urban markets without forcing consumers to travel more than several blocks for their milk supplies.

The results of this study have been modified for changes in prices and wages, and are summarized in Table 137. According to these estimates, the costs of operating specialized milk depots under 1947 conditions would have averaged about 2.3 cents per quart with volumes of 300 quarts per day, and less than 1.3 cents with volumes in excess of 2,000 quarts daily.

[3] W. F. Henry, "City Milk Depots," Storrs Agricultural Experiment Station, unpublished manuscript (1943).

Appendix to Chapter 17

Technical aspects of the consumer surveys

Selection of Sample

The 1943 study of milk distribution in Willimantic resulted in a description of the volume of milk sales in each of 80 subdivisions of the market. In the present study, 20 of these areas were drawn at random and records obtained in each sample area approximately in proportion to the volume of home deliveries. Retail rather than total volumes were used to offset the bias that might have resulted from the chance inclusion of factory or shopping districts with large volumes of wholesale milk. In order to obtain an adequate sampling of store purchases, enumerators were instructed to collect the indicated number of home-delivered records in each area, plus any records of purchases through stores.

Since most of the subdivisions contained roughly one city block, the enumerators were instructed to start at any convenient corner and to take every household along the street that would coöperate until the indicated number of records for the area had been completed. An exception to this procedure was made when the area contained a main street; in that case the area was divided so that all records would not be taken on the main street. While this policy of complete enumeration may be subject to some criticism on the grounds of similarity of adjacent households, it seemed justified on two grounds: (1) the subdivisions were so small as to be fairly homogeneous except in the above-mentioned cases involving main streets; and (2) the complete enumeration eliminated any tendency for the enumerators to select better-than-average homes.

A total of 152 usable records obtained in this fashion covered 272 quarts of home-delivered and 51.5 quarts of store-purchased milk. This represented approximately 25 percent of the retail milk in the 20 sample areas or 6 percent of all retail sales and nearly 5 percent of combined wholesale and retail sales in Willimantic. The 25-percent sample of the areas (20 out of 80) covered 24.4

percent of retail sales for the market. About 16 percent of the volume covered in the survey was purchased in stores; 34 percent of the entire market volume was wholesale, but this included deliveries to restaurants, hotels, schools, and factories as well as sales through stores.

The sampling procedure for Hartford proper was essentially similar to that used in Willimantic. Previous studies had divided the city into 150 subdivisions, and 20 of these were again selected at random. Because the original data did not distinguish between retail and wholesale sales, the apportionment of records among these areas was made on the basis of total sales. The sample areas contained about 15 percent of all milk in the city and were well distributed geographically.

A total of 302 records were obtained in this manner, representing approximately 7 percent of the milk in the sample areas and 1 percent of all milk sales in the city. Some 12 percent of the milk consumed in households included in the survey was purchased at stores.

The procedure used in the six suburban towns surrounding Hartford deviated from the above because milk-sales data were not available by subdivisions. The number of records to be obtained in each town was established on the basis of the relation of the population of the town to the population of Hartford, and within four of the towns the allocation was further broken down in accordance with the enumeration tracts used by the Census Bureau. This procedure added 148 records, making a total of 450 for the metropolitan district.

On the basis of 1940 estimates of milk sales by towns, the 826 quarts of milk covered in the survey represented almost exactly 1 percent of the total volume in the metropolitan area. About 9 percent of the sample volume was purchased through stores.

The Questionnaire

The form of the questionnaire used is indicated below. In addition to specific questions dealing with alternative methods of milk delivery, it included questions on milk consumption, family composition, and family income.

Survey of Milk Delivery Preferences

Date ——————————

Enumerator ————

1. City ————————— Address —————————————

2. Number in household:

   Total —— Under 6 years —— 6 to 15 —— 16 and over ——

3. Milk consumption:

   Total quarts daily —— Home delivered —— Store purchased

   ——————————————

   Distance to store where milk is or would be purchased ————

4. Present delivery system:

   At the same price, would you prefer daily or alternate-day delivery? ———— If a return to daily delivery required a price increase, how much more would you be willing to pay in order to have this service? —— cents per quart. Would square or two-quart bottles change your answer? ————.

5. Store purchases:

   Compared with the present system of home delivery, what savings would induce you to buy *all* of your milk at a store? —— cents per quart. If paper bottles (no deposit, no return) were available at stores, would this change your answer? ————.

6. Exclusive territories:

   Would you be willing to give up your choice of a milk dealer and have your milk delivered under a zoned system if the price was the same? ————.

   What savings would induce you to accept such a program provided that services and quality were satisfactory? —— cents per quart. If the zoned delivery system gave you a choice between two dealers, what savings compared to the present system would make you willing to accept the program? —— cents per quart.

7. Central plant:

   Would you be willing to have milk delivery put on a municipal or public-utility basis (like water and gas) if the price were the same as under the present system? ————.

   What savings would induce you to accept such a plan? —— cents per quart.

8. Family income:
   How many people in household have been wage earners during the past year? —————.
   Approximately what has been the weekly income of the household during the year? $ ———— per week.

Instructions to Enumerators

In addition to giving instructions to enumerators regarding the selection of the sample, an attempt was made to insure standardized and unbiased methods in obtaining information from householders. This was especially important in view of the fact that many people would be unfamiliar with the proposals, and that some explanations would be necessary. The instructions for the original survey are reproduced below:

Intelligent answers on this survey presuppose some knowledge of the matters in question. The enumerator should preface the question with a brief, factual statement where it seems necessary, and may supplement this with factual answers to questions from the householder. *Note:* Keep these short, factual, and unbiased — give all the information possible, but do not answer the questions! A few examples follow:

"Square bottles and 2-quart bottles take up less space in the refrigerator — about four quarts in the space required for three with regular round bottles, or eight quarts in space required for five in round bottles."

"Paper bottles are used in some markets, especially for sales through stores. They weigh less, are usually less bulky (many are square in shape), and you do not leave a bottle deposit or return the empty container."

"Zoned milk deliveries have been suggested as a means of increasing delivery efficiency. It would involve zoning the city and assigning each area to a particular dealer. The volume handled by each dealer would be approximately the same as under the present system. In Willimantic, such a program would reduce the duplication of milk trucks; it would reduce milk-truck travel about 75 percent and increase the efficiency of deliverymen.

"Zoned deliveries may be based on assigning two milkmen to each area. In this case, of course, the savings would be less but the customer would have a choice between the two dealers."

"Some cities have considered making milk delivery a complete monopoly under public ownership (like the mail service and most water systems) or under public control (like the public utilities). A small town in North Carolina is the only place in the United States that has actually adopted this program, and it has been in effect there for many years with apparent success. If such a program were introduced in Willimantic, the daily mileage traveled by delivery trucks could be reduced about 85 percent, the number of milk routes reduced 40 to 50 percent, and the efficiency of dairy-plant operations increased. Under such a program, however, it would be necessary to buy out the present dealers at fair and reasonable valuations."

In general, limit yourself to material such as presented in the bulletins on the efficiency of milk marketing in Connecticut.

Appendix to Chapter 17

Statistical studies of milk sales through stores

Fresh fluid milk has been available to nearly everyone in the United States either through stores or delivered to homes. Products identical in nearly all respects except for the associated services have been offered at differing prices in many markets, so that consumers have been able to express their demands for service (as contrasted to their demands for the physical product) through the normal market channels.[1] It should be possible, therefore, to determine something of the nature of these demands by studying the statistical records of home-delivered and store milk prices and the associated relative store sales of milk in a sample of actual markets.

Data on store and home-delivered milk prices are reported currently for a number of cities by the U. S. Department of Agriculture. Data on volumes sold through these alternative channels, however, are available only for a few markets and a few periods of time. A summary of some recent data on store sales is given in Table 138. These constitute the raw materials from which the analyses of the relation between store sales and store differentials that are described below have been made.

The first analysis made of these data was a simple regression between the percentage of store sales and the store differential.

_____
[1] The physical characteristics of milk available through stores and on retail routes are not exactly identical in most markets. There is some tendency for store milk to be lower in such factors as butterfat content. Moreover, a wider selection of containers and milk qualities, especially the "premium" qualities, is usually available on retail routes.

TABLE 138. Summary of milk sales through stores and store price differentials for selected markets in the United States, 1926–1946.*

Case number	Market	Year	Percent store sales†	Store differential‡
1**	Baltimore, Maryland	1930	14	0
2	Baltimore, Maryland	1935	34	0
3**	Baltimore, Maryland	1940	46	1.8
4**	Boston, Massachusetts	1930	32	2.5
5	Boston, Massachusetts	1935	37	1.0
6**	Boston, Massachusetts	1940	32	1.0
7	Burlington, Vermont	1944	42	0
8**	Chicago, Illinois	1935	25	0.8
9**	Chicago, Illinois	1940	52	3.0
10	Chicago, Illinois	1941	66	3.0
11	Essex Junction, Vermont	1944	23	0
12	Hartford, Connecticut	1940	14	1.0
13	Hartford, Connecticut	1946	12	1.0
14	Hartford, Conn. (suburbs)	1946	3	1.0
15	Ithaca, New York	1940	20	0
16	Jamestown, New York	1942	25	0
17**	Los Angeles, California	1926	8	0
18	Los Angeles, California	1935	42	2.0
19**	Los Angeles, California	1940	58	2.6
20	Los Angeles, California	1943	62	1.0
21	Mansfield, Connecticut	1942	11	1.0
22	New Haven, Connecticut	1942	22	1.0
23**	New Jersey	1935	20	1.0
24**	New Jersey	1940	30	1.0
25	New Jersey (Northern)	1942	26	1.2
26	New Jersey (Southern)	1942	24	1.0
27**	New York, N. Y.	1926	34	4.9
28	New York, N. Y.	1935	39	2.3
29**	New York, N. Y.	1940	56	3.6
30	New York, N. Y.	1942	66	2.4
31**	Philadelphia, Pennsylvania	1935	16	0.6
32**	Philadelphia, Pennsylvania	1940	27	1.0
33**	Pittsburgh, Pennsylvania	1935	48	1.0
34**	Pittsburgh, Pennsylvania	1940	35	0
35**	Portland, Oregon	1935	56	0.5
36**	Portland, Oregon	1940	47	0
37	Providence, Rhode Island	1938	17	1.0
38	Quad Cities, Iowa	1940	36	0
39	Rochester, New York	1942	25	0.6
40**	St. Louis, Missouri	1935	41	1.2
41**	St. Louis, Missouri	1940	38	1.6
42**	San Francisco, California	1926	16	1.0
43	San Francisco, California	1935	62	2.0
44**	San Francisco, California	1940	70	1.2
45	Shelburne, Vermont	1944	67	0
46	Willimantic, Connecticut	1946	16	1.0

TABLE 139. Summary of statistical analyses of the relation between store
sales and store price differentials, selected markets in the
United States, 1926–1946.

Job number	Period	Number of cases	Regression constants*			Correlation coefficient†
			a	b_2	b_3	
1	1926–46	46	27.2	6.21	—	0.343
2	1935	11	30.0	7.21	—	.178
3	1940–46	29	26.8	8.33	—	.393
4	1926–46	46	26.2	6.83	0.64	.360
5‡	1926–40	11	−15.7	9.31	3.85	.912

* Constants for regression equations of the form $X_1 = a + b_2X_2 + b_3X_3$, where X_1 represents the percent that store sales are of total home milk consumption, X_2 the average differential between store and home-delivered prices in the given year and the year immediately previous, and X_3 a trend factor in years. Only the last two analyses included X_3.

† Corrected for parameters in estimating equations.

‡ Based on paired observations for identical markets over a period ranging from 5 to 14 years. In this case, X_1 and X_2 were expressed as the change in store sales and the change in price differentials, and X_3 as the elapsed time in years.

This indicated that sales tended to be higher in markets with high store differentials by some 6.2 percent for each 1-cent difference in the differential (Table 139). Only 12 per cent of the variance in store sales between markets was associated with the differential, making it quite obvious that factors other than price were important in this connection. Unfortunately, detailed information concerning such factors as the type of area, accessibil-

* Sources are given below, where numbers in parentheses refer to case numbers in the table: R. W. Bartlett, *The Milk Industry* (Ronald, New York, 1946) (1–6, 8–9, 17–19, 23–24, 27–29, 31–38, 40–44); T. M. Adams, *Wartime Changes in Milk Distribution and in the Consumption of Milk, Cream, Butter, and Oleomargarine in Vermont* (7, 11, 45); R. W. Bartlett, "Suggested Ways for Lowering Costs of Milk Distribution in Chicago," *Illinois Farm Economics, No. 197*, (University of Illinois, January 1942) (10); L. Horwitz, "Survey of Daily Milk Consumption in the City of Hartford," Hartford Board of Health Mimeograph (1940) (12); *Efficiency of Milk Marketing in Connecticut* (Storrs Agricultural Experiment Station, Bulletins 249, 252, 253, and 257, 1943–1946) (13, 14, 21, 22, 46); R. H. Anderson, unpublished thesis, Department of Agricultural Economics, New York State College of Agriculture (1941) (15); D. A. Swope, unpublished thesis, Department of Agricultural Economics, New York State College of Agriculture (1943) (16); Reports of the Bureau of Markets, California Department of Agriculture (20); Leland Spencer, "Costs of Distributing Milk in New Jersey," New Jersey Department of Agriculture (1943) (25–26); Leland Spencer and S. M. Johnson, estimate (30); S. M. Johnson, based on license applications received by Rochester Health Bureau (39).

† Sales of milk through stores as a percentage of the total store and home-delivered sales.

‡ Simple average of the difference in price between home-delivered and store sales for the given year and the year immediately previous. These are in terms of cents per quart.

** These observations were used in the paired analysis.

ity of stores, and racial characteristics of consumers were not
readily available to expand the analysis.

One factor that could be used to eliminate some of the variance in store sales was time. Casual inspection of the data in
Table 138 indicated that in many markets where data were available for several years there seemed to be an upward trend in
store sales regardless of the differential. Three analyses were
added, therefore, to investigate the nature of such a trend. Two
of these were repetitions of the first simple correlation, but with
trend more or less eliminated by a process of subsorting. Data
were available for 11 markets in 1935; these indicated that store
sales tended to increase about by 7.2 percent as store differentials
increased by 1 cent per quart. Only 3 percent of the sales variance could be accounted for by this relation. In the 1940–1946
period, data were available for 29 markets. An analysis based on
this sample suggested that a rate of increase of 8.3 percent would
account for 15 percent of the variance in store sales.

The fourth analysis used all 46 records in a multiple correlation where the trend was used as the second independent variable. This indicated that store sales had increased an average of
0.6 percent per year in addition to a tendency to expand about
6.8 percent for each 1-cent increase in the differential. The differential plus the trend eliminated only about 13 percent of the
variation in store sales, so that the added trend factor did not
add materially to the accuracy of the description (Table 139).

The fifth and last analysis was an attempt to hold constant or
eliminate the effects of factors not specifically included in the
analysis by pairing observations for identical markets. As already
pointed out, it was clear that price was not the major explanation
of variations in the levels of store sales. A common and accepted
procedure in such a case is to eliminate differences in levels by
measuring *changes* in the variables. This may be accomplished
by pairing observations for given markets with similar observations at later dates. Each pair of observations will then result in
one set of differences.

In the present case, pairing was limited to data from a single
source to eliminate so far as possible differences arising from

methods of estimating.[2] Data were available for 11 markets on this basis: six comparing sales and differentials between 1935 and 1940; two comparing 1930 and 1940; and three comparing 1926 and 1940. As is indicated in Table 138, all of these markets were large cities — a factor which may have given an added measure of similarity. When these data were used in a multiple correlation, the results indicated that store sales changed about 9.3 percent for each 1-cent change in the store differential. In addition, there appeared to be an upward trend of store sales in these cities averaging 3.8 percent per year. Moreover, these factors accounted for 83 percent of the change in store sales.

These results are not to be considered as a final and finished analysis of the problem of store sales. Even the last study is subject to criticism on such logical grounds as the adequacy of using over-all changes without regard for the particular timing of the actual changes and the use of an additive function between the differential and the time when it is probable that the trend itself is a function of price differentials. In view of the limitations of the original sample, however, it seems useless to attempt more refined and complicated analyses at present. The results obtained must be considered preliminary and tentative, but they indicate that there is a significant positive relation between store sales and the price differential and that, at least in larger markets, the average "net" effect of a 1-cent change in the differential has been a change of approximately 9 percent in milk sales through stores.

[2] R. W. Bartlett, *The Milk Industry.*

BIBLIOGRAPHY

BIBLIOGRAPHY

Adams, T. M., *Wartime Changes in Milk Distribution and in the Consumption of Milk, Cream, Butter, and Oleomargarine in Vermont*, University of Vermont, Agricultural Experiment Station Bulletin 527, 1945.

Alexander, W. H., and Ballinger, R. A., "The Distribution of Fluid Milk in New Orleans," Louisiana Agricultural Experiment Station Mimeographed Circular No. 32, 1943.

Anderson, R. H., "Duplication of Delivery Services by Milk Distributors in Ithaca, New York," *Farm Economics*, No. 127 (Cornell University, November 1941).

—————— and Leland Spencer, "Ways of Conserving Tires and Reducing Other Expenses in the Distribution of Milk," New York State College of Agriculture Mimeograph A. E. 386, 1942.

Armentrout, W. W., and R. O. Stelzer, *Milk-Distribution Costs in West Virginia II. A Study of the Costs Incurred by 75 Producer-Distributors in the Clarkesburg, Fairmont, Morgantown, and Wheeling Markets for a Twelve-Month Period During 1934–35*, West Virginia Agricultural Experiment Station Bulletin 270, 1936.

Bartlett, R. W., *The Milk Industry*, The Ronald Press Company, New York, 1946.

—————— and Gothard, F. T., "Measuring the Efficiency of Milk Plant Operations," Illinois Agricultural Experiment Station Mimeograph, 1950.

Been, R. O., "The Definition of Market and Supply Areas and the Production-Consumption Equilibrium for Agricultural Products," George Washington University, Washington, D. C., unpublished thesis, 1939.

Bennett, J. J., Jr., *A Report on the Milk Industry of the State of New York with Particular Reference to the New York Metropolitan Area*, New York Attorney General, 1938.

Bergfeld, A. J., *A Study of Milk Distribution in New Haven with Recommendations*, Stevenson, Jordan, and Harrison Report, 1939.

Black, J. D., *Introduction to Production Economics*, H. Holt and Co., New York, 1926.

—————— and Guthrie, E. S., *Economic Aspects of Creamery Organization*, Minnesota Agricultural Experiment Station Technical Bulletin 26, 1924.

Blanford, C., *An Economic Study of the Costs of Selling and Delivering Milk in the New York Market*, Cornell University Agricultural Experiment Station Bulletin 686, 1938.

Boulding, K. E., *Economic Analysis*, Harper and Brothers, New York, 1941.

Bowen, J. T., *Refrigeration in the Handling, Processing, and Storing of Milk and Milk Products*, U. S. Department of Agriculture Miscellaneous Publication 138, 1932.

Bressler, R. G., Jr., *Economies of Scale in the Operation of Country Milk Plants*, New England Research Council on Marketing and Food Supply in coöperation with the New England Agricultural Experiment Stations and the U. S. Department of Agriculture, 1942.

—— *Efficiency of Milk Marketing in Connecticut 10. Consumer Demands and Preferences in Milk Delivery*, Storrs Agricultural Experiment Station Bulletin 257, 1946.

—— "Transportation and Country Assembly of Milk," *Journal of Farm Economics, Vol. XXII, No. 1*, February, 1940.

—— "Research Determination of Economies of Scale," *Journal of Farm Economics, Vol. XXVII, No. 3*, August, 1945.

—— "Economics for the Natural Scientist," Storrs Agricultural Experiment Station, unpublished manuscript, 1945.

—— "Efficiency in the Production of Marketing Services," Economic Efficiency Series, Research Seminar, University of Chicago, Paper No. 6, 1950.

—— Anderson, E. O., Clarke, D. A., Jr., and Bilenker, E. N., *Efficiency of Milk Marketing in Connecticut 5. Economics and Biology of Alternate-Day Milk Delivery*, Storrs Agricultural Experiment Station Bulletin 247, 1943.

—— Clarke, D. A., Jr., and Seaver, S. K., *Efficiency of Milk Marketing in Connecticut 9. Conservation Possibilities in Retail Delivery in Major Markets*, Storrs Agricultural Experiment Station Bulletin 253, 1944.

—— and Hammerberg, D. O., *Efficiency of Milk Marketing in Connecticut 3. Economics of the Assembly of Milk*, Storrs Agricultural Experiment Station Bulletin 239, 1942.

—— and MacLeod, A., "Connecticut Studies Milk Delivery," *Journal of Marketing*, accepted for publication, 1946.

Brown, C. A., *Costs and Margins and Other Related Factors in the Distribution of Fluid Milk in Four Illinois Market Areas*, Illinois Agricultural Experiment Station Bulletin No. 318, 1928.

Camburn, O. M., *Steam Usage in Vermont Cooperative Creameries*, Vermont Agricultural Experiment Station Bulletin 339, 1932.

Cance, A. E., and Ferguson, R. H., *The Cost of Distributing Milk in Six Cities and Towns in Massachusetts*, Massachusetts Agricultural Experiment Station Bulletin No. 173, 1917.

Cassels, J. M., *A Study of Fluid Milk Prices*, Harvard University Press, Cambridge, 1937.

Chamberlin, E., *The Theory of Monopolistic Competition*, Harvard University Press, Cambridge, 1935.

Clark, J. M., "Toward a Concept of Workable Competition," *The American Economic Review, Vol. XXX, No. 2, Part I*, June, 1940.

Clarke, D. A., Jr., "Wholesale Milk Delivery Costs in Los Angeles, 1950," California Agricultural Experiment Station, Giannini Foundation Mimeograph, 1950.

—— "Cost and Pricing Problems in Wholesale Milk Delivery in the Los Angeles Market," California Agricultural Experiment Station, Giannini Foundation Mimeograph, 1951.

Bibliography 387

—— "Wholesale Milk Delivery," University of California, Berkeley, unpublished thesis, 1951.
—— and Bressler, R. G., Jr., *Efficiency of Milk Marketing in Connecticut 6. Truck Costs and Labor Requirements on Milk Delivery Routes,* Storrs Agricultural Experiment Station Bulletin 248, 1943.
Clement, C. E., *Effect of Plant Arrangement, Equipment, and Methods of Operation in Relation to Breakage of Bottles in Milk Plants,* U. S. Department of Agriculture Technical Bulletin 280, 1932.
—— *Operation and Management of Milk Plants,* Division of Market Milk Investigations, Bureau of Dairy Industry, U. S. Department of Agriculture, Circular No. 260, 1933.
—— *Milk Bottle Losses and Ways to Reduce Them,* U. S. Department of Agriculture Circular 469, 1939.
—— Bain, J. B., and Grant, F. M., *Equipment for City Milk Plants,* Division of Market-Milk Investigations, Bureau of Dairy Industry, U. S. Department of Agriculture Circular No. 99 (Revised), 1932.
—— LeFevre, P. E., Bain, J. B., and Grant, F. M., *Effect of Milk Plant Arrangement and Methods of Operation on Labor Requirements,* U. S. Department of Agriculture Technical Bulletin No. 153, 1929.
Connecticut Dairy Conservation Committee, "Report of the Connecticut Dairy Conservation Committee," *Report of the Milk Administrator,* Appendix D, State of Connecticut, March, 1943.
Crosley Survey, "E. O. D. Satisfaction," *American Milk Review, Vol. 7, No. 10,* October, 1945.
Converse, P. D., *The Elements of Marketing,* Prentice-Hall, Inc., New York, 1936.
Davis, H. M., et al., "An Industrial Engineer Looks at the Milk Problem," mimeographed report of the Civil Works — Emergency Relief Administration in coöperation with the New Hampshire Minimum Wage Office, 1935.
DeLoach, D. B., and Steiner, R. A., *The Portland Metropolitan Milk Market,* Oregon Agricultural Experiment Station Bulletin 388, 1941.
Dow, G. F., *An Economic Study of Milk Distribution in Maine Markets,* Maine Agricultural Experiment Station Bulletin 395, 1939.
—— "An Economic Study of Milk Distribution in Maine Markets," paper presented to the Association of New England Milk Dealers, 1940.
—— *A Preliminary Report on Consumers' Problems of Every-Other-Day Delivery of Milk in Portland and Westbrook, Maine,* Maine Agricultural Experiment Station Miscellaneous Publication 571, 1943.
—— *Milk Distribution Through Stores in the Portland Market,* Maine Agricultural Experiment Station Miscellaneous Publication No. 574, 1943.
—— *Consumption and Marketing of Dairy Products in Portland, Maine,* Maine Agricultural Experiment Station Bulletin 425, 1944.
—— *Size of Load and Delivery Costs for Labor in Milk Distribution in Boston and Portland,* Maine Agricultural Experiment Station Bulletin 437, 1945.
Edwards, C., *Economic and Political Aspects of International Cartels,* Senate Military Affairs Committee Monograph 1, 1944.
Ellenberger, H. R., *Bottled Milk Deliveries,* Vermont Agricultural Experiment Station Bulletin 486, 1942.

Erdman, H. E., *The Marketing of Whole Milk,* The Macmillan Company, New York, 1921.

Federal Power Commission Publication, *Typical Net Monthly Bills for Electric Service — Connecticut,* 1939.

Federal Trade Commission, *Report of the Federal Trade Commission on the Sale and Distribution of Milk Products, Connecticut and Philadelphia Milksheds,* House Document No. 152, 74th Congress, 1st Session, 1935.

Fetter, F. A., "The Economic Law of Market Areas," *Quarterly Journal of Economics, Vol. 38,* 1924.

Galbraith, J. K., and Black, J. D., "The Quantitative Position of Marketing in the United States," *Quarterly Journal of Economics, Vol. XLIX,* May, 1935.

Gaumnitz, E. W., and Reed, O. M., *Some Problems Involved in Establishing Fluid Milk Prices,* Dairy Section, Division of Marketing and Marketing Agreements, Agricultural Adjustment Administration, U. S. Department of Agriculture, 1937.

Hammerberg, D. O., "Allocation of Milk Supplies Among Contiguous Markets," *Journal of Farm Economics, Vol. XXII, No. 1,* February, 1940.

——— "Wartime Problems of Conservation of Transportation," *Journal of Farm Economics, Vol. XXV, No. 1,* February, 1943.

——— Parker, L. W., and Bressler, R. G., Jr., *Efficiency of Milk Marketing in Connecticut 1. Supply and Price Interrelationships for Fluid Milk Markets,* Storrs Agricultural Experiment Station Bulletin 237, 1942.

——— and Sullivan, W. G., *Efficiency of Milk Marketing in Connecticut 2. The Transportation of Milk,* Storrs Agricultural Experiment Station Bulletin 238, 1942.

——— Fellows, I. F., and Farr, R. H., *Efficiency of Milk Marketing in Connecticut 4. Retail Distribution of Milk by Producers,* Storrs Agricultural Experiment Station Bulletin 243, 1942.

Henry, W. F., "Economies of Scale in the Operation of Small Pasteurizing Plants," University of Connecticut, unpublished thesis, 1942.

——— "City Milk Depots," Storrs Agricultural Experiment Station, unpublished manuscript, 1942.

——— Bressler, R. G., Jr., and Frick, G. E., *Efficiency of Milk Marketing in Connecticut 11. Economies of Scale in Specialized Pasteurizing and Bottling Plants,* Storrs Agricultural Experiment Station Bulletin 259, 1948.

Herrmann, L. F., *Milk Distribution Costs in West Virginia III. A Study of the Costs Incurred by 67 Producer-Distributors in the Charleston, Huntington, and Parkersburg Markets for a Twelve-Month Period During 1935–36,* West Virginia Agricultural Experiment Station Bulletin 282, 1937.

Hitchcock, J. A., *Reducing Truck Mileage in Retail Milk Delivery,* Vermont Agricultural Experiment Station Bulletin 491, 1942.

Hoover, E. M., Jr., *Location Theory and the Shoe and Leather Industries,* Harvard University Press, Cambridge, 1937.

Horner, J. T., *The Detroit Milk Market,* Michigan Agricultural Experiment Station Bulletin No. 170, 1928.

Horwitz, Louis, "Survey of Daily Milk Consumption in the City of Hartford," Hartford Board of Health Mimeograph, 1940.

Hughes, E. M., *The Business of Retailing by Producer-Distributors in New*

Bibliography 389

York State, Cornell Agricultural Experiment Station Bulletin 741, 1941.

Jesness, O. B., Waite, W. C., and Quintus, P. E., *The Twin City Milk Market*, Minnesota Agricultural Experiment Station Bulletin 331, 1936.

Johnson, Stewart, *Load Size and Delivery Labor Cost in Milk Distribution*, Storrs Agricultural Experiment Station Bulletin 264, 1950.

―――― and Henry, W. F., "Formulas for Adjusting Milk Transportation Rates," Storrs Agricultural Experiment Station Mimeograph, 1950.

Kettelle, D. I., and Tennant, J. L., "Every-Other-Day Delivery of Milk," Rhode Island Agricultural Experiment Station Miscellaneous Publication 15, 1942.

King, C. L., *The Price of Milk*, The John C. Winston Company, Philadelphia, 1920.

King, G. A., "An Analysis of Wholesale Milk Delivery Operations and Costs," University of Connecticut unpublished thesis, 1948.

―――― and Bressler, R. G., Jr., *Efficiency of Milk Marketing in Connecticut 12. Wholesale Milk Distribution*, Storrs Agricultural Experiment Station Bulletin 273, 1950.

Korzan, G. E., *Costs of Distributing Milk in Montana Markets*, Montana Agricultural Experiment Station Bulletin 462, 1949.

MacLeod, A., *Possible Economies in the Assembly and Distribution of Milk in New England*, Joint publication of the New England Research Council on Marketing and Food Supply, the New England Experiment Stations, and the Bureau of Agricultural Economics, U. S. Department of Agriculture, 1944.

―――― and Clarke, D. A., Jr., *Some Recent Developments in the Connecticut Milk Markets I. Milk Production and Consumption Trends*, Storrs Agricultural Experiment Station Bulletin 254, 1945.

―――― and Miller, C. J., *Efficiency of Milk Marketing in Connecticut 7. Milk Delivery in Rural Connecticut*, Storrs Agricultural Experiment Station Bulletin 249, 1943.

Malenbaum, W., "The Cost of Distribution," *Quarterly Journal of Economics*, Vol. LV, February, 1941.

Marshall, J., Jr., "Changes in Methods of Operation of Milk Distributors in California Which Will Conserve Rubber, Automotive and Other Equipment and Reduce Costs of Operation," California State Department of Agriculture Mimeograph, 1942.

Maxtant, S. L., and Taylor, C. C., *Marketing Fluid Milk in Four Virginia Cities*, Virginia Polytechnic Institute Bulletin 275, 1930.

Meridith, P. W., and Stoltz, R. B., "Bottled Concentrated Milk — A Lower Priced Fresh Milk for the Consumer," *Milk Dealer*, February, 1935.

Ministry of Agriculture and Fisheries, *Milk Report of Reorganisation Commission for Great Britain*, Economic Series No. 44, London, 1936.

Mortenson, W. P., *Milk Distribution as a Public Utility*, The University of Chicago Press, Chicago, 1940.

―――― "Analyze Fluid Milk Distribution Costs," *Annual Report of the Director*, Wisconsin Agricultural Experiment Station Bulletin 442, 1938.

New England Research Council on Marketing and Food Supply in cooperation with the Storrs Agricultural Experiment Station and the U. S. Department of Agriculture, "The 'Rationalization' of Retail Distribution of Milk in Great Britain," 1944.

New Zealand, *Milk Commission Report on the Supply of Milk to the Four*

Metropolitan Areas of Auckland, Wellington, Christchurch, and Dunedin, 1944.

Nixon, A. J., and Reed, O. M., *Municipal Milk Distribution in Tarboro, North Carolina,* Dairy Section, Agricultural Adjustment Administration, U. S. Department of Agriculture, 1938.

North, C. E., *Report of Rochester Milk Survey,* Committee on Public Safety of the Common Council, Rochester, N. Y., 1919.

Ohlin, B. G., *Interregional and International Trade,* Harvard University Press, Cambridge, 1933.

Rinear, E. H., *Milk Distribution Costs of Producer-Distributors and Subdealers in New Jersey,* New Jersey Agricultural Experiment Station Bulletin 663, 1939.

—— and Moore, H. C., *Retailing Milk in Laconia,* New Hampshire Agricultural Experiment Station Bulletin 272, 1933.

Rittenhouse, C. F., *Summary Report on the Cost of Distributing Milk in the Boston Market,* prepared for the Massachusetts Milk Control Board, 1936.

Robinson, J., *The Economics of Imperfect Competition,* Macmillan and Co., London, 1934.

Rockwell, M. V., "Consumers' Attitudes Toward Proposed Changes in Milk-Delivery Service," *Farm Economics, No. 127,* Cornell University, November, 1941.

Rodgers, J. B., Theophilus, D. R., Beresford, H., and Barnhart, J. L., *Distribution of Steam, Electrical Power, and Labor in Representative Idaho Creameries,* Idaho Agricultural Experiment Station Research Bulletin No. 12. 1936.

Rozman, D., *Secondary Milk Markets in Massachusetts in the Period of Falling Prices, 1930–1932,* Massachusetts Agricultural Experiment Station Bulletin No. 304, 1933.

Seaver, S. K., and Bressler, R. G., Jr., *Efficiency of Milk Marketing in Connecticut 8. Possible Milk Delivery Economies in Secondary Markets,* Storrs Agricultural Experiment Station Bulletin 252, 1944.

Sexauer, F. H., "Survey Would Show How Men, Materials Could Be Conserved to Speed War Work," *Dairymen's League News,* The Dairymen's League Cooperative Association, Inc., *Vol. 26, No. 20,* November, 1942.

Spencer, L., "Costs of Distributing Milk in New Jersey," New Jersey Department of Agriculture Mimeograph, 1943.

—— "Views of New York Milk Distributors Concerning Continuation of Wartime Limitations on Delivery Services After the War Ends," New York State College of Agriculture Mimeograph A. E. 508, 1945.

—— *Costs of Distributing Milk in the New York-New Jersey Metropolitan Area,* Cornell Agricultural Experiment Station Bulletin A. E. 528, 1945.

—— *An Economic Study of the Operations of Six Leading Milk Companies in the New York-New Jersey Metropolitan Area, 1941–1948,* Cornell Agricultural Experiment Station Bulletin A. E. 686, 1949.

—— and Luke, H. A., "Consumers' Attitudes Toward Unified Delivery of Milk and the Proposal for a Municipal Milk Plant in Jamestown, New York," New York State College of Agriculture Mimeograph A. E. 404, 1942.

Stelzer, R. O., and Thurston, L. M., *Milk-Distribution Costs in West Virginia*

I. A Study of the Costs Incurred by 22 Plants During 1933, West Virginia Agricultural Experiment Station Bulletin 266, 1935.

Reichart, G., Merkel, H., and Vopelius, O., *The Present State of the German Dairy Industry*, Reich and Prussian Ministry for Food and Agriculture, Berlin, 1937.

Roberts, J. B., and Price, H. B., *Milk Marketing in Lexington*, Kentucky Agricultural Experiment Station Bulletin No. 377, 1937.

State of New York, *Report of the Joint Legislative Committee to Investigate the Milk Industry*, Legislative Document No. 114, 1933.

Stewart, P. W., and Dewhurst, J. F., *Does Distribution Cost Too Much? The Factual Findings*, The Twentieth Century Fund, New York, 1939.

Summers, R. E., and Martin, W. A., "Proration of Power Uses, Dairy Cooperative Associations," Oregon Agricultural Experiment Station, unpublished manuscript, 1937.

Thunen, J. H., von, *Der Isolierte Staat*, Beziehung auf Landwirthschaft und Nationalokonomie, Rostock, 1842.

Tinley, J. M., *An Analysis of the Fresno Milk Market*, California Agricultural Experiment Station Bulletin 559, 1933.

———— and Blank, M. H., *An Analysis of the East Bay Milk Market*, California Agricultural Experiment Station Bulletin 534, 1932.

Tracy, P. H., "Bottled Concentrated Whole Milk," *American Creamery and Poultry Produce Review*, June, 1936.

Tucker, C. K., *The Costs of Handling Fluid Milk and Cream in Country Plants*, Cornell Agricultural Experiment Station Bulletin No. 473, 1929.

U. S. Department of Agriculture, *A Survey of Milk Marketing in Milwaukee*, Dairy Section, Agricultural Adjustment Administration, Marketing Information Series DM-1, 1937.

———— *Farmers in a Changing World*, 1940 Yearbook of Agriculture, 1940.

———— "Fluid Milk Prices in City Markets," Mimeograph, monthly reports, 1946–50.

———— "Changes in the Dairy Industry, United States, 1920–50," mimeographed report prepared at the request of the Subcommittee on Utilization of Farm Crops of the Senate Committee on Agriculture and Forestry, 1950.

U. S. Department of Commerce, *16th Census of the United States, 1940*. Population, Second Series, United States Summary, Washington, D. C., 1940.

U. S. Department of Labor, *Handbook of Labor Statistics, 1947 Edition*, Bureau of Labor Statistics, 1947.

———— *Monthly Labor Review*, Vol. 72, No. 1, Bureau of Labor Statistics.

Viner, J., "Cost Curves and Supply Curves," *Zeitschrift fur Nationalokonomie*, III, 1931.

Weber, A., *Theory of the Location of Industries*, The University of Chicago Press, Chicago, 1929.

INDEX

INDEX

Wellington, New Zealand, 286
West Haven. *See* Connecticut markets, secondary
Willimantic. *See* Connecticut markets, secondary
Willinton. *See* Connecticut markets, rural

Woodbridge. *See* Connecticut markets, rural

Zoned deliveries. *See* Delivery territories, exclusive